FIRST AID FOR

DEMOCRACY AND CAPITALISM

A Plan for World Peace

By

Prof. Fu T. Chen, PhD, CPA
2014/3/23, 1st draft; 2019/7/10, revised

c

IN MEMORY OF

Prof. J. M. Yang
New Asia College, Hong Kong, China

And
Prof. Stanley Pressler
Indiana University, Indiana, U.S.A.

FOR THEIR INSPIRATION

Preface

Many celebrities and the elderly pen memoirs to document their lifetime accomplishments to earn the admiration of their followers and future generations. This author can recall a lot of things, but those worthy of recording are few. However, in the last several decades, I have learned a lot, and my thoughts and responses have been growing daily. Therefore, this book is an attempt to substitute memoirs for something that hopefully will be beneficial to readers, help them better understand the workings of the modern world's development and provide them a basis for appreciation of future evolution.

After one hundred years of independence, America replaced the United Kingdom as the world's largest economy and squeezed into the ranks of world powers. At the end of World War I, the U.S. ascended into a leadership position among the great world powers. After World War II ended, America and the Soviet Union shared global superpower status. Since the collapse of the Soviet Union in 1991, the United States has dominated the world. Besides in politics and the military, over the past century, American technological advances and innovations greatly contributed to improving production. This led to significant improvement in the standard of living, especially in the Western world, a period of unprecedented progress of mankind in history. It was the American century. In addition, America is the champion of democracy and fortress of capitalism. Therefore, to understand the recent century of world evolution, the United States must be the central focus.

Since the 1970s, America gradually lost its economic competitiveness and relied on debt to maintain economic stability and growth. Some of President Johnson's Great Society programs exacerbated social problems. In recent decades, the nation's debt, public and private, has been mounting and unemployment surging. In the past, Japan's trade policy was to blame; now China is accused of being the culprit for serious unemployment. The accusation was unfounded, but it, unfortunately, incited racial hatred and national animosity, which added to the difficulties in securing international cooperation. Moreover, the World Trade Organization (WTO) provides proper channels for mediating trade disputes. Instead of playing the blame game, American leaders should face reality, find out the causes of problems and seek out the solutions to achieve positive results. In the meantime, the U.S. should abandon pursuing military hegemony and economic protectionism policy and actively support the global trend of free flow of goods, labor, and capital. It will not only alleviate America's own problems but will also accelerate the arrival of long awaited world peace and prosperity. No matter how the world changes in the next three to five decades, the United States will continue to play an important role in the international arena but will not be able to control world affairs and do as it wishes as in the past because its economy has been stagnant and unable to meet both its internal and external needs. The rise of the laboring class in national politics will focus on improving the living standards, education, and medical care of the masses; it will deemphasize the military, foreign affairs, and space programs.

Democracy can be traced back to ancient Greece, but the first modern constitutional democracy was the Corsican Republic situated in northern Italy, founded in 1755. However, democracy for all people in Western Europe started after World War II, and in the United States, it was after the passage of the Civil Rights Act of 1964. But, over a period of less than 70 years, with social welfare surging, national debt mounting, and the rich and poor polarizing, democracy in Europe and America has run into serious trouble. If fundamental changes are not forthcoming, democracy will inevitably be replaced by some other systems of government. Therefore, democracy is no longer considered a universal truth, one size-fits-all political system. This book points out the crux of the problems and viable solutions and hopes to benefit the current democracies and enthusiasts of democracy, freedom and human rights.

Most countries before World War II had a closed-door policy with very little foreign trade. Until 1960, the United States' imports or exports did not exceed 5% of its gross domestic product (GDP). In 1944, the signing of the General Agreement on Tariffs and Trade (GATT) eliminated most man-made barriers to trade among nations and promoted the rapid growth of transportation and logistics, leading to mutual benefits and an all parties win effect. World trade grew at a high rate, and people's standard of living also improved considerably.

At the same time, world trade led to global economic competition and realignment of economic activities based mainly on cost advantages. The process has many ramifications, including accelerating logistic flow, plant relocations, product and service outsourcing, improving resource usage efficiency, cost reduction, and increase in output. In the last several decades, the multinationals, especially American businesses, have taken advantage of plant relocation and product outsourcing abroad. This has caused economic recession and severe unemployment at home and exploitation of slave labor and pollution of the environment abroad, merely enriching a tiny group of people. The multinationals are the major culprit for intensifying the polarization of the rich and the poor. Their actions are widening the gap between high income and low income workers and squeezing out the middle class. Capitalism is facing a grave challenge. If no effective reform is forthcoming, capitalism will be replaced by some other economic system, such as the democratic socialism practiced in Venezuela or China's state and private bi-capitalism.

For the past 200 years, the West has dominated the world in science and technology as well as political and economic systems. Western culture prevails, and to some people, it is considered the only viable culture. With the trend of globalization unstoppable, people of diverse cultures are inevitably living and working closer and closer to each other. In the meantime, the Western economic system has shown its weakness and unsustainability. For example, air and water pollution and global warming caused by the industrial revolution have intensified in the last century and is gradually leading to the destruction of our planet. It may not be the time for Westerners to adopt the lifestyle of another culture, but it is certainly time for Westerners to be more understanding of other cultures and to listen and consider the viewpoints of others. Hence, conflicts of interest and clash of cultures may be avoided, and the world may work collaboratively toward world peace and prosperity.

At the end of World War II, world powers renounced imperialism and abandoned colonies. After 70 years' efforts of promoting democracy, freedom, equality, human rights, and a free market economic system, the result seems dismal. There is no democracy among nations; military superiority dictates world affairs; poverty and ignorance in the underdeveloped third world remain almost the same as before; and slave wages prevail outside the Western world. In other words, colonies changed to republics, and their economies changed to free market systems, but their people are still serfs serving the West; their nations do not have an equal voice in the international arena. This inequality and injustice in economics and human rights is the main root cause of international terrorism such as ISIS. Real human rights and equality can be accomplished through new world orders in business, government, social and international organizations, and the United Nations (UN), as well as through the global integration of free flow of all resources.

Ultimately, it is not necessary to have war or revolution; the smooth flow of goods, labor, and capital will provide people of all races with equal opportunity which allows them to pursuit happiness, fulfillment of life, and a better social condition. Thus, it promotes brotherhood and equality among people in the world providing a solid foundation for peace and prosperity in the world. In this book, several key recommendations are suggested that will change the status quo to accommodate world development, i.e., new social and world orders. The suggestions are intended to incite the readers' interest and to enrich and expand the ideas and efforts in order to fulfill this common goal: world peace and prosperity. Even if this goal is unattainable in the near future, our children as well as future generations will benefit from this action. This goal provides a ray of hope that another world war, which will lead to the total destruction of mankind, can be avoided.

This original work was written in Chinese and is intended for Chinese readers because many in China are unaware of what is happening in America. Therefore, a basic and fundamental description of the American system is provided herein. That being said, American readers may choose to skip some parts of the first four chapters. The author translated this work into English with the sincere hope that Western readers will be exposed to the facts from a different point of view. This will help readers to broaden their horizons and place the world as their primary concern instead of having just a national interest, because globalization is inevitable. Furthermore, since a major portion of this book is devoted to America's problems and related solutions, it may be worthwhile for Americans to recognize and familiarize themselves with these problems so that solutions may be developed.

Some of the references were originally translated from English to Chinese. Now, they are translated back to English. Therefore, the citations may not be in their original wording, but the essential meaning remains unchanged. Since the work on this book was started in 2012, some of the data presented herein are no longer current, but an effort has been made to update those deemed to be essential.

At the suggestions of the manuscript's critics, one chapter describing China's major involvement with the world from its beginning and another chapter explaining how the Chinese economic success story was accomplished in the last 30 years are added as an appendix, which might be of interest to those readers who are seeking more knowledge about China.

Prof. William T. Stevens provided a critical review of the book, pinpointing errors and suggesting vital changes which enhance its content. I am grateful for his extraordinary effort. Prof. Kathy Keller edited the entire manuscript; I am sincerely thankful for her thorough and professional work. My gratitude is also extended to Mr. Norman Eng for his editing and revising of the manuscript which enriched the contents and improved the readability of the book.

Sources of data: With date only, *the World Journal*, North American edition, and its website; not dated, the English and Chinese language websites. Unless otherwise specified, amounts are presented in U.S. dollars.

Table of Contents

I. Introduction

Since the beginning of the 21st century, the United States has suffered a series of misfortunes; *Time* magazine called it "the decade from hell". First, on September 11, 2001, al-Qaeda terrorists hijacked four airliners. Two planes attacked the World Trade Center twin towers in New York City, and a third attacked the Pentagon, the Department of Defense, in Washington, D. C. The fourth aircraft, due to intervention by the passengers, didn't reach its intended target and crashed in a rural area of Pennsylvania. All in all, about 3,000 people were killed. Second, in the 2000 and 2004 presidential elections, the Democratic and Republican Party candidates were well-matched and fought inextricably, but after several twists and turns, the election result finally ended up in the U.S. Supreme Court. The Republican candidate, George W. Bush, was declared the winner with a small margin of votes. The radical Democrats condemned Bush for stealing the election. This election result polarized the voters and undermined social harmony and national unity. The third was the 2001 invasion of Afghanistan which supported the al-Qaeda terrorists and was followed by the attack and overthrow of Saddam Hussein of Iraq in 2003. As of May 28, 2010, U.S. military casualties in Afghanistan and Iraq have exceeded 57,000 persons; military spending is over one trillion dollars.

Then, in August 2005, Hurricane Katrina struck the Gulf of Mexico, affecting four U.S. coastal states. Levee failures and government relief inefficiency contributed to the disaster. A total of 1,836 people lost their lives, and property damage amounted to $81 billion. Louisiana suffered the most, with the population of New Orleans reduced by nearly 320,000 people, about 24%. In 2008, two of Wall Street's large financial institutions, Lehman Brothers and Bear Stearns, collapsed. In order to avoid a repeat of the Great Depression in 1929, the federal government vigorously provided relief efforts. Congress, in 2008 and 2009, passed two economic stimulus bills for a total of $939 billion. At the end of May 2010, a total of 831 businesses benefited from the program, mostly from the financial sector but also including General Motors Company. The real estate bubble induced financial crisis, leading to the 2008 national recession and global economic contraction, affected all the major economies except China and India. At present, the U.S. economy has recovered somewhat, but the unemployment rate remains persistently high, 7% as of November 2013. The U.S. seems to be besieged on all sides and facing a major threat to its hegemony.

As a result of its astronomical economic relief spending, coupled with years of military expenditures in Afghanistan and Iraq, the U.S. national debt, by September 30, 2012, surpassed $16 trillion. The United States has become the largest debtor nation in the world, while China has evolved to become the largest creditor for the United States. This phenomenon coincides with the event a hundred years ago of the Anglo/American change of hands in world superpower status, leading to media speculation that China will rise to surpass the United States and become the dominant superpower in the world. This is conceivable because in the past 30 years, China has made tremendous progress, especially in its economy and national defense.

Looking back to the world's major ancient civilizations, Egypt and Babylon are relics; Greek and Roman Empires have become history; and India has been ruled by many foreign powers for a very long time. China is the only continuous major civilization with a long and glorious past. It had advanced commerce and industries, social structure, and a highly organized government system as well as developed social and philosophical beliefs. This led to the highest living standard and the largest gross domestic product in the world for several thousand years until the British Empire eclipsed it.

The philosophy of Lao-tse and Chuang-Tse about the universe and eternal life together with Confucianism in human relations and theory of social governance, even though they are thousands of years old, are viable social ideologies today. Silk, china, and Chinese cuisine are favored the world over. Paper, printing, the compass, and gunpowder contributed immeasurably to the civil and technological advancement in the West. China emerged as one of the world's greatest civilizations a few thousand years ago; it is merely recovering the respect it lost some 200 years ago. China is no longer the prey of today's world powers. But to the majority of Chinese people, they have just left the edge of hunger and poverty not so long ago. The average personal income is very low in China. The Chinese government must work vigorously to promote and improve the standard of living, education, infrastructure, and the environment.

Moreover, Chinese culture advocates and practices benevolence, not hegemony. In China's extensive history, ethnic conflicts and international wars were unavoidable, but to bully and eliminate minorities or to colonize and enslave other nations were activities never practiced. Besides, the Han Chinese majority government and society always observed neutrality and permitted the people involved in the situations to decide for themselves; a hands-off policy on ethnic relationships was practiced, which neither promoted nor restricted ethnic assimilations. As a result, no Romeo and Juliet type tragedy has ever been documented in the long history of China. For more than 5,000 years, the 55 minorities are still alive and well, and maintaining their own cultural identity is the best evidence of this neutrality. The Yuan(元) and Qing(清) dynasties initially did not represent the Chinese tradition but eventually were assimilated into mainstream Chinese culture.

II. The Rise of the United States in Dominating the World

After Christopher Columbus landed in America in 1492, all Western powers competed for a piece of colonial action. The British occupied most of North America; Spain had the most territory in all Americas; Portugal, France, Holland, and Russia shared the rest of the America lands. They converted the Americas into copies of Europe.

2.1. Fighting the British, Forming a New Nation
Thirteen British colonies in North America condemned the practice of taxation without representation imposed by the British monarch in America. In 1776, they announced the formation of the United States of America. Democracy, freedom, equality and human rights were the founding principles, using a presidential system, federation of the states as a political governing body, and a federal and state power sharing system. Over the years, the territory expanded through the creation of neighboring states. And in 1848, signing the Treaty of Guadalupe Hidalgo, Mexico ceded territory (California and parts of the other six western states) to the United States. Then, with the acquisition of Louisiana and Alaska from France and Russia, respectively, and the annexation of the kingdoms of Texas and Hawaii, the U.S. had an area of 9.4 million square kilometers, comparable to the size of China and only smaller than that of Russia and Canada.

In the meantime, the U.S. actively promoted European immigration, imported massive numbers of African slaves for agricultural production, and recruited laborers from China to build the transcontinental railroad for the development of the vast western frontier. Advocating capitalism and a free market economy, by the end of the industrial revolution in the 1870s, the United States replaced the United Kingdom as the world's largest economy.

A U.S. warship was sunk in Cuba, triggering the 1898 war with Spain. The American military overwhelmingly defeated Spanish troops in Cuba and the Pacific, establishing the U.S. as a world power. Spain ceded Guam and Puerto Rico, and received $20 million as a price for the transfer of the Philippines, thereby establishing a precedent for a defeated country to benefit from war. America quickly transformed itself from a group of colonial pioneers oppressed by the British Empire into a new empire with its own colony and controlled territories.

Although the United States was a participant in World War I, North America was unaffected by the war, contributing to economic and military growth and providing the U.S. a leadership position among world powers. During World War II, both sides suffered heavy casualties and losses; the destruction of Europe was massive. A sneak attack was launched by the Japanese on the U.S. Pacific Fleet at Pearl Harbor which was almost annihilated, but the continental U.S. was unaffected and became a world factory, leading to the post war economic boom and widespread prosperity. The economic output grew exponentially, and the standard of living improved almost daily.

2.2. Forty Years of U.S.-Soviet Discord

Soon after the Peace Treaty of San Francisco was signed in 1951, the world was divided into the Western camp, Communist bloc, and neutral countries. The relationship of the United States and the Soviet Union took a sharp turn, from being allies in World War II into becoming sworn enemies. Headed by these two superpowers, military and political struggles were turned into actions which lasted for 40 years until the collapse of the Soviet Union in 1991. The Communists' major offenses were to export revolution and political propaganda. The United States, on the other hand, employed military and economic assistances to non-Communist countries, along with using democracy and human rights ideology as a weapon.

In 1949, the Chinese Communist regime was established and gained control in China, and a quarter of the world's population was placed under the Communist rule. The following year saw the outbreak of the Korean War, which lasted for three years. Although the Americans had modern weaponry, without resorting to using the atomic bomb, it was not easy to win the battle against the Communists who launched masterful strategic human offensive tactics. Finally, the two sides settled for a ceasefire and divided North and South Korea at the North 38 degree latitude.

The Soviet cosmonaut, Yuri Gagarin, in 1961 circled around the Earth and excited the whole world, leaving the United States in disgrace. The American media quipped that "their German scientists are better than our German scientists". True, both the United States and the Soviet Union before and after World War II relied on the expertise of German scientists in developing atomic and space technology. The event led to President Kennedy's request to increase the space budget and his vow to overtake the Soviet Union in the space race. Kennedy's wish was fulfilled less than a decade later when U.S. astronauts successfully landed on the moon to the joy of the whole world. It was not reported whether the astronauts received a warm welcome by the Ladies of the Moon (Chinese folklore).

In 1959, Cuba established a Communist government in the backyard of the United States. In April 1961, the Central Intelligence Agency (CIA) of the U.S. supported the Cuban armed exiles landing at the Bay of Pigs, Cuba, in an attempt to overthrow the Communist regime. It ended in failure. Later, when the Soviet Union installed missiles on the island, it was strongly opposed by the United States and nearly led to a nuclear showdown. The Soviets finally backed down, but Premier Khrushchev vowed to bury the United States.

During the Kennedy administration, the United States increased massive military support to the South Vietnamese in order to contain Communist expansion in Southeast Asia. By 1968, more than 530,000 troops were in Vietnam. Besides the financial burden, the U.S. suffered military casualties of at least 360,000 (58,148 dead and 304,000 wounded) people. Civilian and military deaths of nearly four million people were estimated between 1954-1975 for North and South Vietnam, Cambodia, and Laos. Condemnation of the war in Vietnam was heard all over the U.S. and abroad, leading to a massive anti-war movement at home. President Lyndon Johnson was forced to give up a re-election bid. In 1975, the U.S. military hastily evacuated; the Vietnam War was a painful lesson to the United States and dealt a severe blow to American confidence.

During the Cold War era, both sides accelerated the arms race, especially the development of nuclear warheads (bombs). The U.S. military budget was about 10% of GDP, ranging from $29 to $100 billion in the 1950s and 1960s. In addition to the Marshall Plan in Europe, other foreign military and economic aids amounted to $2.5 billion annually. All this military spending didn't produce the desired result of containing Communist expansion. When the North Vietnamese troops marched into Saigon in 1975, the Communist bloc advanced aggressively; the United States, losing ground, could only parry without the strength to fight back. None of the vast American military aid, democracy, and human rights ideology achieved the desired effect, and it seemed almost impossible to contain Communism's outward expansion.

2.3. Collapse of the Soviet Union: the U.S. Dominates

The Soviet Union Communist regime was founded in 1917, replacing the Czar of Russia, abolishing private property, and establishing public ownership. Besides personal consumption, the government managed and coordinated all economic activities. A series of Five-Year Plans focused especially on the development of heavy industries and national defense. By the beginning of World War II, the output of Soviet's steel, cement, crude oil, pig iron, and tractors topped the world

After World War II, reconstruction and rebuilding the economy were in order. National unity and patriotic sentiment coupled with the Planned Economy system played to its best advantage in this critical period. In addition, the economic plan also included the Communist countries in Eastern Europe as a part of the master plan which gave greater access to sources of raw materials, machinery, finished products, and an expanded market for all Soviet countries. As a result, the rate of economic growth surpassed that of Western Europe and the United States in the 1950s and 1960s.

With 20 years of development and reconstruction, the Soviet people's basic living needs were fulfilled and major social and military construction was completed. However, after the euphoria of building a socialist utopia and the patriotic enthusiasm against the Nazi aggression cooled, the Socialist Planned Economy system revealed its major flaws. Honor and patriotism were the main driving forces for improvement under the public ownership, but they were not as persistent and durable as motivation by self-interest under the private ownership. A planned economy under layers of bureaucracy could not respond quickly and adjust to demand and supply thereby causing severe shortages and waste. Furthermore, it affected the normal operation of a series of related industries, which resulted in a decrease in efficiency and an increase in production costs.

By the 1970s, the economy began to lag; the Soviet Communist Central Committee changed its strategy in favor of light industries to meet people's need for consumer goods but was ineffective. Even though consumer industry was emphasized in the 1970s, shortages were prevalent. In the 1980s, the problem got worse, and a rationing system was implemented to limit consumption. The 1985-86 world oil price slumps greatly reduced Soviet foreign exchange earnings. The Soviet government was unable to pay for imports of consumer goods and external debt. Currency was devalued; the economy was in trouble and the nation was facing bankruptcy. President Mikhail Gorbachev attempted reform was not effective, but instead created more political turmoil.

When President Ronald Reagan took office in 1981, he gave up the old policy of containment and adopted a direct challenge strategy towards the Soviet Union, resulting in a significant military buildup. The U.S. defense budget in 1980 was $134 billion, and by 1989 it had more than doubled to $341 billion, accounting for 31% of the national budget expenditure. The Soviets responded in kind, also accelerating armament expenditure; reported by one website, between 1980 and 1985, military expenditure increased from 22% to 27% of GDP, peaking in 1988. The big increase was also triggered by the massive Soviet military buildup in Afghanistan during the 1980s.

The Soviet Union dispatched its military to Afghanistan by the end of 1979 to support the local Marxist regime against Islamic extremists. President Reagan considered this a part of the Cold War and provided military and financial support to the Muslims. Other Islamic countries and the world Muslim community also contributed funds to the cause of fighting against the Soviets. In the decade-long war, the Soviets had 620,000 troops engaged in the fighting at its peak. Casualties totaled 60,000 and approximately 420,000 personnel suffered from disease. Loss of armaments was heavy: 451 aircrafts crashed, alone. An estimated 100,000 to 1,000,000 Afghan people were killed. The Soviets, as a military superpower with advanced weaponry and massive military personnel, fought a group of amateurs for 10 years. It could not win the war and suffered a heavy loss, exiting ungracefully and empty-handed, like the American retreat from Vietnam. Therefore, the Western media dubbed this as the Soviets' Vietnam War.

In 1986, due to improper operation, the Chernobyl, Ukraine, nuclear power plant suffered an unprecedented major nuclear accident. Radiation spread to all of Ukraine, Belarus, and western Russia, adversely affecting the health of 600,000 people. Although there were only 32 deaths at the scene, deaths from radiation exposure have since reached 4,000 people. Aside from man-made disasters, a 6.8 magnitude earthquake struck Spitak,

Armenia, on December 7, 1988, leveling the entire city and killing more than 25,000 people. The exorbitant number of deaths was attributed to the countless number of collapsed apartments whose builders cut corners and violated building codes during construction. The natural calamity coupled with the man-made disaster hastened the collapse of the Soviet Union.

In March 1990, the Republic of Lithuania was the first to declare independence from the Soviet Union. By the end of 1991, the Soviet Union disintegrated completely. Some Communist regimes in Eastern Europe deserted Russia and joined the West. At this point, Russia could only compete with the United States in its nuclear arsenal, but not in all other areas. The United States emerged as the only superpower in the world.

Disintegration of the Soviet Union was neither due to the Soviet military failure nor the triumph of democracy and human rights ideology promoted vigorously by the U.S. The main reason was the Socialist Planned Economy which lacked production incentive, coordination, and was unable to meet the demand for both civilian and military needs. It gave priority to military spending, up to 27% of the GDP, and failed to meet the demand for consumer goods. In other words, with limited resources, the choice had to be made between guns and butter; you cannot have both at the same time. This demonstrates the fact that a large military establishment without relative economic strength to support it, is like a building constructed on the beach without a solid foundation; sooner or later, it will collapse.

Communists basically subscribe to Karl Marx's doctrine and consider capitalism as a social evil. It not only exploits the fruits of the workers' labor, but also enhances a small group of super rich. The international labor movement, the Communists believe, will inevitably overthrow the capitalist governments on earth, as Premier Nikita Khrushchev vowed to bury the U.S. On the other side, the West painted Communism as a totalitarian regime controlled by party elites who seized people's property and freedom just like hurricanes or tornadoes threatened people's life and property. As reported from a 1954 international conference in Geneva, Switzerland, the U.S. Secretary of State John F. Dulles refused to shake hands with China's Premier Zhou En-lai; hostility toward each other was overwhelming. There was no common ground or possibility to co-exist between these two camps. It was either for or against, and there was no middle ground.

Today, some 50 years later, the U.S. and Russia have a joint space venture and all Communist regimes, except North Korea and Cuba for now, turned the tables and adopted private ownership and a market economy. It is heart-warming and very uplifting to see that people can indeed learn to tolerate different ideologies, to forget stubborn prejudice, and to adopt other workable systems.

III. The World Influenced by the United States

Hegemonies use foreign influence to express their intentions and to implement their policies. Depending on the degree or intensity, power of influence may turn into power of dictation or control. Take Panama, for example. In 1989, President George H. Bush ordered the U.S. forces stationed in Panama to arrest its leader, General Manuel Noriega, and convict him of drug trafficking in Miami, Florida. Because of the Panama Canal's construction, the U.S. has been a major influence in Panama. The dollar is also the national currency of Panama. For years, Noriega worked for the U.S. Central Intelligence Agency. During incarceration, he received much preferential treatment, having his own detention quarters lavishly furnished so that the media called it the presidential suite. After serving his jail term, he was extradited to France where he was tried and found guilty for murder and money laundering. He died on May 29, 2017 while serving a 20 year prison sentence in Panama.

3.1. Social and Cultural Impact

Years ago, I was visiting relatives in Shanghai; they were considering sending their daughter to study abroad. After lengthy discussions, the final choice was narrowed down to the U.S. or U.K. Their daughter was undecided at the moment but said she did not appreciate the American culture, especially the cowboy lifestyle. Culture is the sum of human activity, material and spiritual or concrete and abstract aspects. Substances serve physical needs including raw material, products, tools, machinery and plant equipment. Fulfilling mental and spiritual demands covers the social and natural sciences, literature, art, music, religion, and philosophy. Truly, in the United States, the development of natural sciences is way ahead of mental and spiritual studies. It is not easy to find a famous American thinker or philosopher. However, Lao Tse(老子), Chuang Tzu(莊子), Confucius(孔子), and Mencius (孟子) are only a few in China's five thousand years of history. America was founded less than three hundred years ago; it may be too much to ask for.

Just to name a few major American influences, start with the necessities of life. In ancient times, people used fur and leather for cover and insulation, and later developed the spinning and weaving of natural fiber. Thousands of years ago, the Chinese discovered and produced silk;

and the world of clothing underwent a big change. In 1935, DuPont Co. found a way to convert crude oil into fiber which could be used to produce all kinds of textile products. In 1946, Chinese ladies first used U.S. imported nylon stockings. People were amazed and thought it was God's creation because the stocking was almost invisible; they nicknamed them glass stockings.

Manmade fibers have many advantages, such as being durable, lightweight, and tough; the only drawback is lacking ventilation. Improvement has been made over the last 70 years with a wide range of products. They are inexpensive and popular, and users are found throughout the world. Currently, the production of manmade fibers has exceeded the sum of all other fibers made in the world.

In the 1870s, in western France and northern Italy, a popular blue cotton fabric, both durable and dirt-resistant, was developed, known as denim. It was used for the uniform of the Genoa navy, the birthplace of the jean. In America's early days, jeans were welcomed mainly by farmers and cowboys because of their special qualities. Modified several times, the main feature involved the use of copper rivets to reinforce high areas of stress such as pocket corners, as in today's popular jeans.

After World War II, the blue jean increased in popularity with the global distribution of American western theme cowboy movies. Initially, they were considered outdoor work or casual wear, not formal attire. In recent decades, they have been well-liked by youth and young adults. Jackets, skirts, shorts and other accessories made with denim are fashionable for people of all ages. Today, whether they are worn by a business executive, street vendor, old lady, or toddler, and whether they are worn at the beach, church, office, or for other occasions, jeans are acceptable. It is the only non-class, non-gender specific, popular clothing. Levi, Lee, and Wrangler are the most well-known makers in the United States; other countries also have their own brands.

Food and the art of cooking and eating are highly developed in China. Not only are there a great variety of cuisines to choose from, but they also require a certain color, flavor, form, and taste. In addition to the Beijing, Shanghai, Szechuan, Hunan, Fujian, and Guangdong cuisines, other provinces also have their own specialties, and minorities have their ethnic dishes, too. These foods are the best in the world. As a Chinese restaurateur in London described the Chinese banquet for its rich content in variety, color, taste, and its magnificent form, it is like a symphony; other cuisines, including the French, at most are wind and string ensembles; none can be compared with the Chinese cuisine.

Chinese restaurants, except for a few countries, spread throughout the world. Nevertheless, the American fast food chains have taken over the world much faster than the Chinese. Even the culinary capital of China is no exception, as China's second tier cities are populated with the McDonald's and Kentucky Fried Chicken restaurant chains.

Since the industrial revolution, the United States witnessed the growing rural populations migrate to urban centers to meet the demand for industrial and commercial development. The concept of time also became more stringent. As a result, breakfast and lunch were simplified to meet the work schedules. During World War II, due to labor shortages, women left the kitchen to join the business and industrial workers. As the postwar economic boom continued, only a few women returned to the kitchen. These were two main reasons why the American fast food restaurants grew like wild fire. Their focus was neither excellence nor variety of food offered; rather, quick service, food that was easy to eat, easy to carry, offered for a low price, and a simple menu was the main attraction. Drive-thru restaurants also became popular. Within two minutes you could have a meal on the road. Even if you had to line up for service inside the restaurant, the wait was usually very short.

In 1948 Mac and Dick McDonald developed fast-food operating procedures in their restaurant in California. And in 1955, they teamed up with Roy Kroc to open the first McDonalds in Illinois. Globally, there are over 31,000 McDonald's in 119 countries. Some are company owned; the others are franchised to private operators with daily sales of 4,700 million meals worldwide. The growth of fast-food restaurants also created serious health problems because fast food generally has a high content of salt and fat, less fruit and vegetables. Americans have consumed this food for a long time and have suffered the most. Obesity, diabetes, and heart disease are prevalent.

Human activities are restricted by nature in many aspects, such as when the sun goes down, movements become inconvenient; friends and relatives living in Australia are separated from us by the vast ocean; reunions tend to be more difficult. These time and space limitations are gradually overcome. However, like earthquakes, hurricanes, and tornados, human beings remain helpless, taking it as it comes or relying only on preparation or avoidance.

In 1879, Thomas Edison, a newsboy who did not have a formal education, created the first light bulb in a New Jersey laboratory. Over a hundred years, it gradually lit up every corner of the world. Humans have overcome the darkness problem which has greatly improved the quality of life and productivity as well. The Edison-designed light bulb is still in use today. Due to energy inefficiency, it has gradually been replaced by fluorescent and LED lighting. In the Edison era, several persons made considerable contributions to the light bulb's creation, so the honor should be properly shared by all. After 1878, Edison set up a few electric manufacturing businesses, and then in 1892 merged with Thomson-Houston Co. to form the General Electric Co. (GE). In over one hundred years, the company has become the world leader in technological innovation and manufacture. One of its products, the large commercial jet engine, has no more than two or three competitors worldwide.

Another aspect of nature is climate change. Generally, it is hot near the equator and cold at both poles, while other parts of the globe experience all four seasons. Therefore, sometimes people naked with a fan on cannot keep cool and other times with wool coats in front of a burning fireplace cannot stay warm. In the summer, printers cannot be operated properly because paper became moist from the humidity. Willis Carrier in 1902 developed a system to eliminate moisture in the room in order to dry the paper and avoid the printer's malfunction. In the drying process, the room temperature correspondingly declined, and the air conditioner was born. He did not realize that the originally designed dehumidifier would become the globally popular air conditioner. A lot of Muslims in the Middle East do not like the American way of life, but few would reject the use of an air conditioner.

On the beach of North Carolina in 1903, the Wright brothers (Wilbur & Orville) successfully tested their flying machine. Thus, the distance between places has considerably shortened; and crossing high ridges and a vast ocean is no longer difficult. Flight opened a new page in the history of human life. Aviation became an important part of modern transportation, the war machine, and vehicles for space exploration.

According to archaeologists, the use of wheels can be traced back to 5,500 years ago. The Mesopotamians (now Iraqis) had used earthenware wagon wheels. But the car is characterized by having impetus which was first seen in the late nineteenth century. The engine is its core part, which is the result of Europeans' two centuries of research and development. German Karl Benz created the world's first car in 1886, the Benz Patent Motorwagen. The Mercedes Benz brand continues to this day, and Daimler is the world's oldest car manufacturer.

In the early days, cars were individually made, very expensive, just a luxury toy for a few rich people. In 1913 when Henry Ford launched an assembly line operation with uniform components, streamlining the process. This led to a shortened manufacturing process and a greatly reduced cost per car. Over the years, 15 million units of the most popular Model T were sold; prices plunged from $850 in 1908 to $260 in 1925 which was about 21% of the average person's annual income of that year. This represented a decrease in car price of 70% in 17 years. Hence, cars were no longer the rich folks' toy anymore and became an important mode of people's transportation. The growing number of cars also promoted the emerging automobile-related enterprises and culture, such as gas stations, highways, motels, drive-in theaters, and a host of drive-in services. Today, some are popular around the world and have become the world standards; the others, due to changes in social conditions, are no longer in demand, such as drive-in movie theaters.

The 1790 U.S. census shows 697,897 slaves in America. By 1860 the slave population escalated to 3,953,761, mainly from West Africa. This accounted for 12.6% of the total U.S. population. Gradually, a variety of community and religious groups were formed. Dance and music were essential traditions when religious worshipping, festivals, and other public gatherings were held. With the white influence over the past centuries, blacks began to incorporate the harmony concept and new musical instruments from Europe were introduced in their musical performances which dramatically changed the nature of the West African music. Jazz was born. Jazz first appeared in 1843 during black community celebrations in New Orleans and later spread to New York State and New England. After 50 years of development, in the early 20th century, black jazz bands were accepted in most major American cities. At the end of World War II, jazz was popular around the world and was essential music in nightclubs and ballrooms.

By the end of World War II, integration of jazz, country music, and religious music led to rock and roll music. Stars like Elvis Presley and the Beatles swept the world, becoming young people's idols in the Western world. Their clothing, hairstyles, and actions greatly influenced fashions, which affected the young people's lifestyles much more than the jazz music.

Film and television became an important part of modern life. As he had been in the creation of the light bulb, Thomas Edison made significant contributions in the motion picture industry. Assisted by his staff, Dickson, he created a set of cameras (Kinetoscope) and projectors designed especially for the motion picture industry, and in 1894, exported a large quantity of this equipment to all major European cities.

During World War II, the U.S. film and television industry was virtually unaffected by the war. In the early postwar period, the popularity of U.S. films and television programs monopolized the world market. In recent years, India has vigorously developed its film and television industry, dubbed as the Hollywood of the East, but their products are mostly for domestic consumption, having little effect on the foreign market. The United States still dominates the world film and television industry. In addition, in the 1960s, Walt Disney, world famous cartoon film maker, employed cartoon characters in developing entertainment theme parks. The new concept of blending entertainment and vacation has gained popularity ever since. Currently, there are six Disney theme parks in operation worldwide.

Film and television are important entertainment and they are also tools for broadcasting, communications, propaganda, and education. The United States utilizes these tools effectively to spread political ideology, social values, lifestyles, traditions, customs, religions, and language around the world. Although the British empire was on the decline, English popularity began rising to a higher level than ever before. Not only was English the main language of the U.S., but the global acceptance of the U.S. film and television programs contributed to this English popularity around the world. After World War II, English replaced French as the language of international diplomacy. Although the number of English speakers around the world is only a fraction of the Chinese speakers (328 million people use English versus 1,213 million people use Chinese), English speakers cover broad areas and many ethnicities, and the English language is used in diplomacy and business far more than

Chinese. Consequently, English now has become the unofficial universal language.

With the development and popularization of computer networks, the Internet also began to flourish. In 1973 under Vinton Cerf's supervision, at the Advanced Projects Research Office of the U.S. Department of Defense, he set up a network of computers at the Department of Defense, universities, and research laboratories for the purposes of exchanging information and consulting during research and development (R&D) activities, with good results. Then in 1977, a computer hookup between a research center in California and a college in London, England, was arranged to test the interactions, and the testing was successful. After considerable expansions and improvements, finally in 1983 the Internet operating system was made available to the public.

After 30 years' rapid development, the number of Internet users worldwide has exceeded 2.4 billion by June 30, 2012 (3.4 billion by July 15, 2016). Users in North America account for more than 78% of its population, 63% in Europe, 27% in Asia. China has the most Internet users, totaling 538 million, 40% of its population, and account for 22% of the worldwide users; the U.S. came in second with 245 million users. Recent statistics show that 540 million people worldwide use the English network and 440 million people use the Chinese.

Except for human interventions, national boundaries, regional differences, and cultural diversity posed no restrictions to Internet users. By broadband transmitting, information could be exchanged almost without a time delay, thus significantly shortening the time for communication. The Internet not only fulfilled the goal of information superhighways; now it had become the world's largest information repository, forum, shopping mall, post office, concert hall, and socialized gathering place. In recent years, the Internet has seen theft, defaming, crime, politics and wars, affecting all facets of society, altering people's way of living, but also improving the quality of life. The advent of the Internet age may be the most significant innovation of the twentieth century; its future development may be even more staggering.

Modern civilization is characterized as the electric age. Electricity is vital in every aspect of people's social and economic activities, e.g., television, air conditioner, computer, electric motor, etc. Electricity serves not only as energy but also an element that connects parts to the whole and is just like the nervous system in a human body. Therefore, an intelligent robot can be built to do a complex work. The world advanced from the mechanical to the electrical/electronic age. Among the prominent contributors who are associated with the discovery, production, and distribution of electricity are Italian Girolamo Cardano, Alessandro volta, Englishman William Gilbert, German Otto von Guericke, Serbian Nikola Tesla, and American Benjamin Franklin and Thomas Edison.

Since the civil war in the 1860s, the United States has been the world's richest country, with well-developed industries, good jobs, and living standards continuously improving. Although experiencing World War I and II, the Korean War, and the Vietnam War, the continental U.S. did not suffer the pain of war and social destruction. Modernized urban and superior living and working conditions in the U.S. were recognized by Chinese living overseas as the land of golden opportunity. The U.S. possessed well developed education systems with academic freedom. And in research and development, it was endowed with abundant public and private funding, well-equipped facilities, high salaried jobs, work freedom, with the protection of intellectual property. It was a haven for scholars and scientists -- the envy of the world. Especially after World War II, other world powers were busy rebuilding infrastructure and unable to fund R&D, resulting in a large number of talented scientists and engineers immigrating to the United States. The Nobel Foundation reported from 1901 to 2002, over a hundred years, of all the 684 winners including the prizes in peace, literature, economics, medicine, chemistry, and physics, 270 were U.S. citizens, accounting for almost 40%. Their impact on global social, political, economic, and technological developments is extraordinary. Furthermore, the U.S. maintained strength in global competitiveness.

3.2. Impact of Private Organizations

Hospitality is a major character trait of the Chinese people, particular generosity to friends and relatives. A familiar scene is of both the host and guest rushing to pay the bill in front of a restaurant cashier counter. Chinese billionaires are active supporters of charitable activities, but most of them must consider the welfare of their extended family first. In the matters of community welfare and charitable affairs, they are not as enthusiastically well organized as their American counterparts.

Most newly rich Americans employ foundations as vehicles to utilize their wealth, in an objective, well planned manner, giving back to the community. Their beneficiaries are not limited to their own country, but are also global. By the turn of the 20th century, John D. Rockefeller (1839-1937), Andrew Carnegie (1835-1919), and John D. Rockefeller, Jr. (1874-1960) were the vanguards of fellow American philanthropists. Among other agenda, Rockefeller father and son donated $80 million to establish the University of Chicago (1890); established a foundation to administer philanthropic activities (1913); founded the Peking Union Medical College and Hospital (1919), first of its kind in China, investing $750 million. Andrew Carnegie migrated from Scotland to America in 1848 at the age of 13, taking a factory job for $1.20 a week. He worked his way up to become the steel tycoon owning the world's largest steel corporation. By the age of 66, he sold his business and devoted his money and energy to the causes of improving pedagogy, education, and world peace. His legacy includes the Carnegie-Mellon University (1904), Carnegie Foundation for the Advancement of Teaching (1905), Carnegie Endowment for International Peace (1910), and support of some 2,800 libraries. Currently, the Bill & Melinda Gates Foundation, for example, in 2008, donated $3.6 billion around the world. Particularly in Africa, the foundation provided financial support to fight AIDS, malaria, tuberculosis, smallpox, and other infectious diseases, and provided education, equipment, drugs, and disease prevention assistance. In nine years, smallpox plummeted by 74% in Africa; malaria was cut by half in three years in Zambia. These were considerable and noteworthy achievements.

Recently, one of the richest men in the world, Warren Buffet, initiated a Giving Pledge, supported by Bill Gates. Buffet has donated 90% of his wealth to charities and now invites the world's richest individuals to donate more than 50% of their wealth. Since its inception in 2010, there are 92 pledges globally (2012/9/19). After their daughter was born, Mark Zuckerberg and Priscilla Chan, aged 31 and 30 respectively, donated their 99% holding interest in Facebook, estimated at $45 billion, to a foundation for causes leading to improve the world for the benefit of future generations. The news was received with tremendous jubilation globally. Warren Buffet was the first to extend his heartfelt appreciation on behalf of the world beneficiaries (2015/12/3).

Common Chinese social organizations include school alumni,

homeland and family clan associations, and professional societies for doctors, engineers, etc. Their main objectives were to promote fellowship and improve members' welfare. In America, in addition to fellowship and professional societies, some organizations are especially devoted to promote ideology and religion, improve education and health, harmonize ethnic groups and communities, protect the environment and natural resources, and provide relief during natural disasters and civil catastrophes. The Rotary Club, Red Cross, Boy Scouts, YMCA, and churches are a few examples. These organizations, associating with the local population and being a part of the community, have a profound effect in the long term. Their influences may not be short of the U.S. government's effort. For example, Rotary International, founded in Illinois in 1905, promotes the motto of "service above self in the community, workplace, and in the world." Globally, there are more than 34,000 clubs with 1.2 million members in every country on Earth.

3.3. Diplomatic and Military Impact

After World War II, the United States and other Western powers adopted policies encouraging colonial independence, advocating democracy, and promoting the establishment of the United Nations, to lay the foundation for world peace. Since then, in addition to embassies, this additional global diplomatic platform was made available. But the United States and the Soviet Union quickly turned from being allies into being enemies. The outbreak of the Korean War and the ensuing Cold War only intensified the depth of anti-Communism. After the collapse of the Soviet Union, the United States lost its rival, diverting attention to fighting drug trafficking, and after the destruction of the World Trade Center and the Pentagon on September 11, 2001, devoting its energy to anti-terrorism activities, leading to the wars in Afghanistan and Iraq.

The U.S. State Department's diplomatic goal is to create a secure, democratic, and prosperous world, to ban nuclear weapons, to protect expatriates, and to develop trade and education. The unwritten goal may include the protection and expansion of U.S. interests abroad and to maximize influence and control over world affairs, coupled with the military power to achieve this objective. The State Department's 2010 budget of $51.7 billion, accounted for 1.5% of the total budget, while the budget of the Departments of

Defense and Homeland Security, totaling $706.4 billion, accounted for 20% of the budget. These numbers clearly demonstrate that military force is still the focus of the U.S. influence abroad.

The largest single item of U.S. foreign aid was the Marshall Plan to rebuild Western Europe, at $13 billion, about 5% of the 1948 GDP. The plan was to promote social stability and economic growth. As a result, output in Western Europe increased 35% over what it had been before the war. From 1946 to 1952, U.S. aid to Japan, totaling $15.2 billion, helped to restore infrastructure, to introduce modern equipment and technology, and to promote economic growth. During the Korean and Vietnamese Wars, Japan served as American military suppliers, personnel transition and recreation centers, further promoting product improvement and economic progress. As a result, U.S. markets were flooded with Japanese common merchandise in the 1970s and 1980s. The Japanese automobile industry incursion in America intensified in the 1980s leading to General Motors and Chrysler Motor Company's bankruptcies in 2009. The auto industry failure was contrary to American intentions to promote a strong Japan for the purpose to contain Communist expansion.

During the Cold War, U.S. foreign aid was almost entirely military in nature, mainly establishing military facilities, training military personnel, and supplying arms to friendly nations. The objective was to contain Communist expansion. After the collapse of the Soviet Union, U.S. foreign aid expanded to cover economic, health, and education, but focused on the Israeli-Palestinian region. However, military aid was still the main project. Between 2001and 2006, for example, aid to Israel and Egypt accounted for about 40% of total foreign aid, and 22% of that was military in nature. The Israeli-Palestinian conflict involves territorial, political, racial, religious, social and other problems including terrorism, all complex and cumbersome; no effective solution has been found.

The controversy of the U.S.-South Korea naval exercise with China involved the George Washington aircraft carrier which was built in 1990, at a cost of $4.5 billion. The super carrier can accommodate over 6,000 officers and sailors, more than 100 aircraft, and enough energy to supply a city of one million people, equivalent to the whole naval installation of an average nation. The U.S. has 10 active-duty aircraft carriers stationed at strategic seaports around the world. Most other countries only have one active-duty aircraft carrier (Italy has two small ones). In addition, the

United States has military bases in 191 foreign countries and regions. These bases include air, land, naval, and communication reconnaissance systems. It can be said that America is truly the world's policeman, with its scope of coverage and the ability to respond quickly; no other nation on earth can match it. As a result, with military expenditure mounting, in 2009 the defense budget of $680 billion was more than the sum of the military expenditure of the world's major countries. Fighting terrorists, drugs, Homeland Security spending, and the defense budget reached a total of more than $1 trillion, accounting for 28% of the national budget expenditure in 2009, almost matching the military build-up of the Reagan era in the 1980s.

3.4. Effects of Promoting American Ideology

Democracy, freedom, equality and human rights are America's founding ideals. Soon after the end of World War II, the Western powers, led by the United States, all had given up their colonies, advocated independence, respected human rights, promoted freedom and equality, and required these colonies to set up democratic governments. Democracy is considered by many people in the world as a universal truth, regardless of time and country, a one-fits-all political system. All nations not only can but also should adopt democracy. Also, most people consider democracy as a political goal. All overlook the purpose of politics is building a harmonious society where people are secure and happy with their livelihood and see continuous improvement of their quality of life. The second purpose is improving people's education to promote mental and spiritual well-being. And the last is to safeguard people's rights to life, property, freedom, equality, and dignity. Democracy is one of the means that could possibly achieve these goals. Therefore, the most important question is whether people's lives, education, and civil rights have been improved and enhanced, not whether democracy is implemented or an election is being held.

Nearly 90 years after the founding of the United States, President Lincoln set slaves free, but Blacks really didn't have equal rights until the passage of the 1964 Civil Rights Act, which took another hundred years. American women's political fortune fared even worse; they had to wait until 1920 to claim their voting rights, which was nearly 150 years after the nation was founded. Therefore, 1964 is considered the real beginning of U.S. democracy. For the first 200 years, it was a white male democratic dictatorship. Women and non-whites in America lived under authoritarian ruled. Hence, two systems were in operation and co-existed. Clearly, the U.S. expediently used a dual political system at that time for the purpose of fostering economic and social development. However, ignoring its own political experiences in the United States and without regarding the Afro-Asian social developmental conditions, each country was required to adopt democracy. As a result, there were very few successful experiences.

The biggest impact of the democracy movement was in Asia and Africa, because these two continents had few independent states and contained mostly colonies or semi-colonial regions. Apart from the countries of the Communist bloc, all have become republics, imitating the parliamentary politics of Europe and the United States. However, in emerging republics in Africa and Asia, less than handful nations demonstrated a successful experience. Many of them have a form of election, with presidents at the helm, but ignore the constraints of the constitution and parliament.

Since World War II ended, African colonies and kingdoms, one after the other, converted to these republics. The democracy movement swept throughout the continent; even the two thousand year old ancient kingdom of Ethiopia was not spared. In the last 70 years, the United States and Western powers contributed a large amount of aid to Africa for economic and social development. But in politics, the term president merely replaced the title of king, with not much accomplishment in democracy and human rights. Even worse, between 1971 and 1978, an estimated 100,000 to 500,000 people were murdered by Ugandan President Idi Amin's regime. In 1980, the Rhodesian freedom fighter, Robert Mugabe, overthrew the white regime, changing the country's name to Zimbabwe, and was elected president, serving in that capacity for over 37 years -- life-time tenure? While paving the road for his wife to success his presidency, Mugabe was deposed on November 2017 by the military on account of corruption ending his dynasty.

Except in North Africa and a few other countries developing their natural resources, such as oil and minerals for export, little progress came to other industries in the entire continent. The United Nations 2009 statistics revealed that except North Africa, nearly half of the people in Africa have not surpassed the poverty line of $2 a day per person. Even in

33

the Union of South Africa, the poverty rate is up to 43%; Liberia and Tanzania are as high as 95%. Education in Africa still lags; the illiteracy rate in 25 countries is up to 35%. President Amin was forced to abdicate in exchange for Amin II. Yet, changing leaders without changing substance means the problems persist. As the adage goes, people never have a sense of shame if they are without adequate food and shelter. African people were struggling to subsist; so how could they relish democracy and freedom of speech? Survival was their primary goal. Africa's current priority is eliminating hunger, disease, and improving education, rather than honing politics.

After World War II, Japan under U.S. supervision, renounced militarism, adopting a constitution and implementing democracy. The result was commendable because Japan had a stable social structure and high economic and educational standards before the war. Other Asian countries also restructured to a democratic system. Because the economic and education conditions were somewhat better than in Africa, the political problem was not as severe.

India, hailed by the West as the world's largest democracy, for example, since its independence from Britain in 1947, has accumulated 70-year experience with democracy. However, the caste system is still prevalent. Women often suffer brutal sexual attacks and the worst human rights protection globally, even though Mrs. Indira Gandhi served as India's prime minister for 15 years. Polygamy is not against the law in some areas of India. More than 75% of the people live below the poverty line (2007, $2.00 a day). A February 2015 UN report credits India with meeting the poverty ($1.25 a day) reduction target of 21.9% of its population by the end of 2015, but India is still home of one fourth to the world's poor and one third of the world's malnourished children. Among 40 Asian nations, the literacy rate in India is only better than Bangladesh and Pakistan. Yet, India claims the world's largest private mansion, worth $1 billion; has the world's leading computer software industry; launched a satellite to Mars with space technology; as well, it is the birthplace of some of the world's major religions. Its society is full of extremes and contradictions. India has neither improved the essence of people's lives nor achieved equality of human rights. It is neither a country ruled by a dictatorship nor a democracy. It is simply a land of contradictions.

Indonesia, Pakistan, and South Korea were under military rule for some times under the name of democracy. Taiwan exposed unprecedented presidential corruption after Chiang's dynasty passed on the baton. The Malaysia ruling party employed legal or illegal means to suppress oppositions. China, Vietnam, and North Korea were under Communist regimes. Most of the other parts of Asia were either too poor or too ignorant; they had very little to do with democracy or human rights. In short, except Japan, the effect of promoting democracy and human rights was largely unsatisfactory in most countries in Asia.

Since the early 1970s, the oil exporting countries successfully sanctioned oil embargoes against the United States. The U.S. not only lost influence over these oil-producing countries but had to rely on them for oil supplies at a reasonable price to maintain domestic consumption and economic stability. Other than Egypt and Jordan, who rely on U.S. aid, all other countries in the Middle East showed little interest in the call for democracy and human rights by the United States and other Western powers because they neither needed the financial assistance nor the military protection of the U.S. They maintain authoritarian regimes.

The pro-democracy movement in the Middle East in 2011 set off demonstrations against Egypt, Saudi Arabia, Bahrain, Yemen, Jordan, etc. President Hosni Mubarak, reigning in Egypt for three decades, became a prisoner; other states dispatched military and police to crack down on the protestors. It is not hard to imagine the condition of democracy and human rights in this region of the world.

President James Monroe declared in 1823 that the Americas belong to the American people and warned the Western powers not to interfere with the internal affairs of the Americas, especially colonial expansion. In 1898, the U.S. military overwhelmingly defeated the Spanish armed forces; and after World War I, when the European powers had been exhausted, the Americas then fell entirely within the sphere of U.S. influence. After World War II, except for the Cuban incident causing a conflict with the Soviet Union, the international Communists did not mount any offense in the Americas. Therefore, the U.S. had no political competitor in its hemisphere.

Salvador Allende Gosens, in 1970, advocated the Marxist socialist economic doctrines in the Chilean general election and won the presidency of Chile. He extended diplomatic relations with Cuba and China, and reformed the national economy. Nationalization of the country's key industries occurred, such as copper mines, including the American mining interest. With the assistance of the U.S. Central Intelligence Agency in 1973, General Augusto Pinochet staged a military coup which toppled Allende's government and also ended 43 years of constitutional government in Chile. Pinochet wantonly arrested political dissidents. More than 28,000 people were subjected to torture, with 3,200 deaths in 17 years of his rule.

In 1976, Argentina experienced high inflation and social unrest. General Jorge Rafael Videha saw the opportunity and seized political power. In order to stay in power and to maintain social stability, his iron fist rule resulted in 2,300 deaths and 20,000-30,000 people missing within five years. The other major Latin American countries such as Brazil and Mexico were also ruled by the military on and off. In Latin America, the United States was only opposed to Communism and leftist regimes. When its own interests were not jeopardized, it tended to accommodate the reality and support the authoritarian governments, and turned a blind eye toward human rights violations. President Jimmy Carter's administration was the exception.

Western Europe under the Marshall Plan achieved economic prosperity, social stability, and pressured Germany, Italy, and Spain to complete democratic reform. To the U.S., Western Europe was an important helping hand in fighting the Soviet Union and Eastern European Communist bloc. The Cold War stalemate lasted for more than four decades; both sides made no headway in Europe. It was U.S. President Ronald Reagan who changed the course in dealing with the Soviets, adopting a confrontational policy instead of staying with the containment tactic. The 1980s arms race with the U.S. coupled with the Soviet war in Afghanistan, and a huge oil price slump caused the Soviet Planned Economy to collapse. In 1990, the Soviet Union began to disintegrate, and some Eastern European Communist regimes broke away from Russia. Poland, the Czech Republic, Hungary, and East Germany adopted a parliamentary system. Other countries, including many former Soviet Republics still maintained authoritarian regimes.

IV. The Great Society Legislation Led to a Social Welfare System

After World War II, the Western powers abandoned former colonies and advocated democracy, freedom, equality, and human rights for the newly independent nations. The atmosphere of freedom and equality spread all over the world. The U.S. military personnel who toured in Europe and Asia personally experienced this feeling. They were hailed by the local people as liberators of the atrocities committed by the German and Japanese armies. These soldiers were crowned by the local people as heroes, showered with popular affection, and favored by many local young women who became war brides.

Many U.S. black soldiers upon returning to their hometowns in America encountered racial discrimination and unequal treatment. As compared with the situation they experienced overseas in a foreign land, the difference was huge. Because the South was mainly farming, traditionally embraced slavery, many states had embedded apartheid laws, regulations, and traditions, such as outlawing interracial marriage, segregation on school campuses and public transportation, and special reserved facilities or areas for Caucasians. These restrictions and unequal treatments made Blacks feel disenfranchised, and they were determined to challenge the status quo.

The 1954 Supreme Court decision that segregation in public schools was in violation of the Constitution reinforced the demand from Blacks for equality. They used peaceful means to boycott buses which required blacks and whites to be seated separately. Blacks occupied lunch counters because they were refused dining-in service (termed as sit-ins tactics), and they conducted mass demonstrations to vent their anger towards injustice.

These peaceful protests enticed social sympathy. And they also aroused the guilt of some white people because blacks had done much of the menial labor in American history, especially before farm mechanization, but most of the fruits of farming were enjoyed by white farm owners. It was an unfair system of exploitation. So, a lot of whites openly supported black causes with donations, sympathetic remarks in public, some even joining their ranks as demonstrators. On the other hand, there were a lot of black people taking violent actions to express their anger and revolt, leading to riots, sabotage, arson, bombing, robbery and murder. Because most of these activities were occurring in the black communities, they had become black ghetto disasters.

The most serious events took place in New York City's Harlem district, the Watts neighborhood in Los Angeles, Newark, and Detroit. In the 1967 Detroit riots, fires burned for three days, with 43 deaths, 2,250 injured, 4,000 people arrested, and property losses amounting to millions of dollars. In 1968, when Rev. Martin Luther King, Jr. was assassinated, riots by blacks occurred in more than one hundred cities across the nation. Some blacks took the occasion to express their anger, and some used the opportunity to loot, causing major social chaos and destruction, intensifying people's resentment and prejudice against blacks.

This period of the civil rights movement did not improve the economic or political status of blacks, but it clearly declared to white segregationists that the status quo could not be maintained. It was necessary to make a complete change. The most active organizations were the Southern Christian Leadership Conference, Congress of Racial Equality, Student Nonviolent Coordinating Committee, and the largest black organization, the National Association for the Advancement of Colored People.

4.1. Civil Rights Legislation: the African-American Rises

After President John F. Kennedy took office in 1961, he did not fully realize the seriousness of the civil rights movement. Only after his brother Robert's strong advice did he take the discrimination against blacks as a primary legislative task. In facing the University of Alabama's attempt to prevent black students from enrolling in 1963, his outcry to the nation was: "The United States of America promotes freedom and equality to the world. But in our country, we consider the blacks as second-class citizens, giving them inferior treatment. This is unforgivable and the status quo must be changed immediately". Unfortunately, he was assassinated in November 1963, without accomplishing much in the area of civil rights.

Vice President Lynden B. Johnson (LBJ) took over the office of the President. He incorporated Kennedy's civil rights ideas and extended them to the full range of social issues. He declared that he would build The Great Society in which equality and justice would be extended to all Americans; poverty and crime would be addressed and hopefully eradicated and welfare would be extended to all people who needed it. The whole nation moved towards the Great Society. The reform covered the major areas in politics, economics, health care, education, environmental protection, transportation, housing, firearms, and immigration. During his five year presidential tenure, LBJ pushed through 22 major pieces of legislation which greatly altered American society and people's lives. His influence far exceeds those of all other presidents.

The legislation involving politics were the Civil Rights Act of 1964 and Voting Rights Act of 1965. The Civil Rights Act affirms that every human being in principle was equal before the law. Race, color, religion, sex, age, and place of birth cannot be given a different treatment, especially in voting, education, employment, and the use of public transportation and other facilities. The Act also expanded the Supreme Court decision on public school desegregation to other social aspects and prohibits the use of intellectual qualifications, standards, and procedures as an excuse to deny citizens the right to vote. In the South where blacks were historically discriminated against, it was necessary to get permission from the Department of Justice before the local election laws were changed, and the terms of the supervision in the fourth amendment of the Voting Rights Act was again extended in 2006 to 2031, another 25 years.

In the southern states, civil rights activists set off massive voter registration campaigns. Many blacks for the first time had the right to vote, which changed the 1964 election characteristics in which year voters accounted for only half of the nation's total population. In the South, blacks started to expand their political strength and supported the Democratic Party while on the other hand; whites began steering towards the Republican Party. The political situation in the 15 Southern states has been altered ever since.

In fact, President Dwight Eisenhower's practical actions had significant impact on racial discrimination. As early as 1942, when the Japanese launched the South Pacific offense, Australia asked the U.S. for help, but reiterated the White Australia policy that the U.S. respect their laws and not send any black soldiers. Eisenhower was the military commander at that time and gave them a straightforward reply: "All right. No troops." which forced the Australians into submission. In 1947, President Harry Truman ordered all branches of the military to be desegregated, but by early 1953, five years later, only one-third of the military had implemented the order. When Eisenhower assumed the presidency in 1953, he immediately issued an Executive Order to outlaw racial discrimination in Washington D.C. and the military, and by October 1954, less than two years, no unit in the armed forces was segregated. This was 15 months earlier than the Supreme Court decision on school desegregation. In 1957, when the Little Rock public high schools in Arkansas refused to accept black students, President Eisenhower dispatched the 101st Airborne Division to maintain order and to assist the black students in being smoothly enrolled. Again, this was four years earlier than President Kennedy's confrontation with the Governor of Alabama, George Wallace, on black student admission to a public school (*Washington Post*, George Will column, 2012/2/19). Only because Republicans took a more conservative approach toward civil rights issues, and Eisenhower was Republican, were these significant facts not mentioned by the pro-Democratic Party civil rights activists.

President Kennedy on March 6, 1961, issued an Affirmative Action Executive Order requiring the federal government agencies, businesses, and public organizations not to use race, color, religion, and country of origin as determinants for employment, education, purchasing property, and getting real estate loans. In fact, these were declared illegal acts of discrimination and also were the main features of the 1964 Civil Rights Act that President Johnson later signed. However, on September 24, 1965, President Johnson also issued an Affirmative Action Executive Order, which was precisely contrary to Kennedy's Executive Order and the 1964 Civil Rights Act. The order required all levels of government and public institutions to take positive actions, changing the unfair social conditions caused by historical discrimination to compensate the blacks who were behind in all aspects of life. So, all levels of government, businesses, and public institutions had to be very creative to come up with some plans that would give preferential treatment to the blacks without violating the Civil Rights Act.

The most popular scheme was to set quotas for separate ethnic groups so that blacks would only compete against other blacks, not against other ethnic groups in the selection process. With the implementation of these measures, blacks enjoyed many kinds of preferential treatment, particularly in education, employment, and promotion. For example, the federal government's pay scale was double that of private companies, almost like a tenured position, and blacks then accounted for 20% of federal employees; but their population totaled only 12% of total population (Federal Personnel Office reported in 2010, all federal government employees but not including military personnel). Furthermore, most blacks were not adequately qualified for the jobs they held. Thus, people resented the new system. It represented reverse discrimination. Here is a typical case which shows the whole picture:

Allan Bakke in 1974 sued the University of California, School of Medicine at Davis for discrimination against whites because Bakke was rejected for admission to the school two years in a row while many black students having academic credentials far inferior to him were accepted as medical students. School admission officials cited that the selection plan set aside 16 places especially for blacks; Bakke was not black, therefore, ineligible for consideration. The School of Medicine lost the case in the lower court and appealed to the federal Supreme Court. The court took up the case in 1978. After lengthy hearings, four Justices were in favor of using race as a factor to compensate for the consequences of past discrimination, while the other four cited that not accepting white applicants was in violation of the equal rights of the Civil Rights Act of 1964. The final verdict rested on the views of the ninth judge, Justice Lewis Powell. He declared the quota system illegal and the use of quotas to achieve a multiracial student body would only destroy the true purpose of diversity. He was only in favor of the school developing a diversified student body in order to realize educational benefits. Bakke won and completed his medical education in 1982 at the Davis campus.

In the following years, California, Michigan, and Washington passed legislation prohibiting affirmative action that was discriminatory. However, the practice is still popularly favored today by most public and private organizations. Most recently, 10 elite schools' admission reports, from 1980 to 1997, containing 9,200 student applications, show black students with an average SAT of 1,150, whites 1,460, and Asians 1,600 points. The admission ratio of blacks is more than five times higher than whites, and the whites' admission ratio is more than three times higher than Asians (Princeton University sociology professor Thomas Espenshade, No Longer Separate, Not Yet Equal: Race and Class in Elite College Admission & Campus Life, 2011/8/12). If the SAT scores are converted into a percentile basis, Asians average 100, whites average 91, and the blacks only average 72 points. Although Asian students have outstanding achievements, the chance of being admitted to these elite schools is less than one third of the white students and less than one fifteenth of the black students. This is clearly not fair competition. The Asians do not get the protection but become the victims of the Civil Rights Act. The law should be properly renamed as the Black Rights Act for its true meaning. This Act has existed for 50 years, and middle-aged blacks like President Obama have enjoyed preferential treatment. To continue this policy is certainly not only unjust and unfair to others but also destroys motivation for blacks to move upward but remain a backward group forever, unable to stand up, having to depend on preferential treatment for survival.

4.2. Guaranteeing a Basic Living; Providing Health Care

Regarding people's livelihood, President Johnson declared a War on Poverty. There were four important pieces of legislation: (1) The Food Stamp Act of 1964, supplying the poor with free food coupons of $125.35 per person per month (national average for FY 2014), used as cash for food purchased at any store. As recession and unemployment intensified in recent years, more than 45 million people received the benefit, accounting for 15% of the total population at an annual cost of $58 billion, a 51-month over 45 million recipients record (2015/10/23). (2) The 1964 Economic Opportunity Act designed to provide health, education, and other benefits to the poor so that they could maintain a minimum living standard. Many plans implemented at that time have been abolished, but the Head Start and Job Corps programs still prevail.

The Head Start program was originally designed to make up the deficiency in basic knowledge and skills of 3-5 year old poor children when entering kindergarten to provide them with an equal learning foundation. The project gradually expanded in scope to include other education, health, and low-income benefits. In 2005, 905,000 children participated in 1,604 programs nationwide, conducted in 48,000 classrooms by 212,000 employees and 1.27 million volunteers. The average cost was $7,222 per child per year plus other expenses for an annual budget of nearly $6.9 billion. The Department of Labor is responsible for the implementation of the Job Corps mission which includes counseling poor youth between 16 and 24 years old, helping them find a job or getting them into a college. Food, clothing, shelter, medical care, and pocket money are provided to each without obligation. Nationally, there are 125 centers serving 60,000 youths annually. The 2007 budget was over $1.5 billion.

The other two bills (3 & 4) were the Housing Act of 1964 and the Civil Rights Act of 1968. The former provided $8 billion for low-income government housing, rent subsidies, and home maintenance and repair loans. The latter outlawed acts of discrimination in housing sales, leasing, home loans, etc. In big cities, the government housing accommodated hundreds of low-income families, mostly in high-rise buildings. Because it was difficult to have security control, these buildings soon became breeding grounds for illegal activities, especially drug trafficking. Today few survive, as most have been demolished. In addition, the Appalachian Region Commission (the area extends from western New York State to north of Mississippi covering 205,000 square miles, with 23 million of the nation's poorest whites) was created to help improve the lives of the people in that region.

National health care legislation was a major achievement of President Johnson. The Social Security Act of 1965 established the Medicare and Medicaid systems to insure that people's physical well-being was taken care of. At that time, illegal immigrants were small in number and not a burden to the medical system. Other than the poor, elderly, and handicapped, most people could take care of themselves because medical costs were relatively inexpensive.

The Medicare insurance provided by the federal government to the elderly and
handicapped people is funded by a national labor tax. Regardless of whether payment comes from salaries, wages, bonuses, commissions, tips, fees, or any remuneration for personal services, a percentage of it has to be contributed to the Medicare insurance fund. Medicaid is funded by both the federal (47%) and state (43%) governments to help the poor for their medical needs. The Poor's share of health care costs depends on the size of family and the level of income. The government is just the middleman providing free services to the patients and medical service providers for the Medicare and Medicaid programs. In 2014, Medicare had 54.0 million enrollees and Medicaid, including 6.0 million Children Health Insurance Program participants, had 64.9 million recipients. These two programs combined accounted for 34.3% of the total population. Demand

for medical service outstrips supply leading to medical costs surging. Medicare Insurance receipts were insufficient to meet its expenditure; the Medicare Insurance fund is facing serious financial trouble.

In summary, Johnson's legislation did improve the lives of people: the national poverty rate decreased from 22.2% in 1963 to 12.6% in 1970; the black poverty rate decreased from 55% in 1960 to 27% in 1968. Of course, the general economic prosperity during this period also played an important role in the reduction of poverty in America.

Except for the elderly and disabled, social welfare eligibility was mainly determined by family size and income so that able workers could choose not to work and collected welfare benefits, setting a precedent in U.S. history. This loophole had been amended in the 1990s by the workfare standards which required that the able bodied must be working to be eligible for any benefits. Other drawbacks were common, too, such as having more children in order to collect more benefits and family grants being diverted to buy drugs or luxury goods. A popular slogan at that time, Welfare Cadillac (Cadillac is General Motor's luxury car) referred to this phenomenon. Critics believe that the welfare system does not help recipients strive for self-reliance and a better life, but strengthens their tendency to depend on welfare as a permanent way of life.

4.3. Enhancing Education; Protecting the Environment

President Johnson was an elementary school teacher for several years before entering politics. He personally observed poor students' limitations with education and was convinced that education was the only way to eradicate ignorance and poverty. Therefore, improving education was high on his priority list in The Great Society legislation.

Legislation concerning education included the Higher Education Facilities Act of 1963, Vocational Act of 1963, Nurse Training Act of 1964, Elementary & Secondary Education Act of 1965, Higher Education Act of 1965, Public Broadcasting Act of 1967, as well as the Bilingual Education Act of 1968. These bills strongly supported poor school districts and private schools, college buildings and equipment grants, scholarships, work-study programs, and student loans. To promote literary and humanities development, financial aid was provided to assist museums, artifact storage, libraries, universities, television and radio stations, and humanities scholars.

With the passage of time, many of the projects vanished, but the scholarships, work study programs, student loans, and literary and humanities programs continue to this day. The student loans helped to increase enrollment and created a higher education boom which have become the main source of income for public and private universities alike. The student loans have benefited many young students and professors, but they also provided the opportunity to owners of schools for profit to make a fortune. Today student loans total more than $1 trillion, surpassing all credit card debts (2011/10/26). By the end of 2016, the amount has reached $1.31 trillion (2017/2/18).

To safeguard people's health and to protect ecosystems were the main themes of Johnson's Clean Air Act of 1963 and Wilderness Act of 1964. The Acts set the air quality standards to ensure clean air; restricted factory emissions to prevent excessive air pollution causing ozone depletion; and promulgated regulations to restore natural ecology. It was the first piece of environmental protection law in the U.S. and also created a brand new agency, the Environmental Protection Agency (EPA), which was tasked with the responsibility for enforcing all environmental regulations. Since then, a number of environmental laws were passed in 1970, 1977, and 1990, and now form today's environmental protection regulations.

The Wilderness Act of 1964 aimed at maintaining the natural ecosystem as well as protection of species facing extinction. The Act originally set aside more than nine million acres as wilderness areas and followed by consolidating one million plus acres from other four federal agencies to form the National Wilderness Preservation System. The federal agency published a range of protected species lists enforceable nationwide. Within the national wilderness system, logging, exploration and mining of oil and gas, and operating power equipment were prohibited to ensure clean air and water. As of 2009, Congress passed an additional eight pieces of legislation relating to the protection of wilderness.

4.4. Breaking with Tradition, Changing Immigration Policy

The Immigration and Nationality Service Act of 1965 broke away from the national origin quota tradition and established a system based on an applicant's skill and knowledge or family relationship with U.S. citizens. Although the Chinese Exclusion Act of 1882 was repealed by Congress in 1943, the Chinese annual quota of 105 people was almost meaningless, as though the Act had not been abolished. The whites-favored immigration policy was in full force in the United States before 1965. The new law brought in more Latino and Asian immigrants, and relatively reduced the ratio of European immigrants. As a result, the immigrant population doubled from 1965 to 1970, and redoubled from 1970 to 1990.

The 2010 census showed that people from Latin America have the fastest population growth, totaling more than 50 million, accounting for 16.7% of the national population. This group of people, officially known as Hispanic or Latino, is not a race. All are from Latin America, except Asians even if they were born in the Americas. The majority of them speak Spanish, but other languages are used by different countries, e.g., Brazil uses Portuguese, Haiti uses French, Bahamas uses English, while the original Spanish speakers from Spain are white and not included in this category. Therefore, some media refer to this group as Spanish speakers, which is not quite appropriate. Blacks accounted for 12.0 percent, Asians totaled 4.8%, and the whites 64.0 %. In California, Texas, Hawaii, New Mexico and Washington D.C., non-whites are the majority. Among the 366 metropolitan urban areas, in only nine of them were whites the minority in 1980; today there are 46 cities, including New York, Washington D.C., San Diego, Las Vegas, and Memphis (2011/3/25, 4/15, 7/15).

After over 40 years of accumulated effect, the new immigrant policy significantly altered the makeup of the U.S. population, increasing the proportion of minority voters. *Boston Global* reported that in the 2008 presidential election Obama was the beneficiary of this new immigration Act because the proportion of white voters decreased sharply; according to Simon Rosenberg, this is the most significant immigration bill that has dramatically changed the ethnic makeup in the United States during the last 300 years. The 2010 census showed the immigrant population as 40 million, accounting for 12.9%, the highest percentage since 1920 (2011/8/31, 9/23).

4.5. Brilliant Achievements Lacking Recognition

In a short five-year span, President Johnson's legislation radically changed almost every aspect of people's lives in the United States. Whether it was politics, the economy, education, health, the environment, or immigration, all were materially affected. Its influence is unprecedented and greater than any president's domestic agenda. Imagine, just to raise the national debt ceiling, President Obama had to spend so much effort before realizing his wish.

In the end, where and how did Johnson acquire such tremendous legislative powers? Johnson, benefiting from the enthusiasm of the civil rights movement and sympathy from President Kennedy's assassination, solidly defeated Republican opponent Senator Barry Goldwater in the 1964 presidential election, sweeping the nation with 61.1% of the votes, a record since 1820, and capturing 44 states and Washington D.C. More importantly, the election also produced so many Democratic lawmakers. After the election, the congressional party composition was dramatically altered: 66 Democratic Senators as opposed to 34 Republicans; in the House of Representatives, the Democratic Congressmen outnumbered the Republicans by more than two to one. The Democratic Party had the majority, almost two-thirds, enough to kill any filibuster, a parliamentary maneuvering tactic usually used by the minority party to delay or prevent the passage of legislation. This was the most important factor for Johnson-sponsored bills that sailed through Congress smoothly without any delay. Second, before he became President, Johnson served as a member of the Senate and House of Representatives, each for 12 years, including 10 years as a parliamentary leader. As a result, he became a grandmaster of parliamentary maneuvering, knowing how to avoid pitfalls and selecting the most favorable legislative strategy. Finally, Johnson knew each congressional member's personal and political strength and weakness, likes and dislikes, eliminating the opposition forces one by one by inducement and/or threat. If all of the above measures failed, Johnson would then invite the opposition member to the White House for a private talk, telling him/her what was good for the country and the world. If that still could not convince the legislator, Johnson would use his imperious character, burly body, presidential majesty, White House atmosphere to intimidate the legislator. Legislators were vanquished. This was the famous Johnson Treatment. With these four strategies, the legislation process for each bill was approved as scheduled, bringing in the unprecedented bounty of legislation.

It seemed as if Johnson could easily amend the Constitution, make himself some sort of king of America, and hold onto power forever. But the good times did not last long. The war in Vietnam turned sour. Anti-war sentiment was at its peak both at home and abroad, especially among college students, boycotting classes and holding anti-war demonstrations almost daily. The Hollywood elites were not to be outdone either. Actress Jane Fonda was not only involved in the anti-war movement but also visited Hanoi, North Vietnam to support her beliefs and made her case for the North Vietnamese on U.S. radio stations. She was accorded the title of "Hanoi Jane". Within the Democrat Party there were prominent people, e.g., Robert Kennedy, the former President's brother, and Senator Eugene McCarthy, who supported the anti-war movement. Johnson condemned the press, churches, and college professors for not knowing right from wrong and for speaking without any responsibility. Therefore, even though education and intellectual communities were the second largest beneficiaries of Johnson's legislation, they paid him no gratitude regarding the Vietnam War and, instead, rallied all efforts to smear him. Johnson had little personal contact with black leaders, but referred to Rev. Martin Luther King, Jr., the most revered black leader, in private, as the hypocritical pastor, which might be the reason why the greatest beneficiaries of Johnson's The Great Society legislation, black people, didn't thank him or give him due credit. Moreover, by Johnson's own admission, with his imperious personality he inevitably offended some people in the administrative process. And of course, most Republicans blamed him for turning the country upside down.

After several years' implementation, opposition to the Civil Rights Act and other social welfare legislations mounted. Aside from the ideology, the financial burdens of various Great Society programs had overwhelmed the budget, even at the height of U.S. affluence and prosperity. The government had to temporarily impose a 6% income tax surcharge, heightening people's dissatisfaction with Johnson's overall policy. A January 1967 poll showed that staunch supporters of Johnson were only 16%, forcing him to give up his presidential re-election bid. By the 1972 presidential election, the Republican candidate, Richard Nixon, claimed a landslide victory with 60.7% of the popular vote and winning 49 states, a record of nearly 18 million votes difference from his opponent. The Democratic Party candidate, George McGovern, endorsed the anti-war movement, but only won Massachusetts and Washington D.C.

The vote strongly expressed the people's dissatisfaction with the

Democratic Party and its social welfare programs, with the hope that the Republican new regime would make a fundamental change. However, on June 17, 1972, the Watergate Scandal broke, and people began to debate whether or not to forgive the President if he was also involved in the theft of Democratic Party confidential information. Because of the mistake, Nixon was forced to resign on August 9, 1974. The people's hope that the Nixon administration might reverse the course moving the nation toward a welfare society also vanished.

4.6. Impact of Johnson Administration

Americans generally consider Franklin Delano Roosevelt (FDR) as the greatest president of modern times. The poll also indicated that Roosevelt is only second to George Washington or Abraham Lincoln as the second or the third most admirable president in American history because he led the country out of the Great Depression, then united the Allied nations to defeat the Axis, and helped create the United Nations.

In his long 12 years' tenure, there were also a lot of New Deal legislation, but most were temporary laws enacted to meet emergency needs. During the Great Depression, the emphasis was on restoring people's confidence, stabilizing the banking and financial markets, reviving businesses and industries, reorganizing the banking system, and building public infrastructures. When World War II broke out, FDR promoted justice, gathered resources for war preparations, restructured industries for military needs, and mobilized human resources for the war effort. Once the economy was back to normal and the war had ended, of course, most of the related legislation would not be needed anymore.

President Roosevelt's significant legacy included the founding of the United Nations, building of the largest public utility, Tennessee Valley Authority, which provided electricity and flood control, while improving the regional farmers' lives, and the Social Security Act which gave basic economic security for the elderly and the disable, a milestone in American history. In the financial sector, key legislation included the Glass-Steagall Act of 1933, the Securities Act of 1933 and Securities Exchange Act 1934. The former created a deposit insurance system to assure the safety of depositors' funds and eliminate panic money withdrawals leading to bank failures. The latter two Acts were designed to strengthen securities and exchange supervision, to increase transparency of companies' financial condition, as well as to eliminate security market illegal operations.

In industrial areas, Roosevelt signed the National Labor Relations Act (NLRA) in 1935, allowing trade unions to organize in industries, representing workers for contract negotiation and the right to strike. Companies could not hire new workers to replace strikers, unless the state enacted the Free to Work law. Hence, the Act empowered the unions monopolizing power in the labor market, and they became a formidable political force in national elections. Ever since, the labor unions and the Democratic Party have forged an undeclared political alliance over the last 80 years. The unions enthusiastically supported the Democratic candidate in presidential elections. This bill had profound and far reaching effects on both national politics and the economy.

As great as Roosevelt might have been, his regime committed some serious errors too. In order to accelerate economic recovery, in 1933, Roosevelt signed the National Industrial Recovery Act which repealed the antitrust laws. The Act promoted corporate consultation and cooperation to formulate contracts by each industry on setting production quota and prices in order to avoid competition by business and industry, and encouraged trade unions to organize for enhancing workers' welfare. But an increase in wage rates was the prerequisite for government approval of industrial contracts.

Free competition was the best mechanism for the protection of consumers and also for the healthy development of industry in the long run. The National Industrial Recovery Act which limited free competition and entitled businesses to retain monopolistic power was unanimously declared unconstitutional by the Supreme Court in 1935, a major blow to Roosevelt's legislative agenda. Second, the Japanese sneak attack on Pearl Harbor almost wiped out the U.S. Pacific fleet, causing heavy military and civilian casualties, and inciting people's hatred of the Japanese. In early 1942, Roosevelt issued an Executive Order authorizing the internment of Japanese non-U.S. citizens and their dependents on the West Coast. However, personal freedom in America is a basic human right regardless of citizenship. In recent years, Congress formally adopted a resolution to compensate the Japanese victims and to apologize for the mistake made by the American government.

Besides the Social Security and labor union legislations, President Roosevelt's other achievements included restoring the economy and to safeguard world peace. These significant achievements and contributions were made by Roosevelt when the country and world were in a critical situation. So, his heroic actions were partly created by emergencies.

President Johnson's legislations covered the whole spectrum of social aspects and made great strides towards a welfare society which gave people basic life necessities, civil rights, medical care, education benefits, open immigration, and protection of the environment. Over the last 50 years, the influences continued to expand and changed America significantly. Johnson's legislation promoted social justice and progress, and improved people's livelihood and well-being. However, under a socialist welfare system, it is easy to give people what they want but difficult to expect everyone to contribute according to their ability. Only when people are highly conscientious and dedicated will something be accomplished in a socialist system, so that demand for social services surged and supply lagged, e.g. medical services. Meanwhile, since no obligations were required from welfare recipients, tax payers were responsible for bearing this added financial burden and this situation eventually created serious social problems. Johnson may not be considered by many Americans to be as great as Roosevelt, but measuring the effects of his legislations in both form and substance on American society, Johnson is incomparable to any U.S. president.

V. Challenges Confronting the United States

Within one hundred years after its founding, the United States surpassed the United Kingdom as the world's largest economy. After World War II, the U.S. became a superpower, and since the collapse of the Soviet Union in 1991, the only superpower. More importantly, over the past century, the U.S. made a huge contribution to modern civilization, greatly improving production efficiency and quality of life, and improving the standard of living especially in the Western world. This brilliant achievement is unprecedented in human history, worthy of high recognition. It was the American century. However, since the 1970s, the U.S. has suffered a series of major setbacks and was unable to achieve its goals as planned. Here are a few major examples:

The war between Israel and the Arab countries broke out again in 1973. Because America sided with Israel, the Muslim oil-producing countries initiated an oil embargo against the United States. The oil supply shortages created long lines at gas stations and high gas prices. The government adopted a number of energy saving measures such as bans on Sunday sales of gas, highway speed limits, even limits on decorating with outdoor Christmas lights. Americans experienced resource scarcity for the first time and began to understand the concept of conservation. At that time, the U.S. accounted for only 5.4% of the world population but consumed one-third of the world's energy production, partly attributed to the status of the U.S. as a world factory.

President Nixon announced a policy of energy independence in 1973, comparable to the Manhattan Project (a national program in the early 1940s when the U.S. successfully developed the atomic bomb), investing $10 billion, and vowed the U.S. would become energy independent by 1980. With the passing presidencies of Ford, Carter, Reagan, Clinton, Bush father and son, and now Obama, almost every president declared or initiated legislation for energy independence. Four decades later, the United States has not only failed to achieve energy independence but continues to rely more on imported oil. In 1973, imported oil accounted for less than 35% of the total U.S. consumption. By 2010, it was a whopping 71% (19.2 million barrels of daily oil consumption, 13.7 million barrels imported), more than double the proportion of imported oil in 1973. The supply must exceed the needs of the growing population and economy in order to make overall improvements; otherwise, it will be like boating upstream: if you don't advance you will fall further and further behind.

In recent years, the advancement in horizontal drilling technology made shale oil accessible but at a high cost, economically and environmentally. Data compiled by the U.S. Energy Information Administration show in both 2013 and 2014 that domestic oil production exceeded the production of Saudi Arabia or Russia, and overtook imports. The U.S. was becoming the largest oil producer but moving toward energy independence was being achieved at a very high cost. The oil prices plunged in late 2014 and continued in 2015, hovering around $50 per barrel; by early 2016, it was down to less than $30 a barrel. In the past, when the oil price dropped, the Organization of Petroleum Exporting Countries (OPEC) would typically resort to their tactic of cutting production which reduced supply and thereby jacked up the price. But not this time, Saudi Arabia wanted to keep production as usual even with the low oil price because it would drive off the shale oil producers from the market and allow OPEC to maintain its monopolistic power.

The low oil price rendered shale oil production unprofitable. The Saudi strategy worked, costing America 100,000 jobs in planned layoffs just in the last four months of 2015, with more to come. The Saudis' cost is about $20 per barrel, so they can afford the oil price to drop further. Therefore, the shale oil production cost would have to be competitive with OPEC before the U.S. has a chance for energy independence. In addition, the state of Oklahoma reported more minor earthquakes in recent years when shale oil production increased its activities and more waste water generated from the production contaminating the environment. These issues whether real or imaginary should be resolved before large scale operations resume.

As for the Korean War, the United States could claim a draw. There was no winner or loser. But in 15 years of the Vietnam War, the U.S. forces suffered heavy casualties (58,148 deaths and 304,000 wounded) with astronomical military spending. Local military and civilian casualties were in the millions and there are still health and environmental hazards caused by chemical weapons used in Vietnam and the unexploded ordnance dropped in Laos and Cambodia by the U.S. armed forces during the war. In 1975, the U.S. embassy evacuated in panic, and the North

Vietnamese troops marched into Saigon, ending the nightmare for America. With respect to the war, the U.S. gained nothing but endured domestic and international condemnation, wasted resources and sustained heavy casualties. The war was a fiasco. For the first time, the United States had to accept the lesson of defeat.

In 1953, the CIA, assisted by the United Kingdom, instigated a coup overthrowing the elected Iranian Mohammad Mossadegh regime and installed pro-Anglo/American Shah Mohammad Reza Pahlavi as the ruler. This action certainly was interference in Iranian internal affairs, in violation of its sovereignty. The U.S. and Britain were not even censured by the international community. The following hostages taking instance was certainly part of Iranian retaliation against the United States for violating its sovereignty.

Four years after the Vietnam War ended, on April 1, 1979, Iran established an Islamic regime, ending the Pahlavi dynasty, advocating the supremacy of Islamic religion and culture, and denouncing Western culture for its evil effects. The Islamic revolution began. On November 4, 1979, a group of armed youths invaded and occupied the U.S. embassy in Tehran, Iran, detaining all 52 American personnel. Later, they paraded the Americans through the streets, burning American flags and President Carter's effigy. On April 20, 1980, an unsuccessful rescue mission was launched by the U.S. from the aircraft carrier Nimitz in the Persian Gulf. Two aircrafts and eight U.S. military troops were lost in the failed effort. Mediated by Algeria, Iran released all hostages on January 20, 1981, ending 444 days of American captivity. Iran occupied the U.S. embassy and detained diplomats in violation of international diplomatic conventions. It was condemned and sanctioned by the United Nations.

President Carter was peace-oriented and did not advocate the use of force in solving the dispute, but most domestic and foreign media accused him of incompetence. Compounded with international and economic problems, President Carter lost a bid for re-election to Ronald Reagan. Johnson, advocating war, was hated by the people, and Carter, pursuing peace, was dumped by the voters. Both missed the opportunity to be reelected. Just ten years apart, the elections showed a big swing in people's sentiments.

To promote international trade, a unified measurement system was of primary importance, and almost all countries in the world adopted the metric system except America. As early as 1964, the United States began to prepare for the change. Congress in 1975 passed a bill to adopt the metric system and established the Metric Bureau. Again in 1980, Congress passed another bill, requiring all federal agencies to complete the conversion to the metric system by the 1992 fiscal year. President Bush in 1991 ordered all government departments to use the metric system. Due to strong public opposition, conversion to the metric system was not enforced, and Congress in 2000 abandoned the highway metric sign requirement. Hence, there are multiple systems in use and no uniformity, resulting in the 1998 Mars Climate Orbiter burning incident because the National Aeronautics and Space Agency used the metric system, but the contractor employed British measurement in calculations. Yet, the accident was still not sufficient enough to convince people of the importance of maintaining a unifying measurement system.

On January 23, 2017, President Donald Trump issued an Executive Order to withdraw the U.S. from the Trans Pacific Partnership (TPP) agreement to honor his campaign promise and later informed each of the 11 member nations of the U.S. decision, effectively killing it. The agreement was initiated and vigorously promoted by the U.S. in 2009 to improve economic activities and investment among 12 Pacific Rim nations, excluding China and South Korea. It was also a part of the grand design by the Obama administration to supplement the military alliance in the Pacific in order to contain China's influence. It took seven long years to reach the agreement by October 2015, to be finalized on February 4, 2016 for each member country's approval. The agreement has never reached the U.S. Congress because of strong opposition to the agreement from both Republican and Democratic Congressmen, labor unions, etc. It is another major setback that a serious plan could not be followed through, a blow to the allies' confidence in America. (Refer to 8.6 for more detail on this topic.)

In the 1940s, the Manhattan Project enabled the United States to develop the atomic bomb before Hitler could and avoided a worldwide catastrophe. The bombing of Japan prompted an early end to the Pacific Theater of World War II and saved hundreds of thousands of lives on both sides. The lunar landing program in 1969 also successfully achieved its mission, to the excitement and joy of the entire world. After four decades of such efforts, why hasn't America achieved energy independence and established the metric system? What were the reasons causing the failures in Vietnam as well as the Iranian hostage-taking incident? And why was TPP abruptly cancelled? Whether the reasons were lack of national consensus or collective will, mistakes in policy decision, changes in the world environment, or shifting in national political forces, we'll put these aside for the time being and talk about more specific challenges.

5.1. Declining Economic Competitiveness, Trade Deficit Dies Hard

International free trade markets are the world economic competition arenas for all countries. The strong prosper and the weak fail in determining the survival of the fittest. The markets also set the prices to balance demand and supply for goods and services. Hence, during the last 50 years, 1960-2009, the U.S. international trade data may provide clues about changes in U.S. economic competitiveness.

The national gross domestic product consists of two sectors: goods and services. In the goods sector, including merchandise, machinery and equipment, since 1960 the U.S. maintained a trade surplus, peaking in 1964 when a surplus of $6.8 billion or 1.02% of GDP was realized. However, from 1971 on, except for 1973 and 1975, a trade deficit was incurred every year and has grown rapidly, peaking in 2006 when a deficit of $839.4 billion or 6.26% of GDP was recognized. The services sector, including all level of government spending, education, health care, transportation, finance and banking, tourism, public utilities, etc., on the contrary, had a trade deficit every year before 1971, peaking in 1960 when it amounted to $1.4 billion or 0.26% of GDP. Since 1971, a surplus was registered every year, peaking in 2008 when with $135.8 billion or 0.95% of GDP was achieved. Because the service sector only accounts for about 25% of the total U.S. international trade, the overall trend was consistently dominated by the goods sector.

However, the growth of the service sector within the U.S. in the last four decades has been phenomenal, especially in all levels of government, thus, contributing to the shrinking the goods sector. In the 2013 U.S. GDP of $16,768 billion, the services sector accounted for 79.4%, leaving the goods sector with 20.6%. Total goods produced in the U.S. amounted to $3,454 billion, minus goods exports of $1,580 billion, plus goods imports of $2,329 billion; a total goods sold in the nation was $4,203 billion. Imported goods accounted for 55.4% (2,329/4,203), (68.6% in 2015), of the total sales, i.e., more than half of the products used in the U.S. came from other countries leading to an enormous trade deficit. People wonder why the world's largest economy is unable to make not even half of the product needs for its own country. Is this type of economy desirable? Is there something wrong with the economic system?

The consistent trade deficit with increasing volume leads to two major adverse consequences. First, if the country does not produce, of course, fewer jobs will be available with more unemployed people, eventually bringing about economic downturns or recessions. Second, trade deficits mean borrowing money, resulting in a high national debt. The U.S. debt on July 20, 2016 was $19 trillion, including foreign debts, that exceeded the annual GDP. This is living beyond one's means, on tomorrow's income. When it is time to reconcile this situation it will take tax increases, spending cuts or both, which will threaten to lower the standard of living and/or endanger national security.

Beginning in the 1970s, America was losing its economic competitive edge over Western Europe and Japan. This coincided with the timing of the U.S. trade deficit. The main reason was high labor costs required to maintain a high standard of living in the U.S. It was also the major factor which caused product outsourcing, factories relocating abroad, and ultimately led to serious trade deficits and high unemployment at home. In Bart Van Ark's article, "Manufacturing Price, Productivity, and Labor Costs in Five Economies," he compared U.S. manufacturing productivity and costs with Britain, France, Germany and Japan for 1970, 1975, 1980, 1985, 1990 and 1993. In 1970 the labor unit cost (hourly labor rate divided by the output value) for the United States was 100.0, Britain 75.3, France 66.0, Germany 59.7, Japan 48.1, less than half of that in the U.S. After 1975, Western Europe's cost advantages against the U.S. disappeared, but Japan continued its low cost until 1990. From 1975 to 1993, Japan labor unit costs compared with the U.S. (100.0) were as follows: 79.5 (1975), 78.7 (1980), 65.5 (1985), 99.5 (1990), and 132.9 (1993). The unit cost increases in Japan since 1990 were mainly the result of significant appreciation of the yen (the U.S. dollar exchange rate in 1970 was about 350 yen and in 1993 it was 130 yen). So, since 1990, Japan lost her cost advantage against the U.S., and the general manufactured goods in the American market were subsequently supplied by the Chinese instead of the Japanese.

As a result of international trade conditions, the U.S. manufacturing workforce also shrank. In 1970, there were 17.8 million factory workers, accounting for 25% of the total labor force, and the number peaked in 1979 to 21.0 million. The manufacturing workforces steadily declined since 1979 and in 2005 a total of 14.3 million accounting for less than 10% of the total workforce. By 2010, the factory workers totaled 11.5 million, another 2.8 million jobs lost in five years. And compared to the 1979 peak, 9.5 million manufacturing jobs vanished. Nearly 50% of the manufacturing jobs in the United States were lost during the past 30 years!

Competition can be both tangible and intangible or concrete and abstract. Intangibles or abstracts, such as unity, patriotism, robustness, perseverance, persistence, industry, thrift, lawfulness and friendliness, are favorable traits. In the early days, Chinese transplanted to Southeast Asia not only could make a living, but some also got rich and were better off than other immigrant groups because they were very hard-working and thrifty. After World War I, the Soviet economy grew at a faster rate than Europe and America which was partly attributed to the enthusiasm and patriotism of building a new Communist society. It is evident that the intangible factor is very important and should not be ignored. But the intangible evidence is hard to collect and verify, and easily becomes personal opinion. For the time being, it will be put aside.

The development of the national economy, in addition to meeting the current needs of the people, must invest in infrastructure, education, environmental protection, health care, and research and development in order to improve competitiveness and people's standard of living. Innovation, quality, and cost are the three main competitive factors. New products, improved quality and increased production efficiency are all parts of innovation. Improvement of materials, operating procedures, machinery and equipment can also achieve the goal. Take Apple Inc. as an example. iPod and iTunes sales revived the company from the brink of collapse; then, there came the iPad and the iPhone, enthusiastically embraced by consumers worldwide. Apple Inc. is now one of the world's most competitive enterprises, and its stock price has skyrocketed. Its market value has been one of the tops worldwide. Nevertheless, Apple's products have a lot of competition, no market monopoly power, and patent rights extend for only 17 years in the U.S. Therefore, businesses must continue to make improvements in order to maintain market advantage.

Furthermore, any major innovations attract worldwide attention and competition. For example, 80 years ago, there were at least three individuals who claimed they invented television: the Westinghouse and RCA Russian-born employee, Vladimir Zworykin, Scotsman John Baird, and Utah's Pico Farnsworth. Today, governments, large companies, and universities are equipped with R&D facilities, so the technology monopoly era no longer exists.

For nearly 150 years, the United States has been the world's largest economy, and R&D facilities were commonly located everywhere. The country has the most Nobel Prize winners. In addition, the research and development of new weaponry by the Defense Department, new products such as the Internet and the global positioning system (GPS) were developed and adapted for civilian use. Therefore, the U.S. should remain on the forefront of innovation for the foreseeable future.

Products must cater to the needs of the customers, including factors such as being functional, inexpensive, reliable, durable, beautiful, economical to operate, and properly warranted. Relatively complex products after sale also need to provide buyers with technical, operational, maintenance, and other assistances to secure customers' lasting loyalty. The service industries must comply with trustworthy, inexpensive, and timely principles in discharging their obligations. Regardless of whether product or service industries, they all need to consider the use of appropriate raw materials, parts, machinery, equipment, operating environment, employee compensation, workers' attitude, technical support, marketing, and management personnel. To achieve the goal of lasting customer loyalty, the enterprises must exercise a company-wide collective effort; the lack of it in any department will ultimately mean company failure.

Businesses must also maintain financial health so that employee wages and benefits, suppliers' bills, as well as reasonable returns on capital can be honored. These are all the vendors' operating costs. Therefore, the revenue of products or services must at least cover costs in the long run in order for the business to survive. Financial health of a business is mainly determined by the price (revenue) and cost of its product. Because the price may be restricted by government regulations and competition, the company is most likely unable to adjust at will. But in terms of cost, from raw materials to finished products delivered to the customer, manufacturers have ample opportunities to cut costs, such as bulk purchases of raw materials having a discount and savings on shipping, too; rewarding employees' healthy lifestyle thus improving production efficiency, also reducing medical costs, leading to reduction in overall costs. We'll use the General Motors Company (GM) to illustrate the quality and cost problems in the United States.

In the United States, there is a proverb, "What's good for GM is good for America". GM was formed in 1908 by several independent automobile factories, and business boomed. By 1931, GM had overtaken Ford Motor Company, becoming the world's largest automobile manufacturer. The title of distinction was maintained until 2007: 77 years. At the same time, GM was also the world's largest private enterprise until oil prices dramatically increased and the oil company, ExxonMobil, replaced it. In its heyday, GM had nearly 350,000 employees, 150 plants, 13,000 car dealers, and sales accounting for half of the U.S. auto market. With oversea business in over 157 foreign countries, GM had a total of more than 800,000 employees worldwide.

The automobile industry also sparked related enterprises such as tires, batteries, highways, motels, etc. The above proverb held true. GM seemed to be interweaving with the U.S. economy and best represented its colossal economic power. But since 2004, the company has incurred losses every year and was forced to declare bankruptcy in 2009. In order to avoid the collapse of GM, which would increase unemployment and further erode the economy, the federal government provided $49.5 billion for its transition and reorganization in 2009. GM had a total loss of $80 billion by 2009. At its lowest point, its domestic market share was down to 17.6% as opposed to 50% in its heyday; the company's stock fell to 80 cents a share from $96. In the end, what prompted this historic industrial giant to approach the brink of collapse? There are three main reasons: Products not meeting the market needs, poor product quality, and high product cost.

Products must meet the needs of the consumer. The United States is an emerging country, with many cities built in the last century in its vast sparsely populated landscape. After World War II, the city population migrated to the suburbs, developing highways, new communities, and shopping centers with wide streets and plenty of parking spaces. Europe and Japan, on the other hand, with ancient cities and narrow streets, could not accommodate large cars. Then, the more important factor was the U. S. energy policy which favors low energy prices in order to encourage gasoline consumption. This in turn promoted other industries such as tourism which benefited economic growth. European and Japanese governments levy heavy taxes on gasoline and implement energy-saving measures so that the price of gasoline has always been much higher than in America. In this environment, the American desired big and comfortable cars with high-speed capability. Europe and Japan required small, flexible, fuel-efficient, and easy to park vehicles.

Early in the 1960s, crude oil cost $2 a barrel, gasoline sold for 30 cents a gallon, and the United States produced almost all eight cylinder vehicles, few six cylinders, and no four cylinders at all. However, since the 1973 oil embargo caused oil shortages and soaring gasoline prices, people began to buy fuel-efficient cars. The Detroit Big Three (GM, Ford and Chrysler) were slow to respond and produced no small cars to meet the market needs. This situation provided a good opportunity for the Japanese automakers to invade the U.S. market with cheap products. Toyota, Honda, and Nissan (Dotson before the name change), three major Japanese manufacturers continuously improved the design and quality of their products, and in less than a decade captured 14% of the U.S. market. On top of other Japanese household goods popular in the 1970s and 1980s, auto industry intrusion sparked a strong anti-Japanese sentiment in the U.S. The blame game of trade imbalance on foreign countries played by government officials and congressional members incited racial hatred and national animosity. The following is a typical case.

On June 19, 1982, 27-year-old Vincent Chin and friends attended a bachelor party to celebrate his upcoming wedding in a Detroit suburban nightclub. Mistaken as being Japanese by an unemployed auto worker, Ronald Ebens, an argument ensued between Ebens and Chin. Later, Ebens and his stepson, Michael Nitz, tracked Chin to a McDonald's restaurant. With help from his stepson, Ebens used a baseball bat and attacked Chin, who suffered a serious head injury and lapsed into a coma. Chin died in the hospital four days later. The District Court judge sentenced Ebens to three years' probation and compensation of $3,780 to Chin's family, causing a strong outcry from the Asian community. Although the case was tried again by the federal district court, the killer has never served a day in jail and is still at large. Justice was not served.

Members of Congress responded to the Japanese automobile invasion by threatening legislation to ban the import of Japanese autos, prompting the Japanese companies to set up auto assembly plants in America. By 2008, Japanese made cars, including those assembled in the U.S. and imports, shared a total of 34% of the U.S. market. As of October 2011, with all imports accounting for 33.2% of the car market, 19.7% of the pick-up trucks, coupled with foreign assembled autos in the United States, the Detroit Big Three's market share had been reduced to less than 50%.

Some U.S. products have low quality but a high cost. The United States is a large producer; but also a large consuming country. Consumption necessitates production, and consumption, with certain conditions, can also lead to economic prosperity. For convenience and to encourage consumption, the disposable concept was promoted. Things such as paper plates and cups, plastic forks and knives, even cameras were trashed after use. The average American family in the past usually replaced their old car with a new model in three to five years. Therefore, the emphasis was on eye-catching and functional, not durable and reliable. In this tradition, the U.S. made cars in comparison to Japanese made cars were of low quality, unreliable, and not durable. In 2008 all three American auto companies were asking Congress for funding, followed by GM and Chrysler bankruptcies and reorganizations. In recent years, from top to bottom, whether managers or laborers, there is a struggle for survival, and some progress has been made in the quest for better quality, but still the U.S. lags behind. Data provided by *Consumer Reports* will be used as a basis for analyzing the quality of automobiles on the U.S. market.

Consumer Reports (CR, Consumer Union), founded in 1936, is a very special monthly magazine in the U.S. The magazine reports its test results and the statistics of reader surveys on products and services to provide information to consumers for their decision making. It does not run commercial ads nor accept donations from any company or organization. The magazine relies solely on subscriptions and individual small donations for its maintenance and operating costs to show its independent stance in establishing consumer confidence in its publication. It maintains test labs and sites with professionals on duty, purchases a variety of products for long-term testing, and then reports the results in its publication. It also distributes hundreds of thousands of copies of annual survey to its readers to obtain detailed product and service experiences. After statistical analysis, the findings are also published in the monthly magazine.

Automobiles are the focus of the most detailed investigation, including various models, engines, gearboxes, bodies, electrical and fuel systems, etc., in historical and cumulative base information. Over the past 80 years, some manufacturers sued the magazine because their products were low rated or not recommended, adversely affecting the company's interest. Each time, the magazine's publisher provided detailed test records and survey results to the court justifying the conclusions were based on facts, not subjective opinions, so CR never lost a case. Unless the tests were designed and done improperly, leading to errors, the magazine's reports represent fair, accurate, and authoritative information to consumers.

In its April 2011 issue, *Consumer Reports* assessed all current year vehicles on the U.S. market, excluding commercial, public, and special vehicles, such as trucks, buses, fire engines, etc. Also not included were the newly designed cars because the tests had not yet been done, with no basis for comments. This issue assessed 274 different vehicles on the market, made by different countries in the world. Its findings are summarized as follows:

2013 Recommended Vehicles in America

Automakers	USA	Japan	Germany	Korea	Other	Total
Evaluated vehicles	74	120	43	23	14	274
Recommended vehicles	36	79	19	15	4	153
Recommended rate, %	48.6	65.8	44.2	65.2	28.6	55.8
Recommended market share, %	23.5	51.6	12.4	9.8	2.6	99.9

Recommended vehicles must meet both the minimum level of functionality and reliability standards. Some vehicles are very good functionally but fail the minimum reliability standard, hence they were not recommended. Likewise, reliable cars failing the minimum functionality are also excluded in its recommended group. The functional assessment tests are carried out by CR or outsourced to independent labs which must meet the independence and impartiality tests as observed by CR itself. Reliability assessment is based entirely on the information provided by the

CR readers' survey.

With the Detroit Big Three facing bankruptcy, both managers and workers must struggle to improve quality in order to survive. In recent years, quality has improved some, but it is still far from satisfactory. Even though nearly half of its products were recommended, they accounted for only 23.5% of the market share (of 153 kinds, the U.S. accounted for 36), and the most recommended did not score high on functionality and were rarely the most reliable; and nearly one-third were concentrated in pickup trucks and large sport utility vehicles. Looking back a decade ago, Korean made cars were facing the same quality problem and were unable to penetrate the U.S. market even though the prices were cheap. Improving quality continuously in recent years, Korean made cars now are comparable with the Japanese made ones in quality as the recommended rates for both countries' products were almost equal, and several Korean made models surpassed the Japanese, becoming the best in the world.

Time magazine on December 10, 2008, carried a special article devoted to the U.S. auto industry. The author asserts that the main issues such as quality, cost, etc. were debated as early as 30 years ago. Under the intensive anti-Japanese pressure from the U.S. Congress and the public, Toyota Motor Co. agreed to join GM, co-manufacturing one of its most successful sellers, the Corolla, by supplying all manufacturing, operational, and management systems to the GM plant in Fremont, California, to produce the same car with the name Geo Prism in 1989. It was a success both in terms of quality and cost. But it only served as the automotive industry's showcase; the entire industry remained unchanged, no innovation. Detroit automakers year after year made too many clunkers, and every car produced in North America by them lost money. Compared with Toyota, the average revenue per car was $4,000 less, which was the result of the high cost and high promotional fees that included selling price discount, cash back offers, dealer discounts, and advertising costs. A new labor contract signed with the United Auto Workers union (UAW) in 2007 showed the average wage was $53 per hour, $18 less than before, but still higher than the foreign auto plants in the United States. Finally, citing the views of an auto expert, the main reasons for failure are (1) inability to produce competitive small cars, (2) failure to reduce costs, (3) being too accommodating to the union demands, (4) failure to improve the fuel efficiency, and the biggest failure of the industry is losing learning ability (keeping union's discipline, not adapting to change).

Japanese and South Korean auto plants in the United States were able to improve quality and reduce costs. Why in the U.S. auto plants, after 30 years, were unable to control cost and quality issues. If it is a plant operational issue, the Fremont model should take care of it; if it is poor quality of materials or components, better suppliers can be secured in one or two years; if plant and machinery are out of date, within five or ten years that can be refurbished. Compared with Japanese and South Korean plants in the U,S., the major difference is that workers in U.S. auto companies are members of the United Auto Workers union. They receive higher wages and take orders from the union boss instead of company management.

There is a popular saying in the United States, warning customers not to buy cars made on Friday and Monday, because on Friday, workers are trying to figure out weekend activities and are absent-minded; with a weekend of excessive physical exertion, Monday's work would be error-prone. This is not groundless or absurd. In recent years, workers with an irresponsible work attitude were common. On April 18, 2011 *World Journal* reports that in recent weeks, there were six incidents of air traffic controller (union member too) sleeping while on duty in the United States. Although the pilots circled around in the air and called constantly, they could not interrupt air traffic controllers' dreams, deeply asleep. Some pilots took chances and landed without assistance from the controller; others went to nearby airports for landing.

In Detroit, workers of all automakers must be members of the UAW union. If the union orders a strike, it could paralyze the company because the National Labor Relations Act prohibits the company from firing the strikers and forbids the company from hiring substitute workers, leaving the company with either accepting the union demands or closing down operations. This was one of the main reasons for Detroit automakers to relocate their plants somewhere else. The NLRA does not apply to the 25 states with the Right to Work law, mostly in the southern and Midwestern regions (Indiana, Michigan, and Wisconsin were recently included). It is precisely the reason why the Japanese and Korean auto factories are located in the Southern states so that labor strikes and other union restrictions can be avoided.

For more than 30 years, the U.S. car makers have been unable to improve quality and reduce costs, with the main sticking point being the labor unions. Only when the company faced the threat of bankruptcy did workers begin to get serious and improve quality; unions agreed to cut wages and reduce costs. True, workers like shareholders, managers, employees and consumers should all share the fruits of the company. Yet, workers are also responsible for maintaining product quality and reducing costs, thus enhancing competitiveness and improving company's profitability. Labor unions played an important positive role early in the emerging industry when most workers without statutory protection were unable to get a fair deal from factory owners and were subject to exploitation of all kinds; the union had naturally become the necessary organization for the protection of workers' welfare. However, things have changed completely.

In the last three decades, the United Auto Workers union has become the U.S. auto industry's insurmountable block to progress and regaining its competitiveness, hence, leading to bankruptcy. Labor unions are popular in the U.S. and include virtually every industry and all levels of government. The effect on quality and cost in the automotive industry by the union mirrors the comparable situation in other walks of life, such as the air traffic controller case cited earlier.

Funding for all levels of government in the United States, although not the direct costs of products and services, are passed on to businesses as indirect costs in the forms of administrative fees, sales tax, income tax, property tax, etc. It should be noted that the compensation of American civil servants is generally higher than that of other countries, and compared with developing countries, it is astonishingly high and constitutes a serious problem for economic competitiveness. Federal government employees receive an average annual salary including benefits in 2009 of $123,049 as reported by the Bureau of Economic Analysis on August 11, 2010. Shenzhen in Guangdong, China, is a city founded on August 26, 1980, as a special tax exempt zone for the promotion of the Chinese new economic policy. It is a modern industrial city with the 4th largest economic output in China and the only other stock exchange in China beside Shanghai. The municipal government announced on July 23, 2010, that the average monthly employee salary was 2,750 Yuan; this is comparable to $4,874 annually (exchange rate of 6.77 to the dollar at that time). Comparing the U.S. federal employees' pay with that of Shenzhen city civil servants, it is a ratio of 25 to 1, a staggering 24 times more. This competitive weakness also cannot be overcome in the short run. In addition, huge non-productive expenditures in big government, military, social security, Medicare and Medicaid further weaken the strength of U. S. global economic competitiveness.

To sum it up, American businesses dictated by union contracts cannot deal directly with product quality and cost issues, such as adjusting wages and replacing workers, resulting in a long-term problem of low-quality and high-costs. In addition, high U.S. government indirect costs aggravate the situation, further reducing the global competitiveness of its industries. Although the United States is accorded the innovation advantages, the gap is gradually narrowing. Quality and costs remain uncompetitive. Almost no labor laws are subject to change in the short run, and manufacturers will continue to relocate factories or outsource products abroad in order to prosper. Because all levels of government practice financial austerity, people tend to reduce consumption; product trade may be in a recession, but the trend of the 40 years product trade deficit will not change.

5.2. Compounding External and Internal Crises Threaten National Security

On the United States' northern neighbor is Canada, which was a similar former British colony with a comparable political system, customs, and language, almost like brother states, getting along well, no border conflicts. Some refer to Canada as the 51st U.S. state. To the south is Mexico, which after the signing the Treaty of Guadalupe Hidalgo with the United States in 1848, was aware of its own military capability and wished to be a partner of the United States. With vast oceans on both the east and west coasts, the United States has maintained a naval fleet unrivalled in the world. Therefore, the 48 contiguous states are security proof, not easily subject to foreign attacks.

However, on September 11, 2001, Al-Qaeda activists, hijacking civilian aircrafts, attacked the World Trade Center twin towers and the Pentagon, causing about 3,000 deaths, setting a record for massive civilian casualties by a foreign enemy since the 1848 war between America and Mexico. The vast oceans' natural barriers are no longer U.S. security guarantors. These foreign enemies have neither a country nor a government, leaving without a trace where they came from; almost like the Monkey King's reincarnation (a major character in a Chinese classic novel who, with a magical touch, can convert himself into 72 different forms instantly or with a hop covers several thousand miles). After intensive investigations, it was concluded that the Afghan regime was harboring the enemy, Al Qaeda. President George W. Bush in 2001 ordered an invasion of Afghanistan and overthrew the Taliban regime, but failed to eradicate the Taliban and Al-Qaeda leaders. Afghanistan's newly elected government had a reputation of widespread corruption and inefficiency, leading to Taliban resurgence.

Before the September 11th incident, U.S. intelligence agencies were scattered and fragmented, not fully operating to their capacity and each serving its own purposes without coordinating with one another. So, 22 intelligence agencies were merged to form the Department of Homeland Security with 216,000 employees. As well, other new agencies and facilities were set up to meet the terrorists' new strategy, such as the Transportation Security Administration (TSA) at all airports and security inspection at government buildings and public gatherings. At security checkpoints, people in long lines wait for inspection; domestic air flights require passengers to be at the airport two hours before take-off; international travelers three hours.

In 2012, the Department of Homeland Security's budget of $71.6 billion was greater than the annual output of 132 countries in the world. During the past decade the Department of Homeland Security required an operating budget of $424 billion, plus the military cost of $700 billion in Afghanistan and Iraq, pushed the grand total to $1.1 trillion. In addition, due to security inspection, hundreds of millions of valuable working hours were wasted, causing huge economic losses, ultimately, adversely affecting national competitiveness. To Al Qaeda, the attack had a devastating effect of making millions of dollars in returns for every dollar invested, better than a battalion of warriors.

The 9/11 Investigation Committee recommended the reorganization of the intelligence agency, increased security inspections, etc., to promote more effective action against the terrorists. However, terrorist attacks can have ever-changing strategies, including attacks on public transport, water and power systems, etc. It is almost impossible to defend everything. Therefore, at least some emphasis should be placed on the causes of the terrorist attacks and eliminating the motives for the attacks that would be more cost effective and a once and for all approach. Unfortunately, the Commission did not even mention the motives of the terrorist attack and getting to the root of the causes. Even ants prize their own lives. Why did these people sacrifice their young lives without hesitation, neither for fame nor for money? Why did they harbor so much hatred against the United States?

After the 9/11 incidents, international communities expressed their sympathy for the 3,000 innocent victims. The U.S. dispatched troops and overthrew the Afghanistan and Iraqi regimes in 2001 and 2003 respectively, but failed to find weapons of mass destruction in Iraq, as President Bush declared earlier. As the war casualties in Iraq mounted, including deaths of over 4,000 U.S. military personnel and 100,000 Iraqis, international and domestic public opinion started condemning President Bush for his ambitious and militaristic adventure. Most Muslim countries also opposed Bush's war, causing significant damage and creating disaster to Muslim countries. From the extreme Muslim point of view, the 9/11 incident was perpetrated in retaliation for the death of Muslim compatriots and the creation of Israel in their heartland which oppressed Palestinians. More importantly, the American culture, social values, and ethics were out of tune with the Muslim community and threaten their cultural existence. Finally, slandering their religion constituted unforgivable behavior. These were the causes of the terrorist attack. The United States did not face reality and make the necessary policy reforms. The current measures are aimed at the acts of terrorism and not eliminating the root of their causes. The scourge of terrorist attacks will not be stopped until root causes are eliminated.

On May 2, 2012, Al Qaeda leader, Osama Bin Laden, was killed by U.S. forces who intruded into Pakistan. Did this mean the end of Al-Qaeda and fewer security installations? No. Instead, the Department of Homeland Security issued a stern warning of possible retaliation and advised the American public to beef up security. From the investigation of the 86 terrorist attacks occurring in the U.S. from 1999 to 2009, according to a report released in October 2010, most had nothing to do with Al-Qaeda (2011/6/8), which shows that not only Al Qaeda cells, but other groups were also very active. Violent actions against the West will most likely continue. On August 2, 2013 the U.S. State Department issued a terrorist attack warning, closing 24 embassies and consulates in the

Middle East and North Africa. Four additional facilities in Africa were closed again on August 5th (2013/8/3,6). Large scale attacks could possibly take place sooner or later.

Christians and Muslims fought large-scale wars for the Holy Land between 1095 and 1291, known in Western history as the Crusades; both sides suffered heavy losses. Then, the West focused on the Renaissance and the Industrial Revolution. Significant progress was made in science, technology, and social organization in Europe. Armed with newly developed weapons, European powers began to expand outward, initially plundering gold and silver and other precious resources, then colonizing by force, enslaving the locals, even massacring them, and implementing forced assimilation and cultural aggression. Japan, after the Meiji Restoration, joined the ranks of the Western powers' aggression. All other countries were their preys, becoming colonies, vassal states, or semi-colonies. Large countries in Asia like India and Indonesia were British and Dutch colonies. Chinese coastal cities were dotted by foreign settlements with extraterritoriality, a semi-colonial status. All African nations except Ethiopia were colonized. Aborigine people of the Americas (North, Central, and South) and Oceania met with their worst fate ever with a sharp decline in population, language and culture, and some tribes were lost, almost genocide.

Since the time of the Crusades, Arab countries remained about the same with little improvement, no longer a match against the Western powers, reduced to colonies or vassal states. From the Western point of view, except for oil and Arabic numerals, Arab society was almost irrelevant. Muslim countries were regarded as backward, reactionary, anti-democracy and anti-human rights, such as the King/chieftain system, anti-women's education, pro-polygamy, and anti-women's freedom. On the other hand, the Western powers established Israel in the heart of the Arab world. Israel with the support of the U.S. defeated the Arab coalition forces in 1967 and 1973, and occupied strategic territory, the Golan Heights, threatening Arab security and mistreated the Palestinians. The United States is the primary sponsor of Israel. To the Arabs, Israel was the West, in particular, an agent of the United States. Naturally, the U.S. bore the brunt of the blame for Israel and became the target of their attacks. More importantly, after World War II, the American culture accelerated its incursion into the Arabic world and endangered the existence of Muslim culture and its social system. Ironically, it seems to be a continuation of the religious wars of the Crusades, now expanding to the spheres of politics and culture. Will there be another 200 years of serious conflicts?

The troubles facing the people in the U.S. have not let up yet. According to a June 18, 2011 report, the May Misery index is 12.7 (unemployment rate, 9.1%, plus inflation rate, 3.6%), a 28-year record high. In addition, tornadoes, flooding, and wildfires struck vast regions in recent months, causing serious casualties and property losses. These natural calamities cannot be avoided but are accepted as a matter of fact. However, the greatest continual distress is the rampage of various crimes. The Federal Bureau of Investigation (FBI) reports all crimes into two categories: (1) Violent crimes, including murder, rape, robbery, and assault; and (2) Property crimes, composed of burglary, theft and vehicle theft. Since 1960, the crime rate rose every year, peaking at 758.1 violent cases per 100,000 people in 1991 from 160.9 cases in 1960, nearly a four-fold increase, and gradually declining to 429.4 cases in 2009. The property type also hit a peak in 1991, increasing nearly twice (5,139.7 versus 1,726.3) in the same period; it, too, was down to 3,036.1 cases in 2009. These records did not include drug trafficking, smuggling, prostitution, gambling, fraud and other illegal activities.

King's College in London reported its statistical analysis on May 21, 2011, which showed the incarceration rate per 100,000 people by country as follows: The United States had 743 prisoners, the highest, followed by Russia, 585, England and Wales, 150, China, 120, France, 96, Germany, 88. The Organization of Economic Cooperation and Development Council (OECD) in its 2010 report pointed out that the 34-country average crime rate is 140 per hundred thousand people. The United States' rate is 760, higher than the average by 4.4 times (2011/4/17, 5/21).

Recalling my days of working in New York City in the early 1960s, I often visited friends on the weekends, rode the subway home in middle of the night alone, comfortable and fear free. Not anymore. Especially in the early 1990s, 50 major subway crimes were reported every day (1990). According to New York City official Chief Fox's report in June 2015, subway assault crime rates are down to six per day. Even so, it is best not to take the subway after rush hours, because firearms are popular; a giant would have difficulty overpowering a bad guy with a gun.

Rampant criminals threaten the safety of life and property, and also create significant financial burden to state and local governments. Excluding the police and fire departments budget, the cost of incarceration of criminals is astonishing. It takes $24,000 to keep a prisoner per year because prison must comply with the standard living conditions, the need for professionals to take care of the prisoner's nutrition, and proper rest and exercise time. Otherwise, it is a violation of the law and human rights. The Federal Supreme Court on May 24, 2011, ruled that the California prison system can only accommodate 110,000 prisoners. If no appropriate arrangement can be found, the overflow must be set free, resulting in the danger of releasing early 60,000 repeat offenders.

At present, there are more than two million prisoners in the U.S. Incarceration costs rise every year. In 1977, the state governments spent $63 billion, the local governments, $99 billion. In 2007, the respective amounts were $71 billion and $116 billion, an 11.5% increase over the past three decades. State and local governments are also heavily in debt and facing budget cuts; some stopped building new prisons; others try to sell prisons to cope with the financial shortfall: a dilemma. Building more prisons and detaining more criminals is passive, non-productive, and costly measures. Besides, it only takes care of symptoms and cannot eradicate the root causes of crime. Unless the criminals threaten community safety, imprisonment should be the last resort; judicial innovation in recent years, such as community services and fines, should be promoted. At the same time, effort should be directed toward eradicating the root causes of crimes by strengthening family and social education, improving employment, restricting firearm sales, vilifying violence, promoting access to family counseling, and changing undesirable culture. A cause-symptom, two-pronged approach may be more effective in dealing with crimes.

5.3. Mounting Public and Private Debts Cause Financial Problem

Americans value personal freedom. Any disagreement may break up a marriage, so, the divorce rate is also high. What seems to be the most important factor causing marriage breakdown? It is not due to mistresses or lovers, different life styles or outlooks, nor due to incompatible career objectives, but disputes about family financial affairs. Money is the means, not the end, in life. However, if it is not handled properly, it will destroy the goal of life. This is true for individuals, families, businesses, organizations, governments, and the nation as well, no exception.

In 2009, New York City witnessed the largest individual fraud in history, involving a total of $65 billion, a net loss of $18 billion to the investors. Bernie Madoff was a Wall Street veteran who created a computerized security trading system, adopted later by the NASDAQ Stock Exchange, and also became the non-executive chairman of the Exchange. He was a wizard in security trading; even the federal Securities and Exchange Commission officials had sought his advice. He was highly respected and trusted by his colleagues and the Wall Street financial circle. His investment firm offered a high, guaranteed rate of return favored by wealthy individuals as well as the large financial institutions which used his service to park their idle funds.

Beginning in 1970, Mr. Madoff employed a Ponzi scheme by which he diverted the original clients' investment for his own use and used clients' new investment to pay for the profit of early investments. Four decades passed by before his scheme was uncovered. He was sentenced to 150 years in prison. Not long after that, his eldest son committed suicide because of the scandal. It was not only a disaster to the investors but also a personal failure and disgrace for Mr. Madoff, with a tragic death and ruined his family. Whether it is an individual or the government, if there is no reasonably viable debt repayment plan, just continuing to borrow, resulting in debt piling up higher and higher, this situation is no different than practicing a Ponzi scheme. When the day of reckoning finally arrives, the end result will be the same as that of Mr. Madoff.

There are many types of personal debts, large ones, such as house mortgage and auto loan; small debts, like charging a few dollars for purchases on credit cards, cumulatively becoming a huge debt. In 1970 personal and family debts of all types in the U.S. totaled less than $500 billion; they have increased every year since to nearly $14 trillion in 2010, an average annual increase of 70% -- astonishing. This increasing trend was the driving force behind this period of economic stability and growth of GDP, because today personal consumption accounts for 70% of GDP.

But, the current recession brought about by the financial turmoil differed from the past recessions in several ways besides the economic downturn. First, real estate and stock prices plummeted, a loss of $11.2 trillion to household assets. Second, the recession officially ended in June

2009; by the end of 2011, more than a year and a half later, unemployment stayed above 9%. Third, the S&P 500 Index companies hoarded $800 billion, cash or near-cash, a record high, not investing the available funds. Finally, banks raised lending standards, making credit harder to obtain. Under these economic conditions, family assets shrink, maybe people were out of work for a couple of years, running out of savings, and then there was nowhere to borrow money. Of course, they could not pay the mortgage, resulting in about five million defaulted mortgagers or 9%; and 1.05 million homes have been bank repossessed. Foreclosures were possibly as high as 1.2 million in 2011. At the same time, when the debts are unchanged, assets shrink, with no more income, so personal bankruptcy filings soar. In 2006, before the recession, there were 600,000 people who filed for bankruptcy. By 2010, there were 1.54 million personal bankruptcies, more than 1.5 times, not counting business and non-profit organization bankruptcies.

In 1970, total state government debt was $42.0 billion and local government debt was $101.6 billion, for a total of $143.6 billion. In 2010, their respective debt amounts are $1,115.7 and $1,726.6 billion, totaling $2,842.3 billion, a 47.0% annual increase. State and local governments rely on taxes, administrative fees, and federal grants to meet all expenses, debt repayment, and staff and teacher retirement pensions and benefits. The recession reduced the sales tax, administrative fees, and corporate income tax revenues. Layoffs and pay cuts reduced personal income as well as individual income tax revenue. The decline in real estate prices decreased real estate tax revenue because the tax is levied on house value. The federal government budget cuts reduced grants to state and local governments. All these revenue reductions showed up at the same time and thus presented unprecedented financial difficulties to state and local governments because state constitutions require a balanced budget. Unlike the federal government, the state cannot borrow money to meet its spending, which leads mainly to spending cuts, directly impacting beneficiaries. The federal government is also facing a mounting debt and huge budget deficit, and Congress is unlikely again to pass any stimulus subsidy fund for the states. Hence, the state and local governments must make painful decisions. Due to the short falls' magnitude, the cuts will not be limited to administration, police and fire departments, education, environmental protection; a variety of individual and family subsidies, and even employee retirement pension and benefits, will be affected.

Since the recession officially ended, from June 2009 to May 31, 2011, the local governments have laid off 467,000 employees, including 188,000 teachers. On July 2, 2010, the Committee on Budget and Policy Priorities reported that the 2011 preliminary estimate for all states' budget deficit may reach $140 billion. Some cities unable to meet their financial obligations to creditors and to the generous employee contract requirements mean that over one hundred cities will have to declare bankruptcy in order to refinance and ride out the financial storm (2011/6/7, 12/21).

The federal government debt totaled $380.9 billion in 1970. When President Reagan took office in 1981, the U.S. national debt was less than one trillion dollars. Growing rapidly over the last 30 years, federal budget deficits have accelerated since 2007, exceeding $1 trillion every year; the highest was in 2009, amounting to $1.41 trillion. The total national debt by 2010 was $13.5 trillion, near the national GDP. It is a whopping 88.6% (13.5/.381/40) annual debt increase in the last 40 years. Special expenditure items in recent years include military spending in Afghanistan and Iraq, the Department of Homeland Security, corporate relief, and economic stimulus and recovery funding.

Based on the above data, in 1970 the total American debt, including personal, local and federal governments, was $1,025 billion; by 2010 it was $30,342 billion, a net increase of $29,317 billion in 40 years. This amount averages out to a 74% increase and $733 billion per year pumping into GDP, which was the main force to maintain American economic stability and growth. If there is no viable debt repayment plan, it is like practicing the Ponzi scheme by Mr. Madoff as discussed earlier.

According to the USDebtClock.org calculation, America's balance sheet consists of total assets near $124 trillion and total liabilities of more than $152 trillion as of October 16, 2016. It has $381,143 assets per citizen and $869,843 liabilities per taxpayer. Liabilities are 2.28 to every dollar of assets. The assets include small business, corporate, and household with $11.2, $22.2, and $90.3 trillion respectively; total liabilities consist of federal budget deficit, social security, Medicare, and U.S. unfunded liabilities with $5.6, $15.4, $27.7, and $103.8 trillion respectively. The total foreign owned debt amounts to $6.3 trillion.

In addition to the national debt, there are other financial problems in the making at the national level. In 2010, the social security fund was $45 billion in the red. The deficit will increase to $130 billion in 2011, and it is estimated to go bankrupted by 2037. Medicare, Medicaid, Social Security, and employee retirement benefits totaling $1.6 trillion accounted for 46% of the 2012 federal budget spending of $3.5 trillion, plus another $220 billion in national debt interest payment for a total of 52% of federal outlay. These expenditures are mandatory, not subject to change. Plus, the recently enacted National Health Insurance Act will only aggravate financial difficulties. In addition, the federal government employee, excluding the Department of Defense, retirement pension and benefits liability average more than $700,000 per person (2011/6/8); the total number of employees is over 2 million, for a total debt of $1.4 trillion. However, the federal government does not have to balance the budget; it can employ the usual practice of borrowing to fund spending, create jobs, and maintain economic stability. But this practice will be more expensive and will intensify the debt problem.

Nearly three years since the financial turmoil, people have suffered through the painful experiences of stock price drops, house devaluation, higher gasoline prices, and vanishing jobs. They have begun to tighten their belts, and since August 2008, a net decrease of $180 billion in personal credit card debt was recorded. The Gallup poll of 1,018 people on May 8, 2011, found that up to 47% of them were against raising the national debt ceiling (2011/5/14). The people personally realize that whether individual or government, no one can rely on continuous borrowing to cope with financial shortfalls.

Seventy percent of the gross domestic product comes from personal consumption, with 20 percent from the budget of all levels of government. If everybody cuts spending, it is bound to reduce the total output of the economy, thus reducing the total national income. With income reduced, the next round of spending will be smaller, unless people resort to borrowing or liquidating assets, causing a downward spiral effect. People reducing spending equals lowering the standard of living; government budget cuts would mean fewer warplanes, closing schools, and reducing government services. Eventually, it would lower the standard of living and reduce national competitiveness. Making the choice will be very difficult and painful.

5.4. High Medical Costs and Low Quality of Health Care Service

From a personal point of view, if one is sick, without income, has to be hospitalized, subjected to pain and suffering, and loss of the joy of life; the adverse impact is on time, money, and the meaning of life. If citizens are in poor health, it will mean high absenteeism, more mistakes on the jobs, resulting in a loss of productivity and higher medical expenses. If it is in the military, it affects combat effectiveness and endangers national security. Hence, maintaining public health is a primary task of the government.

Under the current American system, medical bills are paid for by the government medical insurance (Medicare), Medicaid (federal pays 47%, state pays 43%), various health insurances, and the patients' own funds. Costs of free medical services provided to indigents are eventually allocated to all medical services and shared by all who pay the bill.

In the Organization of Economic Cooperation and Development 2011 annual report, American medical costs were shown to be the highest among 34 member nations, accounting for 16% of GDP, as opposed to an average of 9% in the group (2011/4/17). The Commonwealth Fund reported, in comparison with six countries in 2006, the United States topped the medical expenses of $5,635 a year per person, followed by Canada, $3,003, with New Zealand $1,886, the least. On the other hand, the people receiving the most medical benefits are in the following order: Germany, New Zealand, the United Kingdom, Australia, Canada, with the United States, the worst.

Based on the statistics of the Center for Medicare and Medicaid, national medical expenditures in 1970 totaled $75 billion, accounting for 7.2% of the total national output, an average of $356 per person per year. The total medical cost soared to $2,600 billion in 2010, almost 35 times that of 1970, accounting for 17.9% of GDP, $8,402 per person per year, 22.6 times higher than in 1970. Over the past 40 years since 1970, the average annual changes are: total medical cost increased by 86.7% (2600/75/40) per year; per capita cost increased by 59.0% (8402/356/40) per year; and percentage of GDP increased by 6.2% (17.9/7.2/40) per year. This alarming growth trend, especially the per capita cost increasing by 59% per year, forced most small businesses to forego health insurance for their employees; large companies, schools, and local governments also had to cut or cancel health insurance benefits to staff or retirees.

The Medicare Insurance Fund, part A, is unable to make its ends meet, with a deficit growing year after year. If there are no major reforms, bankruptcy will be imminent by 2017 (2011/1/6). This insolvency date has been postponed several times due to legislative actions limiting growth in program spending. Again, based on the 2016 Medicare trustees' report, Medicare funding will become insolvent in 2028. Since the 2008 financial turmoil, the number of unemployed people has increased, many of them applying for Medicaid; by the end of 2009, a total of 47.8 million people benefited from it, accounting for 16% of the total population (2011/4/24), thus putting more financial burden on both the federal and state governments.

According to the U. S. Bureau of Economic Analysis, among the major items of consumption, food was the most expensive back in 1952 accounting for 29% of total personal expenditure followed by housing 16%; transportation and clothing, 11% each; recreation 6%; health care 5%, and financial services 3%. However, 60 years later in 2012, there is a dramatic change. Health care costs took the lead, accounting for 20% of total personal expenditure followed by housing 18%, food 14%, transportation 10%, recreation 9%, financial services 7%, and clothing 3%. During the past 60 years the biggest changes are expenditures for health care, food, and clothing. Cost for food decreased from 29% to 14% and for clothing decreased from 11% to 3%, attributed mainly to the undocumented farm workers in the U.S. and low-priced imported foodstuff and apparel, a benefit from global free trade. The huge increase in health care costs over the years, from 5% to 20%, not only forces people to forego some medical needs and buy less health insurance but also renders people unable to pay their bills. The Commonwealth Fund medical research reports a total of 22 million people in 2005 were unable to pay medical bills and were referred to collection agencies; in 2010, such patients increased to 30 million (AP, 2012/3/5). Medical expenditure is now a serious threat to the fiscal well-being of the federal and state governments, and people's economic security as well.

Medical expenditures are generally indicative of national health, also showing how national resources are allocated. U.S. national health care expenditures accounted for 7.2% of the total output (GDP) in 1970, increasing to 17.9% in 2010. If the growth trend of the past continues for another 40 years, in 2050, medical expenditures will account for 44.5% of the total output (40 years' average growth rate multiplied by the current GDP percentage, 17.9%/7.2%=2.49X17.9%=44.5%). By then, almost half of national resources will be devoted to medical service. Hospitals, clinics, nursing homes, and manufacturers and sellers of drug, medical supplies and equipment are flourishing. If most people are not too busy for their own doctor's appointments, they would be busy performing medical treatment on others or taking care of the sick, handicapped, and aging. Other products and services are bound to be reduced relatively. The United States will become the sick man of North America. Would the country still have much competitive capability?

At the end of World War II, U.S. society was filled with euphoria; general social attitudes were lax, and people demanded freedom without any restrictions. Popular music consumed adolescents, and alcoholism, drug abuse and sexual liberation were prevalent. These activities brought about serious adverse consequences on health and medical care. AIDS (HIV) was first discovered in 1981. Initially, this sexually transmitted disease was mainly confined to the gay community and was considered a special disease of homosexuals. It was not taken seriously by the public, and AIDS quickly spread to every segment of society worldwide. In 1985, Hollywood's popular movie star Rock Hudson announced in public that he suffered from AIDS; his life was in danger. His medical condition took the nation by storm, and authorities began to address this serious public health crisis. As of the end of 2009, the United States had about 1.8 million people suffering from the disease, with the death of nearly 650,000 people; more than 1.1 million people were in medical treatment. Every year 50,000 people are added to this group nationwide. Globally, in 2009, nearly 2 million people died due to the disease; 33 million people had HIV. The funding of treatment and care for this group of people became a heavy social burden globally.

With scientific and technological progress, tuberculosis, malaria, and smallpox have already been conquered in the United States; even tenacious cancer and AIDS mortality have gradually reduced. But, over the past half a century, society is facing the challenges of many new cultural diseases, such as diabetes, chronic pain, asthma, and all types of arthritis. Generally speaking, they are due to the change of people's life style of eating more fast foods and watching more TV, because fast foods contain more fat and salt and watching TV provides little physical exercise. The combination of these two factors brings a host of health problems to the country. Many people are overweight: 25% of adults in 38 states out of 50 are overweight, and out of 12 million young people under the age of 19, one-third of them are also overweight. According to the diabetes department head of the Center for Disease Control (CDC), nearly 26 million people suffer from diabetes, an increase of 10% compared to 2008, and those having early symptoms of diabetes equal 79 million people (2010/6/30, 2011/1/27); both types of diabetes accounted for 34% of the total population. Estimated by UnitedHealth, if this trend continues, by the year 2020 half the country's population will have diabetes, which would cost $3.3 trillion annually (2010/11/24).

The Institute of Medicine announced on June 29 that at least 11.6 million people (about a quarter of adults), not including military personnel and children, suffered such a pain plague. Currently, no effective treatment can be found, and many people must rely on analgesics, such as opium, for relief, at an annual cost of $635 billion; due to prescription drug overdoses, in 2007 more than 33,000 people died, greater than the total number of deaths caused by heroin and cocaine users combined (2011/6/30). In addition, the CDC reported that people suffering from asthma increased by 4.3 million in 8 years, to a total of 25 million people, accounting for 8.3% of the total population. The statistics in 2009 showed asthma medical expenses and economic losses of $56 billion and the average annual drug costs of $3,300 per person.

The 11 million undocumented immigrants rarely have health insurance. Whether for serious illness or not, they use the hospital emergency room for their medical needs to get free service. Secondly, since the 1970s, injuries related to the border patrol, drug trafficking, smuggling, traffic accidents, gang fighting, and personal disputes resulting in injuries, whether major or minor, were all treated by the hospital. Most of these patients have no insurance and are unable to pay their bills. Some became these facilities' long term care patients. For over 40 years, the medical costs relating to these instances have been astronomical. In order to avoid the accusation of not helping the poor and the sick, hospitals will gladly take in anyone, whether legal or illegal, with or without insurance, because it is to their own interest. If the government does not reimburse enough, the remainder will be shifted to increase the rates of all medical services in order for the hospital to stay in business.

Furthermore, for protecting the health of children, before the 2008 recession, almost every state in the union had a plan to help low income and poor pregnant women, whether legal residents or not, with pregnancy education, pre-childbirth nutrition needs, childbirth hospital expenses, after childbirth mother and child health care costs, and other welfare assistance. Such things attract pregnant illegal immigrants because they would not only get free childbirth in a hospital, but also prenatal and postnatal cares and other welfare benefits. More importantly, their children will automatically become U.S. citizens who have the legal right to remain in the country, with themselves becoming the citizens' parents and having the priority to remain in America. It is "killing two birds with one stone", so to speak. No wonder there were so many illegal immigrant women giving birth in America. In the first half of 2011, 46,486 illegal immigrants with American children were repatriated, while 21,860 people with the same status were told to leave. In the Department of Homeland Security inspector general's report in 2009, it was estimated that between 1998 and 2007, a 10-year span, more than 100,000 people who gave birth in the U.S. were repatriated, not including those who gave births but not repatriated (2012/4/6). Since the 1970s, the number of illegal women who gave births in the country would definitely be more than 100,000 people. Although the government footed the cost and there were no unpaid medical bills, this contributed to an overall demand for medical service, thus pushing up the price, i.e., hospital service rates and health insurance premiums. It is another important factor why a sharp increase in health care cost and insurance premiums has taken place in the last 40 years.

Based on any report, the United States' medical costs are the highest and most expensive in the world, and the resulting medical benefits are the lowest or the worst in developed countries. The rates of medical service as well as health insurance premiums have soared to the point that most people are unable to seek service or buy insurance at their own expense. The small and medium size firms cannot afford to pay for the full benefits of their employee health insurance. Since businesses are cutting back employee medical benefits, which has set off a health care heated debate nationwide. It has become one of the major issues in 2008 presidential campaign.

After being elected to the presidency, President Obama devoted his energy to the passage of the national health care bill, the Patient Protection and Affordable Care Act (ACA). This piece of legislation, which eluded his several predecessors, finally got through Congress and came into effect on March 23, 2010. It is the Obama administration's major legislative achievement. However, from government officials to the patient, there was no consensus as to why health care costs increased so rapidly with low medical results and how to make the program work better. Before the bill was passed, 54% of people polled were opposed to it (Rasmussen Reports); after the bill adoption, 49% were in favor of it (*USA Today*/Gallup Poll). After the bill was passed, 14 state Attorney Generals filed lawsuits or vowed to oppose the Affordable Care Act. As of June 20, 2011, a total of 43 states with over 200 items of complaints were filed against the federal health insurance, ACA. After the start of the new Congress in 2011, the Republican leaders vowed to overturn this bill. It seems that the road leading to the national health insurance is very rocky.

President Obama called a White House press conference on November 1, 2013, and announced that he made errors in the implementation of the Affordable Care Act and asked the insurance companies to extend existing health insurance policies to their current holders for a year, regardless of the provisions of the new healthcare law; he made several apologies to canceled policyholders, acknowledging his responsibility.

There were several reasons for the debacle. First, the new healthcare law website (HealthCare.gov) became operational on October 1, 2013, but nearly all of those who applied for health insurance found that the site was paralyzed and unable to carry out the procedures for the purchase of health insurance. In Alaska, by October 29th, nearly a month after its inception, only three individuals successfully completed the insurance purchasing procedures online. Secondly, President Obama, during his election campaign, had repeatedly assured the voters that people could keep their existing health insurance. However, in a review of the new healthcare law, insurance companies found that most existing health insurance policies did not meet the new health care insurance law requirements of more insured items and less choices of care providers. As a result, 3.5 million existing health insurance policies were canceled as of November 3, 2013. Finally, for the purpose of drumming up support for the vote and new health care law, the most important feature of the law was concealed which plans for healthy young people to support some of the health insurance cost of other groups. For example, the Maryland Bowie State University student health insurance program last year cost $100 per student per year. In 2014, the premium per student skyrocketed to $ 1,800 per student. The school had no choice but to cancel the health insurance program and let 5,500 students take care of their own unaffordable health care insurance (2013/11/19).

For the new health insurance website (HealthCare.gov), cost $678 million and 16 companies were qualified to bid for the project. However, the government took advantage of a regulatory loophole, by-passing a competitive bidding process, and only reviewed and awarded the project to CGI. Toni Townes-Whitley, senior director of CGI and the First Lady, Michelle Obama, were in the same graduating class at Princeton University, and both are members of the Black Alumni Association at Princeton. CGI worked for the Ontario, Canada government on establishing a network of people with diabetes, which could not be completed on time. The contract was canceled in 2009 by the government. The company also designed a health website for Vermont, with many complaints; the state is considering levying fines (2013/10/24). Even if the government project managers did not violate any law, the selection of this contractor apparently was an unwise administrative decision.

The health insurance exchanges were authorized in 2011 with $2.4 billion federal loan with intention to provide competition to the insurance companies to bring insurance premiums down. By the end of 2014, 21 out of 23 exchanges operated at a loss, 11 seriously; eight had been shut down. Government officials admitted that there will be more problems to come. Thus, just in New York State, there are more than 200,000 people who lost their health insurance (2015/10/18). *Bloomberg Businessweek* reported that on November 2, 2015, the total value of federal loans to co-ops which have failed has exceeded $1,027 million and Colorado HealthOP 80,000 customers will go to the insurers still in operation. There will be more chaos to come.

Democratic Congressmen proposed changes to the Affordable Care Act, and the House, controlled by Republicans, passed a bill (39 Democrats defected) authorizing the health insurance companies to ignore the ACA and continue their business as usual. Twenty-six states refused to expand Medicaid, causing more than 50 million poor people to be without health insurance (2013/10/19). The Kansas Insurance Commissioner summed up the present situation saying that "it is now a big chaos, and I do not know how to tell people". Fewer choices for doctors and hospitals, more compulsory insurance items, higher amounts of co-pays and deductibles with higher insurance premiums besides the disabled website brought grievances from all over the country.

The effort to repeal the Affordable Care Act was carried out by the Republican lawmakers in both the House and Senate several times. However, the bills failed to pass the Senate before arriving on the desk of the President; and Mr. Obama vowed to veto any such bills. Other oppositions to the ACA including conservatives, state Republicans, small businesses, labor unions, and the Tea Party Movement, besides numerous litigations, had run their course in the last four years. The U.S. Supreme Court's decision on June 28, 2012, upheld the constitutionality of the ACA's individual mandate (ACA requires people to buy health insurance); and, again, on June 25, 2015, the Court affirmed the law's federal subsidies to individual health insurance applied nationwide, not just to those states which have set up co-op insurance exchanges. Thus, it paved the way for implementation of the ACA nationwide.

As Obamacare (ACA) enters its fourth full year of operation, it encountered a major threat to its survival. It is not constitutionality or law suits against ACA but lacking choices and surging insurance premiums. *Bloomberg Businessweek's* August 22, 2016, article cited that four major insurers who participate in offering the ACA program will suffer a significant loss in 2016 and will pull out of the market in 2017. UnitedHealth will likely lose $850 million, and Aetna, Anthem, and Humana will suffer a loss of at least $300 million each on their Obamacare plans in 2016. UnitedHealth will stop selling ACA policies in 31 out of 34 states. Humana will leave eight out of 19 states keeping only 156 counties instead of 1,351 a year ago. Aetna will leave 11 out of 15 states where it sells ACA policies. A Washington D. C. health care consultant Avalere estimates that one third of the nation's states will have only one insurer; 55% of the country will have less than two insurers to choose from; and some counties will go without an ACA insurer (2016/8/20). ACASignups.net, a website keeping up with health care law, projects a 24% increase in health insurance premiums in the November 2016 open enrollment season (*Bloomberg Businessweek,*

2016/8/22).

The Covered California ACA program experiences testify that the insurers' financial loss was caused by three major factors. First, the open enrollment admitted too many people who were over-qualified for subsidies, ending with 90% of the insured having government subsidies. Second, pharmaceutical companies jacked up drug prices, especially lifesaving drugs. Lastly, the federal government substantially reduced subsidies in 2016 and will end its subsidies next year (2016/8/8). There is no easy fix to these problems. The new health care law had the potential of becoming a major milestone and legislative achievement for the Obama administration. Judging from the current development, the outcome remains uncertain.

Before President Lyndon Johnson's medical legislation was enacted, medical services, just as with any other product or service, were allocated by money; and the price regulated the supply and demand of the service. At that time when poor people were unable to pay for the medical cost, there were no services for them. Of course, it was an unreasonable system and changes were warranted. Since Medicare and Medicaid were enacted, the entire medical service community and its operation were changed dramatically. Demand for medical services skyrocketed not just to cover the existing underserved population, the poor and the old, but also to take care of the influx of illegal immigrants and drastic reduction in industrial employment, causing unemployment to surge and a demand for Medicaid. By the end of 2015, Medicare had 55.5 million enrollees, and Medicaid had 56.4 million recipients, which together accounted for 34.7% of the total population. The government paid virtually everything for these two medical programs. These free medical programs had potentially induced an elevated demand for medical services; and as a result, both costs and the prices for services soared.

High costs and prices of medical services did not halt the growth of demand as with other services or products. When the price goes up, people tend to use less or find some alternatives to bypass it. But not in this case, because the federal government pays 100% of Medicare and 47% of Medicaid bills, and does not have to balance the budget; it becomes a bottomless financial pit; it is able to pay as much as the demand asks for. Hence, money and high medical prices do not serve as an adjuster of the demand and supply function as a resource allocation measure anymore, almost without any allocation basis; thus, this leads to a skyrocketing demand for medical services as well as medical costs and insurance premiums at the same time. Individual medical expense increased so alarmingly, like a runaway horse without reins, by 59% per year every year in the last 40 years, creating a major financial problem for both the local government and private sector. Even the new insurance legislation did not include undocumented people, but their medical costs eventually became a social burden. With more illegal immigrants forthcoming, the problem will definitely be intensified. If the growth rate continues to be unchecked, by 2050 medical costs will account for 44.5% of the national GDP. The nation will face a crisis with medical services.

It is politically correct to say that life is priceless. Whether rich, poor, young, or old, society should provide the best medical care in order to achieve the goal of equality and non-discrimination in medicine. This objective is in line with the interests of hospitals and the medical profession. With limited resources, hospitals and doctors try to perform as many services as possible, because more services mean more income to them, further deteriorating the already depleted supply. With all resources being limited, therefore, the concept of an all-encompassing medical service for all is unsustainable. A new allocation basis must be sought to replace the money basis so that the demand for and cost of medical service can be reasonably contained, aiming at more equitable and effective results.

Taking kidney transplants as an example, only a number of hospitals in the country are capable of performing kidney transplants, and the supply of kidneys is also scarce.
U.S. Congress passed the National Organ Transplant Act of 1984 and the Transplantation Amendments Act of 1990 which set up an organ procurement and distribution networks. The guidelines relating to organ transplants most were directed at patient's and hospital's conditions for the organ transplant operations. Kidney International Supplements updates its 2017 clinical practice guideline for the diagnosis, evaluation, prevention, and treatment of the disease. And in 2007, the Center for Medicare and Medicaid Services published guidelines pertaining to hospital conditions of participating organ transplant programs. At the present, only the location of kidney donor is the distribution determining factor which calls for to be used by the local procurement organization in conjunction with

the transplant centers in the areas first, then regional, and finally national (Kidney Failure and the Federal Government, Institute of Medicine, 1991). Other important factors have not been taken into consideration, thus, the goal of effective medical care has not been achieved. People who are waiting for transplants, rich or poor, young or old must line up in chronological order to receive the operation in their areas. Should the first one be an unhealthy older person, it may be a waste of medical resources and does not achieve the desired benefit. Major medical procedures of this type should be based on a cost and benefit analysis instead of on an equality basis so that maximum benefits to society may be achieved for the resources used. The Department of Health and Human Resources should develop a set of guidelines to determine a patient's priority for the transplant, to be used nationwide. Factors should include a patient's age, health condition, bad habits, and contributions or potential contribution to society, etc.

Except for preventive medical services such as immunization shots and annual physical checkups, the co-pay, co-insurance, deductible, and maximum limits systems should be strengthened to achieve the fair and reasonable use of medical services. Even for the very poor, there should be a token service charge to deter waste.

Furthermore, to achieve the reasonable use of medical resources, a responsibility system must be in place to reward those who carried out the policy effectively and ended up with savings of medical resources, and to penalize those who did not fulfill their duties which resulted in waste and mismanagement of medical resources. That should include everyone, from the federal and state governments to the insurance companies, health care organizations, hospitals, doctors, and beneficiaries. Especially, patients have the primary responsibility for their own physical and mental well-being, and they ultimately determine the overall demand for the medical services. Therefore, a set of rules should be instituted to reward and provide incentives to those people with healthy lifestyles and to penalize those with bad habits that adversely affect their health. For example, each person should have a medical expense allowance account with an account limit of, say, $4,000 per year excluding accidents and major operations. The allowance would vary by each individual according to their age, gender, health condition, occupation, location, etc. If the total medical expense exceeds the limit during the year, the first $200, the patient pays 10%, the next $200, 20% and so on, till 100% is reached. On the contrary, patients who do not run out of limits, would get a 10% bonus for the first $200 from the limit, a 20% bonus for the next $200, and so on, till 100%. A healthy person who does not use medical services during the year, for example, would get $1,100 for the first $2,000 allowance and 100% for the remaining $2,000 allowance for a total of $3,100, a help to recoup some of the premium. There may be a few, who would forego necessary medical service to get a bonus, but in general, it would help to reduce unnecessary medical services, and more importantly encourage people to maintain healthy lifestyles. In addition, there should be a lifetime maximum medical service amount for each person, and the amount decreases as age advances. Special considerations to the maximum limit should be given to those who have made or will make a significant contribution (defined and guidelines devised by experts) to society and those who use their own funds to cover medical services.

The patient responsibility system, including the account limits and other rules, should be determined by a panel of experts, taking into account factors such as age, gender, occupation, location, and health condition. People who have special circumstances may petition for an individual review. The system should be reviewed and revised with input from the public at least once every three years to eradicate the loopholes and to correct the inadequacies so that a fair and reasonable use of medical resources may be attained. And, at the same time, it provides an allocation basis so that demand for medical resources is placed in check.

Finally, medical doctors and hospitals do not post price lists. It is true that many medical procedures vary from person to person; and it is not one price fit all situations. However, a report published by the University of California, San Francisco, examining hospital records shows that the lowest cost for appendicitis circumcision surgery was only $1,529; and the highest reached was $182,955 (*Archives of Internal Medicine*, 2012/5/28), nearly 120 times which might have involved with other complications. Medical professions should be required to provide more transparent pricing information so that the consumer can make a wise choice. Huge differences in service charges reflected unfair practices to patients and unjust profits to providers. Definitely, there is a need for improvement.

In conjunction with various medical professions, the Department of

Health and Human Services should develop a set of medical service rate standards, adjusted by variations in region and size of medical operation, to be implemented nationwide by medical providers. Thus, it will provide pricing information to the consuming public so they can make a better choice in their medical needs. Those providers who deviated from the standard by an allowable margin, say 15%, would bear the responsibility to justify higher charges to patients. This policy would be able to contain some of the escalating rise in medical costs. Since it is a type of price control, congressional action may be required. As discussed earlier, price and cost no longer serve their function as adjusters for demand and supply (free market mechanism) in medical services. Hence, price controls are justifiable to curb the run-away increasing price trend.

5.5. Education Substandard and Labor Market Imbalance

Generally speaking, there are three stages of education in a lifetime for each individual: family education, school education, and social education. Family education mainly aims at the formation of personal character and value of life. Traits such as care, love, tolerance, honesty, justice, simple life style, industriousness, optimism, charity, contribution, and creativity can be molded into a child's conscience and behavior, which will raise their awareness and inspire them to seek knowledge and to diversify their interests in order to enrich the course of their life. School education is designed to provide knowledge and skills, so as to broaden a student's horizons and to acquire expertise for serving society. Working in the society involves getting jobs done which requires interactions with people and other organizations. It is an ongoing course of comprehensive application of character, value, knowledge, and skills. While interacting with people, based on the reactions received, one constantly revises his/her attitudes and behavior to make improvements and to achieve perfection, which is the personal social education. Of course, it does not mean that in the family and school, there are no personal interactions, but these are not their main focus.

The importance of education is second only to people's livelihood. It is the basic foundation for technological progress and economic development, and the necessary condition for a free, democratic, civilized and harmonious society. Yet, its result is abstract and difficult to measure in the short run; as the old saying goes: it takes ten years to grow a tree, but hundred years to make a man. It is so often neglected. For the time being, we will leave the family and social education aside, and concentrate on school education.

America has public and private schools. As the constitutional separation of powers between national and state governments dictated, the federal government, except in Washington, D. C., is neither allowed to establish schools in any states nor to interfere in school affairs. Therefore, all public schools are set up by states and municipalities. Military academies, even though established by the federal government and designed to train officers, are not considered regular educational institutions.

As to the implementation of the national education policy, the Department of Education relies on financial incentives, such as grants, student loans, etc., in exchange for compliances with the federal policy by the public and private schools throughout the nation. Apart from a handful of church-supported schools, the compliance rate is almost 100%. Second, in the United States, accreditation is neither a necessary condition to operate a school nor is it administered by the government. The filing for school accreditation is completely voluntary and handled by a private organization. Therefore, operating a school is very free, with almost no restrictions. As a result, there are all kinds of schools flourishing and academic freedom prevailing that makes the United States the leader of the world's best comprehensive and research universities. Freedom of operating a school, on the other hand, also makes America the world's largest diploma mill and the capital of bogus universities.

After the end of World War II, the world was filled with the atmosphere of freedom, and it also spread to the education institutions. In addition, civil rights legislation resulted in significant education system reform in all levels of public education. In 1954, the U.S. Supreme Court, in the Brown v Board of Education decision, overturned the 1896 ruling which allowed segregated public schools but provided equal financial support. The new ruling declared racial separation in public education unconstitutional. Thus, it set off a massive nationwide school integration movement, particularly in the southeastern states inhabited by most blacks. The school district had to buy fleets of buses and reassigned black and white students to meet the requirements for school racial mix (school busing plan). Some children had to be bused to schools outside their own community in order to meet the quota that might take up to several hours of traveling, creating many practical hardships and causing some families to send their children to private schools.

After 40 years of implementation, in general, it had the effect of promoting racial integration and social harmony. It was also a pilot program for children of different races to learn to live together. From an educational point of view, a hefty price was paid for this experiment because children had to spend valuable time on the school bus; the school districts ran bus companies; and the cost of transportation surged. Because public primary and secondary education are compulsory, except for extracurricular activities, they are all free including school bus transportation. A more serious problem was a racially mixed student body having a varying degree of academic competency. It was necessary to lower standards and to adopt a no repeater system (social promotion) to avoid the majority of black children failing the grade and reinforcing their sense of inferiority. As a result, a large number of unqualified primary and secondary school graduates were produced. Once they entered college, even participating in remedial courses could not make up the deficiency. The university also had to lower standards and graduation requirements; significantly watering down the quality of public education at all levels. Over the last decade, these ill effects have become conclusive, with even a majority of blacks supporting the community school system. Children are no longer long-distance transported and the no repeater policy is also nearing its end.

The Organization for Economic Cooperation and Development just published the 2010 Pisa Study, which includes 470,000 15-year-old student test results in 65 countries and regions. The tests covered reading, math, and science. American students ranked 14th among the 34 countries in OECD, better than Mexico and 19 other countries. Their scores are 500, 487, and 502, comparable to the average scores of the organization's 493, 496, and 501. Worldwide, the United States ranked the 17th, while Shanghai City students were named the champion, scoring 556, 600, and 575 respectively. Per capita student costs and all primary and secondary schools funding as a percentage of GDP are as follows: OECD average, $8,271 per student, 3.6% GDP; U.S., $11,301 per student, 4.0 % GDP. According to the Washington Education Foundation bulletin, 23 % of high school graduates do not meet the military enlistment exam minimum standards. Of 17-24 year old youth applying to enlist, 75% were disqualified because their test scores were too low, were physically unfit, had no high school diploma, or had criminal records (2010/12/22), endangering military readiness and national security. American College Testing Company (ACT) is a non-profit private institution, specializes in testing high school students' academic ability before entering college. (Approximately half of the students' nationwide take the ACT and the other half take the SAT tests.) ACT reported the 2011 test results in English, reading, math, and science in which only 25% of all students taking the test passed all four subjects; 75% failed. The passing rate for all four subjects among the ethnic groups shows Asian students having the highest passing rate at 41%, white 31%, Hispanics 11%, African American, only 4% (2011/8/18). These test results should be the policy review subjects for government education officials.

This mediocre, at best, student performance did entice national attention and President Obama signed the Every Student Succeeds Act into law in 2015. With a Race to the Top program established by Education Secretary Arne Duncan, the policy provided incentives to states to develop more charter schools and to hold teachers, principals, and schools accountable for students' achievement. However, this responsibility policy to improve students' academic standards was not well received by the teacher union leaders and middle class families who opposed more testing and higher standards, ending with a stalemate. In the 2016 presidential campaign, the Democratic Party's education agenda promised to give more funding but demanded less results. Major Republican candidates, Donald Trump, Ted Cruz, and John Kasich, renounced Presidents Bush and Obama's education agenda, will not hold states responsible for student performances as reported by *Bloomberg Businessweek* on May 2, 2016. It is most likely that there won't be much improvement in education in the U.S. in the coming decade.

The Intel Science Talent Search Competition has a pre-Nobel prize reputation, because in the past, seven Talent Search Competition winners have become Nobel laureates. This award was initiated by Westinghouse Electric Corporation in 1942. In 2011, approximately 1,700 high school students nationwide participated in the annual contest. The 300 local and state finalists and their schools received $1,000 each, from which 40 national finalists were selected. The first ten prizes range from $100,000 to $10,000 and the remaining 30 finalists each received $7,500. Chinese American students were incredible that year with 16 placing among the 40 finalists, accounting for 40 % of the total. The Chinese comprise 1.2 % of the U.S. population, yet garnering 40 % of the honorees; definitely, this is no accident. It would be worthwhile for educators to explore the reasons why. It may help to improve academic achievement, especially for African American and Hispanic students.

Most American families pay little attention to children's education. People have a much keener interest in athletics, not academics. Take the local television news, for example; except for the weather, which concerns everyone, the only regular program is sports. Moreover, Super Bowl madness far outweighs any major event, even the presidential election. When family and community pay little attention to education, of course, student achievement will suffer. Life needs diversification so as to broaden interests and to enrich living. Ball games are good, clean entertainment, but to regard them as the most important event in life would certainly lower one's life horizon.

Education funding, quality teachers, equipment and facilities are important, but they cannot guarantee the quality of education. Family and community enthusiasm for education and a willingness to make sacrifices for the benefit of children's education must play an important role as well.

Since the 1960s, college student movements began to boom, some confined to a region, while others involved nationally. From wars to exploitation of workers became the focus of these student movements. Of course, the students' own interests such as tuition, academic evaluation, school administration, and student rights were also on the agenda. These movements raised students' awareness of social issues, resulting in a political force to be reckoned with, also inducing school policy and administration reforms.

On May 4, 1970, students at Kent State University, Ohio, demonstrated against the U.S. invasion of Cambodia; the state of Ohio's National Guardsmen responded by using firearms to maintain order, killing four students and injuring nine, with one permanently paralyzed. This unwarranted incident incited demonstrations and boycotting of classes carried out by college and high school students all across the nation. The protest lasted about a week; 900 universities/high schools and four million people participated, setting a record for student protests in

U.S. history and also changing the U.S. direction of the war in Vietnam.

In the meantime, students started to participate in school administrative decision-making processes such as becoming members of the school board of directors, the appointment of school executives, teaching and administration reforms, prompting school administration transparency, and professors becoming more conscientiousness. However, many students, as a part of the student movements, devoted a great deal of time and effort trying to improve the school, country, world, and the environment, but overlooked their main purpose in school which was to enrich themselves with knowledge and skills. At the same time, it also brought in a small group of professional students who intended to sway the student movements, paving the way for their intended purposes.

During this period of student unrest, the student gained two new rights which greatly diluted the quality of higher education. First, it was the freedom of classroom attendance. True, with many college subjects, students can study by themselves, with no need for classroom meetings, and some unprepared professors lecture about irrelevant topics, such as ball games, in class. It was really a waste of students' time. However, many disciplines/subjects, except for few well prepared and very bright students demand and require professors' help; that is the reason for classroom meetings. Otherwise, individual tutoring would be needed for each student, requiring more professors and a higher financial cost to the school and student as well. Furthermore, some subjects, especially in science and technology, require previous knowledge as the foundation for future building, from simple to complex situations. Therefore, missing one class may cause learning difficulties, and certainly it cannot accommodate freedom of classroom attendance. If the students have the competency and do not need to attend the class, they should get the credit by taking the necessary examinations. Both classrooms and teachers can be reduced, saving school funding and students' money, a winner-for-all solution.

Second, it was the students' evaluation of the teacher (student evaluation). Evaluation included subject materials, lecturing, examination, grading, etc., usually in the true and false and multiple-choice format to gather students' opinion and became an important document for faculty evaluation by the administration. For fair and easy comparison, regardless of the disciplines/subjects, such as swimming, art appreciation, calculus, or comparative political systems, all used the same survey form; the result was just like comparing apples to oranges. Furthermore, the questionnaires were mostly subjective, such as whether the textbooks were good and the professor's lecture was clear, etc, lacking specific facts, like how well lessons progressed in accordance with course syllabus, the quantity of course assignments, and the professor's absence and on time record, etc. As a result, it became a professor's popularity contest. In order to be popular with the students, some professors reduced the course requirements, some gave easy tests, and most simply awarded students a higher grade. Students generally got As or Bs, Cs and Ds were rare, and Fs were nearly nonexistent, resulting in high grade inflation. Grades didn't carry much meaning anymore. Medical schools maintaining strict admission standards with limited places under a special environment suffered the adverse effects at a minimum. Colleges of Law and Engineering require higher admission standards, and some graduates had to pass professional examinations in order to obtain a license, so they were not at liberty to lower standards at will. Each of the other colleges showed that student grade levels improved but the actual quality of education dropped. If the student evaluations were properly designed and its findings used appropriately, it could have been a useful tool for promoting teacher and student understanding and improving the overall quality of education.

The United States is a constitutional republic. There are rules, regulations, civil law, criminal law, and the constitution. Small matters, such as personal behaviors, or big events, like presidential elections, most have expressly been provided for in writings by law. Of course, it is unlawful to assault someone, but cursing people sometimes may be unlawful, too. While studying, school rules must be observed. When at work, company and government rules and regulations must be complied with. Life is filled with legal implications. From congressional legislation to the government executing the law, and the court interpreting the statutes and making judgments, every step in the process requires legal knowledge. Of course, lawyers know the most and have become the most influential group on national policy. Attorneys representing people and the community, seeking fairness and justice for all, perform an indispensable social function. Although most lawyers' incomes fall below that of doctors', and they are not held in as high esteem (social value) as doctors', the legal profession has nonetheless become the most attractive profession to young Americans.

The legal profession has greater working flexibility and more choice during a career than most other occupations. For example, a lawyer can join a law firm, corporation, or government, especially the federal government, because most departments are regulatory agencies which require some employees to have a legal background. In the meantime, a lawyer has the time, while still on the job, to run for a congressional office, even the presidency. In the last 50 years, among the ten presidents of the United States, Nixon, Ford, Clinton, and Obama are graduates of law schools. There are even more congressmen with legal backgrounds. Hence, many of the bright and outstanding talents are attracted into this profession. According to the National Center for Education Statistics report, in 2009 there were 44,159 people passing the Bar exam, but only 26,239 lawyers properly employed; more than 40% were unemployed or working without using their expertise. New York State had the worst situation, with 2,100 out of 9,787 lawyers in the legal field, 78% of the learning going to waste; and this does not include those law students who did not pass the Bar Exam. Thus, the significant surplus of lawyers constitutes a major personal sacrifice and society's loss, and creates serious social problems such as ambulance chasing and frivolous lawsuits.

On the other hand, there is a general shortage of professionals in the technology sector in the U.S, including scientists, engineers, technology assistants, and technicians. During World War II, the United States relied heavily on German scientists to develop atomic weapons and space exploration, and in the last 70 years, foreign students became the U.S.' main sources for scientists and technicians. According to the Semiconductor Industry Association official data, foreign students accounted for half of master's degree graduates in electrical engineering and 65% of PhDs awarded (2011/5/14). In recent years, international competition for technology talents intensified. The American ability to attract talents has diminished gradually, especially after the financial crisis causing severe unemployment. The staff in the tech sector was not exempted either, accelerating the U.S. brain drain phenomenon.

According to OECD, in 2010 the United States had 691,000 university foreign students with an annual payment of tuition and fees to schools and foreign student living cost of $20 billion, the largest foreign exchange revenue item from the U.S. service sector. However, the worldwide foreign students increased by 85% between 2000 to 2008 to a total of 3.3 million, but the United States' share fell from 24% in 2000 to 19% in 2008. America was losing ground to Europe, Japan, Australia, Canada and others (2011/6/24). Chinese and Indian students accounted for most of the technology foreign students in the United States. Since the 2008 financial crisis, the number of repatriates surged; not only was the employment outlook better in their home countries, but also the entrepreneurial opportunities were brighter as well. According to Wang Huiyao at the Student Exchanges in North America, Chinese returnees were about 50,000 in 2008, which jumped to 100,000 in 2009, and 120,000 in 2010 (2011/5/15). At present, although the unemployment rate was high, the United States provided relaxed regulations to foreign scientific and technical personnel, adding computers and medicine to the tech category, and extended their stay to 17 months, while waiting for the six years H-1B work visa, enticing them to remain in America (2011/5/14).

The PayScale website conducted a 2016 survey of 960,000 workers in the U.S. The survey results revealed that: (1) 50% of the respondents consider themselves underemployed; (2) 75% of them do not use the knowledge or skills they acquired in college; (3) 25% consider themselves a temporary worker and are looking for a permanent job. According to Accenture Consultant, less than 50% of the 2016 college graduates found employment in their fields of study which is worse than 41% in 2015 (2016/7/1). A serious human resource dislocation and labor market imbalance is getting worse than ever.

Demand and supply of a professional is much more complicated than that of a commodity. Salary (price) adjustments cannot be completely relied on to achieve a balanced demand and supply. To select a profession, in addition to salary, there are other important determinants, such as personal interest, the field's prospects, the work environment, ease of learning, social values, etc. It may require a preparation period after graduating from high school, ranging from a minimum of three to five years, and as many as eight or ten years. This is the biggest decision in the life of young students, and they will have to live with it for the rest of their lives. Parents and the government should not make the decision for them. However, the nation must provide all kind of workers and professionals in order to meet the needs of society and to achieve the balance of supply and demand. Shortage of workers presents a problem and surplus also becomes a waste. Ideally, the goals should be that people work in their rightful capacity, no talent is wasted, and everyone's potential is fully realized. This responsibility lies with the family, government and community leaders besides the individual involved.

To reverse overemphasizing sports, to improve education standards, and to balance disciplinary demand and supply, the task cannot be accomplished in three or five years by any means, legislation or demonstration. It will take a long term, consistent, and concerted effort of leaders from family, school, government, and community in order to change the undesirable culture. It may need three to five generations to accomplish this goal. Taking a hundred years to make a man is not an exaggeration. Second, the government should initiate testing and counseling services to school children, providing parents and students with the vital career data as guidance. The information should include children's interests, abilities, potential, weakness, and manpower supply and demand trends for making timely educational choices. Underutilization of one's ability will likely make an unhappy worker, or entering into a surplus labor market will result in a waste of talents. Both constitute a significant loss to individual and society that should be vigorously prevented.

5.6. Family Structure Breakdown: Educational Function Disappearing

Since time immemorial, the family has been the basic unit of the tribe. With the development of society, various organizations also rose, such as the clan, alumni, trade associations, labor unions, charitable foundations, as well as promotional organizations, including church, Rotary Club, YMCA, etc. However, none have arisen to replace the family's major social function which is to foster new members in order to continue and expand common social goals. Therefore, a healthy family is vital to national prosperity and social stability.

A healthy family must meet all three of these conditions. First, the family must have enough income to meet basic living necessities so as to not have to worry about food and shelter. Second, there should be a stable marriage and happy family. If parents quarrel and fight often, it would be hard to raise a child with a civil and loving character. Finally, parents must be willing to serve as mentors, prepared themselves with considerable knowledge and willingness to go all out to achieve the goal of their children's education as their primary concern.

Parents should incorporate three stages, parenting, teaching, and supporting, to accomplish the task of fostering a useful member of society. That includes good health, knowing right from wrong, basic civic requirements, the skills of self-reliance, motivation for innovation, expanding horizons for making wise decisions, and developing successful personal characteristics. The three stages should proceed basically according to the development of children's physical, psychological, and intellectual conditions. From staying at home to independent living, from home teaching to participating in social activities, from family supporting to making one's own living, parents must play different roles with different attitudes, from strict and loving parents to mentors and good friends in dealing with children. In the traditional Chinese culture, it is natural to be strict and loving parents, but more difficult to be mentors and good friends. But everyone has only one life to live and everyone also has his/her own destiny. Unless faced with a great danger, parents should not force their decisions on children. When children are matured physically, psychologically, and mentally, the full stage of development, parents should respect the views of children in choosing their friends, occupation, and spouse. Whether the choices end up in happiness or misery, they will have to live and accept the outcome, with no other person to blame for how things turn out.

Probably before children enter junior high school, all aspects of their faculties are in the developing stage. The choices they make mainly are responses to their physical and psychological needs, rarely representing rational decisions, because of a lack of intellectual training and reasoning experiences. Therefore, parents need to make wise choices, calling the shots and not complying with child's unreasonable requests. On a hot summer day one year, I gave some watermelon juice to my one year old daughter; she wagged her head in the walker while drinking vigorously and enjoyed the juice tremendously. Later, when given milk, she refused to drink in protest. Only after several attempts at persuasion did she accept the milk again. Toddlers, though very young, are able to detect intention and to make a pretension. Parents must work together, setting an example to teach them, and developing good habits early to achieve maximum effectiveness.

When children are in secondary school, they should gradually assume more responsibilities of taking care of themselves and planning for their own activities. Skills and abilities for independent living and decision making should also be developed, such as assuming some of the housework and participating in social activities. Parents should gradually relegate themselves from the decision maker to the position of inducer so as to complete the transition. Graduating from high school is the time for children to develop their self-reliant ability. Parents should help them complete their career needs, become successfully employed, and select a spouse. At this time, parents should be the most reliable mentor, good friend, and trusted adviser. If children would tell their parents about academic difficulties, friend disputes, and romantic development, clearly the task of being a mentor and good friend will be accomplished, for parents are in the position to help them successfully become new members of society.

Using the training of a nautical captain as an illustration, in the first stage of development, parents serve as a captain, children as trainees. The main task is to familiarize trainees with sailing knowledge and skills, facts of business management, and leadership skills and attitudes toward peers; parents lead by example and children learn from actual operation. The second phase focuses on the ability of children in training trials, where parents serve as instructors pointing out errors and providing correction in navigation, operation, and management. In the final stage, children complete the training and assume commander responsibility, with parents relegated as advisers to assist in navigation.

After the end of World War II, the sexual revolution, women working outside the home, and rock and roll popular culture prevailed in America, altogether seriously altering the family structure and its members' relationship, and greatly impacting family function and social stability.

Food and sex are human nature. This simple fact has been known as an important part of life since ancient times. If people do not face reality, don't discuss it, lack accurate information, and have no in-depth study, it will not be easy to find the right answers to sexual problems. Kinsey Reports: *Sexual Behavior in Human Male*, and *Sexual Behavior In Human Female* by Dr. Alfred Kinsey, Wardell Pomeroy and Others, were published in 1948 and 1953 respectively. The books unveiled the survey results of the sexual behavior of men and women in America, startling people in all walks of life. People no longer regarded sex as a dirty thing or a forbidden topic anymore. Then *Playboy* magazine, published in 1953, was widely welcomed by many adult males in most professions and was the first not to be regarded as an adult magazine. The trends expanded sexual freedom and also changed people's attitudes toward sexual behavior. Women's sexual needs and status began to be recognized, having the effect of improving women's rights. Nudity, premarital sex, contraception, etc. were gradually accepted by society. Abortion and homosexuality have also been recognized by society, and are no longer a taboo.

Gay rights and same-sex marriages have been a controversial issue in American society for a long time. In recent decades, propaganda, demonstrations, and litigation by gay rights advocates have heating up, and acceptance by a majority American society was achieved. On June 26, 2013, the U.S. Supreme Court handed down a ruling that accorded the same legal rights to same sex marriage as heterosexual marriage. Again, on June 26, 2015, the U.S. Supreme Court declared same sex marriage legal in all 50 states. The decision was a 5-4 vote by the judges on Obergefell v. Hodges, brought by Jim Obergefell, and overturned the decision by the 6th Circuit Court of Appeals. The case was an outgrowth of a dozen gay couples who challenged same sex marriage bans in Ohio, Kentucky and Tennessee, the only states with bans that had been upheld by the federal appeals court. Before the 2015 ruling, gay marriage had already been made legal in 37 states and the District of Columbia, by legislation, voter action or federal courts that overturned a state's bans. The ruling was hailed by supporters as a step to assure equal rights for all and opposed by those who feel state rights guaranteed by the Constitution had been violated.

In 2004, a sex video made by Paris Hilton and her boyfriend circulated on the Internet and was also available for sale in Denmark, the U.S., and Japan. Paris Hilton is the 23 year old heir to the Hilton hotel and real estate consortium, a socialite. Soon, the incident turned into a social topic. She also turned into a celebrity, becoming a name brand spokesperson, doing film and television performances, and creating other business opportunities. If this had happened before the sexual revolution, Paris Hilton's behavior would have been regarded as immoral, degrading herself and her family, becoming a social outcast. Today, unmarried sexual relations are considered as a matter of normal behavior, indicating a significant change in sexual attitudes in American society.

President Franklin Roosevelt on September 11, 1941, ordered the U.S. military to attack German warships in the Atlantic Ocean, which was tantamount to a declaration of war against Germany. In the same year, on December 7th, the Japanese launched a sneak attack on Pearl Harbor, destroying 16 warships, causing military and civilian deaths of nearly 3,000 people. On the following day, the United States officially declared war on Japan, leading the U.S. to formally enter into World War II. A comprehensive effort was called for that included mobilization of manpower, resources, machinery and equipment, as well as political propaganda. Thus, automobile and aircraft factories were retooled to make military hardware, and all males of military service age were conscripted to the armed forces, resulting in a severe manpower shortage in civilian society. The government appealed to the public asking women to take a job in the community in order to make up for the labor shortage in all social sectors during wartime.

After World War II ended, most of the demobilized soldiers returned to their original positions but did not squeeze out women in the workplace. The war destroyed the world's major economies, but North America was unaffected by the destruction. Therefore, the United States became the world's largest factory, supplied current domestic consumption, compensated for inadequate supplies during the wartime, as well as fulfilled the needs of the current international demand. These factors contributed to the extreme post-war economic boom and rapid growth, which reinforced the need for workers, including women currently on the job.

With the atmosphere of democracy, freedom, equality, and human rights, women did not want to be men's accessories anymore and demanded equal rights. One of the most important conditions was the ability to make a living not relying on men for help. As divorce became more common, the need to have a job to maintain self-dignity reinforced women's career emphasis. But most American men still maintained the tradition of the female taking care of the home, refusing to help with housework. As a result, working women became two full-time workers; both physical and mental stamina became overloaded, seriously affecting family life and children's education.

According to the Bureau of Labor Statistics, in 2009 women accounted for 46.8% of all workers who concentrated in the secretary, assistant manager, nurse, school teacher, cashier, and medical assistant profession. From 1950 to 2005, the employment rate for women increased from 34% to 60%; that is, six of every ten women over the age of 16 worked outside the home; men went from 87% down to 76% for the same period. Women-owned or majority-owned businesses grew by 43.3% between 1997 and 2006; almost double the national average of 23.3%. In 2012, 15 women were the chief executive officers of *Fortune* magazine's 500 U.S. leading companies. Over the past 70 years, the social status of women has improved considerably, but not quite on equal footing with men.

Not long after the end of World War II, rock and roll music became popular in the United States. Soon after Elvis Presley's first show in 1954, he was worshiped by youth at home and abroad. In 1960 after their Liverpool debut, the Beatles (John Lennon, Paul McCartney, George Harrison and Ringo Starr) became the idols of youth throughout the Western world. Jazz music, mostly confined to the indoors, was enjoyed by adults and young people. Rock and roll brought out tens of thousands of young fans and the concerts sometime lasted for several days, no longer a simple music show, but a festival. The Woodstock Music & Art Fair was held from August 15 to 18, 1969, in New York State. Two hundred thousand concert goers were originally expected, but 500,000 youth showed up to participate in the four day and three night party, causing a significant security problem to the state and local law enforcement departments. Under the influence of this environment, young hippies and the American Bandstand culture were nurtured.

Hippies originally inhabited the Haight-Ashbury district of San Francisco. They held anti-traditional social values, advocating a return to nature and pursuing a different lifestyle. Hippies also had their own community, enjoying spiritual rock and sexual liberation, and using drugs, such as cannabis, LSD, etc. in order to pursue different forms of consciousness and ideology. Soon these ideas spread to the world's developed countries. The movement made its greatest impact on entertainment, music, and the arts, as well as clothing, health food, environmental protection, and sexual freedom. Hippies were also the backbone of opposition to the Vietnam War; "Make love, not war" was their loud, anti-war slogan.

Jazz lovers mostly are adult, young and old. Adolescents show little interest in jazz. Rock and roll fans are mainly young people and teenagers. In order to meet the market needs, the American Broadcasting Company (ABC, one of the three major private television companies) in 1952 began broadcasting the American Bandstand program which consisted of the most popular music sold or most widely played music by the radio stations in the last week, known as the Top 40. The music was accompanied by teenage dancers as well as singing stars, greatly beloved by fans throughout the nation. The program lasted 37 years until 1989, and the host, Dick Clark, also became a household name. This program became the focus of teenagers' social and cultural activities, somewhat like Facebook today, impacting teen clothing, hairstyles, vehicles, and coining some special languages, creating a unique sub-culture.

The Pew Research Center released its survey in 2011 that in the U.S. with under 45-year-old fathers, almost half had an illegitimate child, African Americans as high as 72%; and 20-24 year old fathers even higher, up to 75% (2011/6/19). The country each year has about 470,000 newborn babies belonging to teenage mothers (babies having babies), abortions not counted. A bulk of 82% of the newborns were unplanned, lacking prenatal medical care, causing premature births, deformity, and other serious problems which increased long-term medical burden to family and society. Alcoholism, smoking tobacco, and drug use were no longer an adult privilege; school children also participated in these activities. According to the report by the National Center on Addiction and Substance Abuse Research at Columbia University, 75% of high school students used tobacco, alcohol, or drugs in the last year, one-third of them becoming addicted (2011/6/30). The federal National Institute on Drug Abuse surveyed 46,482 students taking marijuana; 13-14 years old accounted for 16%, 17-18 years old, 20%, higher than the smoking rate of 19.2% (2010/12/15). The federal Substance Abuse and Mental Health Services Administration released its study for 2010; the number of people over 12 years old who used drugs reached 22.6 million and accounted for 7.3% of total population, an increase of 8.9% over the previous year, a growth rate higher than the previous two years, 8.7% in 2009, 8.0% in 2008 (2011/9/9). The U.S. Department of Justice estimates that 450,000 minors run away from home each year, and within 48 hours, one-third of the youth wandering the streets will be induced or coerced into prostitution. Anti-vice operation since 2003 resulted in saving 2,700 minors, 1,350 pimps conviction, ten of them sentenced to life imprisonment, and confiscation of $3.1 million (2013/7/30). The Opportunity Nation Alliance reported that there were six million 16-24 years old youth nationwide, or 15% of them, both unemployed and out of school. Nevada, Michigan, and New Mexico were the most severely impacted states, and almost all major cities across the country had unemployed and out of school youth totaling more than 100,000. These youth will become an economic burden to the community (2013/10/22), creating problems for community security and services as well as for human resource development.

After the war, sexual liberation, women leaving home, and rock music changed society; in more than 70 years, the cumulated effect has dramatically changed family structure, family function, and parents' relationship with their children. Cohabitation became prevalent among young people, with marriage no longer considered necessary anymore. The sanctity of marriage gradually disappeared, and extramarital sexual activities increased, leading to a breakdown of marriage. The divorce rate surged, fueling the growth of single-parent families.

Families composed of two parents were down from 78% in 1950 to 48% in 2010, a decrease of 30% in 60 years (2011/5/27). Today more than half (52 %) of families are single-parent families. According to the U.S. Bureau of Labor Statistics data, in 1975, working mothers with children under the age of 18 accounted for 47%; the rate kept rising, reaching 73% in 2003. Recent economic downturns, accompanied by high unemployment, showed a slight decline in 2008 to 71%, and this did not include those women having no young children.

These working women were already exhausted after a day's work, and men did not pitch in to help with the housework; getting life together would be a challenge, let alone teaching children and helping them with school homework. Although women's employment improved family finances, it also neglected parenting responsibilities that cannot be compensated for with money. Meanwhile, young people's thinking and behavior became influenced by the new rock culture with intensified peer pressures; parental influence was reduced to minimal.

Technological advances over the past century accelerated, and scientists began to explore other planets, but in providing a stable and prosperous society, no innovation can replace the function of the family. It still relies on the old system to accomplish the task. Observed from the data above, many American families merely are a child's restaurant, hotel, and bank. Motherly love and fatherly discipline, as well as family education, have almost disappeared, replaced by popular culture and peer pressures. This likely is the main reason why the U.S. investment per student tops the world and academic achievement lags behind many countries, and the per capita crime rates and security costs are way ahead and leading all nations.

5.7. Disrespecting Rules and Regulations: Misplacing Responsibility

The fate of the nation is everyone's responsibility. This responsibility consists of three aspects: the responsibility to oneself, to one's family, and to society. Individuals must follow appropriate living rules and maintain an optimistic attitude to achieve overall well-being, both body and mind. One should actively pursue knowledge and skills to achieve at least basic civil obligations and to serve the community so as not to become a vagrant or a burden to society. In the family, people must show respect to their parents and elders, and volunteer assistance to them to repay them for their upbringing. To one's children, one should practice nourishing and teaching coupled with love and discipline to make them not juvenile delinquents but contributing members of society. To a spouse, siblings and peers, one must show caring and tolerance, with no consideration for personal advantage and self-centeredness. In society, one should show warmth and sincerity, be humble in learning, loyal to duty, be bold to innovation, and maximize the potential to pay back society. From individual conduct to work attitude, if people don't take their responsibility seriously, it not only affects individuals and families, but also affects society and the nation. There is nothing that the national leaders can do about it. Therefore, peace and prosperity are everyone's responsibility.

In society, to ensure working standards and to encourage creative initiative, there must be a responsibility system complete with reward and punishment. An employee's duties must be itemized in writing to insure complete understanding. Regular evaluation should focus on objective matters, such as the amount of work, on-time completion rate, error rate, days of tardiness and absence, and special performance and contributions so as to avoid evaluation becoming a human relations contest. Reward and punishment must be fair and reasonable to inspire enthusiasm in the workplace and to strengthen the sense of responsibility.

Let us look at how private industry handles the responsibility problem. April 20, 2010, a deep sea oil well explosion occurred in the U.S. Gulf coast; 11 workers lost their lives, 17 were injured, and about 53,000 barrels of crude oil per day leaked into the Gulf of Mexico, creating an unprecedented deep sea oil exploration disaster. The leakage was plugged by September 19, five months later, causing extensive pollution along 491 miles of the coast line bordering four states and 4,200 square miles of sea life. Crude oil carried by waves intruded inland harbors; some sank into the sea beds. Despite great efforts to clean up, it remains uncertain whether the natural ecology can be restored.

The federal government fined British Petroleum (BP) $20 billion to compensate the losses sustained by people living along the coast and to clean up the pollution. BP, two contractors, Halliburton and Transocean, the four coastal states, and the federal government were all anxiously investigating the causes of the explosion and trying to stop the leakage so that damage could be minimized. It was difficult to clearly pin down the causes and to determine who was at fault. All parties refused to accept responsibility, and the government was also implicated for lacking proper regulatory enforcement.

On January 5, 2011, the White House Oil Spill Commission issued its final report accusing BP and two contractors of using inferior materials and rushing to complete the well for early oil production as the main causes of the accident. The report also criticized BP for committing nine errors, acknowledged not enough government supervision, and called for the oil and gas industry to improve safety awareness to prevent serious accidents from happening again; but no specific individual was held responsible for the disaster. BP chief executive, Tony Hayward, toured the site, apologized to the families for deaths and victims of the accident, and declared that he needed to resume his regular routine, eventually flying back to England for vacation.

In summary, the accident was due to improper operation and management, and the company paid for the damages. No company employees or government officials were prosecuted in the accident. The end result is that BP may recover the $20 billion fine by raising oil prices; otherwise, it will be paid for by the shareholders. Gasoline consumers and company shareholders had nothing to do with the well explosion, but were brutally punished, while the company executives and government officials who were involved in the accident bore no responsibility at all.

Are civil servants taking their responsibility more seriously than private business personnel? President Obama, campaigning in Chicago, answered a reporter with "Some government employees are basically do-nothing lazybones"(2011/4/16). *The World Journal* on April 18, 2011, reported that in recent weeks, six incidents of airport traffic controllers sleeping on the job endangered aviation safety and alarmed tourism and government officials. In 2009, Medicare and Medicaid overpaid beneficiaries and care providers a total of $110 billion; that is the sum of the annual budget of the Department of Education and the Small Business Administration combined (2010/7/23). The 2008 financial crisis was triggered by real estate's bad loans. The semi-official mortgage agencies Fannie Mae and Freddie Mac suffered an estimated loss from 2008 to 2013 of $363 billion and received a $154 billion bailout from the government to keep them solvent. However, the Federal Housing Finance Authority revealed on March 31, in 2008 and 2009 the two mortgage agencies' chief executive officers (CEO) received a total of $17 million in bonuses; six other senior officers got $35.4 million (2011/4/2). Companies suffered losses; executives got rewards. In 2010 the Securities and Exchange Commission (SEC), complying with Sen. Chuck Grassley's investigation request, found that over the past two and a half years, there were 31 serious disciplinary cases, including 17 senior staff with annual salaries between $100,000 and $222,000. During this period of financial crisis, it would have been their excellent opportunity to utilize their expertise in finding the causes and impact of the crisis, providing rehabilitation recommendations and necessary policy changes. However, these officials were busy browsing porn sites, up to eight hours a day. Their computers issued by the government were full of pornographic images, and their offices piled up a large number of pornographic video discs. The average federal employee remuneration, including benefits in 2009, was $123,049, more than double the private sector of $61,051, and retirement pension benefits of $700,000 per person. It is an exceedingly generous compensation.

To sum up these four cases: Employees have serious disciplinary problems; lack accountability and responsibility concepts; have no regular performance evaluation; and reward and punishment are inverted. Furthermore, these officials' compensation packages form a significant part of the national GDP. However, they not only did not contribute any useful service, but may have created an economic loss.

Recently, the scandals of the Department of Veterans Affairs (VA) and the Center for Disease Control and Prevention broke out. The magnitude, scope, severity, and duration of irresponsibility or wrong doing far exceed the four cases cited above. It was not just a few bad apples; it became a culture within those departments for years, costing the VA Secretary's job on May 30, 2014 and the Lab Director's resignation thus far.

Success depends on people. People are the key to the success or failure of any endeavor. If the reward and punishment system is not directed towards the individuals who are responsible for the results, it will not have much effect. If the workers are irresponsible, disregarding operating procedures and regulations, and are not committed to their execution, even if there are perfect systems with excellent machinery and equipment, the outcome still will be sub-standard. The rise of a nation and the prosperity of society depend not only on competent leaders but also rely on each individual member to assume their responsibility, from personal well-being to completion of the assigned task of society with concerted effort so that the goals may be achieved.

5.8. Powerful and Rich Line Own Pocket: Widening Income and Wealth Gaps

Pursuit of a better life with perseverance and trying with the utmost effort for one's own happiness are the driving force behind the progress of human society. Self-interest is also the prime mover of the capitalist economy by which one makes progress; society is also improved--the effect of the invisible hand described by Adam Smith in his book, *Wealth of Nations*. If it will benefit all people, of course, it is on a higher level of achievement.

Today, whether it is in the government or private industry, many utilize their positions to further their personal interests. Some do not hesitate to violate the law to achieve their objectives. Public servants may become community thieves, which may result in disciplinary action or a jail term. Former President of Taiwan, Chen Shui-bian, embezzled public funds and seriously violated financial regulations; he was convicted and imprisoned. But he does not monopolize corruption. Chinese mainland government officials have been prosecuted for corruption almost daily. Just in 11 months this year, seven ministers in Brazil lost their jobs, only the defense minister resigning not due to corruption (2011/12/6). American politicians are not to be outdone either. The former governor of Illinois, Rod Blagojevich, was sentenced to 14 years in prison for peddling Barack Obama's Senate seat. He will soon become the prison roommate of another former Illinois governor George Ryan because he, too, was convicted for corruption and sentenced to six years in prison--two consecutive former Illinois governors sentenced to prison and also the state's fourth governor jailed in 40 years (2011/12/8). Some business executives are not that much more honest either. Tyco International Ltd Chief Executive, Dennis Kozlowski, colluded with Financial Officer, Mark Swartz, and expropriated company funds for his personal use: a $6,000 shower curtain, $2 million spent for his wife birthday party, all totaling $600 million. He was sentenced to 25 years in prison in 2005.

These crimes should not be ignored, but the more serious trend is to set business executives' own interests as a priority with legal procedures to realize personal gain. In order to achieve their goal, a group of senior business managers are cultivated to implement their plans. Of course, they would need to be rewarded handsomely, creating a group of new elite in society. The same phenomena also prevailed in the federal government. This group's income is among the highest, which is the object of the Occupy Wall Street movement.

There are legislative, executive, and judicial branches under the U.S. federal government. The executive branch is the largest among the three, which consists of Defense, State, Homeland Security Departments, etc. Next is the legislative branch including the Senate and House of Representatives. The judicial branch is the smallest among the three, which comprises the Supreme Court and the lower federal courts. The current federal civil service pay system is predominated by the general service pay scale which covers 71% of civilian personnel; the other pay schemes cover the blue-collars and the very high-end executives. The general service pay scale is divided into 15 grades, with 10 steps each. Federal employees are also provided with a living expense allowance (locality adjustment) in all cities, ranging from 14.16% to 35.15% in 2013. First grade minimum annual salary with the lowest allowance is $20,324 and the highest salary at   Grade 15 with the highest allowance is $175,042. Special executive remuneration could go up to $242,865. An average annual retirement benefits of federal employees is $70,000.

Excluding the Department of Defense, the federal government currently employs 2,003,000 people, with the average annual salary and benefit of $123,049 in 2009, which is more than double that of $61,051 in the private sector. According to the U.S. Department of Commerce, in 2008 the average annual federal employee benefit per capita is $40,785, more than triple that of $9,882 paid by the private sector. Federal benefit includes dental, vision, health, long-term care health insurance, pensions, life insurance, sick leave, and child care, etc. (2010/8/11). The President's annual salary has also doubled to $400,000.

The legislative branch consists of the Senate and the House of Representatives. Two senators are elected from each state for a total of 100 senators, serving a six-year term. The number of the House of Representatives from each state is apportioned by the population in that state. There are 435 House members altogether for a term of two years. In 1946, the legislators were paid $10,000 per year. Over the last 70 years, they continually raised the pay for themselves, now drawing an annual salary of $174,000. It is nearly a 25% pay raise per year for 70 years in a row.   On top of that, there are fringe benefits including free mail, domestic and international travel, and first-class employee benefits and pension, for an estimated total compensation of $285,000 per year; as compared with the private company employee average income of $50,875, it is 5.6 times greater. Among 13 developed countries, the U. S. congressional pay is only second to Japan. It is more than double than the group average and it is 2.3 times higher than that of business employee's compensation. In addition, each member of Congress drew an average annual allowance of $1,353,205.13 (2012) that paid for staff personnel salary of $944,671, enough for 18 full time positions and other office expenses both in Washington, D. C. and at home.

Judiciary pay is classified into four categories: Supreme Court justice salary, $213,900, Chief Justice, $223,500, circuit court judges, $184,500, district court judges, $174,000. Their compensation is comparable to the members of Congress and is adjusted at the same time.

Although many families in Washington, D. C. have to rely on government food stamps to get by, the 2010 census shows that the greater Washington D. C. area, including part of the three neighboring states, mainly the home of federal government employees, has an average annual household income of $84,523 plus super fringe benefits, the highest in the nation, more than the national median of $50,046 by $34,477, or nearly 70%. It would have been much higher if not diluted by so many food stamp collectors in the nation's capital, higher than San Jose's Silicon Valley. The country is currently under economic recession, high unemployment, and the Occupy Wall Street movement, but the employees of the federal government and financial communities are handsomely rewarded, leading to Kevin Zeese, director of Prosperity Agenda, to claim that "Currently there is a big divide separating the reality of life between Washington D. C. and other parts of the United States; people in the capital have become more and more alienated from ordinary people's hardships and suffering" (2011/12/20).

Even though there are layers of control, many local government officials use their positions to enrich their personal gains. For example, an uproarious incident from Bell, California caught national attention in 2009. With a population of less than 40,000, the city manager took office ten years ago, and his salary was less than $60,000. Since then, he gave himself raises every year; now his salary is close to $800,000, double the salary of the U.S. President. In addition, assistant manager drew $376,288 a year, close to president's compensation; in the police department with 46 employees, the chief was paid $457,000; and part-time city councilmen's remuneration was nearly $100,000 each. This undoubtedly is a case of a clique getting together using legal procedures to gain their high pay. After the matter was exposed, the California Attorney General, Jerry Brown (governor elect), ordered an investigation of local officials whose annual salary exceeded $300,000. Recent reports indicate that in the California League of Cities, there are another four city managers earning more than $300,000 a year. It is evident that the high local official's pay is not an accidental phenomenon, an isolated case.

Since 1602, the Dutch East India Company paid its shareholders an annual dividend of 16% for 48 years without interruption. The stock gradually gained investors' confidence. In the last 400 years, the stock markets continue to improve; large enterprises did not need to rely on wealthy families or financial consortiums for their capital needs. Instead, by pooling resources from the masses, they can accomplish the same objective. Thus, with a small price per share, even blue collar laborers could become investors, resulting in hundreds of millions of shareholders. Today, almost all of the major private companies have adopted this method of financing with a few exceptions, such as Ford Motor Company. Since 1903 after its founding, Ford Motor Co. has been a family-owned business. Its stock was not available to the general public until 1956 when its share was first traded on the stock exchange. Now Ford has about 3.8 billion shares of common Stock held by all investors, including the Ford family. The market price is about $12 per share, or, the company total market value of $45.6 (3.8x12) billion.

With the changing method of financing the enterprises, shareholders were no longer corporate managers, instead developing a group of senior officers who specialize in managing private companies. The business executives are company's nominal employees but are the real bosses in charge of the company's overall operation for its absentee owners.

According to the general corporation law in America, the general shareholders' meeting is the primary source of power. Common shareholders have one vote per share in electing the board of directors and deciding the company's major policies. The Board in turn, decides on corporate strategies, the appointment of president and chief executive officer, and supervision of operating performance. In reality, few shareholders, except large ones, participate in the company's annual general meeting; all in accordance with the company's proposals, they commission the company to vote on their behalf, or proxy. Generally, candidates for the board of directors are nominated by the company's officers, and the vast majority are their corporate peers. Usually, the chief executive also chairs the board, and a few company executives also serve as directors.

Except employees of the company, all directors are part-time positions. According to the consulting firm Towers Watson, the median compensation of directors of Fortune 500 companies in 2011 was $234,000, an increase of 10% over the previous year. The National Institute of Company Directors survey shows that directors work on average 4.3 hours per week, less than five hours, and mostly are business chief executives or retired CEOs. Critics believe that the remuneration is too high, serving just as window-dressing, providing little oversight of management for the shareholders and offer few operation strategies to the company (2011/10/27). Therefore, from nomination of candidates of the board of directors to the policy decisions, almost all are within manipulation of the company executives. The board of directors rarely discharges their duty in policy decisions and management supervision. They exist in name only, merely serving as the CEOs' rubber stamps.

A report published by the Policy Studies and United for A Fair Economy in 2007 contended that American CEOs of large corporations having an average annual income of $10.8 million which is 364 times the average annual salary ($29,544) of full-time and part-time workers. If using $40,000 as the full-time non-managerial employee pay, it is approximately 270 times, but back in 1989 it was only 71 times. The highest was 525 times in 2000. The dramatic increase was due to the 1990s computer software booms (Dot com bubble) with software company stock prices rising, making executives believed that it was time to handsomely reward themselves for their performances. Also, the Economic Policy Institute survey in 2006 compared the highest 20 CEO's annual average salaries of $36.4 million with the 20 highest remunerations in other industries or professions. It was 204 times that of U.S. generals, 38 times that of non-profit executives, and three times that of European company executives with sales higher than the U.S. firms. This does not include annual benefits averaging $438,342 and pension. The GMI Assess Company reports that in S&P 500 companies in 2011, the average CEO salary increased by 36.5%, the highest honor belonging to John Hammergren of the McKesson Company with an annual salary of $145 million. If he is dismissed, his severance pay is $469 million (2011/12/16). The next layer of business executives are the general manager and operating manager. According to Labor Department statistics, in 2009 the average annual salary for these positions for all companies in the nation was $134,590; the highest reached $173,120 per year plus generous benefits and pension.

The federal government and private companies often claim that it is necessary to raise compensation in order to compete for the needed talents in the labor market. This ultra-high reward is clearly not the result of market competition but the outcome of the executive clique scratching each other's backs.

The business CEOs neither have term limits nor are supervised by their respective boards, have long tenure at the helm with unchallenged power. It would be unusual if they were not corrupted. The serious offense is an outright violation of the law, such as with the Tyco International Co. scandal mentioned earlier, or else, it is executives ganging up with high level cadres and fighting for their collective unwarranted gains and ignoring the interests of the shareholders, employees, consumers, and community.

A joint report prepared in 2010 by the Congressional Budget Office and the Census Bureau analyzed the richest 1% from 1979 to 2007. After adjusting for inflation, their assets increased by 275%. Their household income (after tax) in 2007 accounted for 17% of total national income, but only 8% in 1979, an increase of more than 100% (2011/10/16). Fidelity Institutional Wealth Services reports that currently 5% of the U.S. population owns more than 55% of the country's wealth. In 2009, the number of the richest 10% grew by 56%, higher than 49% in 2005. *Forbes* magazine estimates the Walmart family of six now amassed approximately $93 billion, more than the total assets of the lowest 30% of people combined (2011/3/15,4/5,7/26,12/15). The U.S. Census Bureau data also shows that in the last 40 years, the highest-income households (more than $100,000) increased from 9.0% of total population in 1970 to 22.7% in 2000, and 21.4% in 2010, averaging 3.4% increase annually.

Since the 1970s the U.S. lost its productivity advantage to Western Europe and Japan, and in the 1980s, major U.S. corporations began to relocate their factories and to outsource products abroad. The implementation of the North American Free Trade Agreement (NAFTA) in 1994 accelerated the pace of relocating manufacturing facilities, small or large, by U.S. business to take advantage of cheap labor in Mexico, like GM and Ford automobile plants in Mexico. And in recent decades, the multinationals, bypassing investment and management of factories, simply contracted overseas manufacturers to make what they needed (product outsourcing). They intensified the outsourcing operation in recent years. This is actually nothing new because small merchants have always been following this path. The major difference is that it is not possible to produce these products at such low cost at home and the quantity purchased is usually large. The imports by the multinationals into the U.S. have seen a dramatic increase in the last few decades. According to AmericanEconomicAlert.org, multinational foreign trade between 1982 and 2008 showed increases in exports of 264.57% and imports of 536.03%. Their foreign trade balance in 1982 registered a favorable balance of $42.62 billion, and in 2008 it turned into an unfavorable balance of $172.46 billion, showing the import growth at a phenomenal pace in recent decades. For example, GM's cars and Apple Inc.'s iPhones are made in Mexico and China, respectively, but are mass imported into the U.S.

Let us use the iPhone to show its economic impacts both at home and abroad. Based on Robert Reich, the former U.S. Secretary of Labor, using the Asian Development Bank Institute study, it provided the following cost, profit and country benefit from the 2009 iPhone, as discussed in the ThomHartmann.com website on February 27, 2013.

2009 iPhone Cost, Price and Nations Benefited

2009 iphone per unit	Nation benefited:		China	U. S.	other
U. S. regular selling price	$550*	100.0%			
Cost: Part A	61	11.1			$61 Japan
Part B	30	5.5			30 Germany
Part C	23	4.2			23 S. Korea
Part D	24*	4.4			24 Other
Patent	11	2.0		$11	
Labor	6	1.1	$6		
Factory overhead	24*	4.4	24		
Price paid to contractor	179	32.5			
Gross profit	371	67.5			
Marketing and administration, warehousing, freight	41*	7.5		41	
Net profit	330	60.0		330	
Total	$550	100.00	$30	$382	$138
	100.0%		5.5%	69.5%	25.1%

*Estimates. Worldwide sales, 2009: 25.7 million units
Total net profit: 25.7 m x $330 = $8,481,000,000

This is not an income statement of Apple Inc., and not all iPhones are sold for $550. Unit sale price depends on model, phone co.'s service contract, and the location where the phone is purchased, but it helps to illustrate how a multinational benefits from outsourcing and its overall impact on both domestic and foreign economies.

Hartmann inscribed: "From the Robert Reich piece in the *Huffington Post*, using 2009 data, Reich wrote: Researchers from the Asian Development Bank Institute have dissected an iPhone whose wholesale price is around $179 and to determine where the money actually goes. Some shows up in Apple's profits which are soaring. About $61 of the $179 price goes to Japanese workers who make key iPhone components, $30 to German workers who supply other pieces, and $23 to South Korean workers who provide still others. Around $6 goes to the Chinese workers who assemble it. Most of the rest goes to workers elsewhere around the globe who make other bits. Only about $11 of that iPhone goes to American workers, mostly researchers and designers. So, 34% (61/179) goes to Japanese workers, 17% to German workers, 13% to S. Korea workers, and 3% to Chinese slave wages. 6% goes to American workers, highly specialized white collar researchers and designers and I wonder how many of those are H-1B workers. Further, the Japanese, German and S. Korean contributions aren't "cheap labor" contributions, it's high-end manufacturing which was what WE WERE SUPPOSED TO BE DOING, once we shed all those low-skill jobs offshore. Well, seems Japan, Korea, and Germany got those. We got neither. What did we get? We still supply most of the brain dead consumption, by people who can't afford them. They argue that China revaluing the Yuan wouldn't help much because using the iPhone as an example, so much of the manufactured goods from China use subassemblies from elsewhere. That is, everywhere EXCEPT the U.S. In fact, they argue that it's greed of the U.S. multinationals, not the Chinese currency manipulation that is the cause of job suction to China. If U.S. high-tech companies, such as Apple, were willing to share their profits with low skilled U.S. workers by keeping assembly jobs in the U.S., it would be a more effective way to reduce the U.S. trade deficit than by targeting the exchange rate policy of the PRC. They go on to argue that Apple's 60% profit margin – yep, 60% - would only drop 10 percentage points to 50% by being made in the U.S. 50%, of course we'd have starving executives then. The bigger question is, considering Apple's record of manufacturing and business practices – hmmm, let's see, rampant off shoring, slave wage labor, tax evasion, stock option fraud – why do they still continue to enjoy unconditional fawning over by liberals, including prominent liberal media figures? A once-in-a-lifetime product blockbuster designed and conceived in the U.S., yet the productive U.S. economy is pretty much shut out of any of the benefits? And nobody questions anything about it? That's your problem with the economy, sir."

The above quotation provides a better understanding and corrects misunderstanding of outsourcing operation on several issues. First, the gigantic net profit margin of 60% made by Apple on iphone is attributable to product innovation and low manufacturing cost, which is the result of slave wages and less governmental and environmental regulations in China. Design, marketing, freight, and administration cost of $52 per unit benefits Apple and its related employees at home. The entire awesome profit of $330 per unit generated from iphone goes to Apple's executives and its shareholders and explains partly why assets of the richest 1%'s, from 1979 to 2007, after adjusted for inflation, increased by 275%; their household income (after tax) in 2007 accounted for 17% of the total nation's income, but only 8% in 1979 (source above), a major factor causing the widening of the income and wealth gaps in the U.S. in recent decades. Second, in 1979, U.S. manufacturers employed over 21 million workers. By 2010 the number dwindled to 11.5 million, a net loss of 9.5 million jobs or 47% in 30 years (see 5.1). Factories relocated and products outsourced abroad are the major factors contributing to the loss of jobs and to the shrinking of the middle class. The culprit is neither greed of the multinationals nor Chinese workers, but the force of global economic competition. Third, Apple iphone production operation is just like sweatshop operators in Brooklyn, New York or farm owners in Sunnyvale, California, who depend on illegal farm-hands; all derive profit from slave wage labor. It does not matter whether the workers are willing or where the locations is; the fact is someone is benefiting from labor exploitation. Finally, for how much does China actually export iphones to America? Is it $550, $179, or $30? Although Foxconn (contractor) bills Apple for $179 apiece and that amount is also used in determining the international balance of payment, China has to import $149 of iphone parts from other countries, leaving a net export of $30. However, China is blamed for the U.S. trade deficit of $179 and the factory smog crossing the Pacific to America from the operation of making the iphone. In summary,

American receives almost 70% of the iphone revenue, 60% of that is paid to the business elite and shareholders; 25% is paid to other advanced tech foreign countries; China ends up with less than 6% of iphone revenue.

Outsourcing or relocating factories abroad is a very lethal two-edged sword. It drastically reduces the large number of factory workers and good jobs at home, causing unemployment or a settling for low-pay service jobs, and resulting in economic recession. On the other hand, the company elites profit tremendously from slave labor and pollution in a foreign country because of lax environmental regulations. This is the main culprit of the evil effects in recent decades of persistent high unemployment, of widening income and wealth gaps, of shrinking of the middle class population, and of growing international trade deficits in the U.S. and other advanced economies.

To sum it up, product outsourcing and factories relocated abroad created massive unemployment at home by exploitation of slave labor and damaging the environment on foreign soil, handsomely enriching a tiny group of elite; it is capitalism in its worst form. Is it helpful to demonstrate against Apple, like the human rights activists do? Apple may be forced out, but some other multinationals will replace Apple's position. Only when man made restrictions on labor movement, such as national boundaries and labor union rules, are removed, allowing a free labor movement globally, will the exploitation of slave labor vanish.

The flames of the Middle-East Jasmine revolution spread to Wall Street. The disparity of income and wealth is no longer an economic academic topic, but prominent newspaper headlines. Pew Research Center released the latest polls showing that two-thirds of the people believe a strong conflict exists between the rich and the poor, an increase of 50 % compared with 2009. The believers are mostly white, the middle class, and independent voters. They also vent their frustrations because the government ignores the inequitable income distribution and social injustices. The current unfair economic distribution is the core crisis of the U.S., stressed by Lawrence Summers, the former Treasury Secretary and Harvard University President, (2011/12/3). The Occupy Wall Street movement was the prelude; the main act is yet to be staged.

5.9. Middle Class Dwindling Led to Social Instability

The middle class is not an American social caste system but a group of people having certain common characteristics as defined by sociologists. According to Dennis Gilbert's analysis in 2002, the country is divided into the affluent, including the most senior managers of large enterprises, prominent politicians, and rich families, about 1% of the total population. The next group is the bourgeois, upper middle class, high level managers, highly paid professionals, such as doctors and lawyers, accounting for 15%. Then, semi-professionals and artisans, middle managers, and senior staff of schools form the lower middle class, which constitutes 30%. Ordinary staff and working class laborers, accounting for another 30%, are the fourth group. The minimum wage workers, comprising 13%, are the fifth group. Finally, people with little income, mainly relying on government subsidies, accounting for 12 %, comprise the last group. Most sociologists consider the middle class family income to be between $50,000 and $100,000. If using this income as the basis for classification, Gilbert's six categories may be summarized as follows: the top two income levels, the affluent class, accounting for 16%; followed by the next two income levels, the middle class, 60%; and the two lowest income levels, the laboring class, 25 %.

From an economic point of view, the affluent class income is greater than consumption, the surplus going to investment (income=consumption+investment) and will benefit economic expansion. The middle class spends most income for consumption, little savings (income=consumption+savings) and will stabilize and improve economy. The laboring class cannot make ends meet and has to rely on government benefits for living (income+benefits=consumption), thus having a negative impact on the economy. Because income means production (income=wages+profit+interest+rent=GDP), welfare benefits provided by the government are taken out of taxpayer's income and reduce taxpayers' consumption or investment. Besides, spending from welfare benefits interrupts the production, consumption, and production cycle, resulting in inflationary and economic contraction tendencies because demand is greater than supply.

The middle class is characterized by professional skills, economic security, considerable work autonomy and a stable family. It advocates traditional values, independence and innovation but does not rule out non-traditional practices and ideals. It is more enthusiastic than other groups in participating in political activities, has relatively moderate political outlooks, actively promotes community welfare, and is the founder of many social trends. Due to its sheer number, these people serve to promote economic prosperity, to prevent extreme policies, to stabilize politics, and to improve society as a whole. They are the main driving force behind national prosperity and social stability.

The recent economic downturn intensified the polarization of income and wealth distribution. In 2009, the top 20% income earners received 49.4% of total income, and the bottom 20% accounted for only 3.4%, an income gap of 14.5 to 1, nearly double 7.69 to 1 recorded in 1968 (2010/9/29, 10/26). People living below the poverty line in 2010 (family of four with annual income of $22,314) numbered 49.1 million people, and those living within income twice the poverty line totaled 97.3 million, a sum of 146.4 million people, accounting for 47.4% of the total U.S. population, an increase of four million people from a year ago. Among Hispanics the poor accounted for 73%, followed by Africans and Asians, with whites the least; and children suffered the most with 57%, followed by seniors over 65 years old (2011/12/15).

The Federal Reserve Bank data indicated that since the housing bubble burst in 2008, the nation's wealth shrank by one-third, back to the early 1990s level; the national median household assets dropped from $126,400 in 2007 to $77,300 in 2010, a net decrease of 38.8%. The middle class suffered the most (2012/6/12). The recent economic recession accelerated personal bankruptcy, according to the National Bankruptcy Research Center data; there were 1.53 million people filing for bankruptcy in 2010. Families with no net worth but debt reached 24.8% of the total households in 2009, higher than 18.6% in 2007, widening the gap between the haves and the have-nots. In the last 29 years, the assets of the 20% highest income people increased by 65%, and the 20% lowest income people increased by 18%, with the remaining middle 60% of households increasing less than 40%.

According to the CNNMoney website, there has been no real income growth for the middle class since the 1970s, and an actual decline from 2000 to 2010. The middle class was hardest hit by the real estate bubble because real estate was their main wealth (2011/9/22, 10/26). The Brookings Institution 2006 survey indicated that the middle class communities in the major U.S. cities shrank from 58% in 1970 to 41% by 2000. The U.S. Census Bureau data also showed that in the last 40 years, the middle class families (income between $50,000 and $100,000) declined almost every year from 34.9% of the total population in 1970 to 29.1% in 2010, a net decrease of nearly 6%. The Pew Research Center survey of 229 U.S. metropolitan areas, between 2000 and 2014 and after the cost of living adjustment, showed that the middle class population declined in 203 areas; the affluent class increased in 172 areas; and the laboring class was up in 160 areas. During this 15 year period, workers' income dropped by 27% in Springfield, Ohio, 18% in the Detroit-Warren-Dearborn, Michigan area, and manufacturing jobs lost by 29% nationwide. The researcher concludes that the middle class was shrinking in almost every city, representing the national trend (2016/5/12).

Whether using income, wealth, population, or the total number of households as a measurement, the middle class was shrinking. In early 2016, government statistics show 7.85 million people unemployed (those who despaired of employment prospects and left the job market were not counted), actual unemployed over 15.5 million; 45.1 million using food stamps, and over 1 million bankrupt (U.S. National Debt Clock). Newly created jobs were mostly low paying positions, and at the same time, people were facing high prices, high tuitions, and high medical costs. Economic insecurity and future uncertainty reduced an optimistic outlook. Some moved up to the affluent class, but most fell back to the laboring class. Polarization of income and wealth distribution squeezes out the middle class. Thus, it weakens the sources for national economic prosperity and political and social stability. The deteriorating trend over the past decades was accelerating. The major culprit was the relocation of factories and outsourcing of products abroad by the multinationals, as with the iphone case discussed earlier. And the only sensible way to combat this culprit is by improving America's global economic competitiveness.

Some may think that the United States does not face serious challenges, and these phenomena are the usual incidents encountered by a super power, just like the moon changes its shape or people have joys and sorrows: normal occurrences. No need to worry or to fuss. Since the 1970s America has suffered an economic and social setback by European and Japanese economic competition and the Great Society program. The public feeling of general economic and social deterioration intensified in the 1980s. Elliott Currie and Jerome H. Skolnick stated in the introduction of their book, *America's Problems*, Little, Brown and Company, 1984:

"Today, we still feel that all is 'somewhat not right', but the national mood has shifted from uneasiness to alarm, from indifference to resignation. For many of us, the past few years have brought a gnawing sense that things are out of control -- from our neighborhood streets to our foreign policy, from the most distant workings of international economy to the most intimate aspects of our family lives". In the last 40 years, the scope and intensity of social decline have expanded, as *The Washington Post* columnist George Will expressed on September 11, 2011, that "Since the 1970s, on the whole, the country is facing setbacks and demoralization, generally people's feelings of impotence, vulnerability and decline were pervasive". The 911 incident only intensified this deep and emotional degeneration.

As we look back at the past 40 years since the Watergate incident (1972), when President Nixon was forced to resign (1974), several major events occurred: The Arab oil embargo (1973) caused gasoline price to surge; the United States retreated from Vietnam (1975); the Iranian occupied the U.S. embassy and detained U.S. citizens for 444 days (1979); the Soviet Union collapsed (1991); the outbreak of the first Iraq war occurred (1991); the 2000 Presidential election lawsuit decided by the Supreme Court; the September 11, 2001 terrorists attacked the New York World Trade Centers; the War against the Afghan Taliban started (2001); and the second Iraq War began (2003). In addition, there were the dotcom and the housing bubbles explosions (2001, 2008), Hurricane Katrina catastrophe (2005), and the Gulf of Mexico oil leaking disaster (2010). Besides, events which did not get much public attention were in the process of becoming serious problems including a welfare system out of control, rampant illegal immigrants, health care costs surging, declining economic competitiveness, soaring national debt, widening income and wealth gap, the middle class shrinking, sexual laissez-faire, a drug epidemic, crime pandemic, education deterioration, family malfunction, and a great decline in responsibility and morality.

These above events provided more anxiety and less joy. They polarized people, sometimes advocating conservatism, sometimes liberalism. Turbulent partisan forces ignored the national long-term interest, each promoting its own agenda; society elites enriched themselves and misdirected national resources and efforts; and political forces transitioned from the middle class to the laboring class, prompting policy decision uncertainty as well as the vast changes taking place in other parts of the world. All in all, the cause of so many incomplete national policies might be attributed to people not knowing what to believe, letting alone what to do; the lack of a social consensus, losing national direction, political parties struggling to a stalemate, society elites growing rampant, the change in the political dominant force, and the rise of developing nations. As a result, so many U.S. important policies and plans could not be implemented or carried out as planned.

VI. Illegal Immigrants Swarmed in: Transforming America

In the early days, European powers adopted two kinds of immigration policies, colonialism and labor immigration. Colonialism called for occupation, control, and assimilation of indigenous peoples as the goal. In other words, destroying the local cultures and replacing it with the European culture instead. Since Christopher Columbus first set foot in the Americas in 1492, 525 years ago, the original inhabitants of the Americas not only had their population reduced drastically, but some tribes vanished altogether, along with their languages and cultures. All of the Americas and Oceania had become copies of continental Europe.

The other type of immigration was labor recruitment for the purpose of economic development. In the early part of American history, a large number of African slaves were imported for agricultural development, helping America becoming the largest economy in the world. And the recruitment of laborers to build the transcontinental railroad accelerated economic and social development. The railroad was completed on May 10, 1869, which reduced traveling time between the east and west coasts from six months to one week, twenty six times faster than the previous mode of transportation, a net time savings of 25 weeks (2014/5/11). It greatly enhanced the flows of peoples and goods, accelerating immensely the speed of social and economic development. The Chinese labor contributed a high of 12,000 men in 1868, comprising at least 80% of the construction workforce but the Chinese were slapped with the Chinese Exclusion Act of 1882 by the U.S. Congress after the railroad was completed.

The United States actively pursued the labor immigration policy, resulting in the rapid development of its economy. By the 1870s, America had replaced the United Kingdom as the world's largest economy. In a historical retrospect, Canada has a social system very similar to the U.S. but is endowed with much more territory and natural resources than America. Prior to international trade being highly developed, consumption was done mainly by the domestic population, and before production was mechanized, labor was the most important factor of production. Canada didn't have as favorable a labor immigration policy as the United States, therefore the consumers (people) and producers (workers) were both insufficient. As a result, it slowed down Canada's economic development. Currently, Canada GDP is about one tenth of America's, hardly any comparison.

6.1. Significant Events in U.S. Immigration

Beginning with Christopher Columbus landing in Americas in 1492, the European powers scrambled to invade and colonize the new world. Masses of Europeans arrived in Americas to populate and control the new territory. Europeans alone would not fulfill the enormous manpower required for the colonial expansion; so, a large number of slaves from Africa and laborers from Asia were brought in to support the development and maintenance of colonial establishments. Immigration to Americas accelerated at high speed and large volume. By the early 19th century, there were half of a million black slaves in the U.S. alone.

For different reasons and under different circumstances, immigrants also had a reflux phenomenon in America. In the early 19th century, before the American Civil War (1861-65), slavery and black people were controversial topics of society. At that time, many political leaders advocated the repatriation rather than emancipation of slaves because black people would be able to get more freedom and equal treatment in Africa. The American Colonization Society promoted and sponsored the repatriation of non-slave black people to Africa, establishing a free country. From 1817 to 1867, about 13,000 participants returned to Africa. In 1847, they established the Republic of Liberia, adopting the U.S. constitutional system, using English as the official language, and naming Monrovia as the capital in honor of President James Monroe's (term 1817-25) contribution to the nation's founding. This group of people called themselves Americo-Liberian, distinct from the indigenous population. Although accounting for only 5% of the population, the group has occupied many government key positions since its founding, until the 1980 military coup.

In the early 1930s, the United States faced the Great Depression, banks closed their doors, factories shut down, and the unemployed overflowed the streets. To meet the serious unemployment, the press agitated a public anti-Mexican movement and prompted actions taken by government officials. Whether legal immigrants or not, coercion or other means were used to force people of Mexican heritage to move back to Mexico, lasting until 1937. A total of 500,000 people were forced back to Mexico, including many Mexican-American citizens and their dependents. It was known as Mexican Repatriation in United States history.

During World War II, the U.S. encountered a severe labor shortage, and in 1942 signed the Bracero Program with Mexico importing various temporary workers to meet the emergency. The agreement expired in 1947, was revised to allow only agricultural labor, and terminated in 1964, but the quota extended to 1967. During these 25 years, there were 4.5 million Mexicans who came to work in the United States; about 14% of them remained in the United States. Under the Bracero Program, the U.S. government determined the annual labor quota, and U.S. employers signed a labor contract with the Mexican government, setting the wages, food, accommodation, medical, and other standards, which provided workers some protection from abuse.

Soon after the Bracero Program implementation, as news of good jobs in America spread, many Mexican workers followed their peers into the United States to find work without government approval. Meanwhile, U.S. employers, prompted by quota shortages or self-interest, hired the undocumented workers at low wages without fringe benefits, bypassing both governments' red tape, leading to increasing rampant inflows of undocumented workers.

In 1954, shortly after taking office, President Dwight D. Eisenhower ordered the execution of the Operation Wetback, because the undocumented workers had become a serious problem. The repatriation under this program of over one million Mexican illegal immigrants made the border temporarily quiet and peaceful for a while.

The U.S. immigration policy was based on a national quota system and had always favored Europeans until new immigration legislation passed in 1965. The new law changed to the family and skill oriented immigration policy. A great part of the American Southwest and West was originally ruled by Mexico, populated with Hispanic residents. Hence, Mexico benefited from the new policy the most, leading to the rapid growth of the Latino population. Meanwhile, illegal immigrants continued to enter the United States in search of work. By the early 1980s, the problem had become worse. Opponents contended that illegal immigrants took away local jobs and tended to depress wages, while those in favor were mostly the farm owners, worrying about insufficient illegal workers to meet their farm needs. Eventually during President Ronald Reagan's tenure,

Congress passed the Immigration Reform and Control Act of 1986. The law required that a company with three or more employees must verify the status of employees and intentionally hiring illegal immigrants constituted a criminal offense. The government granted amnesty to three million illegal immigrants who were in the country five years or more, including 1.3 million farm workers and 1.7 million others. It was considered a once and for all solution with the expectation that illegal immigration problems would never appear again.

Because the U.S. Chamber of Commerce strongly opposed businesses being responsible for worker's status, employers only examined whether workers had the documents; they did not verify the document's authenticity. Thus, the U.S.-Mexican border was flooded with forged documents. Furthermore, the farm owners, instead of hiring farm workers, changed to the contractor system, compensating the contractor on a project-completion basis. If the contractor had legal status, the farm owners could ignore all labor and immigration laws because the workers were not their employees. After the three million illegal immigrants were granted legal status, it did not put an end to the influx of illegal immigrants. Instead, it intensified the inflow creating a population of 11 million undocumented workers today.

Latin America currently is the main source of legal and illegal immigrants, so that the number of Latinos in the United States surged. From 1970 to 2010, the Census Bureau statistics showed the total number and percentage of Latinos as a part of the total U.S. population were as follows: 1970, 9,589,216 people, 4.7%; 1980, 14,608,673 people, 6.4%; 1990, 22,354,059 people, 9.0%; 2000, 35,305,818 people, 12.5%; 2010, 50,477,594 people, 16.7%. During the past 40 years, the Latino population increased more than 40 million people, a growth of more than 4.3 times.

6.2. Influx of Illegal Immigrants: Government Losing Control

Since the 1970s, the illegal immigrant influx picked up speed; in the 1990s, the annual influx had outnumbered the legal immigrants. The total number of illegal immigrants is not easy to determine. Muzaffar Chishti of the Institute of Immigration Policy at New York University pointed out that the entry of illegal immigrants from Mexico exceeded 500,000 people each year before 2008; due to the U.S. economic recession, this year only

100,000 people arrived (2011/12/11). The 2010 census estimated the total number of illegal immigrants to be 11.2 million, 400,000 people less than in 2007, accounting for 4% of the U.S. population, consisting of 8 million workers, 71.4% of the total. Among this group, there were 6.5 million people originating from Mexico accounting for 58% of the total, other Latin America 23%, Europe 4%, and Africa 3% (2011/2/2). California has the most illegal immigrants, comprising 25% of the total, followed by Texas 14%, and Florida 8%. From 2000 to 2009, the states with the fastest growing rate of illegal immigrants were Georgia, increasing by 123%, Washington 65%, Arizona 52%. Illegal immigrants generally have a low level of education, 49% lacking a high school diploma, as compared to 25% of legal immigrants and 9 % of natives who did not graduate from high school. *USA Today* reported in 2006, that general services attracted most illegal immigrants, accounting for 21%, followed by construction-related employment 19%, manufacturing and repair 15%, sales 12%, management 10%, transport 8%, agriculture 4%, and others 11%.

Smuggling was the most common method for illegal immigrants entering into the United States, accounting for 60%, followed by those who stayed in America with expired visas, about 40%. The third category was those who came from Canada or by sea accounting for only a few. Most smuggling takes place on the U.S. Southwest border with Mexico. Some were disguised as cargo transported in airtight container trucks; deaths due to suffocation or heat were common. Another entry from the desolate U.S. Southwest desert involved a trek lasting several days; thirst and heat exhaustion frequently took their tolls. And those who tried to enter by sea through Cuba and the Bahamas often were overloaded on boats that capsized where many drowned. Most illegal immigrants were arranged by underworld organizations and conducted by a leader. The fee could be as high as $40,000 per person and had to be paid before immigrants regained their personal freedom.

In the 2011 fiscal year, a total of 327,577 smugglers were arrested, about the same as it was in the early 1970s. The peak year occurred in 2000; a total of 1.6 million people were apprehended, concentrated in the Southwest border of the United States, Mexicans making up 90% (*Washington Post*, 2011/12/5). In recent years, about 40,000 people were repatriated annually, and over 30,000 people (2007) not repatriated were jailed in the country's 200 detention centers. In 2010 the federal government sent back 390,000 people at a total cost of $2.55 billion, or $6,538 per person (2010/12/29). Drug lords mix drug trafficking and illegal immigration into one, having double benefits. As a result, among the repatriated criminal illegal immigrants, drug traffickers led the pack. In 2011, 396,906 people were repatriated, including 216,698 criminals consisting of 44,683 (21%) drug traffickers, 35,927 (17%) drivers under the influence, 5,848 (3%) sex offenders and 1,119 (1%) murderers. Beginning in 2012, the Obama administration ordered the Justice Department not to detain and repatriate non-criminal illegal immigrants and criticized the states of Alabama and Arizona for their immigration-related legislation.

Even though the United States possesses enough nuclear arms capable of destroying the earth several times and the technology to land men on the moon, it can not safeguard national boundaries, pursue travelers with expired visas, and can do little about illegal immigrants. In the 2008 presidential campaign, Mr. Obama promised to enact new immigration legislation if he were elected, but failed to fulfill his promise. The federal government has lost its control over illegal immigration. The situation is out of control, no viable solution in sight.

6.3. Economic Impact of Illegal Immigration

Immigration is part of international affairs and should be under the jurisdiction of the federal government. But some illegal immigrants draw benefits on and use facilities of the state and local government, such as public schools, hospitals and community services. And the others may have committed crimes requiring detention or imprisonment by state and local government facilities, thus becoming a financial burden to them. In the recent economic downturn, most state and local governments faced a serious budget shortfall. Arizona, Alabama, Georgia, Mississippi, Oklahoma, Nebraska, Missouri, Indiana, South Carolina, Utah, and Pennsylvania introduced legislative control of illegal immigration to reduce state government expenditures (2011/1/2, 2012/2/2).

Little attention had been paid to illegal immigration until the 2008 financial crisis. When the unemployment rate rose to 9%, this was used as a powerful weapon by those who oppose illegal immigration. They contended that illegal immigrants took away the jobs of local workers and called for strengthening immigration law enforcement so as to provide employment opportunities for local people. On the other hand, human rights activists and pro-Latino groups strongly claimed that illegal immigrants made contributions to the national economy of $66 billion annually through the spending of 11 million people and with 8 million jobs equivalent to about 5% of the national workforce. Although very few are subjected to income tax and real estate tax, all illegal immigrants had to pay sales tax and gasoline taxes which helped state and local government finances.

Because the pay is too low or the work is too harsh, most Americans do not desire the jobs that the illegal workers do. Therefore, these types of workers are still in great demand. In June 2011, Alabama had a 9.9% unemployment rate and implemented the state new immigration law which forced the illegal farm workers to leave. Potato farmer Keith Smith began to hire local workers to replace them. He said that most American workers came in late, were slower than those experienced farm workers, and were ready to call it a day after lunch or in the afternoon; some workers resigned only after one day on the job. Tomato buyer Spencer said that a group of four Latinos can pick 300 boxes of tomatoes a day, at a rate of $2 each for a total of $600; that is $150 per person per day. Recently, a team of 25 American workers picked 200 boxes of tomatoes a day, $3 each for a total of $600, and each earned $24 a day. In addition, local workers can get unemployment benefits of $265 a week. If they choose to work, (with a minimum hourly wage of $7.25) for 40 hours a week, this pays $290; of course, it is better to take the unemployment benefit. According to an analysis conducted by the University of Alabama economist Samuel Addy, the new law resulted in 80,000 job vacancies, $10.8 billion in economic losses to the state (2011/2/2, 10/22). This is not an isolated case. Georgia also had a 9.9% unemployed population, and 70% of its crop had not been harvested due to a severe shortage of farm hands. Stanley, a farm owner, says that local workers were not available, and they were unwilling to work for two hours and it was too hard a job (2011/5/28).

Cesar Chavez organized the National Farm Workers Association in 1962 to vent their grievances and injustices, and to demand higher wages and better working conditions for farm workers. And in 1965 they joined a strike with the Farm Workers Association against the Delano, California grape growers. Later, these two unions merged into the United Farm

Workers union (UFW). They advocated non-violence and an anti-illegal immigrant policy in the labor dispute with the growers, enticing public sympathy and support with a consumer boycott of buying grapes. The strike also gained national attention and consciousness of the farm workers' plight. As a result, on July 29, 1970, it made the 26 Delano grape growers allow them to unionize their workers and enhanced public support so that the landmark statute, the California Agricultural Labor Relations Act of 1975, was enacted.

During those years, the UFW made a considerable gain in their demands to improve members' welfare and expanded membership to 50,000 workers at its peak. However, by the mid-1980s, UFW influence had diminished, with its membership dwindling to around 15,000, a 70% drop. There were several important factors contributing to the decline. First, the influx of undocumented workers surged. They ignored the union rules which became unenforceable by the union or the government. Second, the growers switched to the contractor system; there were no labor contracts for the union to sign. Hence, the union became irrelevant. Third, California grape growers' opposition and a series of hostile governors undercut the effectiveness of the law. Finally, the federal government preferred to keep food prices low and inflation in-check. They ignored the deplorable conditions of the migratory farm workers, a human rights violation; even though, a Senate subcommittee held a hearing, no legislation was proposed. As a result, the ground gained for the migratory farm workers during the Chavez farm labor movement was lost almost entirely.

In a study entitled *"Farm Workers in the U.S."*, by Eduardo Gonzalez, Jr., State University specialist, Cornell University Cooperative Extension released on October 5, 2015, the paper pointed out that the Bracero program began to entice Mexican farm workers to America in 1942 and ended in 1964. It was replaced by the agricultural guest worker program (H-2A) in 1952 which accounted for a part of the legal farm workers in the U.S. today. Every year one to three million farm hands entered the U.S., mostly from Mexico and Central and South Americas. Today, 52% of the farm workers enter without documentation and 61% of them live below the poverty line. Their median annual income is less than $7.500 (way below $11,770, 2015 the Federal Poverty Level Guidelines for one person). Farm workers' pay, including large farm American workers, is the second lowest pay among all American occupations, only better than domestic services. Most of the undocumented farm workers are subject to foremen's abuses, harmful agricultural chemicals, unsanitary and unsafe living condition, violence, and threat of deportation if employed by farm owners so that they take other jobs the first chance they get or return home when they have saved enough money. The harsh working conditions coupled with low pay for the illegal farm workers explains why there are only four million of them in America even though millions of them enter the U.S. every year.

Almost all migrant farm workers are seasonal, temporary and mobile; once the crop is harvested, they move on to another farm. These are almost all contracting jobs, based on piece rates, with low wages, headed by a contracting foreman; they are not employees of the farms. Therefore, the statutory labor laws and regulations do not apply, such as minimum wage, health care, retirement, unemployment, and holidays -- a lot worse than the previous Bracero Program. Migrant farm workers are living without a home, eating at irregular hours, most are exploited by the contractors, are rarely with their family unless their children also work with them, and live a life much worse than that of the former American black farm slaves; so many return home after acquiring enough savings or change to other occupations. Regardless of whether these farm activities are condoned by the U.S. government or the farm workers are willing participants, it is simply a revival of farm slavery of a different form in America. Yet, the U.S. State Department never includes this serious human rights abuse in its annual report to Congress on the human rights violations around the world.

The Congressional Budget Office, conducting an investigation of 29 cases on illegal immigrants in the last 15 years, concluded that state and local governments spend more on illegal immigrants in various services than the illegal immigrants pay in taxes and fees combined. Former Mexican President Vicente Fox said that international remittance is Mexico's largest foreign exchange income, more than oil exports, tourism, or investment income. The World Bank reported that in 2005 foreign remittances into Mexico totaled $18.1 billion mainly income from the Mexican immigrants, legal and illegal, in the United States who sent money home. This income is neither consumed nor saved in a U.S. bank, thus, causing the overall U.S. economy to shrink by $18.1 billion, a negative impact. On the other hand, illegal immigrants rarely rob jobs from local workers, and their presence or absence has little impact on the nation's unemployment rate. In May 2006, the *New York Times* and CBS poll shows that 53% of people polled believe that local people will not do the work of illegal immigrants, as also evidenced by what occurred on Alabama and Georgia's farms. Yet, both the above two arguments, economic contribution and robbing local jobs by illegal immigrants, do not fully support the facts.

Illegal immigrant workers mostly are paid by piece rates which are much lower than the statutory minimum wage, having a lowered cost impact on the related industries. In agriculture, their low labor costs greatly benefit food price stability, especially fruits and vegetables. In real estate construction related businesses, illegal immigrants supply cheap labor, resulting in low costs in housing construction, thus accelerating the real estate bubble expansion, making a lot of millionaires and also creating tens of millions of home foreclosures. Of course, this was not the fault of illegal immigrants; they were just innocent participants.

6.4. Political Impact of Illegal Immigration

The U.S. Constitution does not specify the number of political parties that can be formed, but in reality the Democratic and Republican Parties took turns governing the country; a third party almost had no chance to assume power. In the past 50 years, the Democratic Party moved the country towards a welfare society advocating a larger role of government in people's life; promoting workers' rights and welfare policy; permitting abortion; and conditionally restricting firearms in order to protect community safety. The Republicans support capitalism and the free market ideal, contending free enterprise has a far better efficiency than bureaucracy; promoting military superiority, fiscal conservatism, and less government; consider abortion as the killing of lives; and believe that firearm ownership is an undeniable and indispensable civil right. Since The Great Society legislation of the 1960s, the U.S. political map has been greatly altered. In general, the Southern states, which were originally dominated by the Democratic Party, switched to support the Republican, and the mid-section states also tilted toward the Republican Party. Both the east and west coastal states were the strongholds of the Democratic Party. This general trend has prevailed ever since.

After 1965's implementation of the new immigration law, those who benefited the most were Mexicans. The Mexican-American population in the United States surged from 760,000 in 1970 to 31.8 million people in 2010, a close to 41 fold increase in 40 years; so did the Latino population of 9,589,216 people, accounting for 4.7% in 1970 and increasing to 50,477,594 people, 16.7% of the total population in 2010, (2012/4/24). Of course, Latinos expanded their political muscle. In the 2008 presidential campaign, Senator Barack Obama promised the Latino voters that immigration legislation would be his No.1 priority if he were elected, and ultimately he received 67% of the Latino votes. To compensate for not being able to honor his promise in time on the immigration legislation, President Obama appointed Sonia Sotomayor in 2009 to the federal Supreme Court, the first Latino justice in the U.S. history. In 2005 Antonio Ramon Villaraigosa was elected mayor of Los Angeles, the country's second largest city, setting a precedent for being the first Latino mayor of Los Angeles in 130 years. He was re-elected in 2009 and was named the chairman of the 2012 Democratic National Convention, which demonstrated the importance of Latino voters to the Democratic Party. Most Hispanics are Catholics who strictly prohibit abortion and emphasize marriage and family, but 73% of them are low income people, in favor of the social welfare system, supporting Democratic Party policies.

According to the National Hispanic Foundation, in the 2012 presidential election, there were 12.2 million Hispanic voters, higher than 9.7 million in 2008, and now there are 50,000 Latinos reaching 18-year-old voting age every month (2012/2/9). The cover of the March 5, 2012, *Time* magazine says, "Yo Decido. Why Latinos will pick the next President". In the 2010 national census, the ethnic composition was as follows: whites 64%, Latino 17%, blacks 12%, and Asians 5%. In Arizona, Florida, Nevada, Colorado, Virginia, and North Carolina, neither party would have a clear advantage in the 2012 election; therefore, these would be the hottest contested states, and the Latino votes would be a major determinant of the presidential election. The vast majority of illegal immigrants come from Latin America, accounting for 81%. Mexico alone accounts for 58%, ranking as first place. Therefore, illegal immigration became the Hispanics' greatest concern.

In 2001, the Democratic and Republican Parties reached a preliminary agreement supporting the Senate proposed the Dream Act, Development,

Relief, and Education for Alien Minors Act. As the name suggested, it was aimed at developing the talents of undocumented young people for employment in the United States while addressing part of the illegal immigration problem. The qualifications of the illegal were: under 36 years of age, coming to the United States when a minor, residing in America at least five years, of good character, and a high school graduate plus two years of college or military service, can apply for temporary residency for six years. Within six years, those who are in school must complete a university degree or two years of military service; those who are in the military must attend two years college; then they could apply for permanent residency.

Supporters of the Dream Act legislation contended that more young intellectuals will help national competitiveness; universities will get more tuition fees and reduce the fiscal burden on government; also, it will provide more recruiting sources to the military. Since 10 states have accepted undocumented college students, implementation of this plan should be able to proceed smoothly. Opponents to the Act asserted that this is tantamount to rewarding illegal behavior and there will be a greater influx of illegal immigrants; increased education and welfare burden; and intensified local government financial difficulties. Limited federal education grants will reduce local students' education opportunities. Furthermore, identity and documents are hard to verify, thereby increasing implementation difficulties.

Illegal immigration became a political tug of war between the two political factions. On one side, the liberals and the emerging Latino political forces claim that the entire nation's population is comprised of foreigners. Therefore, immigration is a divine right; refusing to accept these useful people already in the country constitutes an act of discrimination, especially against Hispanics. On the other side, the traditional conservatives assert that the existence of illegal immigrants proves that the government has been unable to control the borders and the flow of travelers, which endanger people and national security. The 9-11 incidents are the best evidences. The Republicans strongly opposed illegal immigration, causing the bill to be killed. Five years later, in 2006, Congress revisited the old issue; again, it was rejected. Since then, the same bill has come up in Congress every year for six years in a row and was met with the same fate every year until 2011. It demonstrates that illegal immigration has become a major national political issue greatly influencing Hispanic voter's decisions.

While illegal immigrants do not have the right to vote, the 2010 census includes illegal immigrants, and on this basis reapportions House member seats for all states, resulting in an increase of four seats in Texas, two seats in Florida, with six other states each gaining one seat. In contrast, New York and Ohio each lost two seats, and another eight states each lost one seat. Louisiana refused to accept the seat reduction, maintaining that illegal immigrants are not citizens, so, of course cannot participate in American politics. To include the illegal immigrant population in determining House of Representatives seats is unconstitutional and was appealed to the U.S. Supreme Court, but the appeal was not accepted for consideration.

According to 2007 statistics, the U.S. national fertility rate was 52.3 per thousand, while Hispanics had more than doubled the average, at 108.4. Along with the large number of Latino legal and illegal immigrants flowing into the U.S., this situation will dramatically alter the future composition of the population. By 2050, the makeup of the U.S. population is expected to be: 46% white, 30% Hispanic, 15% black, 9% Asians. In addition, Hispanics are more comparable in beliefs, ideals, habits, education, and income, besides their unity and cooperation. To the contrary, whites have a wide disparity of income and education, and are polarized as liberals or conservatives, each having their own ways. Thus, Hispanics demonstrate a high degree of political efficacy, and their political influence will likely surpass the whites by 2050.

Today is not 1953, and it is not a politically acceptable policy to repeat President Eisenhower's repatriation of a large number of illegal immigrants. Even if it worked, it would be futile because the repatriated would simply turn around and reenter the United States. It just means more work and cost to the federal agencies ($6,500 cost per repatriate) and solves no problems. Therefore, total repatriation is no longer a viable option; the focus should be placed on how to make the majority of illegal immigrants into useful productive members of society and to reduce the burden on government finances. But sooner or later, they will become citizens, with 81% of them coming from Latin America, 49% having no high school diploma and economically disadvantaged. They will definitely enhance the political influence of Hispanics and the laboring class political force.

6.5 Impact of Hispanic Language and Culture

Since Christopher Columbus landed in America in 1492, the European powers, one after another, carved up the Americas. Each vigorously expanded colonialism, military occupation, cultural invasion, and miscegenation and assimilation. North America and the Caribbean were under the sphere of British control. Central and South Americas were Spain and Portugal's world. The French ruled Haiti; Russia occupied Alaska; and the Netherlands had a part of the Caribbean. European languages, religions, and customs replaced the indigenous culture. Spain and Portugal promoted miscegenation in order to achieve assimilation.

In the first 150 years of European rule, the indigenous population dwindled from 50 million to 8 million people by 1650, a net decrease of 84%. The main causes were the Old World diseases brought by the Europeans, such as smallpox, measles, and other infectious diseases, resulting in a large number of deaths. In only one hundred years, between 1518 and 1618, there were nine major plague outbreaks, because the natives lacked immunity to foreign diseases, causing an extreme high mortality rate. With an estimated death of 10-20 million people, there also vanished many of the local languages and cultures. Wars, genocide, and forced labor accounted for the second largest number of deaths. Therefore, from the aboriginal perspective, this was an unprecedented catastrophe in the Americas. Columbus was the major culprit, not the hero who discovered the New World.

For long-term peace and stability, Spain and Portugal promoted a miscegenation policy. Interracial marriage eliminated racial differences; of course, there would not have racial conflicts. Fusing local and foreign peoples in one family, no more "ours" and "yours" distinctions existed; cultivating all ethnic cultures in one pot, it would thus create a harmonious society. This seemed to be the pursuit of the noble ideal of universal brotherhood, but it was the implementation of Europeanization. After 500 years of assimilation, resulting in a special Hispanic population, some of their physical appearance is almost the same as white Europeans, others are nearly identical to African blacks; most come in between, but there is a special distinction, because most of them have Native American Indian features.

Hispanic is not a race, but a social group as classified by the United States Census Bureau. Of course, they have their cultural identity. Following Spanish and Portuguese traditions, most of them are Catholics, accounting for 70%, together with other Christian sects, Jewish, Muslim and other foreign religions; believers in the native religions are few. In language, English dominates in North America except Mexico. French is popular in Haiti and Quebec, Canada. Portuguese is the official language of Brazil. The Caribbean uses Dutch, English, and French. And all the other parts of the Americas use Spanish. Indigenous languages exist in the desolate and remote mountain areas, such as in parts of Peru, Guatemala, Bolivia, and Paraguay, as well as small areas of Mexico, Panama, Ecuador, and Chile. The postwar civil rights movement drew attention and protection to the native languages; today, some have been declared as official languages.

Texas Sen. Ralph Yarborough recognized learning difficulties of Latino children because of language barriers. He proposed the Bilingual Education Act in 1967, accelerating the school children's, aged 6-8, ability to master English in order to be integrated into the normal school curriculum. Since 1968, when President Johnson signed it into law, there have been five revisions and expansions of the Bilingual Education Act, which significantly altered the original objective. The budget for bilingual education increased from $7.5 million in 1968, to $162 million in 2000; California benefited the most, up to $58 million in federal subsidies. The new law authorized acceptance of all children having difficulty in English, including the children of illegal immigrants, into a program that developed the bilingual education curriculum, faculty, and information centers. So, it was no longer a mere transitional measure to assist children in mastering English, but became a parallel bilingual education system.

Bilingual education emphasized using the native tongue for all immigrants; Hispanics accounted for the vast majority of immigrants and most of them use Spanish, thus strengthening the importance of that language. For convenience, government agencies, businesses, and community groups have adopted Spanish, so that official forms, advertising, signs, telephone service, and a variety of automated machines have English and Spanish selections. America was moving towards an English-Spanish bilingual society.

The development of multi-languages facilitates contact with different cultures, enhanced mutual understanding and cooperation, and promoted favorable thinking and experiences leading to ethnic harmony and social progress. It should have been praised and encouraged. However, under the current bilingual development trend in the U.S., it will have serious adverse effects. First, it is fueling Hispanic inertness; no longer actively learning the local language, they become difficult to integrate into the local community, resulting in an ethnic divide, opposition, and even conflict. Second, communication between citizens must rely on translation, which inevitably reduces some national unity and cohesion. More importantly, with the technological development and the growing trend of globalization, English is not only the main language of the United States; it is the world's most prevalent language. Inability to use English means missing many favorable opportunities such as employment, business, politics, science and technology, research and development, and even the convenience of travel abroad. Therefore, those who lack English skills will find it hard to get a good job in the United States and will become the low-income segments of society forever, leading to second-class citizenship. It will inevitably create the potential for social conflict, class confrontation, ethnic friction, and community anxiety and unrest.

The Republicans may have sensed the serious trouble ahead. Once President George W. Bush (term 2001-2008) took office, he initiated bilingual education reform and tried to steer the trend back to its original objective in 1968. With the Senate Democratic leader Edward M. "Ted" Kennedy's support, the No Child Left Behind Act, English Language Acquisition, Language Enhancement and Academic Achievement Act of 2002 quickly got approved by Congress. The focus was on accelerated English learning in elementary schools for non-English speaking students, the reduction of the bilingual education budget, and the implementation of a unified test for subsidy standards to schools. Due to shortages of bilingual teachers in math and sciences, and the rapid influx of school children of illegal immigrants, low student test scores reduced benefits from federal grants. On the other hand, parts of the new bill contradict the Civil Rights Act of 1964 and the Equal Educational Opportunity Act of 1974, so that the Act became highly controversial and could not be implemented in all bilingual education campuses without review and approval individually by the court or federal agency. The entire bill was in limbo.

The United States is a military superpower. Facilities preventing terrorism are everywhere, and fighting drug trafficking is carried out both at home and abroad, but it could not protect its own borders. Before the 2008 recession, more than 500,000 illegal immigrants entered into the country every year; terrorists and drug traffickers could easily be smuggled into the country with the illegal immigrants. Counter-terrorism and drug fighting efforts were almost in vain, so was it not a big joke? Massive repatriation is no longer politically acceptable. Members of Congress suggested an amnesty program for over 11 million illegal immigrants already in the country, doubling immigration quotas, erecting a Mexican border wall, strengthening border patrol, heavy fines for hiring illegal immigrants, and computer control of work permits and other documents. But the majority failed to achieve bipartisan support. Then, the Obama's White House also restricted enforcement actions against illegal immigration, and the Supreme Court began hearings on immigration related legislations of Alabama and other states, resulting in a complicated mess.

Los Angeles, America's second largest city has a Latino mayor; a Hispanic also serves as Supreme Court justice; Hispanics are members of Congress and many local government officials. In the future, no doubt, some will be governors, vice-presidents, and even the president. Mexican food has long been a requisite on school lunch menus favored by young students. Tacos, Tortillas, Fajitas, Enchiladas are the most popular items, and Taco Bell and Azteca chains can be seen everywhere. Spanish has been adopted by government and business, and has become the second most common language in the United States. Hispanic traditions, such as being family oriented, devoutly Catholic, opposed to abortion and other social influences, will expand. With the rapid increase in number, by 2050 Hispanics will account for 30% of U.S. total population (see 6.4); many communities in the United States based on the British language, culture, and traditions, could soon be converted to a Spanish culture-based society. From another point of view, Mexico was defeated by the United States in the past, ceding territory for peace. Now, by exporting a huge population with Latino heritage, it will soon transform America inside out and remake this North American giant somewhat closer to a Latino's image.

6.6 Implementing a New Marshall Plan: Preserving American Tradition

An emergency occurred on the Texas-Mexican border because, since October 2013, there has been an influx of a large number of minors into Texas from Honduras, Guatemala, and El Salvador. The total influx has exceeded 52,000 people, doubling last year's number, causing severe shortages of government personnel, facilities, and creating a border crisis. The Obama administration requested $3.7 billion to deal with the situation, including $1.8 billion for the resettlement of these youths and the rest for increases in border patrol, immigration judges, and other programs to discourage people from attempting to enter into the United States (*Reuters*, 2014/7/8).

According to the current statutes, this group of teenagers, unaccompanied by adults, must be reviewed by a judge before any decision can be made about their status in the U.S. If repatriated, by law they must be sent back to their home country by airplane, which is time-consuming and expensive. The Obama administration blamed extreme poverty, drug and other violent crimes, and lack of community security as the causes for the exodus of these young people looking for stability and happiness in America. Republicans accused President Obama of policy mistakes, because beginning 2012, detention and repatriation of innocent illegal immigrants were halted, equal to a halfway amnesty, giving much encouragement to illegal immigrants, especially women and children who enjoy more humanitarian protection. Repatriation will offend the Latino community and immigration activists, but no repatriation will result in a long-term burden on American society. The Obama administration found itself in a dilemma.

True, these young people escaping poverty and crime at home and seeking happiness in the United States is an undeniable fact. However, the harsh social conditions in Central America have long existed, so why wait until now before migrating northward in droves? It is hard not to attribute the cause to the repatriation policy suspension which gave more incentive to the illegal to enter America now.

In September 2014, the office of the United Nations High Commissioner for Refugees notified the U.S. House Judiciary Committee and also proposed to the International Organization for Migration regional meeting in Nicaragua that these young people are mainly escaping armed gang fighting and other violent crimes, similar to traditional political and ethnic conflicts, in line with the conditions for asylum. And the United States and Mexico should follow this asylum principle. The border crisis may turn into a humanitarian crisis and may become a more difficult problem.

In order to win over Hispanic voters, President Obama in 2012 ordered no sending back of any non-criminal illegal immigrants, leading to the current crisis. Now he cannot afford to offend the Latino community and must find ways to accommodate these young people, enhancing future Hispanic political strength, and must cater to their desires in the future. This democratic electoral process mainly based on voters' interest has become a major weakness of democracy. It created a cocoon, got bogged down and is now unable to extricate itself. The condition appears hopeless.

On July 25, 2014, three Presidents from Central America were in the White House for a meeting. The main focus was on how to prevent youths from seeking refuge in the U.S.; a pilot plan for young refugees will be introduced in Honduras to accommodate a selected few as a measure to combat the current influx of youth. It seems that all efforts are directed toward deterring people from entering America, such as constructing a high wall and increasing border patrols, but none has been aimed at the causes of the exodus, i.e., poverty and drug violence.

If drugs can be traded commercially, just like any other merchandise, there will be little drug related violence. And if improvement is made to the local economy so that people can make a living at home, there will be very few willing to leave their family and friends, risking their lives to venture into a strange country. So, illegal immigrants from Central America will be diminished, even cause of some to return to their homelands.

With drug trade commercially normalized, violent crimes related to drugs would greatly decrease. The U.S. should initiate another Marshall Plan to be implemented in Central America to improve people's livelihood, social conditions, and community security so that there would be every reason for people to stay home and not become a problem to the U.S. Taking into account the savings relating to illegal immigration, such as border patrol, detention centers, repatriation, settlement, etc., as well as a part of fighting drugs both at home and abroad, and parts of the homeland security budget, it will be wise to invest in a new Marshall Plan in Central America. The success of this plan will not only keep out illegal immigrants from Central America, but might also entice some Latinos to return home. And that is a once and for all solution. Thus, it will alleviate the major illegal immigration problem and preserve American traditions, not being dominated by Hispanic culture in the future, if that is what most Americans wish. But people must keep in mind not to repeat the mistake made in the Alliance for Progress in the 1960s which enriched American business and overlooked the main goal of the project, ending up in failure.

Illegal immigration is no longer a mere colonial and labor issue; it is becoming a major political, economic, human rights, and national security problem, extremely impacting the development of the United States. Especially, if it turns into a humanitarian crisis, it is bound to intensify and become more difficult to solve, thereby adversely affecting society. Illegal immigration renders America helpless, unable to make the desired choice, but it must face reality. First, as President Obama mentioned, illegal immigrants account for 50-60% of farm workers. Without them, the agricultural sector will be paralyzed with not much food on the American family table. Second, the pro-illegal immigration, especially Hispanic, political force must be appeased to win national elections, and the force is getting stronger by the day. The illegal immigration problem will not go away even if the 11 million currently in the country are allowed to stay because there will be more illegal immigrants entering the United States. Unless a new Marshall Plan is successfully carried out or the global free flow of all resources are implemented, as suggested later in this book (see 9.2), there will be no end in sight of illegal immigrants from Central America.

VII. Prospects for the United States

At the end of World War II, all imperialists led by the U.S suddenly turned themselves into advocates of democracy, freedom, equality, and human rights. English became the most popular international language together with mass media, such as movies and TV programs. America broadcasted political ideal and social value and tried to convince the world that the system advocated by the West was the only choice as a political and social system leading to freedom and prosperity. Other forms of government were perceived as illegitimate, harmful, and had to justify for their existence. However, 70 years later, the reality has proved otherwise: Greece and some other democracies are in political trouble; big nations dominate the world scene and there is no democracy among nations. People in other parts of the world, even though they are under democracy and capitalism systems, are almost as poor and ignorant as before World War II, and they are tilling and weeding to subsist in serving their former masters, the developed nations. The Edward Snowden and NSA scandals and the slave farm labor prevailing indicated that even in the U.S. human rights were not honored. Democracy is no longer regarded as the only option, and America has lost its moral high ground in the calling for human rights.

The American world superpower hegemony is basically supported by four pillars which are ideology and culture, technology, military, and financial power. Except ideology and culture, the other three pillars are anchored mainly on an economic foundation to maintain their effectiveness and to expand their influences.

In the past one hundred years, America made a tremendous contribution to science and technology and improved people's living standard especially in the West. It was the American century. Beginning in the 1970s, America lost its economic competitiveness which gradually eroded its economic base. Since the 2008 financial crisis prompting all levels of government to cut their budgets, R&D funding has not been fully restored. Russia, China, and India are tracking close behind American space technology. American cyber superiority is challenged by Russia and China. Development of supercomputer technology, which is vital to all R&D, is currently led by the Chinese. Wired.com reported on June 21, 2016, that China just unveiled its Sunway (divine mighty) supercomputer with Chinese-made chips, more than three times faster than the previous leader, Tianhe-2, and nearly 20 times fastest than the U.S. supercomputer, Titan. More world top 500 supercomputers are in China than in any nation in the world, including the U.S. On May 22, 2017, *Boston Globe* carried an article, "*America second? Yes, and China's lead is only growing.*" which might cause disbelief, dismay or denial to most American. The author, Graham Allison, director of Harvard Kennedy School's Belfer Center for Science and International Affairs, stated that in a 2015 annual ranking by *US News & World Report*, China's Tsinghua University dethroned MIT as the top engineering university in the world. There were three more Chinese universities ranked among the 10 top engineering schools in the world, the same number as the U.S. universities. In the STEM fields (science, technology, engineering, and mathematics), China produced four times graduates as many as the American universities (1.3 million vs. 300,000). And Chinese universities awarded more PhDs in STEM fields than US universities every year since 2009. The American technology lead is shrinking.

After the collapse of the Soviet Union in 1991, the U.S. emerged as the only super power. Russia can only match with the U.S. in her nuclear arsenal. America is the true world policeman. The U.S. is leading the world in all facets of the military except ground forces.

And after the Bretton Woods Conference in 1944, the U.S. solidified her control on the world financial system. As America gained world prominence so did U.S. global financial control and the dollar supremacy. Thus, it provides the leeway for America, unlike the Soviet Union or Greece, to be able to maintain economic stability and growth on debt. However, the global trade and financial development in recent decades has gradually reduced American global financial control and will be further eroded as its economy withers.

Except ideology and culture, the other three pillars require economic strength to sustain their effectiveness and to expand their influence. Hence, a close assessment of the U.S. economy will provide much insight to the future U.S. superpower hegemony.

7.1. What Does the GDP Measure?

Gross domestic product is the sum of the national goods and services produced and consumed in a year. The goods sector consists of tangibles and intangibles which includes agriculture, fisheries, forestry, mining, construction, manufacturing, copyright, patent, etc.; the service sector covers all levels of government, education, healthcare, transportation, information, finance, leasing, food, entertainment, travel, fitness and beauty, and utilities industries. If the consumption or expenditure method is used to present GDP, total output equals to personal consumption, government spending, gross investment, and net of import and export (GDP=C+G+I+XM). If using income as a basis for GDP measurement, total output is the sum of wages, profits, rent, and interest, plus sundry adjustments including corporate income tax, dividends, and unallocated profits adjustments (GDP=W+P+R+I+SA). The two methods of calculation have the same result. Of course, all countries use local currency for recording their GDP which then are converted into U.S. dollars for international agencies' statistical purposes.

As technology advance and living standards improve, people began to seek luxuries. After basic material needs are satisfied, human beings start to pursue intellectual, psychological, and spiritual fulfillment. Demands for entertainment and education; visiting temples and churches; donations to charity and causes all flourish. From an economic point of view, this trend proportionally reduces the product industries and increasingly emphasizes the service sector; it is also the general trend of economic development in the West.

In 1960, the U.S. service sector surpassed the product sector and accounted for 57.2% of GDP; with the accelerated growth of the last 50 years, and by 2011, the weight of the service sector reached 80%, which also accounted for 80% of the private national labor forces, becoming the major source of employment in addition to the public sector's employees. There were five main factors contributing to this phenomenal growth in the service sector: (1) The Johnson Great Society legislation greatly increased government regulatory and enforcement agencies leading to big government and more employees; (2) Medicare and Medicaid services surged, resulting in a huge demand for medical institutions and their personnel; (3) The military buildup during the Cold War and continuing on to this day escalated defense spending as well as its personnel; (4) The information and the Internet age, information enterprises and networks, especially the software industry, flourished prompting more start-ups and staff; (5) Finally, the U.S. manufacturing competitiveness weakened, leading to factories being relocated abroad and products outsourced overseas; shrinking product output relatively enhanced the service sector.

Goods can be stored and transported, and production and consumption can be done at different times and in different places. Because of booming international trade and fierce competition in recent decades, huge differences in product prices have been eliminated. However, due to the impact of freight, duties, regulations, and social customs, etc., the price differentials among regions and nations still exist. Hence, the International Monetary Fund (IMF) makes the purchasing power parity (PPP) adjustment for a more realistic comparison of GDP in different countries.

Production and consumption of services are inseparable, cannot be saved and used or exported later, and are subjected to time and place restrictions. However, with the rapid Internet development, the service sector will, in 3-5 years, dramatically expand its reach beyond the national boundary, and more service industries will become exportable, e.g., global retailing and banking. But for now, they are mostly for the local people's current consumption. The exportable services accounted for by a tiny portion of foreign trade (5.2% of total service in 2015), and they will have to compete with international peers in order to survive. So, their cost is in line with international standards. For example, for many airlines operating between Shanghai and New York City, the high fare, high cost, and poor service carriers will be eliminated sooner or later, but don't count on government-subsidized airlines.

The non-exportable government and non-profit organization services, with a lack of local and international competition, their prices and cost of services may have a vast variation as compared with their foreign counterparts.

Non-export service entities can be divided into two categories. One group is the private service enterprises in finance, entertainment, food, etc., such as retailers, banks, restaurants, private schools that would need to compete in the domestic market for their business; so, price and cost structures are more in line with local standards. The other group is all levels of government, publicly-funded institutions, and nonprofit organizations, including federal, state and local governments, post offices and public school systems, and private foundations, which mostly have no competitors and no cost limitations, but are only subject to budget control.

Governmental and not-for-profit sectors are not subject to competition and regulation by the price mechanism and free market force. Hence, there is uncertainty about the adequacy of services and their economic value which constitute major pitfalls. If government services are underprovided, it means that people's needs are not completely met and society is not fully functioning, such as waiting several days to get a driver's license. On the other hand, more government services than are needed means more bureaucratic and regulatory hurdles for business and industries to cross, adding to their cost of operation and hindering their ability to compete globally. Therefore, more services than are needed are worse not better for the economy. Like the Greece case, in the last several decades, political parties used government payroll to boost employment and hence GDP to show their accomplishment in order to win an election. Most of these spending were funded by national debt and did not produce much useful economic service. Thus, they only contributed to the growth of the current year GDP, but promoted little to the future economic activities or GDP. The extra payroll spending widened demand and supply, causing inflation, mounting national debt, economic dislocation, unemployment, revenue shortfall and budget deficit -- followed by economic, political and humanitarian crises.

Second, since most governmental services have no competition, as a result, their economic values are difficult to establish. The value of GPS and the Internet developed by the U.S. Defense Department personnel is incalculable, much more than employees' compensation over the years. On the other hand, those air traffic controllers while sleeping on the job produced no economic value, but created potential public disaster and economic loss. However, regardless of whether their services have any value or not, their compensation is a part of the national GDP. As a result, the true economic value in this sector is very much in doubt.

Expenditures on big government administration, large military forces, and the Department of Homeland Security produce a corresponding high amount of GDP. They may indicate military might, but not necessarily produce any economic output. These non-economic and non-productive outlays will not promote the second round of GDP, and it is likely causing the persistent huge amount of federal budget deficit year after year. The non-economic nature of GDP, which includes expenditures for administration, military, public security, etc., should be separately reported from the economic sector.

As society progresses, it tends to grow with division of labor or work specialization in the service sector and create additional GDP, e.g., house cleaning and gardening, but sometimes it may not provide additional economic benefit, mainly illusive—shifting work from one group of people to another group with no measurable services enhanced. Suppose two neighboring families decide to swap cooking for gardening and charge each other $10,000 a year; GDP grows by $20,000 without the benefit of additional service. Hence, the higher degree of service specialization in a society tends to produce higher GDP and may not create that much economic value. This phenomenon is also applicable to the goods sector in the less developed countries for their infant market economies. Therefore, some adjustments to GDP in the less developed economies for the barter and self-produced and self-consumed sector are warranted because they are completely excluded from GDP computation.

Furthermore, recording the goods sector for GDP is based on the products sold, excluding the defect units, an output concept; their values have met an objective market test. Whereas, services performed by government, not-for profit organizations, medical facilities, educational establishments, etc. are measured by spending, not the result, an input concept. And most of these services do not have to compete for market; thus, their objective values are in doubt because spending on services may include waste and inefficiency which obscure their true value. Besides in some cases, high service costs produce high GDP and may not indicate social improvement; instead, it may be the result of worsening social conditions. For example, the 2014 Ebola outbreak in West Africa caused medical costs to surge; so did the GDP in these six African nations. The increased medical expenses were no indication of improvement in people's well-being in West Africa. On the contrary, it was the result of a grave public health crisis, a disease pandemic that required a large amount of medical outlay.

The service sector should also be measured by its output and a universal unit value, for example, college degrees granted, adjusted for quality. And overall well-being in health, community safety, etc. should be used to measure changes in national GDP, not the amount of spending. And by adopting a universal standard unit value on non-market value items, such as a college degree, it will eliminate the differences in goods prices, labor rates, waste, and inefficiency among nations from GDP statistics. An adjustment item in the GDP is needed to accommodate the difference between adjusted and reported values. Thus, more comparable GDP data may be provided for better assessment of economic strength, military might, and social vitality. Details of the methodology reform rely on the experts' inputs.

At present, GDP includes economic and non-economic, productive and non-productive sectors such as agriculture, transportation, education, medical service, government administration, and military expenditure. It does not provide clear vital information needed to assess a nation's economic strength, military might and social vitality. Instead, it confuses the issue, confusion of production and consumption, leading to erroneous decisions. For example, government spending (consumption) increases gross domestic product (production), (consumption=production), and a large GDP is the rationale for a higher government budget. This circular reasoning process eventually leads to the national debt crisis like the situation in Greece. This confusion also leads to erroneous implication that spending means production, thus, spending alone can achieve economic prosperity.

The method of reporting GDP needs a fundamental overhaul. It should have separate sections to provide information on how much GDP resources were provided (goods sector + exported services + non-exported services) and how GDP resources were used (goods and service sectors + imports – exports). The economic strength is basically driven by production and determined by nation's ability to produce-- economic advantages, absolute and comparative. This section should indicate production result, tangible and intangible products, and exported services which is insignificant now. This includes wheat, car, movies, software, foreign student spending, etc. The non-exportable services are for domestic use and are determined by the nation's ability to consume which is limited by current income and available financial resources including debt increases. These services do not have to compete with foreign providers. Therefore, they present nation's ability to consume and do not constitute economic strength. These services are accounted for as both source and use of GDP. For example, government payroll is shown both as national income and expenditure.

The resources used to maintain, improve, and achieve personal wellbeing, community safety, national security, and social objectives are individual/private and public/collective consumption. The social vitality section should cover the cost of maintenance and improvement of people's physical and mental well-being which includes expenditures for living, education, and health care. It is private/individual consumption. Costs of federal, state, and local government functions, law and order, and community safety should be separated in another section as costs of social governance. Investment in long term assets such as housing and infrastructure construction are for social improvement. It is private/individual and public/collective consumption during the year except for the military. The military might section is basically concerned with national security which includes the defense budget, cost of wars on drug and terrors, and related expenditures such as military intelligence gathering. It is public/collective consumption on military. Thus, it might be able to shed some light on the vital questions of economic strength, military might, and social vitality. A statement using this approach is presented as follow.

2015 U.S. and China GDP

Sector	Nominal GDP in Billion* U.S.		China		China/ U.S.	Adjusted GDP in Billion U.S LRP*	China PPP*	China/ U.S.	Per Capita In Dollar U.S.	China
Goods	$3,625	20.1%	$5,267	47.1%	145%	$3,625	$8,445	233%	$11.1	$6.1
Services	14,412	79.9	5,915	52.9	41	9,656	9,485	98	29.6	6.9
Total	$18,037	100%	$11,182	100%	62	13,281	$17,930	135	$40.7	$13.0

Sources of GDP:

Economic Strength: Goods and Exported service

Goods	$3,625	20.1%	$5,267	47.1%		$3,625	$8,445		$11.1	$6.1
Service	751	4.2	218	1.9		751	218		2.3	0.2
S-total	$4,376	24.3%	$5,485	49.1%	125%	$4,376	$8,663	198%	$13.4	$6.3

Consumption Capacity: Non-exportable

Service generated: Private and public consumption

	$13,661	75.7 %	$5,697	50.9%	42%	$8,905	$9,267	104%	27.3	$6.0
Total	$18,037	100%	$11,182	100%	62%	$13,281	$17,930	135%	$40.7	$13.0

Uses of GDP:

Personal Wellbeing: Household consumption

	$12,283	68.1%	$4,260	38.1%	35%	$9,044	$6,831	76%	$27.7	$5.0

Social Governance: Public consumption except military*

	$1,999	11.1%	$1,375	12.3%	69%	$1,474	$2,205	150%	4.5	1.6

Social Improvement: Capital formation

	$3,662	20.3%	$5,043	45.1%	138%	$2,696	$8,086	300%	8.3	5.9

Military Might: Defense budget

	$598*	3.3%	$146	1.3%	24%	$438	$233	53%	1.3	0.2
Total	$18,542	102.8%	$10,813	96.7%	58%	$13,653	$17,338	127%	$41.9	$12.6
Export	$2,327	12.9%	$2,359	21.1	101%					
Import	2,832	15.7	1,990	17.8	70%					
Net	$505	-2.8%	$369	+3.3%						

Import Dependency	U.S.	China
Goods Produced	$3,625	$5,267
-Export	2,327	2,359
+Import	2,832	1,990
=Used, consumer & business	4,130	4,898
Import/used	68.6%	40.6 %
2015 population	326 m. (1.0)	1,375 m. (4.2)

* Due to rounding, totals may be off. PPP=8,445/5,267=1.6, based on U.S. prices; LRP=8,048/12,075 = 0.67, based on Chinese labor rates, see 7.2 for detail. Social governance includes public education funding. Defense budget does not include budget for Homeland Security and nuclear weapons of $38.2 billion and $59.8 billion (in Dept. of Energy budget), respectively.

Sources: UN Conference on Trade and Development and Wikipedia websites.

The Chinese goods' sector is 45% greater than the U.S. After the International Monetary Fund's PPP adjustment based on the US. price level, it is 233% of America's. In the service sector, before the labor rate parity (LRP) adjustment, China is 41% of the U.S. size and 2% lesser than America after the adjustment. The detail of the LRP adjustment is discussed in 7.2.

The sources and uses of GDP statement is also presented in the nominal and adjusted format. The source section indicating the Chinese economic strength is 25% and 98% stronger than the U.S before and after the adjustment respectively. The U.S. consumption capacity is 42% greater than the Chinese but 4% less after both the price and labor rate adjustment. In the uses of GDP four sections, both countries spent about same proportion on social governance and national defense but varied widely on household consumption and social improvement. U.S. consumers spent 68% of GDP and 20% of U.S. GDP was destined for capital investment vs. 38% and 45% for the Chinese respectively. It clearly indicated that the Chinese people forwent consumption in favor of investment. After these four sections being adjusted for price and wage variations, China's military budget and consumer spending are 53% and 76% of the U.S. sizes, but social governance and investment are 150% and 300% of America's. However, China has more than four times population than America. On a per capita basis, comparing the American with Chinese, these four areas are: Consumer, $27.7/$5.0=5.5; government, $4.5/$1.6=2.8; investment, $8.3/$5.9=1.4; and military, $1.3/$0.2=6.5. The American has military superiority aspiration and global coverage which lead to a large budget and is 6.5 times of the Chinese. Consumer spending is 5.5 times indicating a higher living standard in the U.S.; social governance is 2.8 as large as the Chinese representing a big U.S. government. Investment shows the least disparity among the four between America and China, equivalent to 1.4 time per capita.

The above data show that in 2015 except investment, America outspent China in other three areas, leading China in consumer and military spending, and topping all four areas on the per capita basis. Thus, its income could not keep up with spending resulting a 2.8% GDP deficit which required the imports to make it up. The result indicated that 68.6% goods used in the nation was of foreign origin which implies American economic competitive weakness and its economic strength is declining. China on the contrary scored a 3.3% GDP surplus and relied only 40.6% of its product need by foreign suppliers. This provided the Chinese economic aid or loan to other nations.

this reporting would provide what concrete items GDP consists of instead a simple vague notion of gross domestic product. However, without making improvement in the GDP design and datum collection as suggested above, it will not be able to provide an accurate report. Hence, it is lacking vital information for crucial decisions making.

7.2. How Big is the U.S. GDP?

GDP consists of product and service sectors. Prices of products differ in regions and countries. IMF provides price parity adjustments (PPP) for a better comparison among nations. Because service compensation varies widely among nations, lots more so than product, a labor rate parity (LRP) adjustment is in order to provide a proper comparison, in addition to the purchasing power parity adjustment for the product sector. And for less developed economies, non-monetary or non-market economic activities such as barters and self-supported production and service need to be added to GDP to provide a more accurate economic reality to determine real economic condition.

Compensation of U.S. government employees generally are higher than their foreign counterparts, and medical treatments are also much more expensive in America. For example, the former city manager of Bell, California, was paid nearly $800,000 annually, not including fringe benefits and pensions. Medical procedures, like an appendectomy may cost as much as $182,955 (see 5.4 for medical expenses), which is a lot higher than what would be charged by a foreign hospital. They are all parts of the U.S. GDP, and they are not representative of the real social benefits. As a result, the U.S. GDP is overstated. The positive effect of high salary and expensive medical charges will provide the recipients more income, improving their living standards as well as a higher national GDP. At the same time, higher salaries allow the federal government to skim the cream of human resources so that the National Security Agency can get all math PhDs it wants, leaving business, industry, academic and research institutions with less available talents and at a higher cost, thus impeding their competitiveness. The bad news is that government spending and health care costs are ultimately passed on to business and industry, increasing their indirect costs, and reducing their competitiveness. Thus, it causes a migration of   factories to foreign lands and products outsourced, leading to trade deficit, massive domestic unemployment, and economic recession. Furthermore, since salary/wage is an important part of GDP, a higher salary will produce a higher GDP, and higher GDP is the rationale for a bigger budget and another round of pay raises. This reciprocating cycle produces superficial economic growth results, seriously affecting economic planning and evaluation, which will lead to major policy decision errors, such as the huge U.S. federal budget deficit experienced every year in the recent decades. Therefore, the personnel costs of non-export services must be adjusted, in addition to the PPP and exclusion of non-economic sector adjustments, to reflect a more accurate economic reality.

According to the International Monetary Fund estimates, the U.S. GDP in 2011 totaled $15.094 trillion, consisting of $3.019 (20%) and $12.075 (80%) trillion for the product and service sectors respectively. Although the United States has a large number of foreign students (foreign students' spending in America counts as part of services exported), education topped the list of foreign exchange earnings in the service sector, higher than transportation, finance, tourism and other services. But in 2011, the total foreign exchange income from all services only amounted to $606 billion, 5% of the service sector total. Therefore, almost all of the services produced in the year were for domestic use not exported, accounting for 95%.

The service sector, in 2011 GDP terms, consists of 13.2% for all levels of government spending, 12.6% for business services (lawyer, consultant, accountant, etc.), 11.7% for wholesale and retail, 11.6% for leased property sales, 8.7% for education, health care and social services, 8.0% for finance and insurance, 14.2% for all other services. Service industries usually require a lot of personnel with the exception of public utilities, such as power companies, railroads, etc., which need a huge amount of investment and operating materials, often a small proportion of manpower costs. For most other service industries, such as law firms and consulting companies, a big chunk of operating costs attributed to personnel compensation, only a small proportion for other expenses.

As of 2010, the United States has 22.5 million civil servants at all levels of government (including public school employees, but excluding defense and postal personnel) which exceed the sum of employees of agriculture, fisheries, mines, construction, forests, manufacturing, and utilities, and almost double the 11.5 million manufacturing workers. It was just the opposite situation in 1960 when manufacturers employed 15 million workers, and only 8.7 million people worked for the government (2011/4/2). In this 50 years, government employees at all levels in the U.S. increased by 13.8 million, nearly 1.6 times, which also contributed to GDP growth, because government spending made up 13.2% of GDP.

The city of Shenzhen, China, reported on July 23, 2010, that its average civil servant monthly salary of Y2,750, at the dollar exchange rate of 6.77 at that time, amounted to an annual salary of $4,874. According to the Bureau of Economic Analysis' report on August 11, 2010, the federal employee average annual salary and benefits total $123,049. Taking the Shenzhen salary data as a comparison between China and the United States, it is 25 to 1 (123,049/4,874): civil servant compensation in China is 24 times less than that of the U.S. federal employees. This compensation accounted for a major part of GDP that was the basis for a high standard of living, contributed to the high cost of goods and services, and produced a negative impact on U.S. international economic competitiveness.

The U.S. federal government's payroll data will be used as a basis for the labor rate parity adjustment. The 2011 federal government budget outlay of $3,834.0 billion may be divided into three parts: (1) Direct payment, $2,626.5 billion, (2) defense and military spending, $825.0 billion, and (3) all other government costs, $382.5 billion. Direct payments consist of Social Security, Medicare, Medicaid, interest on U.S. bonds, welfare benefits, state and industry subsidies, foreign and military aid, and other direct funding. Defense and military spending mainly includes the Departments of Defense budget and other military expenses, such as fighting terrorists and drug traffickers. All other government costs cover the budget for Congress, federal courts, and all executive branch civic functions such as the Departments of State, Education, Federal Bureau of Investigation, etc.

The total federal government workforce, excluding defense and military personnel, totaled 2,002,900 people in 2010. The average annual salary including benefits of $123,049 per person amounted to $246.4 billion annually; it was 64% (246.4/382.5) of all other government budgets. In other words, apart from the military personnel (Postal Services was a semi-public entity, not in the federal budget), employee payroll expenses accounted for 64% of all other government offices' total budget; the remainder, 36%, was for non-payroll expenditures, such as utilities, office equipment and supply, repair and maintenance, etc. Assuming this rate for all non-export services, the estimated personnel expenditure for non-export services was $7.34 trillion ((total services-exported services) x rate of personnel expenses) or ((12,075-606) x 0.64)). Using the Chinese wage standard, the United States personnel expenditures should be $293.6 (7,340/25) billion, $7,046.4 (7,340.0-293.6) billion overstated, and total U.S. GDP should be $8.048 (15.094 - 7.046) trillion consisting of $3,019 billion for the goods sector and $5,029 billion for the service sector.

The following table summarizes the 2011 GDP data using a population of 309 million and 1,339 million for the U.S. and China respectively, including the IMF estimates, purchasing power parity (PPP), and labor rate parity (LRP) adjustments.

2011 U.S. and China GDP, Adjustments for PPP and LRP

	2011 GDP	PPP based on 2011 U. S. market price				LRP based on 2010 China wage rate	
		GDP	Goods	Service	Per Capita	GDP	Per Capita
	U.S.$*	U.S.$*	U.S.$*	U.S.$*	U.S.$	U.S.$*	U.S.$
U. S.	15.09	15.094	3.019 (20%)	12.075 (80%)	48,848	8.048	26,045
China	7.29	11.300	6.441 (57%)	4.859 (43%)	8,439	11.300	8,439

*Trillion U.S. $; Changes: China 7.298+4.002=11.300, U.S. 15.094-7.046=8.048

Commodity prices in China were generally lower than the U.S.; after the PPP adjustment to the U.S. price level, China's GDP rose by about $4 trillion, or 54.8%; the Chinese product sector was more than twice that of the U.S., $6.4 vs. $3.0 trillion ($4.2 vs. $3.0 before PPP adjustment). The 2015 data showed that 69% of products used in the U.S. were imported, which shows the U.S. goods sector was dwindling as opposed to the service sector (refer to 5.1). American labor was more expensive; using the Chinese wage standards, there was a net decrease of $7 trillion U.S. GDP, approximately 46.7%, which was mostly represented by the federal and local government employees' payroll. After both PPP and LRP adjustments, the GDPs were $11.300 and $8.048 trillion for China and the U.S. respectively, a 29% difference in favor of China. This was a preliminary estimate, because Shenzhen and U.S. federal employee's salaries were both higher than the national averages.

According to the University of Pennsylvania economist Arvin Subramanian of the Peterson Institute's research report, PPP adjustment by IMF using the price index of 11 major cities in China, which is sizably higher than the average price in other parts of the country having much larger population, resulted in a low estimate for China's GDP. After the appropriate adjustments by purchasing power parity, 2010 GDPs for China and the U.S. were $14.8 and $14.6 trillion respectively. Knoema.com showed 2014 GDP after PPP adjustment, $17.6 trillion for China and $17.4 trillion for America. China has surpassed the United States as the world's largest economy according to the PPP calculation. *The Economist* evaluated 21 economic indicators, such as exports, manufacturing output, energy used, fixed asset investment, new car sales, patent applications, and cell phone usage, etc.; China has surpassed the United States in more than half of the indicators (2011/12/30). Mainly because goods produced in America amounted to $3.019 trillion in 2011, which is 72.66% of China's $4.155 trillion merchandise production and 46.87% after PPP adjustment.

In light of the above estimates, it is no wonder that in the Gallup poll taken in the U.S. for the past two consecutive years, the majority of American believe that China has overtaken the U.S. to become the world's largest economy. The 2010 poll showed 53% voted for China, 33% voted for the U.S. In 2011 the ratio was almost the same, 52% vs. 32%; only the over 65 population still believed that the United States is No.1, China second; the ratio is 50% vs. 41%. Those choosing Japan, EU, or Russia did not exceed 7%. Looking ahead 20 years, American are still optimistic about China's economic development, but the gap between the two countries is getting narrower, 46% versus 38% (2012/2/11).

China has the largest population among all nations in the world, more than four times that of the United States. China's per capita GDP after the price adjustment is about one-sixth, and after the wage adjustment, is less than one-third of the United States per capita GDP. The U.S. is still far ahead in people's living standards. Moreover, in the past 150 years, except the four years of the American Civil War, the U.S. enjoyed economic prosperity, social stability, and completion of all needed community facilities, infrastructures and basic social construction. In contrast, in the last 150 years, China was prey to world powers, brutally invaded, defeated and humiliated, ceded territories, paid reparations, and was forced into the opium trade. During World War II, the Japanese military campaigns conducted widespread massacre, massive pillage, and total destruction, followed by the civil wars, the Great Leap Forward, and the Cultural Revolution. Devastation and impoverishment prevailed. Almost all of China's economic progress began with the 1980s economic reform movement.

GDP consists of non-economic expenditures, such as administration, military, public safety, education, health care, etc., which should be separated from the product sector to determine its true economic strength. The 2011 U.S. GDP is composed of 71.2% personal consumption, 20.3% government spending, 12.3% investment (may include government construction), and 3.8% net import (U. S. Bureau of Economic Analysis). Therefore, to measure economic activities, all levels of government spending should be excluded, but adding back government funding for public education of all levels to arrive at its GDP economic component. Because in the U.S. elementary and secondary public schools are funded by state and local governments, it is free of charge to its citizens, no tuition fee. Public higher education institutions do charge a tuition fee but generally require government subsidy to keep them operating. These transfer payments to schools are unlike Medicare or Medicaid transfer payments because they don't show up as education expenditure whereas the latter would ultimately be reported as medical expenses under the personal consumption component.

GDP is a country's annual economic gross income and the basis of the national budget expenditure. Since government spending is a part of GDP, higher spending will boost GDP, and a larger GDP is the rationale for another higher government budget. Non-economic component will not produce income in the next run of GDP, causing income to be overestimated. When the next year's GDP is overestimated, it tends to lead to a budget deficit. That is one of the reasons why the U.S. budget deficit occurred year after year and intensified in the recent decade, a deficit of more than $1 trillion per year. The U.S. national debt has exceeded $16 trillion, averaging over $50,000 per person. Accumulating a large amount of debt inevitably causes an adverse effect. For example, in the late 1980s, economic dislocation, soaring military spending, mounting debt, and inability to repay foreign debt prompted the collapse of the Soviet Union.

7.3. U.S. Economic Outlook

Community critique Larry Little discussed the nation's economy in his September 16, 2012 column. He stated that the government recently announced the creation of 96,000 jobs, but since the financial crisis, there are 12 million people unemployed, and household income is in the fourth consecutive year of decline. In the 1980s, the Reagan White House launched an arms race, with the strong economic strength of the U.S., and forced the Soviet Union onto the road toward its collapse. Today, we seem to have lost confidence because our economic strength is insufficient to support healthy families, good schools, and favorable foreign policy (2012/9/16). The U.S. economic stagnation and decline have become well recognized facts. As discussed earlier, the U.S. depended 69% on foreign imports for its product needs in 2015, and the U.S. 2011 GDP after adjustments for price and wage parities was about 71% that of China's. Due to a stable domestic political system, global superpower status, and world financial institutions dominated by the U.S. and the dollar supremacy, the country is still able to survive and maintain economic stability on debt. But the state and local governments are trapped by high debt and budget deficit, requiring the implementation of austerity measures, including expenditure cuts and benefits reduction, which will suppress economic growth.

In recent years, approximately 70% of U.S. GDP comes from people's consumption. Spending of all levels of governments except fixed assets construction accounts for 20% of GDP, which consists of 8% from the federal and 12% from the state and local governments, and public institutions for education. The remaining 10% is economic investment that is an addition of new real assets. Most government direct payments, such as Social Security benefits, Medicare, Medicaid, welfare benefits, etc., are accounted for as medical and other household expenses in the personal consumption category. Thus, these direct payment items are excluded from government spending, and federal spending is reduced to one third of its budget. On the income (production) side of GDP is the sum of the goods and services produced during the year. Taking total consumer and government spending (businesses are middlemen, spending excluded) plus economic investment compared with the year's production, if spending is greater than production, the result is debt increases or assets including savings decreases; conversely, increases in assets or decreases in debt.

Since 1970, household debt in the U.S. increased from $460.2 billion to $13,500.0 billion in the 3rd quarter of 2010, an average increase of 73.3% per annum. State and local government debt in 1970 totaled $143.6 billion and increased to $2,842.3 billion in 2010, excluding employee retirement funds and credit market instruments, an annual increase of 49.5%. The U.S. Treasury in 2010 had debt of $13,528.8 billion, more than $13 trillion increase compared to $380.9 billion in 1970, an increase of 88.8% per year (see 5.3). The total debt of both the private and public sectors has increased by almost $29 trillion since 1970. During 1970-2010, the U.S. foreign direct investment (FDI) totaled $4,021 billion; deducting foreign direct investment in the U.S. of $3,318 billion for the same 40-year period, the net amount was $703 billion (Bureau of Economic Analysis, U.S. Department of Commerce). After deducting the net FDI outflow, there was a net increase of more than $28 trillion in private and public debt in 40 years, averaging $700 billion per year. This was the main force which maintained stability and growth of the U.S. economy during the past 40 years. This is like playing the Ponzi scheme by Mr. Madoff as discussed earlier but on a national basis. It is true that not all of the $28 trillion debt was used in consumption; a portion of the debt was in public and private investment such as construction of infrastructure and private housing, or addition to foreign financial assets. However, unless these assets are sold to a foreign entity, they are non-recoverable because selling fixed assets or securities to its own nationals only involves changes in owners, nothing else.

It is evident that in the past four decades, U.S. production could not keep up with consumption and investment, and mainly relied on borrowing to maintain economic stability and growth. It also led to an unfavorable trade balance of $8.2 trillion in these 40 years. Will the United States be able to continue the borrowing maneuver in order to maintain the current economic status? When Congress refused to raise the debt ceiling, the S&P lowered the credit rating of U.S. Treasury bonds in 2011 and has been criticized as unpatriotic because the lower credit rating increases the cost of borrowing, resulting in a higher financial burden. President Obama reiterated that the United States is not Greece. True, in the short run, except for acquisitions of resources, property, business, and infrastructure construction loans to foreign countries, the U.S. debt is safer than European and Japanese bonds and is still the choice of investors. But the U.S. debt is no longer considered default free. This road is still open, but rugged and with higher borrowing costs. The impact of heavy debt on national security and the burden to future generations must also be seriously considered.

Due to the state constitution's requirement, state and local governments in the U.S. must balance their budgets. The recent recession drastically reduced revenue, so state and local governments had to implement budget austerity, retrenching expenses or declaring bankruptcy to avoid contractual financial obligations committed in the past. Three cities in California filed for bankruptcy in 2012, including Stockton with nearly 300,000 people. The mayor of Scranton, Pennsylvania, announced on July 6, 2012, that due to municipal finance shortfalls, 400 city employees must take minimum wage pay ($7.25 per hour). Wisconsin had a deficit of $3.6 billion in 2010. In order to balance the budget, Governor Scott Walker followed the legal procedures to reduce or limit government employee union benefits, including the statewide teacher union, triggering strong opposition from unions and the state Democratic Party, which demanded his resignation. The 2012 Wisconsin referendum showed that the majority of voters support the governor's action that the government must maintain financial health, too.

After the housing bubble-induced financial crisis led to a recession, the government provided $700 billion in bailouts to the financial industry and General Motors. Congress in 2008 and 2009 passed two more economic rescue packages, a $152 billion Economic Stimulus Act and a $787 billion Restoration and Reinvestment Act, for a total of more than $1.6 trillion. So far, the results seem weak, with no significant economic recovery and unemployment remaining high, mainly because the vast majority of money was spent on non-productive projects. The 2008 Economic Stimulus Act provided $120 billion for a tax rebate that accounted for 80% of the total, and the 2009 Act was also used for major tax cuts of $288 billion (37%), state and local government grants of $144 billion (18%), $111 billion for infrastructure construction (14%); only $43 billion (5%) were spent on new products development.

If the beneficiaries put their tax rebates and unemployment benefits into their saving accounts or used them to pay off their debt, resulting in no demand in the marketplace, the economic benefit was equal to zero. If they chose to use the benefits on consumption, the demand increased by one time only and subsequently stopped. If funds were spent on making producer goods (non-consumer goods), demand may be increased by more than one time, creating continued and expanded demands. For example, if funds were used to manufacture aircraft by Boeing Co., all costs of an airplane constitute one demand; and more flights may be scheduled by the airline leading to increased passenger traffic, thus increasing additional demand for hotels, restaurants, and other services. If aircraft are selling well, the business would have to expand production facilities, like Boeing building a new plant in South Carolina, resulting in sustained and expanded economic demand, leading to economic expansion, high employment, and prosperity. However, domestic businesses with international competitive capability, like Boeing, are already in full production and need no government incentives. Because the U.S. has been losing its competitive edge in cost and quality, to create a company with international economic competitiveness in the short term is almost an impossible task.

Two bills providing tax rebates and subsidies, etc., may create a one-time economic demand, and corporate income tax cuts do not necessarily plow back to production. According to BIRINYI data, the S&P 500 Index companies currently hoard $800 billion in cash, doing nothing, not being put into production, setting a new record (2011/6/24). Infrastructures, such as roads, bridges, airports, etc., though not consumer goods are for long-term use purposes; they are unlikely to yield all of their economic benefits right away. If the construction is completely useless, such as a bridge to nowhere, it is tantamount to consumer goods; demand increases by one time only.

Application of John Maynard Keynes' economic theory during the 1930s relied heavily on government spending (fiscal policy) and helped the United States get out of the Great Depression and restored employment and economic stability. At that time, all business and production were at a halt, and government spending was needed to start the production engine. Besides, production facilities and infrastructures were not as complete as today; therefore, new investments were able to achieve the benefits of increased production. Today, there is excess production capacity and complete infrastructures even though replacement and upgrading are in dire need. Government spending on infrastructures will create one time demand and would be difficult to stimulate other economic activities except construction related industries because few startups and business expansion are forthcoming. So, public spending will improve the economy temporarily but will not be an effective way to stimulate economic growth leading to prosperity. The economic outlook is less optimistic.

The Federal Reserve Bank (Central Bank) maintained its interest rates close to zero to commercial bank borrowing and launched the third round of the monetary easing policy (QE3, monetary policy) on September 13, 2012, in order to promote early economic recovery. Low interest rates have a tendency to encourage investment and consumption but are not a major factor. For example, making a car purchase is mainly determined by the ability to make monthly payments, to have income or employment security. The interest rate which affects how much to pay is a secondary consideration. The monetary easing policy promotes dollar devaluation, equivalent to reducing the price of products and services to foreign purchasers enabling local enterprises to increase export production, but it also raises import prices, adding to the burden on people's lives and reduces actual consumption. Production increase and consumption decrease cancel each other out; the benefit to economic growth is debatable. The currency devaluation definitely alleviates national debt, especially to foreign lenders because the amount of debt is unchanged, the dollar value has shrunk.

Secondly, from the early 1990s, the U.S. public discovered a new economic paradise. Internet entrepreneurs received funding from overly enthusiastic private investors, without regard to the cost and profit prospects, establishing various Internet software companies. Newly formed company's stock, one after another, was listed with the stock exchange (IPO); with overly optimistic public investors, stock prices rose every day to strengthen the grounds for highly overblown activities and significantly rewarding the executives themselves. At the 2000 Super Bowl, 17 Internet companies each spent $2 million for a 30-second ad, heralding extreme economic prosperity. The good times didn't last long.

By 2001, Internet companies, one after another, collapsed, and the NASDAQ (mostly small technology companies' stock) stock index plunged to 1,114 from 5,046; 78% of the total listed enterprises market value evaporated, causing 90,000 people to be unemployed and a severe economic recession. Investors and pension funds were looted almost completely: The Dot-com bubble or Dot-com bust.

Then, the government, Congress, banks, real estate companies and developers were pushing the real estate market as a means to rescue the failing economy. It ignored the minimum requirements for loan approval in order to increase the number of potential homebuyers. When the lax home loan practice was questioned by some financial media, they were severely criticized by prominent congressmen for suppressing the American home ownership dream. As a result, there was a high demand for real estate, leading to rising home prices. Speculators, fearing the loss of an opportunity to make a fortune, scrambled to buy houses, triggering another round of price hikes. Real estate prices rose and home construction boomed. This endless cycle led to a high demand in construction workers, enticing a large number of illegal immigrants, and brought about general economic prosperity. By the later part of 2007, the housing bubble exploded, followed by a recession, rising unemployment, homeowner installment payment defaults, a surge in bad home loans, and home foreclosures and bank repossessions. All this brought down Bear Stearns and Lehman Brothers, two large Wall Street financial companies, leading to financial turmoil, which eventually spread worldwide. Home prices felled an average of 35% nationwide, in six major cities by 50%, with Las Vegas the worst, dropping by 61% (2012/5/10). Under-water homes (home loans greater than the market value) abounded, and foreclosure (homes repossessed by the bank because owners were unable to pay installment loans) notices could be seen everywhere. The residents of California, Arizona, Nevada, and Florida lost the most. Fabulous homeownership dreams turned into nightmares, and people suffered heavy losses.

The Federal Reserve Bank of Dallas' analyst reported this on the fifth anniversary of the financial crisis: The total loss of $6-14 trillion nationwide; each family lost $50,000-120,000, equivalent to 40-90% of annual income. The net decrease in non-agricultural employment of 8.7 million workers, 14.7 million people unemployed, 10.6 million not fully employed. Since December 2007, it is the first time since the 1960s economic recession that more and more people believe that their future income will be less (2013/9/12).

An emergency was sounded on Social Security funds because in 2011 there were 2.94 million people who applied for disability benefits, a 51% surge to the total of 8.7 million people. Most of the new applicants were people who ran out of unemployment benefits and despaired of future employment prospects. Since 2007, the total number of unemployed who are actively seeking employment fell to 63.6% from 66.0% (2012/5/7); coupled with those who have left the job market, the overall employment situations did not improve much. However, the Dot Com and housing bubbles did serve as strong boosters, creating work and employment, helping the U.S. economic recovery, but with a hefty price. Because most Dot Com firms during those years either produced no useful products or their businesses plans were unsustainable, as a result they eventually went bankrupt. The housing bubble created jobs and built homes at an accelerated speed but could not fulfill the strong demand for housing. The situation was basically triggered by the unqualified homebuyers and housing speculators, which ended up with huge unpaid home loans and the financial crisis. Can another bubble be found to save the current predicament? At the present, a student loan bubble is in the making, amounting to $1 trillion total ($1.31 trillion by the end of 2016), but only portions of college students, schools, and banks are involved. It is too small and will not be able to solve the current difficulties. Furthermore, these bubbles provide illusory economic outcomes, causing significant losses, only creating opportunities for a few to get rich; it is a disaster to most people that does more harm than good.

The Center for Economic Research of the Census Bureau and Ewing Marion Kauffman Foundation conducted a joint investigation. In the past, the startup companies (formed within five years) provide a lot more jobs per firm than established businesses, hiring 20% of workers in 1980, down to 12% in 2010. The proportion of startups to the established also decreased from 13.02% in 1987 to the current rate of 7.87% (2012/5/3), which is another reason why the unemployment rate stays persistently high.

The U.S. Trade Representative Ron Kirk recently released a list of Priority of the Observed Countries and pointed out that the intelligence products and copyrights such as computer and network software, movies, TV programs, video games, music, and various manufacturing patents, currently account for over 60% of the total value of U.S. exports, supporting 40 million domestic workers and are crucial to the overall economy (2012/5/1). The importance of these products has surpassed aircraft, armament, soybeans, and corn in export and the U.S. economy is moving toward high-tech intelligence enterprises. Basically, this is the right direction because American wages are too much higher than the developing countries and are uncompetitive in general merchandise production.

Once the prediction of transition to the intelligence industries does come true, it will only aggravate the difficulties for the United States because intelligence industries require personnel with competent technical education. Even if the United States has the innovative genius, generally it provides poor education quality, and there is a shortage of qualified technical personnel. At the same time, automation and computerization are bound to replace a lot of the labor force, aggravating the unemployment situation. The latest technology star, Tesla Motors Co., makes all electric vehicles like the Tesla Roadster, a two-seater sport car with superior performance, all assembled by robots with a base price tag of $109,000. From 2008 to June 2012, there were 2,350 of these vehicles sold in 31 countries. Because the price is almost five times more than an ordinary car, the Tesla is becoming the toy of the world's super rich. In four and a half years, with no more than 3,000 units sold, there has been little impact on the overall U.S. economy. In June 2012, the company introduced Model S, priced at $69,900, available with a $7,500 income tax rebate; quite popular, the company expects 21,000 vehicles to be sold in 2013 (2013/8/10). However, since the company uses robots in manufacturing, the Model S does little to boost employment.

Bloomberg Businessweek reported in its April 20, 2015, issue that on the Java Sea, a new Shenzhen has been born. Indonesia is poised to duplicate the Shenzhen, China, success story because its manufacturing labor cost per hour is only $0.50 as opposed to $2.06 in Vietnam, $3.25 in China, $6.83 in Mexico, $9.88 in Brazil, and $38.13 in America. Therefore, advanced economies with high labor costs will lose jobs unless the product is high-tech, no competitor, or with low labor content, such as expensive jewelry, high cost drugs, or can be made with an automated production process; otherwise, shipping costs and marketing advantages will not offset higher labor costs. Chinese wages in recent years have increased, and a number of labor-intensive and low-tech factories have moved to Indonesia, Bangladesh, and Vietnam. The advanced economies cannot and should not compete on these labor-intensive and low-tech products. However, to retain the long-term advantage of intelligence industries, an advanced education system coupled with sophisticated research and development communities must be maintained. Currently, the U.S. generally has low education quality; the ability to attract foreign talents gradually declines, and governments at all levels and universities slash research and development budgets; the U.S. advantage in the high-tech intelligence industries is unlikely to last very long.

The Commerce Department released a report on 2010 U.S. multinationals: Multinationals accounted for 20% of the total private sector and employed 2.3 million workers in America, an increase of 0.1% over last year. The U.S. overseas' companies (at least 10% ownership) employed more than 1.1 million people, up 1.5% from 2009. Since 1999, these U.S. multinationals reduced about one million personnel in the American workforces. On the other hand, in 2010 foreign companies in the United States cut 1% of their personnel, while investment also decreased by 1.7% (2012/4/19). According to the Bureau of Economic Analysis, Department of Commerce statistics, the U.S. foreign direct investment in the most recent decade (2003-2012) totaled $2.89 trillion, and foreign direct investment in the U.S. totaled $1.85 trillion (including the immigration investment program, also called the EB-5 Green Card Visa Program which requires foreigners to invest $500,000 to $1 million and to employ 10 people for two years in exchange for a green card). Except in 2005, the United States' foreign direct investment was greater than the foreign counterpart each year for the entire decade, resulting in a net capital outflow of $1.04 trillion, or 56% greater than inflow. In summary, assuming the Greenfield projects were the primary investment, more American capitalists believed that the overseas market was more lucrative than the overseas investors who felt the U.S. market was more profitable. The main determinants for choosing location may be low production costs, plentiful human resources, being close to raw materials and finished good markets, sound infrastructures, and good coordination of labor, community, and government. According to the Immigration

Naturalization Service data, since the inception of the immigration investment program in 1990, a total of $2.3 billion foreign capital was absorbed and created 46,810 jobs in the first 20 years (2012/6/12). The immigration investment program helps a little but cannot reverse the general trend of capital outflow.

Recently the Obama administration strongly advocated the recovery of U.S. manufacturing, urging the multinationals to move their overseas operations back to the U.S. in order to create jobs and to promote economic prosperity. These ideas stir up public excitement, and the media start to paint a rosy economic future. They also cited that multinationals, such as Caterpillar, Ford, GE, etc., as having recently moved plants back from China; as well, news came out on the latest technology, including robotics, artificial intelligence, 3D printing, and nanotechnology, etc. that will be widely used, reducing labor costs; and the trend of cheap energy in the U.S. will continue because of shale oil production. According to these reports, the U.S. manufacturing reflux will be the inevitable trend of the future (2012/7/24).

Since 2006, Ford Motor Company invested a total of $4.9 billion in China, including in Chongqing, its largest overseas facility. In April 2014, Ford announced an additional plant would be built in Hangzhou, China, at a cost of $760 million, expected to go into production in 2015. So the report that Ford moved its plants back to the United States does not provide the evidence that it is the beginning of a large number of American manufacturers repatriating!

President Obama's call to revitalize the manufacturing sector may provide exciting news to the voters, but the high budget deficit, huge national debt, large trade deficit, factories relocated abroad, product outsourcing, and slow economic growth have been a foregone conclusion and cannot be reversed in the short run. When the two political parties could not reach an agreement on a national budget, the automatic federal government spending cut of $1.2 trillion kicked-in (known as the sequester) in 2011. At the same time, almost every state is also in budget deficit, which has a negative effect on economic growth. To solve the government budget deficit and the huge national debt, it will take at least five to eight years. Economic competitiveness cannot be improved in the near future. It will accelerate factory relocation and product outsourcing abroad. Long-term economic slowdown is likely and no significant growth can be expected

America is not Greece, by virtue of its superpower status and global financial domination; it can still survive on debts but only to maintain economic stability. Unless a large new bubble is created again, it will not be able to return to economic prosperity. The main reason is wages are too high, resulting in most domestic enterprises losing their competitiveness, factory relocating and product outsourcing abroad, fewer startups, and net capital outflows. Even during the bankruptcy of General Motors in 2009, the labor union only agreed to a pay cut of 8%. In 2011 new contracts provided UAW workers an average wage of $56 per hour, equivalent to $9,707 (56x40x52/12) a month, the envy of most college graduates because a lot of them are out of work. If they do find a job, the average monthly salary does not exceed $6,000. In addition, there is an average of more than $25,000 worth of student loan on their backs.

All level governments practicing austerity budget cuts, public and private debt mounting, household assets shrinking, and uncertain employment prospects are hampering enthusiasm for consumption. High labor costs, lack of scientific and technical personnel, capital outflows, reducing startups, all hinder a positive attitude toward new business development. Therefore, only by eliminating the labor union monopolistic power in the labor market is there hope to bring fundamental improvements in the U.S. economy.

7.4. The Main Crux of the Problem

Within the American capitalism economic system, the supply and demand for all resources are regulated by a price mechanism in the free market to achieve equilibrium, the balanced condition. For example, if there is gasoline shortage, prices will rise, while encouraging oil production, at the same time promoting energy conservation, so that supply and demand move toward equilibrium and halt the price movement. The exceptions are the labor and medical service markets.

Years ago, as a means to protect worker's minimum living standard, the federal and state governments adopted a minimum wage statute. Today, people who are unable to maintain a minimum standard of living are provided with various public financial assistance and welfare benefits, such as food stamps, Medicaid, rent subsidies, etc. Therefore, the minimum wage becomes an extra social assistance. It not only disrupts the normal functioning of the supply and demand in the labor market but also threatens the development and survival of small businesses. Hence, minimum wage has outlived its reason to exist; complete abolishment is in order.

Twenty-five states, mostly in the Southeast, Southwest, and Midwest, have the Right to Work law; businesses are free to hire or fire workers without union restrictions. In the other 25 states under the National Labor Relations Act (NLRA), matters concerning workers such as hiring, dismissal, wages, benefits, working conditions, work evaluation, etc. are mediated between the company and the union. Companies cannot fire striking workers and cannot hire new people to replace them; the only choice is either accepting the union conditions or closing the operation. This labor stipulation provides the union with a monopoly power in the labor market so that wages are dictated by the union's desire and not as a reflection of the demand and supply condition in the labor market.

Higher wages without high productivity, resulting in higher production costs, undermine competitiveness, leading to job losses and high unemployment. The last 30 years of economic development in Detroit provides the best illustration of this situation. If wages are set too low, there will be problems, too; qualified job candidates cannot be found, resulting in many vacancies and the work cannot be carried out as planned.

Since 1935, when President Roosevelt signed the NLRA, the Democratic Party has always supported a high wage law. Because it not only entices workers' voting support, it also claims to improve their income and ability to consume. Consequently, there will be a need to expand production, promoting employment, economic growth and prosperity; it cycles endlessly. This was one of the main factors for the rapid growth of the U.S. economy and a rising standard of living since NLRA was enacted, which was the envy of the world. None of the previous wage heights caused any economic problems because the recovery from the Great Depression, to be ready for World War II, post-war reconstruction, and the Korean and Vietnam Wars, brought about such great demand and created insufficient supply on all resources including labor. In the post-World War II era, while the United States had no economic competitor and monopolized the global market, all products regardless of price could be sold throughout the world.

The American global economic domination ended when Western Europe and Japan completed their economic rehabilitation. Since the 1970s, increasing international competition expanded to most industries, and the U.S. hegemonic monopoly has disappeared, mainly because worker's compensation was too generous, resulting in a high cost of production. Currently, except Boeing aircraft and agricultural products, the United States only thrives in the military arms industry, dominating the world arms trade. In 2011, total arms export sales were more than $66.3 billion, accounting for 78% of the global arms sales (2013/1/2). In addition, a small number of high-tech products, such as medical supplies, precision machinery and mechanical equipment are still leading the international market. However, due to a lack of foreign demand, national security, industry secrecy concerns or export restriction, the total value of high tech product exports has a minimal overall impact on the economy.

In a globalization economic environment, it is reasonable to link wages with the international exchange value workers created. If wages are higher than the exchange value, extra allowance is equivalent to social welfare; this results in non-productive additional consumption, expands the supply and demand imbalance, leads to inflation, and creates a vicious cycle of wage and price hikes, an upward spiral effect. At the same time, if the product cost is too high, it is bound to lose competitiveness, leading to economic recession, increasing unemployment, reduced consumption, and then reduced production. It is a chain reaction, or a downward spiral, causing economic contraction.

Compensation of American manufacturing workers is 76 times that of Indonesian workers (U.S. hourly wage rate $38.13 vs. $0.50 for Indonesian). Is productivity also 76 times higher? Why should Indonesia provide the world with slave labor? In fact, international workers should be entitled to equal pay for equal work, the true meaning of equality and human rights. This serious violation of equality and human rights is basically created by the current world order which restricts labor free movement and is ignored by the Western powers, but they only complain about trade imbalances.

Although U.S. manufacturing productivity is higher than other industries, the productivity growth rate was 1.5% from 1987 to 1990, 4.1% from 1990 to 2000, 4.7% from 2000 to 2007, and 1.8% from 2007 to 2015 (U.S. Bureau of Labor Statistics). There was no amazing progress made in productivity gain but a decreasing trend in recent years. It demonstrates that mechanization, automation, and computerization of operations have not or do not have universal applications. Without lowering wages, hence living standards, the U.S. cannot remain competitive, leading many businesses to make a difficult choice: to close factories, relocate them abroad, or to outsource products to survive. No wonder the market is flooded with imported goods, previously most from Japan and now from China. As a result, the data show that in 2013 more than half (55%) of products, both consumer and producer goods, used in the country are imported leading to U.S. product trade deficits (refer to 5.1) and in 2015, the imported shot up to 68.6%. Since 1970 the trade deficit grew year after year, becoming the country's fundamental problem. Therefore, elimination of the union monopoly power in the labor market and allowing global labor free movement is the only viable solution to the trade deficit and slave labor worldwide.

Politicians, blaming exchange rates or other trade barriers for the trade deficit, are reluctant to face a reality that requires a reduction in wages and a lower standard of living, because the most important responsibility of members of Congress is representing their constituents and fighting for voters' interests; social and national interests are a secondary consideration. Workers are congressional members' basic voters and their political bosses. If they do not act to please them, especially members of the House of Representatives, when their two years term is up, "please find yourselves another job". This is a fatal drawback of the democratic election system, making a self-destructive cocoon. Regardless of who is being elected as the president, this reality cannot be altered; besides, the president is also required to follow the same election rules. A more thorough discussion of this issue is presented in 9.1 and 9.2.

Although the unemployment rate was over 9% in 2011 and work was hard to find, a serious shortage of agricultural workers exist because unemployment compensation and welfare benefits are better choices than working. Therefore, local workers will not accept those low-pay and hard-labor jobs. Instead, they must be filled by illegal immigrants. The White House estimated that 50-60% of farm workers are illegal immigrants (2013/7/30). Once these illegal farm workers obtain their U.S. residency, they, too, will do the same things as the local workers, filing for unemployment and welfare benefits. Farm owners will need another group of undocumented farm workers. This cycle goes on and on, leading to widening the gap of the haves and the have-nots, intensifying the public financial burden, and eventually creating class antagonism and social conflict. The result of this process will increase unemployment claims and welfare recipients, put a heavier burden on the community, strengthen the political power of the laboring class and intensify the self-destructive cocoon process, going deeper and deeper, unable to extricate itself. In the meantime, regardless of the U.S. government's intention or illegal immigrants' willingness, it simply creates an exploited laboring class. As mentioned earlier, these illegal farm workers are working and living in a condition worse than that of the previous black farm slaves. It is a serious violation of human rights.

The U.S. Chamber of Commerce on June 19, 2013, sounded the alarm that the amazing growth of Social Security, Medicare, and Medicaid totaled $1.6 trillion and will reach $3 trillion within a decade. This is a time bomb. If we do not face reality and make early reforms, the United States will go bankrupt (2013/6/20).

7.5. Rise of the Laboring Class: Leading the Political Force

The table below summarizes selected items of the 1970 and 2010 U.S. census and the 2008, 2012, and 2016 presidential election statistics from the Wikipedia web site and the exit poll taken by CNN.

Items of 1970, 2010 U.S. Census & 2008, 2012, 2016 Presidential Elections

Category	Census % 1970	Census % 2010	Pres. Elections 2008/2012/2016 Voting	Dem	Rep	2012 Dem	2012 Rep	2016 Dem	2016 Rep	2012-16 net Dem	2012-16 net Rep
Gender											
Male		49	47/47/47	49/45/41	48/52/52		7		11		4
Female		51	53/53/53	56/55/54	43/44/41	11		13		2	
Race											
White	83.1	64	74/72/71	43/39/37	55/59/57		20		20		0
Black	11.1	12	13/13/12	95/93/89	4/6/8	87		81		-6	
Asian	0.8	5	2/3/4	62/73/65	35/26/27	47		38		-9	
Other	0.4	3	3/2/3	66/58/56	31/38/36	20		20		0	
Household income, in thousand											
$00 - $29		32	18/20/17	60/63/53	37/35/40	28		13		-15	
$30 - $49		19	19/21/19	55/57/52	43/42/41	15		11		-4	
$50 - $99		29	36/31/30	49/46/46	49/52/50		6		4		-2
Over $99		20	26/28/34	49/44/47	49/54/48		10		1		-9
Age *18-24; #25-44											
18-29		10*	18/19/19	66/60/55	32/37/36	23		19		-4	
30-44		27#	29/27/25	52/53/51	46/45/41	8		10		2	
45-64		26	37/38/40	50/47/44	49/51/52		4		8		4
Over 64		13	16/16/16	45/44/45	53/56/52		12		7		-5
Education											
Non-col. graduate			55/53/50	52/51/37	46/49/58	2			21		23
College graduate			28/29/32	50/47/49	48/51/32		4	17		21	
Postgraduate			17/18/18	58/55/58	40/42/18	13		40		27	
Religion											
Protestant			54/51/52	45/43/40	54/56/58		13		18		5
Catholic			27/25/23	54/50/45	45/48/52	2			7		9
Other			8/11/10	74/63/62	22/34/30	29		32		3	
None			12/12/15	75/70/68	23/26/26	44		42		-2	
Community size											
City > 49,999			30/32/34	63/62/59	35/36/35	26		24		-2	
Suburb			49/47/49	50/48/45	48/50/50		2		5		3
Rural area			21/22/17	45/39/34	53/58/62		19		28		9
Political view											
Liberal			22/25/26	89/86/84	10/11/10	75		74		-1	
Moderate			44/41/39	60/56/52	39/41/40	15		12		-3	
Conservative			34/35/35	20/17/16	78/82/81		65		65		0
Union affiliation											
Yes			21/18/18	59/58/51	39/40/42	18		9		-9	
No			79/82/82	51/49/46	47/48/48	1			2		3
Party affiliation											
Democratic			39/38/36	89/92/89	10/7/8	85		81		-4	
Republican			32/32/33	9/6/8	93/93/88		87		80		-7
Other			29/29/31	52/45/42	44/50/46		5		4		-1

Change over 3% in Demographics of 2016 over 2012 Presidential Elections

Demographics $ in 1,000	% of Total vote	Loser, % Dem/Rep	Gainer, % Dem/Rep	Weighted vote value vote x loser/gainer
Less educated	50		23	1150-R
College graduate	32	21		672-D
Postgraduate	18	27		486-D
Union member	36	9		324-D
Income over $99	34	9		306-R
Protestant	58		5	290-R
Income under $30	17	15		255-D
Republican	33	7		231-R
Catholic	23		9	207-R
Male	47		4	188-R
Age 45- 64	40		4	160-R
Rural areas	17		9	153-R
Democrat	36	4		144-D
Age over 64	16	5		80-R
Age 18 - 29	19	4		76-D
Income $30-$49	19	4		76-D
Black	12	6		72-D
Latino	11	6		66-D
Asian	4	9		63-D
Net gain				74-D 2,067-R

Population: 1970, 203,211,926; 2010, 308,745,538 people
2010: 115,904,641 units' household, 2.66 people per unit;
median income, $49,445, average income $69,530.

Presidential candidates:	Democratic	Republican
2008	Barack Obama	John McCain
2012	Barack Obama	Mitt Romney
2016	Hillary Clinton	Donald Trump

In 2008, the most important voters who elected President Obama were the ethnic minorities and laboring class. Although white voters enthusiastically participated, accounting for 74% of the votes with only 64% of the population, and even though 55% of them voted for McCain versus 43% for Obama, it was not enough to overcome Obama's overwhelming advantage with the minority votes, at least 62%, blacks, up to 95% of the votes. As reported by the *Boston Globe Daily*, Obama was the beneficiary of the 1965 Immigration Act because this bill led to an influx of a large number of minorities, thus substantially decreasing the ratio of whites which accounted for 83% of the population in 1970, now dropping to only 64%, almost 20% less. Second, those with an income of $50,000 or less accounted for 51% of the population with only 37% of the votes, but 55-73% of them voted for Obama, showing that the political potential of the laboring class has not yet been fully developed. Among Democratic and liberal voters, 89% favored Obama, so did two-thirds of young people. Hispanics, 17% of the population, accounted for only 9% of the votes; some did not participate, and others might not qualify to vote but have a great voting potential. Income of $30,000 or less accounted for 32% of the total population, only 18% of the votes cast, with room for 14% of additional voting potential.

The 2012 presidential election was almost a rerun of the 2008 edition. President Obama still relied on the laboring class (income less than $50,000), minorities, women, and under 40-year old voters to get re-elected with 55-93% favorable margins. Latino, Asian, aged 30-40 voters were even more enthusiast in supporting Obama than in 2008. A portion of youth under 25 years old deserted Obama, votes dropping from 66% to 60%. White, male, above 40 years old, of all political persuasions, and income over $50,000 voters were all in favor of Mitt Romney. However, their vote margins were insufficient to overcome the huge leads that Obama enjoyed in the laboring class, minorities, and people under 40 years old; the smallest lead was 57% and the blacks as high as 93%. Democratic and Republican Party voters supported their own candidates at least with 92% votes, no more than 7% voting for other party's nominees, a net drop of 3% from four years ago. It indicates that party hardliners surged and compromisers dwindled; more party stalemates will be expected in the future.

Before the 2016 presidential election season began, most people thought the election process would merely be an official coronation formality for Hillary Clinton to the presidency because she would have been in the White House if Sen. Ted Kennedy had not supported Barack Obama in the 2008 presidential nomination. Now, she was the favorite in and out of the Democratic Party, especially among intellectuals, the young, and women voters. And most polls showed Clinton's big lead over her potential Republican opponents. When Bernie Sanders, a little known Senator from Vermont, entered in the primary race for the Democratic Party presidential nomination, he was thought as a sidekick to Clinton's show. However, after Sen. Senders garnered a sizable delegation to the

Democratic National Convention before conceding the nomination to Clinton. It was the first surprise of the election.

After strong opposition by the Republican Party establishment, Donald Trump went on to win the Republican nomination anyway. Polls showed that Clinton was far ahead of Trump in the race for the presidency. Mass media also favored Clinton to win the election; Republicans worried that Trump could pull their other candidates on the ballot to their defeat in the election. Few gave Trump a chance to win the presidency. By the early morning of November 9, 2016, it was a big shock to the nation and world, a nightmare for Hillary Clinton which ended her dream of the White House. Although Clinton won the popular votes by more than 2.8 million winning the city vote by 59% vs. 35% for Trump, but losing the suburb and rural area by 45% vs. 50% and 34% vs. 62% respectively, she garnered only 232 electoral votes as opposed to Trump's 306 votes, thus losing the election to Trump.

Comparing the last three Republican presidential elections' record according to the above table, Trump's big weakness was with the intellectuals and his own party voters. He was behind McCain by 16%, 22% and Romney by 19%, 24% for college graduate and postgraduate voters respectively. Republicans gave both McCain and Romney 93% of their votes versus 88% for Trump. The strong suit of Trump was with non-college graduate, low income, rural area, and religious group's voters; he led the other two Republicans at least by 9%, 3%, 4%, and 2% of the voters. Overall, Trump's performance was not much better than McCain in 2008 or Romney in 2012. On the Democratic side, Clinton's vote-getting ability was behind Obama 2008's record in all categories except Asian voters which accounted for 2% and leading Obama in 2012 by a slight margin only 5 out of 29 sub-categories. Obama beat her in women's vote by 56% and 55% versus Clinton's 54%. Therefore, as compared with her peer Democratic contenders for the presidency, Clinton's performance was subpar and Obama's administration record may be partially to blame for her poor showing attributing more to the Democratic loss.

Analyzing voter demographics in the last two elections shows that Democratic lost 8 and gained 2 whereas Republicans lost 3 and gained 6 among 19 categories exceeding 3% vote differences, a net gain of 74 vote value for the Democratic vs. 2,607 vote value net gain for the Republicans. These factors and the geographic vote distribution tell the story why the election startled almost everyone. The Republicans' biggest gain was in voters without a college degree. Less educated voters supported the Republicans with 49% and 58% vs. Democrats 51% and 37% of the vote in 2012 and 2016 respectively, a 2% advantage turning into 21% deficit for the Democratic, a 23% net gain for the Republicans (1150 vote value). Ironically, it is just offset by the two intellectual group voters gained by the Democratic in 2016 with 21% and 27% each (1158 vote value, this combined value is overstated because highly educated voters may also be high income voters too). The under $30,000 income voters also deserted the Democratic Party, which accounted for 255 weighted vote value. It was a startling phenomenon of social polarization that those having knowledge and money voted for Democratic and those having less knowledge and money voted for Republicans. This big switch was out of the ordinary because in the past the poor and less educated always enthusiastically supported the Democratic and the educated and rich always voted for the Republican. The next biggest voter revolt was the union members which reduced 9% of their support to the Democratic. Then, came church members' vote; the Republicans gained 290 and 207 weighted vote value in Protestant and Catholic votes.

Voters in the 2016 election expressed their rejection of the status quo. The CNN election exit poll showed voters dissatisfaction with their government at 69%, the highest expressed, following by the poor economy and wrong national direction, both by 62%, and ISIS threat at 53%. They desired to have a change for the future. The theme of the 2008 Obama campaign was CHANGE. However, in his eight year tenure as the president, few domestic changes had taken place except Obamacare, which is saddled with serious problems (refer to 5.4). More voters repudiated the Democratic Party and traditional politicians because lots of their promises in the past did not turn into reality. Jobs and polarization of income and wealth became the hot issues. Trump seized voters' sentiment and campaigned on creating jobs, raising import duty, preventing factory relocation abroad, reducing corporate and individual income tax, investing in infrastructure, canceling the free trade agreement (NAFTA) with Canada and Mexico, resigning from TPP, deporting all illegal immigrants, building a Mexican border wall, and withdrawing from world engagement except Asian Pacific. These measures which were enthusiastically embraced by the laboring class will keep or create jobs, they believe, at home for their benefit. Thus, his campaign eroded the traditional Democratic voter base among the low income, less educated, and union members. Democratic liberal policies such as requiring Catholic and Protestant institutions to comply with contraception and gender-neutral facilities to the public greatly challenged religious core values and turned off church members' support for the Democratic. Despite the great showing of support by intellectual and social elites, these were not enough to win the election in favor of the Democratic.

The middle class voters no longer played a decisive role in the 2016 election. The low income and less educated favor employment and living improvement, an inward needs demand. Trump's appeals for jobs and a better life were enthusiastically embraced by the laboring class. Whereas, the high income and well educated aspire to American greatness and U.S. world supremacy, an outward looking desire. The intellectual voters were also turned off by Trump's manner and language toward women. It was a fierce struggle and well matched between these two groups. The balance was tipped over in favor of Trump by churchgoer and rural voters, and he went on to victory.

The election provided the evidence that the laboring class has replaced the middle class in setting the American political agenda. However, the agenda may not be faithfully implemented by the intellectual and social elites who are in charge of government functions-- policies making and key operations.

Candidate Trump's pro-Russian and anti-Chinese policy may be based on the fact that Russia posts only a military threat but China is a potential challenger to the American world super power status. Since the North Atlantic Treaty Organization (NATO) was set up to counter the Soviet's military forces, the Soviet Union is no longer in existence. So, NATO is irrelevant, out of date. This American attitude bewildered NATO members. China was labeled as a currency exchange manipulator, the culprit of America's huge trade deficit and high unemployment. Overturning the established one-China policy, Trump's camp initiated a telephone conversation with Taiwan's president. And Stephen Bannon, Trump's close advisor, asserted that the U.S. would go to war with China in the South China Sea. Weeks after the inauguration, President Trump's travel bans were twice suspended by the federal courts; the Republicans had to withdraw a healthcare bill intended to replace Obamacare; and hearings on Russian interference with the U.S. election were being held in Congress, plus numerous domestic anti-Trump protests and overseas uproars about his nationalism and protectionism. Then, NATO's secretary was welcomed in a meeting with President Trump who proclaimed NATO's vitality; China was removed from the list of currency manipulators by the Trump administration on April 11, 2017; Mr. Bannon is reported out of presidential influence. Reality has set in and may play a major factor in setting the Trump administration's policy.

7.6. Prospect of U.S. Politics
   The table below shows the U.S. party political makeup after the 2008, 2012, and 2016 elections.

Party Control on U.S. Government, 2008, 2010, 2016

Party	Democratic	Republican	Other	Total
Year	2008/12/16	2008/12/16	2008/12/16	
U.S. Senator	57/53/48	41/45/51	2/2/1	100
U.S. House of Representative	257/201/194	178/234/240	0/0/1	435
Governor	26/20/15	24/30/34	0/0/1	50
Control both state chambers	27/17/13	15/28/33	8/5/4	50
Both governor and chambers	18/13/6	10/25/26	22/12/18	50

   Because most immigrants and the laboring class live in metropolitan areas, the demographic mix does not change as much over time as in other parts of the country. And lots of these newcomers for one reason or another didn't participate in elections. Therefore, most of the House, governors, and state legislatures are under Republican control. Democrats controlled the White House in 2012 but lost the Senate majority in the 2014 election, resulting in both federal legislative chambers being under Republican control. This caused increasing impasses with the White House, as well as federal and state government policy conflicts, and prevented some policies being implemented nationwide. In recent years, many state legislatures enacted statutes limiting illegal immigration. The situation not only reduces administrative efficiency but also affects the government's credibility. The 2016 election spells disaster for the Democratic Party which not only loses the White House and Senate majority but also greatly reduces its political power at the state level as the above table shows. The Republican Party showed an overall election winning trend from 2008 to 2016.

Although a Republican occupies the White House and Republicans control both chambers of Congress, it will not be easy to make a fundamental change like President Johnson did in the 1960s. Mr. Trump barely won the controversial race, did not have people's mandate, and oppositions to his presidential policy came from many social segments, including some from his own party. In the next four years it is likely that a strong international alliance against ISIS is forged; a military presents in the Pacific is strengthened; income tax is reduced for all; and infrastructure and border wall building are promoted. These measures will definitively stimulate economic activities, create jobs and honor his campaign promises. The military spending and infrastructure investment will create jobs and boost GDP for the current year but may not promote economic activities in the future because of the U.S. economic competitive weakness. Therefore, the fiscal policy of government spending coupled with income tax cut will further widen budget deficits and increase national debt which are normally disavowed by the Republicans. Thus, the fiscal policy may not set well with his own party.

The influx of illegal immigrants will vary with changes in the U.S. economy. In recent years, when the construction industry slumped, many were hesitant to enter America or return to their homeland. But the service industry, agricultural workers, and other laborers are still in high demand, requiring many illegal immigrants to fill the gap. While the U.S. auto workers union members substantially dwindled in recent decades, other sectors, especially the service union members, will continue to grow. They will strengthen the laboring class political force, expanding their role in the United States political decision-making.

With the recent fiscal crisis intensifying income and wealth polarization, the Census Bureau reported that in 2010 the poverty rate continued to grow, reaching 49.1 million people, together with 97.3 million low income people (100-199% of the poverty line, income for a family of three of $17,568 - $35,136) for a total of 146.4 million people, 47.4% of the total U.S. population (2011/12/15). This group of people includes a sizeable portion of blacks, Hispanics, Asians, most labor union members, minimum wage workers, and all welfare recipients.

There are currently 50 million Hispanics; 21 million of them have voting rights with an additional 600,000 voters per year in the future (2011/7/15, 8/11). The current 11 million illegal immigrants are waiting for the legal status, and there will be a steady stream of illegal immigrants in the future. Most of these people belong to the laboring class; in time, they will organize themselves to replace the middle class, strengthening their dominant political status and deciding the fate of the nation. Of course, these people will use their immediate needs, life experience, and social values as major factors in making choices. Attention will focus on livelihood issues, expansion of welfare, improving living standards of the poor, universal education and health care, hosting illegal immigrants, military and international spending cuts, including defense, foreign aid, space budgets, the withdrawal of troops from Iraq and Afghanistan, and reducing American global policeman's role.

Here are a few examples that show the footprints of the new political force. President Obama announced in February 2010 to give up the Constellation space program (no further exploration of the moon as a preparation to enter Mars) that was strongly opposed by the aerospace community, especially Neil Armstrong (the first man on the moon) in the congressional hearings. The U.S. has completed a return of its military personnel from Iraq and withdrew its entire troop from Afghanistan by the end of 2014, except 9,800 men as trainers and advisors to the local forces. The Department of Defense has cut $487 million spending in 2011; if the two parties cannot reach an agreement, a further cut of $500 billion military expenditure will occur in the next decade.

In the 2013 nationwide midterm elections, the New York mayoral candidate Bill de Blasio campaigned on breaking the disparity of wealth, opposing the huge income gap, prohibiting racial profiling, raising the minimum wage and general salary, and increasing taxes on the wealthy to pay for free Head Start services, youth extra-curricular activities, elderly services, and distributing identity cards to illegal immigrants. He was elected to the office. The 99% Occupy Wall Street movement shadow had reappeared, giving many low-income people a ray of hope, but causing concerns for high-income earners. It carried a strong socialist and idealistic sentiment (2013/11/6).

Since 1970, all level of government in the U.S. expanded rapidly, especially the federal government. The total government employees reached 22.5 million in 2010 which is 2.56 times of 8.7 million in 1960 (7.2). Thus, the U. S. GDP is heavily padded with government payroll. America, the world's largest economy, is unable to produce enough goods to meet its own household and industry needs and has to heavily rely on foreign producers. In 2013, more than half, 55.4% (68.6% in 2015), of all products used in America were imported (see 5.1). The 2010 census shows 47.4% of its population, 146.4 million people, lived under the 200% poverty line with almost one fourth (25%) of families with no net assets but debt in the richest nation on earth (5.9). OECD 2010 Pisa report shows American students ranked 14th among 34 nations, having test results only better than Mexico and some other developing countries (5.5). The ACT testing reported in 2010 that 75% of high school students failed to pass all four subjects (5.5). The OECD study of 2010 criminal record shows that America tops the 34 nations with 760 criminal incarcerations per 100,000 people, 5.4 times the OECD average (5.2). The U.S. National Security Agency (NSA) put the whole world under surveillance, including its own citizens (9.6). On the other social fronts, federal agency statistics indicate a total of 22.6 million drug abusers in 2010, representing 7.3% of the nation's population (5.7); nearly half the nation's fathers under 45 years old had an illegitimate child, 20-24 years old reaching 75% (5.7); a revival of farm slavery occurred (6.3) and a prevalence of grave irresponsible behavior in and out of government. On the other hand, the U.S. military expenditure in 2012 amounted to $711 billion, accounting for 41% of the world total, more than the major nations' spending combined (8.7). The American armaments trade accounted for 78% of 2011 global sales (7.4). Under repeated vows to reduce nuclear arms by President Obama in recent years, Reveal website reported that during the past four years of research and development by Lockheed Martin Corp., the B61-12 nuclear warheads (bombs) have been successfully trialed and tested, and are approved by the National Nuclear Security Administration for full production by 2020. The B61-12 is the most deadly (up to 50,000 tons of TNT) and most expensive nuclear warhead (400 bombs costing $11 billion) in history. It certainly will terminate foes and eventually destroy world civilization and mankind as well.

The U.S. has neither improved the living standards of its general population nor uplifted their education level nor safeguarded the human rights of its people. Polarization of wealth and income and deterioration of moral and social fabric are prevailing. Apparently, the great nation's resources and efforts were grossly misdirected by the ruling political and social elites. Maybe they intend to revive the British Empire without the colonial burden, to dictate the world by force, and to maintain dollar supremacy for unlimited borrowing power. These conditions suggest that something is wrong with democracy, capitalism, or the Western culture. Changes of status quo will take place in several possible ways. The U.S. might follow Venezuela's democratic socialism path through its growing laboring class political force, e.g., New York and Seattle elections, and the 2016 Iowa presidential primary socialist movements and the Trump phenomenon in the 2016 general election from within. The globalization force of free flow of goods, labor, and capital will bring about a new world order which will be discussed in a later part of this book. Large scale international wars would cause massive destruction and alter current social and world orders. Or, through the slow process of the diminishment of the dollar supremacy and U.S. world financial control, this will limit its ability to finance debt, forcing a major national policy change to take place.

In a transitional period, changes often represent the conflicts between the old and new forces in customs, ideals, beliefs, values of life; correspondingly, they bring about class antagonism, ethnic conflicts, social unrest, violence, etc. The growing trend of the laboring class to become the U.S. major political policy maker will significantly impact society in many ways which include increasing public fiscal responsibility, generally lowering education and living standards, reducing national competitiveness, leading to recession and social decline, and domestic concerns alienating foreign involvement: more negative impacts than positive. The U.S. will find it difficult to sustain superpower status for long.

VIII. International Outlook

Defamation of Islam's Prophet Muhammad in a film circulated in the West caused uproar in the Muslim world. People in 20 Muslim nations rallied, protested and attacked American embassies, consulates, and other American interests, leading to the deaths of the U.S. ambassador to Libya Chris Stevens and three embassy staff. In the Pacific, a storm of territorial sovereignty disputes rose involving Russia, Japan, South Korea, and China in the north. And China, Vietnam, the Philippines, Malaysia, and Brunei disputed over island sovereignty in the South China Sea. Israel and the Palestinians continued trading missile raids with air bombings. Syria's civil war was extended into another year. In 2013, the Al Qaeda Iraqi branch broke away from its leader, forming the ISIS Islamic State and threatening the Iraqi regime. Egyptian president Mohammed Morsi, inaugurated years ago, was deposed by the military because of the strong opposition to his regime which triggered a wave of political turmoil. Abdel Fattah el-Sisi, a military strong man, was elected as president on June 8, 2014, to restore law and order and to revive the Egyptian economy. The Yemeni civil war intensified and turned into a multinational involvement. Policies of the Turkish Prime Minister met with massive demonstrations nationwide, and in July 2016 a military coup was crushed. North Korea's nuclear issue has intensified, and the Americans will install the controversial THAAD system in South Korea. Russia annexed Crimea during Ukraine political unrest. Some European countries are still steeped in financial/economic difficulties and political unrest and are besieged by international refugees. In the southern hemisphere, Venezuela and Brazil are in political and social discord and class confrontation. Brazil's President Dilma Rousseff was impeached and replaced by the vice president in August 2016. Crises are emerging around the globe.

The world economic development will show further integration and cooperation in trade and investment among nations by forming various bilateral and multilateral agreements. Most noticeably, there are the Transatlantic Trade and Investment Partnership (TTIP) and Trans Pacific Partnership (TPP) promoted by the U.S. The TTIP and TPP are designed to strengthen economic ties between American and EU and the 11 Pacific Rim nations. The Chinese have a grand economic plan for the next decade around the world. Major projects include the China-Pakistan corridor, a part of the "One Belt One Road" plan, high-speed rail system construction, and the 10 economic and social aid plans to aid Africa. In addition, there are many economic and investment accords signed by China and other countries globally.

What will these changes bring about in the next decade?

8.1. Changes in Europe

The European Union (EU) has 28 member States (on July 1, 2013, Croatia became the newest member state), with a total of 500 million people, accounting for 7.3% of the world population; a 2011 economic output of $17.6 trillion, about 20% of the world GDP. The EU continues to accept members, so it is continuously expanding.

The financial turmoil in 2008 leading to recession greatly impacted the European continent. Besides the recession, democracy is in trouble, too. Because the governments depended on borrowing to maintain continuous improvement in workers' benefits and social welfare, resulting in huge national debt and the inability to cope with it, this led to political and humanitarian crises. These EU members are not the United States and cannot continue borrowing to maintain economic and social stability.

Greece, Ireland, Portugal, Spain, and Italy were the most seriously affected by the financial crisis. Economic recession, rising unemployment, government budget cuts, and state retrenching expenses resulted in demonstrations by tens of thousands of people who opposed reducing benefits and lowering living standards. On June 16, 2012, in Italy, 200,000 people took to the streets to protest budget austerity. From 2008 to March 2012, Greece's GDP declined by 17%, youth unemployment was as high as 48%, and more than 33% lived below the poverty line. European media reported: "The scene is young men leaving Greece, the elderly searching trash for food and committing suicide. From the national debt crisis, Greek has marched into an economic crisis, leading to political crisis, which is now becoming a humanitarian crisis". Protests and riots were Greeks' daily rituals, while the Prime Minister announced a May election for the people to decide on austerity measures for debt relief. No party won a majority of the seats in the election; multi-party consensus could not be reached; and no cabinet was formed. A June re-election produced the same result. Teamster Pandelis said: "I am tired of the New Democracy and Pan Greek Social Movement Parties. In the past 30 years they took turns ruling the country and both hurt the economy badly. In order to entice voters, disregarding reality, both parties out bided each other to offer the voters more and better public subsidies and welfare benefits. At the same time, both Parties expanded government payroll for an already overstaffed and inefficient civil service workforce for the sake of higher employment records" (2012/6/18). Using government benefits and spending to buy votes may be considered the price the Greek people paid for implementation of the democratic election.

Lately, the European Central Bank announced the buy-back of bonds issued by any EU member nation without limit, and a German court also approved the continuing operation of the European Stability Mechanism, easing the Euro and EU crisis temporarily. The European Central Bank is revising its financial regulatory mechanism to meet the current challenges and requires beneficiary countries to implement austerity measures.

Recent political development in Ukraine put a dent in the relationship between the EU and Russia, which may cause Russia to reduce ties with the EU and to reinforce its ties with Eastern Europe, the Middle East, and China. The development will not be confined to the economics but military and national security as well. Military activities by the North Atlantic Treaty Organization along the EU and Russian border have been surging, which incited Russian response in kind. Turkey, Saudi Arabia and Iran will play an increasingly important role in their region. Driven by U.S. policy as well as their own interests, Russia and China will increase their cooperation in all aspects.

On the June 23, 2016, referendum, the British voters decided to leave the European Union (Brexit). The event produced a shocking wave and a negative stock market reaction throughout the world. By law, within two years the British exit must be completed, which will alter the British relationship with the rest of the world, rendering some parts of the bilateral or multilateral accords to be ineffective or uncertain. Due to the size of the U.K. economy, people see the negative impact on both the EU and U.K. But more importantly, Brexit dampens the aspiration for a united Europe, which is the goal of EU. U.K. politics is further complicated by the Scottish independence movement and its desire to remain in the EU.

Illegal immigration from Eastern Europe, North Africa, and the

Middle East is also a common issue in European society, but it represents a small proportion to the total population and not in one large group like Latino in America; therefore, it does not constitute a major social problem as it is in the U.S. However, the wars in the Middle East and Africa intensified lately, and they accelerated illegal immigrant and refugee flows into Europe. Boats heading to Italy and Greece capsized in the Mediterranean, and caused the deaths of over 1,000 people in May 2016, triggering international attention; the EU parliament convened a special meeting to deal with the influx.

The political tension and military conflict in the Middle East and North Africa have seen an increase of refugees, especially from Syria. The UN High Commission for Refugees (UNHCR) estimated that by the end of 2015 there will be 400,000 migrants moving into Europe, twice the number as in 2014. The deteriorating situation in 2015 prompted the European Commission President Jean-Claude Junker to propose a quota for member nations to take in 120,000 asylum seekers and relocating 40,000 already in Europe (*Bloomberg Businessweek*, 2015/9/14). This crisis is so complex that will not be easily resolved anytime soon. The refugee problem will certainly intensify.

Serious disparity of wealth and income in Europe is less than in the United States so that the middle class of most EU member countries still dominates national politics. Despite the democracy trouble, with a balanced budget and the necessary fiscal constraints to prevent using government handouts as baits for getting people's votes, there is no immediate need for democratic reform. But for the long-term benefit, a thorough change must be made, because the existing democratic election system is based on the majority's personal interests; it will inevitably follow the footsteps of Venezuela where the laboring class determines the political agenda. Arab Spring and the Jasmine Revolution could topple weak constitutional governments like Greece, but such extremes will miss most of the EU member nations.

8.2. China's One Belt One Road Plan and High Speed Rail System

Nearly 10 years have passed since the financial crisis, and most advanced economies have not recovered from the pre-recession peak of the first quarter of 2008 except Germany and the U.S. Germany suffered a sharp economic decline in 2009, but by 2011 it rebounded due to its superiority in the automobile, machinery, and chemical industries, which dominated the world market. America resorted to its fiscal and monetary policies to maintain its economic stability; it was basically financed by public and private debts, about $730 billion per year from 1970 to 2010 (see 5.3).

The Euro zone economies are still in the negative territory, unemployment exceeding 10%. Despite the annual G-7 and G-20 efforts, the results seem dismal; economic recovery is elusive and they are out of options. As a result, some politicians have turned to trade protectionism to save jobs and income for their workers. Waves of anti-globalization activities swept through Europe. Right after his inauguration, U.S. President Trump signed an order withdrawing from the Trans Pacific Partnership agreement. And on June 1, 2017, President Trump called a Rose Garden press conference in the White House proclaiming "we are getting out of the Paris Climate Accord and I was elected by the citizens of Pittsburg" because it was an unfair deal for America and he wants to save coal miners' jobs. The Accord has 195 nation signers, virtually every country on earth except Syria and Nicaragua. These actions in essence, declare that America is pursuing protectionism and leaving the world economic stage. It is effectively handing the world economic leadership over to China, whether China likes it or not.

Since most world economies are in recession leading to government austerity measures and budget cuts, there seems to be no way out. At the 2014 Asian Pacific Economic Cooperation summit, China pledged $1.6 trillion in the next decade for the One Belt One Road plan. The plan will connect Asia, Europe, and Africa with modern infrastructure along the 40 countries in the Road's paths. On October 24, 2014, the Asian Infrastructure Investment Bank was established with 57 member nations by the March 21, 2015, application deadline and boosted to 77 nations by May 13, 2017. In the meantime, numerous investment projects have been carried out around the world by China in the last few years. Among them, the China-Pakistan Economic Corridor (CPEC) with a price tag of $54 billion was partially operational by November 13, 2016. And an inaugural ceremony was held on August 29, 2017 to celebrate the operation of the Dawood wind power project which provides 50 mw electricity enough for one half million households' need, a much welcome news for acute power shortage in Pakistan. The project also created

300,000 local jobs mainly devoted to manufacture the wind towers. After completion of the entire CPEC project, it will immensely improve Pakistan's economy, shorten the distance to west Asia, the Middle East, and beyond for China, Korea, and Japan. When the Greek government auctioned the Piraeus Port to raise funds for the national debt repayment, the China Ocean Shipping Company (COSCO) was the only bidder. Over the years, COSCO spent $1 billion and promised another one-half billion dollars to upgrade the port making it more efficient. However, it was met with a labor strike lasting for a month and half and "COSCO go home" signs in its early operation. The port operation has enhanced cargo traffic and created one thousand additional jobs; it is the bright spot for the Greek struggling economy and is now welcomed by the locals. The port is a strategic gateway to Europe, an important link in the Belt Road plan.

These facts demonstrate to world leaders that China was not just providing some lip service about world prosperity and peace. China is willing to use its resources to promote global economic growth and to achieve world prosperity and peace. Thus, it laid the foundation for the Belt Road Forum for International Cooperation in Beijing, China, on May 14-15, 2017. The forum attracted 29 government leaders, chiefs of the UN, World Bank, and IMF. Over 1,200 participants came from 110 countries, including 92 high ranking government officials and many world business leaders.

The Chinese initiative promotes the Belt Road spirit, which consists of the following principles: (1) All-inclusiveness. The Belt Road plan extends from the 40 nations along the path to every nation on earth which desires to participate and enlarges the scope to include areas other than infrastructure; (2) Equality. Nations small or large enjoy the same rights based on their contribution. China, the promoter and the major contributor, will not be entitled to any special privileges such as a veto power; (3) Non-intervention in another nations' internal affairs. Donors should not attach any string imposing ideology or political system on others; (4) Non-predatory mutual benefit. Most multinational organizations other than the UN promote self-interest at the expense of other nations or have the purpose of eliminating or reducing strength of perceived enemies or competitors. Participants of this plan should subscribe to mutual benefit, not self-interest, and non-predatory practices; and (5) Cooperation consensus. Mutual consultation, mutual respect, mutual effort, and sharing the fruits should be faithfully observed by all participants.

After 70 years' effort, the current world economic system provides affluence to a small segment of population in the world leaving a large population living in poverty. Slave wages prevail in all third world countries in addition to serious environmental damage which moves the earth toward its destruction. These world economic conditions are unsustainable; changes are imminently needed. The Belt Road spirit promotes world economic equality and justice besides growth and prosperity, and sets it apart from the existing world economic order. It is hoped that the new spirit of world cooperation and mutual benefit will achieve its goals of improving living standards and providing economic justice for all people in the world in sustainable economic development. The Chinese initiative was met with some skeptics as to China's political motivation, investment sustainability, business conduct transparency, and environment consideration. Certainly, there is room for concern and improvement. Nonetheless, the Belt Road spirit is one step in the right direction toward international economic cooperation leading to world prosperity and peace as well as economic equality and justice for all mankind.

One of the Chinese's newly developed enterprises that will play a very important role in the Belt Road plan as it begins to evolve is the high speed rail system. Over the past decade, the development of rail transport in China has astonished the world. The British *Daily Telegraph's* lengthy article praises the achievement of the former Minister of Railways, Wang Lijun, who within nine years, took an old and large railway system with an average speed of 30 miles per hour and transformed it into the world's largest high-speed rail system (HSRS), with an average speed of 200 miles per hour (2013/7/9). China absorbed advanced high-speed rail technology, discarding the shortcomings, mastering the strengths, with its own research and innovation; it has excelled and become the purveyor of the most advanced high speed rail system. With its vast region, China has accumulated a plethora of experiences in construction and operations in various topographies, geologies, climates, temperatures, and social structures. By the end of 2015, China will have 19,000 km of high speed rail, 60% of the world's running mileage. Chinese construction cost is two thirds of other countries, as reported by the World Bank (2015/10/27).

China's HSRS technology and its development set a few records in recent years. In 2008, China exporting HSRS motor car parts to Germany set a precedent for the return of high tech products to that advanced country. Harmony trains run at a top speed of 487 km (302 miles) per hour, costing $26 million per km to build. Japan's maglev trains clock a speed of 507 km (315 miles) per hour, costing $253 million per km, both setting amazing world records (2013/11/20). Hence, the Chinese have a price-performance ratio advantage of 9.34 to 1.00 as compared with the Japanese. Therefore, whether it is cost, technology, or safety, China has the absolute advantage in the world in HSRS technology.

By the end of 2014, there are three major HSRS outside China under planning and construction by the Chinese. The Pan Asian HSRS consists of east, west, and central lines. The east line starts from Kunming, China, passing through six countries, ending in Singapore; sections of it will be in operation in 2016. The Europe-Asia HSRS, beginning in Beijing, crossing seven nations and ending in London, is slated to start construction in 2017. The third is the Asia-Minor HSRS, which starts in Xingjian, China, traveling through seven nations, with its last stop in Bulgaria.

In 2014, China's involvement in foreign HSRS construction included the 421 km first section of the Pan Asian HSRS from Kunming to Laos' capital and four lines in Thailand, a 400 km HSRS between Budapest and Belgrade, a HSRS connecting Ankara and Istanbul, Turkey, and other works in Malaysia, Iraq, England, and India. In the meantime, China negotiates currently with the U.S., Russia, Brazil, Saudi Arabia, Turkey, Poland, and Venezuela on HSRS projects (2014/1/10, 18, 2/16). On May 7, 2014, Nigeria signed a contract with China to build HSRS, connecting 10 states along the coast line. The project will provide 1,385 km HSRS with 22 stations at 120 km/hr for a total price close to $13 billion. New China News reports that on October 23, 2014, the Massachusetts Bay Transit Authority has approved a contract to purchase 284 subway trains to be used in the Boston subway system from the North Locomotive Group of China for a price tag of $660 million. The company has outbid the world's leading manufacturers from South Korea, Japan, and Canada by a wide margin and plans to build an assembly plant in the state providing 250 local jobs with an investment of $60 million. It is the company policy to become a locally-operated business to expand its activities in other American cities as well as to branch out to rail construction operations. The North Locomotive Group's export sales in 2014 exceeded $3 billion, an increase of 73.5% over 2013 (2015/1/27). In 2014, the South Locomotive Group and the North Locomotive Group, both from China, are competing for a $566 million contract relating to HSRS in California. The two Groups merged recently.

In addition, there are some bright spots for China's HSRS. The long contest between Chinese and Japanese interests for building 150 km, $5.3 billion HSRS linking Jakarta and Bandung, Indonesia, was won by a Chinese consortium. Thailand and China reached an agreement on exchange of one million tons of rice and 200,000 tons of rubber for 867 km of HSRS at a top speed of 180 km. The project will be managed by a joint enterprise to begin full operation by next May (2015/12/4). A bullet train delivery ceremony was held on November 15, 2015, in Macedonia, Europe, by the country's premier and Chinese CSR Zhuzhou Electric Locomotive Co. executives to commemorate the first delivery of its six high speed trains. The train is designed according to Europe's rail interconnect TSI standards with a maximum speed of 140 km and a life of 30 years. It opens the door for the Chinese HSRS export to the European Union (*wenweipo.com*, 2015/11/16).

The inaugural ceremony of the first African electric modern railroad was held on October 5, 2016. The roadway which connects Ethiopia's capital Addis Ababa to Djibouti will help to reduce traveling time from seven days by highway to 10 hours. The railroad with 45 stations, 752 km in total length, at 120 km per hour was designed and built by two Chinese companies using all Chinese standards costing $4 billion in less than six years. The Chinese plans to take six years to train local personnel to assume all operating and maintaining of the railroad. It was exciting news to East Africans (2016/10/5). On May 31, 2017, President Uhuru Kenyatta of Kenya also inaugurated a Chinese-built railroad between the port of Mombasa and the capital Nairobi. The $3.2 billion 480 km railroad, 90% financed by China, is the biggest project since Kenya's independence in 1963. The new railroad was completed in two and a half years and is affordable, having a higher payload besides its speed, which will bring costs down 79% to cargo and 40% to passengers and will reduce travel time in half. The project is a strategic gateway to East Africa and a part of a master railroad plan to link five other nations. Currently, the project has generated 46,000 local jobs and an estimated

1.5% GDP growth rate per year in the future. It is perceived as a significant event in Kenya's economic development as the President proclaimed in the ceremony: "Today we celebrate one of the key cornerstones to Kenya's transformation to an industrialized, prosperous, middle-income country". Amid the jubilant celebration, accusations of corruption, concerns over the impact on wildlife, high project cost, economic sustainability, and Chinese influence have also dogged the project.

In addition, there were two more railways built by China in Africa completed and operational in the recent years: The 1,344 km project costing $1.83 billion linking Lobito and Luau, Angola, was completed on 2015/2/14 and the 186.5 km project with a price tag of $850 million connecting Nigeria's capital Abuja and the state of Kaduna was in operation by 2016/7/26 (*Al Jazeera and Wenweipo* websites).

Recent reports indicate a number of setbacks in the HSRS overseas development for China. Mexico cancelled its $4.3 billion contract with a Chinese builder because of a bribery scandal. A Colombian proposal for HSRS to replace the Panama Canal four years ago has been silenced. HSRS operation in 2012 promised by the Venezuelan government years ago is now only half way complete due to local government financial difficulty. The ambitious transcontinental HSRS negotiated by Brazil, Peru, and China has also met with uncertainty. The main factors are the Chinese economic slowdown requiring fewer raw materials from Brazil, political and economic deterioration in Brazil, and environment concerns (2015/10/5). A memorandum of understanding was signed by India and Japan to build a 508 km HSRS between Mumbai and Ahmedabad, India, at a cost of $15 billion. Japan will provide $12 billion financing at 0.1% interest for 50 years, with a 15 year grace period. This memorandum is awaiting government's approval (2015/10/27). Early in June 2016, XpressWest announced ending a joint venture with Chinese companies to build a HSRS linking Las Vegas and Los Angeles for an estimated price of $5 billion.

High speed rail technology and nuclear power station exports dramatically changed China's foreign trade pattern of the past (exporting billions of shirts in exchange for an airplane) and boosted domestic related-enterprises, technical aid to foreign countries and technology services for the future. The operation of HSRS will definitely facilitate the flow of goods and people, reducing the cost of transportation, promoting economic development for the affected regions, and speeding up globalization. In addition, Chinese personnel are needed to help with construction and operation in the host country, and local staff will be sent to China to familiarize themselves with the operating knowledge and skills. These exchanges will enhance understanding of people in the different cultures and will be beneficial to global integration and world peace.

8.3. Prospect of China's Economic Development

The 2008 recession in the U.S. and Europe reduced their demand for imports, impacting the growth of emerging economies so that all countries in the world were either in recession or at a slowdown. China no longer had a two-digit rate of economic growth. The Chinese government began adopting policies to boost domestic consumption and to modernize urban transportation for improving people's living standard. Second, in addition to signing trade agreements with individual countries, efforts were directed to expand free trade areas, e.g., the Association of Southeast Asian Nations (ASEAN) countries, the free trade zone of China, Japan, and South Korea, and the Regional Comprehensive Economic Partnership (RCEP). Third, the economic diplomacy policy was pursued to aid underdeveloped countries building infrastructures, developing natural resources, and achieving industrialization, providing technical and financial assistance.

Due to China's huge population, traffic congestion and pollution have been the fact in the past. It was somewhat tolerable because more than 80% of its population were dispersed in the rural areas. The industrialization and urbanization in the past three decades have moved the people to the urban areas and made the problem worst as most of China's cities do not meet air and water quality standards (see A2.6). For the sake of people's health, China is in dire need to reduce pollution and congestion in the cities. One of the 13th Five-year Plan (2016-2020) calls for modernization of city rapid rail transit (CRRT), i.e., building mostly underground rail systems. A total of 3,127 kilometers were authorized at an average cost Y500 million ($75 million) per km, the most expensive type of urban transit construction. Lately, the emphasis has been shifted to build more aerial railways as opposed to underground operation because it not only costs a lot less to build but also it is causing lots less destruction to the environment and community. By the end of 2014, CRRTs were operated in six cities, 11 cities under construction, and 20 cities gaining authorization to build. Recently, many more cities were added to the CRRT authorization roll, including 50 third tier cities, but some projects are scheduled to finish beyond 2020. Between 2013 and 2018, the annual CRRT investment requires Y310 billion ($47 billion), creating another construction boom in China. Building CRRTs will certainly alleviate city congestion and pollution, improve efficiency, utilize China's excess capacity such as steel and cement, and propel economic growth. When they are all done, China will have modern intra-city transportation to supplement its HSRS intercity transportation system, which will greatly enhance efficiency and improve its economic competitiveness.

As announced by President Xi Jinping of China at the 2014 Asia-Pacific Economic Cooperation (APEC) summit, China will invest $1.6 trillion in the next decade in the land and sea silk routes, "One Belt One Road" plan to Europe and Africa, involving some 40 countries and regions along the path. Most of these investment projects will be provided by grants or favorable long-term financing either from China, the Asian Infrastructure Investment Bank, New Development Bank or other international institutions. These projects offer favorable conditions for social improvement and economic activities along the 40 countries' path, enhancing diplomatic and cultural relations with China as well as Chinese domestic economic activities: a winner for all.

The British *Daily Telegraph* lists important infrastructure projects to be funded overseas in the near future by the Chinese. In addition to the $40 billion Grand Canal of Nicaragua, to be completed by 2020, there are the China-Pakistan corridor, including highway, railway, oil and gas pipelines, fiberglass cables and airport, which will become an important hub connecting China to the Middle East and Africa, costing $32 billion. Also, there is the Nigerian high speed rail road, $13 billion; Algerian six-lane east-west highway, $11.1 billion; new Baltic city for 35,000 people in Finland, $1.7 billion; Texas turbine wind farm, $1.5 billion; and Nigeria hydroelectric power stations, $1.2 billion (2014/7/9). These projects promote economic development abroad and at home, mutually beneficial to the guest and host countries, having an "all winners" effect. It will speed up the global logistics flow and cultural exchanges, promoting world prosperity and harmony.

After President Xi Jinping of China paid a state visit to the U.S., signed an accord with America on cyber security and a contract with Boeing Co. to purchase 300 airplanes worth $38 billion in late September 2015, he attended the United Nations' General Assembly meeting at its New York City headquarters to commemorate its 70th anniversary on September 26, 2015. The Chinese announced in the meeting the setting up of South-South Cooperation and Assistance Funds to help less developed countries in their economic and social development with an initial funding of $2 billion, aiming at $12 billion by 2030. At the same time, President Xi also declared in the meeting to forgive all unpaid interest-free loans which end in 2015, to the world's poorer, small island, and landlocked nations. Both announcements were welcomed by the UN members.

The Queen of the United Kingdom invited President Xi as a guest to Buckingham Palace in late October 2015. The British and Chinese reached an agreement on cooperation and investment of 40 billion pounds covering energy, tourism, medical and health, finance, and cultural areas: notably, the construction of $24 billion Hinkley Point nuclear power project in England, the most expensive of this type in history by a Chinese and French consortium, and a cruise ship three times larger than the Titanic, a $4 billion venture financed jointly by the Carnival Cruise Lines and the Chinese. Following Xi's visits to the U.S. and U.K., the King and Queen of Holland paid a state visit to China on October 25 to 29, 2015. The royal couple was accompanied by 250 businessmen and ended up with 15 cooperation agreements ranging from finance, trade, aviation, technology, and panda protection. In the meantime, it was German Chancellor Angela Merkel's eighth visit to China. The German was reinforcing their eminent trade ties with China by 15 business deals, worth $22 billion. Then, French President Hollande came in for a meeting with President Xi on Cop-21 Climate Summit in Paris, nuclear waste recycling, and accelerating Chinese investment in the French energy sector, also a $22 billion deal. China Nuclear Engineering Co. signed an agreement with Romania National Power Co. to jointly invest, construct and manage the No. 3 and 4 reactors in the Carnivora nuclear power plant, with a 7.2 billion euros price tag. It is the Chinese first step into the EU with nuclear construction (*wenweipo.com*, 2015/11/12).

China will provide $60 billion in aid to Africa, as announced by

President Xi on the Forum on China-Africa Cooperation held in Johannesburg on December 4-5, 2015. Under the principle of non-interference in the internal affairs of each nation, the aid will be used between 2016 and 2018 to finance 10 major plans covering economic, education, medical, and social areas.(2015/12/4).

In the last decade, China vigorously promoted the transformation of its enterprises from a "made in China" to a "created in China" economy. It was carried out by heavy investment in research and development, and through acquisition and joint venture of foreign advanced businesses to enhance China's international competitiveness. Today, China is not only the major supplier of consumer goods but also the provider of equipment and infrastructure to the world. And in 2014, China became the world's second largest foreign direct investment (FDI) nation and also turned itself into a net investment capital exporter, even though China was the most favored FDI recipient. From 2003 to 2013, China's FDI overseas averaged $46.4 billion per year. In the meantime, it is beginning to promote the policy of transplanting its enterprises to foreign land to become a part of local community economic development.

According to *Bloomberg Businessweek's* report that mergers and acquisitions of foreign businesses by the Chinese interests had been less than $20 billion every quarter since 2011, the pace has picked up dramatically in the 4th quarter of 2015, which amounts to over $40 billion. In 2016 by February 26th, the amount of investment by the Chinese has reached $77 billion (2016/3/7). This phenomenon overwhelms and alarms the advanced economies. It presents both a challenge and opportunity to the Chinese and the host country.

China's economic expansion abroad, which includes mergers and acquisitions (M&A), Greenfield projects, and other economic or financial aids, has been met with success and failure, heartily welcomed or outright rejected. Data compiled by the American Enterprise Institute show that about 25% of Chinese investment projects overseas from 2005 to 2014, worth $246 billion, have been stalled by snafus or failed (*Bloomberg Businessweek,* 2015/9/30), such as the half-completed Venezuela HSRS discussed earlier. On account of national security, China's State Grid Corporation and Hong Kong-listed Cheung Kong Infrastructure's bidding to acquire Ausgrid was denied by Australian Federal Treasurer Scott Morrison on August 20, 2016. The Chinese commitment of 800 million pounds to build Manchester Airport City was met with great reception in this rusted, early Industrial Revolution city of northern England, providing a good opportunity for economic revival.

The Committee on Foreign Investment in the U.S. (CFIUS) is chaired by the Treasury Secretary, including members from department heads of Justice, Homeland Security, Commerce, Defense, State, and Energy as well as the Offices of the USTR and Science and Technology Policy. The committee has the final authority to approve M&As, including foreign-owned businesses operating on American soil. It is often becoming a major obstacle for both M&A parties in the U.S. The grounds of national security to exclude Chinese interests may include protection of its businesses, preserving trade and technology advantages, and keeping local employment. Some investments by the Chinese in developing countries, especially in Africa, were branded as plundering local natural resources and practicing new colonial economic exploitation. Because of its economic size, some people consider Chinese investors as economic predators, not welcomed. Also, there is a cultural difference between the Chinese business and the local community. Therefore, the ventures into the global economy by Chinese enterprises are not smooth and successful in many cases.

The high speed rail systems, city rapid rail transits, nuclear projects plus the One Belt One Road and other infrastructure construction plans in China and around the world will require an astronomical amount of materials such as steel, aluminum, copper, concrete, lumber, carbon fiber, etc., which in turn will create a commodity production boom in natural resource rich areas, such as Russia, Canada, Brazil, Australia, America and many Asian and African nations, reviving the sagging commodity sector and the surplus production capacity since the 2008 recession throughout the world. And the recently signed accords with the U.K., the Netherlands, Germany, France and the aid to Africa together with other basic infrastructure development around the globe will enhance economic activities and improve social condition both in China and around the world. Since China has the financial resources and is willing to use them, most of these projects will be carried out as planned. In the next decade, China will lead the world to economic growth and prosperity, keeping production machines humming all over the globe.

On July 13, 2017, Liu Xiaobo, human rights activist and Nobel peace prize winner died of liver cancer in a Chinese jail. China again became the target of criticism by the global human rights group for violation of individual freedom. To be fair and reasonable to this criticism, the world development and the Chinese history must be taken into account. Before the world total disarmament is realized, peoples need national sovereignty to protect their life and property from foreign aggression. Therefore, national security and collective freedom should come first before individual rights and freedom will be assured. Patrick Henry's speech, "Give me liberty or give me death", in 1775 was for seeking collective liberty from the British bondage and fighting for national sovereignty. After the White House was set on fire by the British troops in 1814, America soon became a world power and never again experienced its sovereignty in jeopardy. Then, it was time for people in America to seeking individual freedom.

In the last 150 years, China's history was full of foreign invasions, devastation and massacres. More than 300,000 innocent Chinese were slaughtered in Nanjing, China, the massacre committed by the Japanese military in 1937. What good is freedom of speech or freedom of assembly if people's lives were not assured? Today, it is the first time in the last 150 years that China is able to defend its sovereignty and protect its people's life and property from foreign aggression. Therefore, most Chinese hold dearly and above everything national security because they realize that without collective freedom, individual freedom means nothing.

Recently, Chen Kunchen taking refuge in the Beijing U.S. embassy again incited newspaper headlines around the world. Chinese intellectuals, who number 119.6 million people, 8.9% of the total population in 2010, yearning for Western democracy and freedom, have not subsided in their fight to be heard. Will Communist China's one-party dictatorship be able to survive? Will the Arab Spring Jasmine Revolution flames also spread to China? The American *Christian Science Monitor* website published a lengthy article, "Why China Won't Collapse", authored by Daniel A. Bell, American professor of philosophy at Tsinghua University in Beijing (2012/7/12). The author pointed out that since the 1989 Tiananmen Square incident, Western experts believe that a non-popularly elected regime lacks legitimacy; sooner or later, it is bound to collapse. Since 1990, several Western scholars have launched extensive field investigations into this subject. The major findings are: Most people support the system of one party rule; the Chinese political system and the central government have a high degree of legitimacy; and most public discontents are directed against the local governments. There are three main reasons why people are comfortable with the current political system. First, major achievements have been made in improving people's livelihood; general poverty and illiteracy have become history. Second, most people believe that having able and caring political leaders is more important than the right to vote. Finally, the regime has restored the dignity of China as a nation. Prof. Bell goes on to say that the Chinese Communist regime has not collapsed and will not collapse. If the above observation is accurate, China will have a stable political climate for years to come, which is a necessary condition for economic growth and prosperity

8.4. Vigilance of the Muslim World

The Tunisian coup in December 2010 triggered the Arab Spring Jasmine revolution, which quickly spread to North Africa and Middle East, resulting in social turmoil, disrupting the economic order, and greatly affecting people's lives. These earth-shattering upheavals caused death of between 49,790 to 63,182 people. After a nearly 30 year reign in Egypt, President Hosni Mubarak was sentenced to life imprisonment; Libyan strongman Muammar Gaddafi's 42 years of iron-fisted rule also came to an end. Some governments made concessions and changed policies to meet the people's demands; some increased welfare benefits to appease public sentiment; others used force to suppress the revolt. By the end of 2011, four governments were overthrown, eight countries had extinguished the flames of revolution, and the people of nine other countries continued carrying out protests and demonstrations.

In the fierce civil war in Syria, both sides have suffered heavy casualties. The UN estimated on January 15, 2015, the death toll of 220,000 people, with millions displaced, the majority becoming international refugees. The conflict has its international implication; both Russia and America are involved in addition to the regional powers such as Turkey, Iran, Saudi Arabia, Israel and ISIS.

President Mohammed Morsi, who was elected on June 24, 2012, to replace President Hosni Mubarak in Egypt, failed to improve the economy and people's livelihood, to accommodate opposition parties, and to take overall national interests into consideration; he instead placed a great emphasis on his party, the Muslim Brotherhood's interests that triggered people's massive protests demanding Morsi step down. The turmoil lasted for a year, and Morsi was ousted by the military in early July 2013. This coup intensified the conflicts, with the Muslim Brotherhood on one side, demanding Morsi's reinstatement, and the people and the military on the other. Fighting quickly spread outside Cairo to other parts of Egypt. The country was facing a civil war. The economy was much worse than the Mubarak era. On June 8, 2014, field marshal Abdel Fattah el-Sisi was elected President of Egypt hoping to end chaos and to restore social and economic stability.

In 2013, Abu Bakr al-Baghdadi, chief of Iraqi al-Qaeda operation, also representing Sunni Muslims' interests, broke away from the tradition of hit-and-run tactics and started occupying territory, setting up a governing regime. In April, 2013, it declared the formation of an Islamic State, ISIS, inspired by the revival of an Islamic emirate straddled across Iraq and Syria. In less than two years, it has conquered the eastern region of Syria and a great portion of Iraq. By June 2014, the second largest city in Iraq, Mosul, fell and ISIS posed an imminent threat to Baghdad, capital of Iraq, alarming the world. The reality made the U.S. go back to the Iraqi battlefield to prevent the complete takeover of Iraq by ISIS and forced Prime Minister Maliki, a Shiite, out of office. Beginning in October 2016, a coalition led by the U.S. which was joined by various local factions mounted an offense assisted by warplanes, against ISIS in Mosul. Furious fighting and bombing lasted for nine months and reduced the second largest city in Iraq to piles of rubble. The Prime Minister of Iraq declared a victory in Mosul on July 10, 2017, basically recapturing the city from the terrorist control.

ISIS not only attracts Sunni Muslims but also Western sympathizers, numbering 7,000 people including at least 100 Americans; some of them join their fight in the front lines. The regime has amassed immense financial resources, including oil field revenues from eastern Syria and northern Iraq and the assets of Iraqi central bank in Mosul in addition to other sources of revenue. It is estimated to have about $2 billion and a fighting force of about 100,000 people.

ISIS instigated coordinated attacks on several public places in Paris, Franc, and its suburb causing 130 deaths, including seven of the ISIS perpetrators on November 13, 2015. Also, the terrorist group destroyed a Russian airliner above the Egyptian Sinai Peninsula with 224 people on board on November 17, 2015. These incidents triggered French and Russian revenge with air strikes on ISIS installations. France also initiated an anti-ISIS alliance by the Western powers that prompted the British and Germans to join in with their air power against ISIS. However, none promised to commit ground forces in the Middle East.

As ISIS carried out its brutality against humanity recently, it set off a public outcry and global condemnation, and led to a world joint effort to eliminate the terrorist organization. Saudi Arabia has announced a coalition of 34 Islam nations against terrorism which includes countries in the Middle East, Asia, and Africa, but excluding Iran, Iraq, and Syria. The coalition's objective is to protect its members from threat and harm caused by terrorist organizations including ISIS. Riyadh, Saudi Arabia, is the joint operation center to coordinate and support military actions especially in Iraq, Syria, Egypt, and Afghanistan. Military operations will be in cooperation with the local government and international community. It does not rule out sending ground forces to carry out its missions. This coalition seems to be a self-defense mechanism rather than setting a goal to eliminate terrorism, a compromise with the ISIS posture.

Syria's Assad government is defended by Russia and Iran; the West and Saudi Arabia want Assad to step down and support the rebels. ISIS is the third party fighting both of them. The three parties tangle with each other; all may have harbored wishful thinking that they may rely on others to eliminate their enemies. Turkey, adjacent to Syria, also stepped up its involvement in the war. Apparently, there are nations or organizations who serve as an outlet for ISIS's oil revenue and profit from it. There are many interest groups with different objectives involved, leading to a very complicated situation. Therefore, without a unified front and concerted effort and lacking ground operations by all against it, ISIS is not going away anytime soon. ISIS is a viable force in the region and certainly is another source of turmoil in the Middle East.

The Kurds' claim of 30 million people dispersed mainly in Iraq, Turkey, and Iran signifies the largest ethnic group on Earth without a nation. On September 27, 2017, the independence election committee announced a 92% yes vote of 3.3 million in Kirkuk, Iraq and the neighboring areas in a referendum for independence. The referendum was prohibited by the Iraqi central government and denounced by Turkey and Iran. The Kurdish movement will be the additional cause of conflicts in the region.

The Yemeni civil war escalated into international involvement with a 10 Arab nation's coalition against the rebel, Houthi, supported by Iran. Saudi Arabia took the lead, launching air strikes on military targets of Houthi and may send in ground troops. Conflict will certainly be intensified if Saudi Arabia and Iran have a military showdown. However, with the oil market slumping and Iran just coming out of the sanctions, there is little incentive for either party to escalate the war. The Syrian civil war has intensified; the Turkish government was under massive protests and in 2016 survived a military coup; Palestine and Israel are still deadlocked; and the Arab Summit, in its March 25, 2014 meeting, announced that it will never recognize Israel as a state. France initiated a 70 nations' conference on January 15, 2017, in Paris, France, to promote the Israel and Palestine two nations' coexistence concept. It is perceived as the crucial step to resolve the conflict. The conferees consisted of nations from Europe, Arabia, and permanent members of the UN Security Council but not attended by the two parties involved.

In 2010, nearing the 9-11 anniversary date, the Florida Christian pastor Terry Jones instigated a burning of the Koran campaign sparking worldwide Muslim public outcries. Recently, U.S. resident Nakoula Basseley slandered the Prophet of Islam in a video circulated on the Internet. The United States again became the public enemy of the world's Muslims, leading to massive protests in more than 20 countries across North Africa, the Middle East, and Asia. The U.S. ambassador to Libya and three embassy employees were killed during these anti-American rallies. Demonstrations had extended beyond embassies and consulates to include American interests and British, French, and Germany embassies. Around September 20, 2013, the Muslim militant group, Izz ad-din Al Qassam, launched hacker attacks on Wells Fargo, Chase, US, PNC and other American banks and the New York Stock Exchange, causing difficulties or paralysis on their website operations. Hackers vowed to continue attacks until the video was withdrawn from the Internet (2012/9/28). The U.S. President and Secretary of State have repeatedly condemned such acts of publicly insulting religion and declared that the government has nothing to do with them. However, to Muslims, these acts are considered the same as an undisciplined child running wild hurting others; parents should shoulder the responsibility. It is clearly a conflict between freedom of speech advocated in the West and religion sacredness and cultural differences subscribed to by the Islamic world.

Except for few oil rich countries, most Muslim nations suffer from economic underdevelopment, high unemployment, poverty, rising prices, and social unrest. People are dissatisfied with government officials who do not improve their lives and make social progress, enrich them and use national resources just for consolidating their position. The revolutions were mainly directed at corrupt and incompetent rulers and their governments. Young people, connected to the new information technology, have been aware the significant changes in the world and the rise of emerging countries, especially China, which not only lifted its huge population out of the plight of the hungry but also regained its national dignity. The Arab and Muslim countries remain in almost the same old feudal condition, with not much improvement to speak of. Many of them realize that they must keep pace with world progress to be viable members of the international community.

Although new Muslim regimes adopt the democratic electoral system, they are not modeled on the Western freedom and human rights ideology. They intend to establish Islamic nations with the main thrust of improving people's livelihood, carrying forward Muslim traditions, and reviving the dignity of their nations. However, various approaches have been advocated by different factions or nations. Some maintain authoritarian tradition without any reform, such as Saudi Arabia and Jordan. Others promote the Islamic theocratic regime, mixing politics with religion, like Iran and Morsi's Egypt. Youth and intellectuals prefer Western-oriented democracy. In addition to the traditional military influence, the situation is further complicated by the historic animosity between Shiite and Sunni Muslims, militant and terrorist groups, and Arab and Jew conflicts. It certainly will not be easy to integrate all political and religious factions, to improve people's livelihood, and to make social progress while achieving a consensus with the overwhelming support of the people.

The democracy movement throughout the Middle East has not yet produced desired results for the masses who fight for jobs, food, medical care, security, and peace. The social condition has been getting worse. Experts believe that the movement raised people's expectations, destroyed existing law and order, with the new system and order requiring a long time, even several generations, to establish (2013/8/15). The situation will inevitably bring corresponding turbulence to the new regimes, leading to political instability and social unrest.

The internal and external problems of the Muslim world have intensified. In the past, they closed their doors to outside influences, maintaining their inherent religious beliefs and social values. Today, with advanced information technology and the expanding trend of globalization, isolationism is no longer possible. Therefore, the biggest challenge facing Muslim countries is how to adopt foreign technology and culture for improvement of people's living standards and social condition, and at the same time, how to prevent them from conflicting with Islamic cultural values and to integrate them into their own culture. In addition, there is the Israel problem. This is not an easily solvable task. Thus, conflict, unrest, turmoil, and fighting will be the regional norm for years to come.

8.5. Latin America's Rebirth

Most of Latin America after World War II was underdeveloped, where poverty and illiteracy were just as bad as in Africa and Asia. Economic and social development was in dire need for the whole region. In 1959, Cuba established a Communist regime which was a thorn in the eye of the United States. On April 15, 1961, a group of Cuban armed exiles supported by the U.S. Central Intelligence Agency landed at the Bay of Pigs, Cuba, in an attempt to overthrow the Communist regime, but was unsuccessful.

In 1961, the Alliance for Progress was initiated by President John Kennedy to be established within the Organization of American States. Its purpose was to improve social conditions, living standards, and education. It was believed that eradication of poverty was the best weapon to combat Communist expansion. Twenty-two Latin American countries participated. After nearly a decade of effort, the Alliance for Progress program was declared a failure in the late 1960s. It was mainly due to: (1) Except Cuba, Communists did not actively operate in Latin America; as a result, the United States lost its main interest; (2) The authoritarian regimes supported by the U.S. as a defense against the leftist forces were not received well by the local people; (3) The economic assistance of $1.4

billion per year provided by the United States, of which a whopping 90% of the aid was managed by American business; thus the U.S. corporations became the aid's major beneficiaries. For example, including U.S. economic aid, Brazil's balance of payments to the U.S. showed a net capital outflow. It turned out to be Brazilian economic aid to the U.S.; (4) The stubborn old local forces opposed to the new tax laws and land reform, so the poor were still poor.

Latin American societies still maintained the status quo with no significant changes until 1994 when the North American Free Trade Agreement (NAFTA) was implemented. When the U.S. and Canadian manufacturers relocated their plants to Mexico to take advantage of cheap labor and improve their competitiveness, this agreement also promoted other multinationals, such as Japanese, to set up shops in Mexico. It helped to develop the Mexican economy and improving people's living standard there.

In 2004, Venezuelan President Hugo Chavez and Cuban Prime Minister Fidel Castro initiated a free trade zone in Latin America and the Caribbean Islands; Bolivarian Alliance for the Americas (ALBA) was intended to replace the Pan American Free Trade Zone proposed by the United States. By the end of 2004, the two founding countries signed a health care and education in exchange for oil accord. Bolivia joined in 2006; Nicaragua, Ecuador, the Dominican Republic, Antigua and Barbados, and St. Vincent and Grenada subsequently became member states. In February 2010, the General Assembly approved Suriname and St. Lucia as guest members. The Alliance aimed to consolidate regional resources in order to accelerate economic, political, and social development. Specific measures were: (1) promoting barter, exchanging goods for goods or services and vice versa; (2) creating a regional currency, SUCRE, to replace the dollar as a regional currency; and (3) fostering regional economic mutual assistance and improving social welfare. The organization was advocated by the socialist left-wing activists; one of its intentions was self-reliance so as to protect itself against the U.S. economic threat. Years of efforts produced rewards; the new economic model proved quite effective.

When the U.S. suffered a financial crisis and a sluggish economy, this led President Obama to announce on March 15, 2010, that the U.S. might consider joining this organization, becoming a member of ALBA.

This would alleviate the plight of the U.S. economy and contribute to the development of Latin America. The move will not only remove the more than 60 years of U.S. economic sanctions against Cuba, but will also make America Cuba's close economic partner. In December 2014, Cuba and the U.S. both announced their intention to normalize diplomatic relations with each other, ending the cold war animosity.

More importantly, 12 participating nations in the 2004 South American Summit released the Cuzco Declaration, announcing the establishment of the South American alliance. After years of planning, finally on May 23, 2008, in the Brazilian capital, the alliance charter was signed. When Uruguay became the ninth nation whose Congress approved the Charter on December 1, 2010, the existence of the alliance was officially declared on March 11, 2011, and was named the Union of South American Nations (UNASUR). The alliance members consist of Bolivia, Colombia, Nicaragua, Peru, Argentina, Brazil, Paraguay, Uruguay, Venezuela, Chile, Guyana, and Suriname. It is modeled on the European Union to establish a common market, to eliminate tariffs and borders, to use a common currency, and to coordinate defense and military cooperation. It is expected to take 15 years to complete the integration. In 2010 the Union mediated conflicts between Colombia and Venezuela, preventing them from developing into a full-blown war, and in September of the same year provided $100 million assistance to disaster relief in Haiti: beneficial effects from the new alliance.

Mexico, Chile, Colombia, and Peru signed a treaty on June 6, 2012, to form the Pacific Alliance. It intensified economic integration for the four countries in an attempt to develop new trade relations with Asian Pacific countries, but will not conflict with the efforts of other Latin America regional organizations. The alliance will strengthen the overall economic development in Latin America.

The major problem that Latin America will face is the democratic electoral system, which has been adopted by most countries in the region. As with the Venezuelan case discussed earlier, the system will inevitably develop into a democratic socialist society. It will improve people's living standard and social conditions to a point where consumption outpaces production and investment leads to demand surging and supply lagging. A sagging economy will be crippled by high inflation, commodity shortages, political polarization, class antagonism, corruption, and social unrest.

Even with the oil wealth Venezuela has, it could not keep its system going for long, causing high inflation, commodity shortages, and economic dislocation. The recent development in Brazil has shown the symptoms that Venezuela has experienced. Other Latin American countries will also be infected with the Venezuelan syndrome when they, too, develop to that stage, perhaps a decade later.

Latin American countries do not rely on U.S. aid and no longer look up to America as a savior. Now they want to be self-reliant, paving roads for their good fortune, improving people's livelihood, popularizing education, and harmonizing society. They want to be respected internationally with full rights. As Venezuelan Foreign Minister Nicolas Maduro (current President) put it: "The ALBA's achievement, in addition to our unremitting efforts, is based on solidarity, cooperation, and spirit of mutual reciprocity of member states". From 2000 to 2009, the ALBA eight member states have more than doubled their economic growth rate. Latin America will have its own mouthpiece and play a rightful role in the international arena. South America's 12 nation alliance, UNASUR, will enhance internal prosperity and strengthen its impact internationally; Brazil has the potential to become a world economic super power. People of Mexico and Central America will continue their northward movement, transforming the United States.

8.6. Global Economic Influence and Outlook

Because of merchandise production declining and social welfare program expansion in the last several decades, the growth of the service sector in the developed economies has accelerated. Currently, almost in all developed countries the service sector exceeds 70% of GDP, with some reaching 80%. Most government services are non-economic, non-exportable, and non-productive in nature, such as administration, military, public security, welfare benefit, etc., having no international exchange value. These government expenditures will create a one-time demand and will increase the current year GDP, but nothing for the future economy (see 7.3). The non-exportable services, except military and foreign service, like police and fire departments have almost no effect on the foreign economy. Thus, global economic influence would not depend on the size of national GDP but more on its size of international trade and foreign direct investment.

The recent years' service sector, trade, and foreign direct investment data of the 12 leading economies as reported by the World Bank and the United Nations Conference on Trade and Development (UNCTAD), including its preliminary report on 2015 FDI, are shown below. The 2015 final FDI report has been released, an increase of $63 billion (less than 4%) in world total inflow over the preliminary version but on a different format not comparable to the 2014 FDI report. Updating is skipped.

2013 Service Sector, Trade and 2014-2015 Foreign Direct Investment

Nation Region	2013 Service GDP %	2013 International trade Export	Import	Total	Im/use%	2013 trade GDP %	2014-2015 FDI Inflow 2014	world%	2015	world%
U. S.	77.7*	$2,242	$2,761	$5,003	65.3	29.8	$86	6.8	$384	22.6
China	46.1	2,414	2,279	4,693	45.9	49.6	236#	19.0	299#	17.6
Germany	68.4	1,759	1,506	3,265	161.9	87.2			10	0.6
Japan	73.2	860	995	1,855	68.8	37.9				
France	78.5	816	870	1,686	103.8	60.0			44	2.6
U. K.	79.2	835	829	1,664	89.8	65.9	61	4.8	68	4.0
Brazil	69.3	279	333	612	44.7	27.2	62	4.9	56	3.3
Russia	59.8	588	466	1,054	61.7	48.3				
Italy	74.4	628	584	1,212	120.1	58.5				
India	57.0	464	591	1,055	63.3	56.2			59	3.5
Canada	70.8	536	579	1,115	68.4	61.0	53	4.2	45	2.6
Australia	70.7	305	304	609	69.1	40.5	49	3.9		
EU		7,819	7,326	15,145			267	21.2	426	25.1
ASEAN		1,558	1,457	3,015			151	12.0	146	8.6
NAFTA		3,223	3,743	6,966			139	11.0	429	25.3
C. & S. America		1,226	1,287	2,513			153	14.5	151	8.9
World total		$23,316	$2 2,606	$48,937			$1,260a	100	$1,699	100

$ Billion dollars.   * 2012.   # includes Hong Kong 2014, $111; 2015, $163.
a Data from different sources, 2014 world total varies with the following table.
Im/use: Import as a percentage to total goods used, service trade insignificant.

2014 and 2015 Foreign Direct Investment, Inflow

Region Year/%	2015 FDI inflow = 2014	2015	%	M&A, 37.9% 2014	2015	%	+ Greenfield,42.4% 2014	2015	%	+ Corp.Rec.,19.7% 2015	%
World	$1,245a	$1,699	100	$398.9	$643.7	100	$714.3	$720.7	100	$334.6	100
Developed	493	936	55	274.5	566.8	88	229.6	247.5	34	121.7	36
EU	254	426	25	160.6	269.2	42	122.4	139.8	19	17.0	5
N. America	146	429	25	44.1	242.3	38	77.7	76.6	11	110.0	33
Developing	703	741	44	120.1	67.6	11	459.1	439.4	61	234.0	70
Africa	55	38	2	5.1	20.4	3	88.0	71.1	10	-53.5	-16
L. America	170	151	9	25.5	10.1	2	89.3	68.6	10	72.3	22
Dvlg. Asia	475	548	32	89.3	35.3	5	280.6	299.3	42	213.4	64
Transition	49	22	1	4.2	9.3	1	25.7	33.8	5	-21.1	-6

$ Billion dollars.   a Data not from same document, 2014 world totals vary.

International trade is the arena of economic competition for the purpose of improving standards of living throughout the world. The flow of goods and service is mainly determined by each nation's natural endowment and economic advantage, absolute and comparative. Countries import crude oil because they lack the natural resource or are too expensive to produce. Large jet airliners are made by a few countries in the world, and these few countries have the absolute economic advantage in trading the jet airplanes. The comparative economic advantage will be discussed later in 10.1 of this book. These are the basic factors determining the international trade flows and trade balances.

Importing indicates the country lacking the natural resources or competitively being disadvantaged to produce particular goods or service. Imported items may be for business or consumer use. If it is for consumer use, it ends the economic activities. Otherwise, it is incorporated into other product or service used locally or exported to a foreign country. On the opposite side, the exporter claims the absolute/competitive advantage to seek out profitable markets in a foreign land. Exporting countries who are producers will be required to set up production where the economic activities will be carried out leading to economic growth and prosperity. Therefore, compared with an importer, an exporter has a greater influence on the global economy.

The Im/use column in the above table shows 2013 each nation's dependency on foreign goods for its domestic needs, both consumer and industry. America and Japan recorded at 65.3% and 68.8% for their goods needed from foreign suppliers respectively. EU member nations in this 12-nation group had the highest import dependency: Germany 161.9%, the highest, and the U.K. 89.8%, the lowest. This didn't necessarily mean that they imported more for domestic consumption, but mostly due to EU was moving toward a higher degree of economic integration. Thus, more division of labor and specialization of production were carried out among member nations and the final products were mostly for use by another country including EU member nations. Brazil and India imported more goods than they produced to meet their domestic need. China had a trade surplus and a 45.9% import dependency, second to the lowest. China imported more raw material and parts to be used in production than Brazil and most of these goods were destined for foreign markets, not for local use. For example, iphone major parts were imported from Japan, Korea, and Germany and the Iphone's main market was America. Hence, China would have a lower import dependency for domestic consumption than Brazil.

The 2013 world trade amounted to $48,937 billion, both goods and services, of which the advanced economies accounted for just about 50%, including 30.9% for EU, 10.2% for the U. S. Except Germany, most advanced economies imported more than they exported, which means more production was carried out in the developing countries, leading to fewer jobs in the developed economies. Thus, it brings about high unemployment, trade deficit, budget shortfalls, and economic downturns in the advanced economies if it is not supplemented by debt and investment.

Economic growth and prosperity depend on technology, capital, and cost of production in a stable political and social environment. The advanced economies enjoy the technological advantage, but machinery and production technology are transferable in today's global economic setting. Capital and skilled labor are the only issues. Global private capital flows basically are determined by reward and risk. The financial crisis in 2008 demonstrated that advanced economies were not immunized to financial risks as developing nations. So, private investors took the reward, shifting their attention to the developing nations for profit. As a result, the capital flow which was mainly included in the foreign direct investment contributed to developing economies' growth and prosperity.

Foreign direct investment is the movement of financial resources across the national border, which involves financial investment for business only. Therefore, personal remittances sent to relatives, portfolio investment in stocks and bonds, and purchases of real or personal property by foreign individuals are not parts of FDI. There are three components in FDI, namely merger and acquisitions of business (M&A), Greenfield projects (GP), and corporate reconfigurations (CRC).

The 2015 UNCTAD preliminary report shows that the world inflow of FDI reached $1.7 trillion, a 36% increase over 2014 and the highest level since 2007. The total inflow consists of merger and acquisitions $644 billion, 38%; Greenfield projects $721 billion, 42%; and corporate reconfigurations $335 billion, 20%. The U.S. raked in $384 billion, 23% of world inflow and also regained the top spot as a FDI recipient lost to China in 2014.

The big surge in FDI in 2015 was attributed to several extraordinary factors: The Syrian, ISIS, Yamani, and Ukrainian conflicts' escalation and dense cloud of potential wars in the East and South China Seas; the biggest oil price plunge since 1980s; Chinese Yuan devaluation; European and Japanese negative interest rates; and Chinese state and private capitalists eager for overseas expansion. Reported by the *New York Times*, in 2015 a $1 trillion fund, business and individual, exit China due to uncertainty over the Chinese currency exchange rate, just for one example (2016/2/14). Besides the business motivation, all the aforementioned factors led capital to seek safe havens, high returns, and easy convertibility. And the dollar became the favorable choice. The report also pointed out that this same phenomenon is unlikely to repeat in 2016.

Merger and acquisitions involve business investment in a foreign entity resulting in effective control of the enterprise, normally requiring at least 10% equity; otherwise, it is a portfolio investment. The M&A end result is consolidation of operation, such as combining two or more businesses into one or absorption of one or more corporations by another one. Business consolidations usually eliminate duplication or excess capacity, resulting in reduction in economic activities and employment. In the Chinese M&A cases, the purposes are more of gaining market, technology, and expanding their business operation abroad. M&A also means selling business equity to a foreign party, losing some economic and technological control power. Hence, from the national interest point of view, these transactions may not be good to the country and its economy for giving up the control. Of $384 billion the U.S. received in 2015, $228 billion, 59%, was for M&As, no more than $77 billion, 20%, for GPs, and about $79 billion, 21%, for CRCs.

M&As in Europe were even more active than in America. In 2015, the EU taking in $269 billion together with North America, and the other developed economies' inflow accounted for $567 billion, 88% of the M&A total. This means that the developed economies were selling out their businesses, an indication of business and/or economic weakness, to developing nations or to other developed nations. China in 2015 reportedly spent $131.7 billion to acquire American business equity for economic transformation and global economic development (2016/2/25).

Greenfield projects implied by its term are plans to build plants and facilities on a virgin soil. These projects enhance production capacity and stimulate economic activities beside infusion of money to the nation. It is where the economic activities will be carried out and jobs will be created that in turn will provide economic growth and prosperity. As the table above indicated, in 2015 GPs accounted for $721 billion, 42% of total inflow. Developing Asia led the pack with $299 billion, a slight increase over 2014, and accounted for 42% of total GPs, followed by the EU 19%, U.S. and Canada 11%. According to fDi markets of *Financial Times*, the first 6 months in 2015, India topped the 10 leaders in GPs with $31 billion, China second with $28 billion. It shows the investors' confidence in Asian economic development and where economic actions will be in the future.

Maybe it is for operational, tax savings, or safety reasons. Costs of corporations to relocate or set up headquarters and divisions in another country are FDI corporate reconfigurations. CRCs do not get involved with another business entity, nor do they affect actual financial resources movement. It is merely a bookkeeping transaction which makes adjustments to the national accounts of the international balance of payments. It enhances the financial position and corporate administrative activities in the recipient countries. In 2015 the CRCs reached to $335 billion, 20% of the total FDI. Developing Asia, excluding Japan and South Korea, was the major beneficiary, receiving $213 billion or 64% of the total. U.S. and Canada came in second place with $110 billion, 33%. It is likely that in 2015, multinationals relocated headquarters or set up shops in developing Asia mainly for operational needs and in America and Canada possibly for safety and stability because of wars and oil market turbulence in the Middle East.

The underdeveloped countries, which are almost absent from the above FDI tables, generally suffer an elevated risk and low profitability economic condition, shying away from big global private investors, especially where war, political turmoil, and social unrest prevail. Therefore, their economic growth and social improvements were mostly funded by their government, foreign aid, and the international financial agencies. In the next decade, China, with its state capital, will extend her help to those countries in Asia, Africa and Latin America for basic infrastructure construction, economic development, industrialization, and social improvement, as discussed early. It might prove to be a mutually beneficial engagement. Although their economic contribution is not highly significant, it will boost some economic growth.

Participants in the 2016 World Economic Forum held in Davos, Switzerland, from January 20 to 23, 2016, proclaimed the forthcoming 4th industrial revolution which is preceded by the mechanical, electrical, and electronic industrial ages. With digital and cyber applications as a background, the new era will usher in more automation, such as robotics, which requires more investment in capital and human brain. Employment in science and technology sectors will expand, but other sectors will diminish. The net result will be reduction of jobs, between 5 and 7.1 million, in the 15 major economies in the next five years. Female will most likely be adversely affected.

In general, the developed economies are in the 4th industrial revolution process, transitioning from producing general merchandise to high-tech and intelligence products. Mainly because high labor costs are uncompetitive in producing common goods, it leads to importing of more goods than exporting for domestic use, except in Germany. German labor costs were not lower than most advanced economies. However, Germany possesses excellent automobile, heavy machinery, and chemical industries which helped to make Germany the world's top exporter until 2009. German brands such as Audi, BMW, Mercedes Benz, and Porsche dominate the luxury car segment worldwide; Volkswagen's Beetles (people's cars) are beloved by the young and old alike. And electricity generators as well as chemical products are welcomed globally, helping Germany to maintain a trade surplus.

As pointed out by a U.S. trade official, intelligence products have become the most important export items, accounting for 60% of the value, more so than aircraft, armament, corn, soybean, etc. and providing 40 million jobs in America (see 7.3). However, the transition to the high tech and intelligence industry has not produced significant enough benefits to support the domestic economy and employment. Like the iphone case cited earlier, it caused high unemployment, a huge trade deficit and polarization of income and wealth in the U.S. Therefore, maintaining economic stability and growth by the advanced economies is mainly supported by consumer and government spending, and investments powered by public and private debt. In the U.S.A. from 1970 to 2010, 40 years in a row, it was averaging $730 billion debt per year (5.3). It is somewhat like the Ponzi scheme Mr. Madoff played except it is for the nation.

With a sluggish economy, low competitiveness and high labor costs coupled with the diminishing ability to attract tech talent to the U.S., Robert Gordon of the U.S. National Bureau of Economic Research points out that the United States no longer enjoys a 3.2% GDP growth; from 2012 to 2032, a 1.9 % growth rate is expected. Nanotechnology, 3D printing, gene sequencing, and automation technology could replace human workers. In any case, growth of GDP will be snapped, creating a new era of economic stagnation, for not only the U.S., but the whole world in the next 20 years (2013/10/26). Brain power and capital investment will replace manpower and some materials, leading to high unemployment, under consumption and an economic slowdown in the advanced economies.

The Conference Board also projects a slow growth for the mature economies and predicts by 2018 China will replace America as the top world GDP. The global economic growth will mainly be generated by the developing economies in Asia and Africa. The projected world economic development data by the Conference Board are summarized in the following table.

World Economic Development, 2015 to 2025

GDP	% of World GDP			Rate of Growth, %				
Year	2015	2018	2025	2015	2016	2017	2016-20	2021-25
U.S.	16.7	16.2	14.9	2.4	1.7	2.0	2.0	1.6
Europe*	18.5	17.9	16.7	1.9	1.8	1.7	2.1	1.7
Japan				0.5	0.5	0.1	1.4	1.6
Mature Economies				1.9	1.7	1.8	2.1	1.8
China	15.6	16.3	17.2	3.8	3.8	3.9	4.5	3.6
India	6.7	7.3	8.2	7.3	6.8	6.5	6.0	5.5
Other Asia				4.8	4.5	4.6	4.6	4.2
Latin America				-0.7	-1.1	1.3	2.5	2.4
Brazil				-3.9	-3.8	0.0	2.2	2.3
M. East & N. Africa				2.9	2.6	2.8	2.3	2.2
Sub-Saharan Africa				3.1	2.6	3.0	5.0	5.2
Russia, C. Asia & S.E. Europe				-1.0	0.3	1.6	2.4	2.3
Emerging Market & Developing Economies				3.1	3.0	3.6	4.0	3.6
World Average				2.5	2.4	2.7	3.1	2.8

*28 EU member nations plus Iceland, Norway, and Switzerland.

In the meantime, the U.S. promotes two grand economic development accords for the near future. The Transatlantic Trade and Investment Partnership (TTIP) were initiated by President Obama on February 11, 2013, in his annual State of the Union message. It was agreed on by the EU Commission President Barroso. The proposal will further integrate the American and EU economies. Estimated benefits of TTIP are an additional two million jobs, $150 billion trade increase, and GDP growth of 5% and 3.4% for the U.S. and EU.

Both the U.S. and EU are developed economies that tend to compete more instead of supplement each other. For example, Boeing and Airbus are against each other and the agriculture businesses on both sides of the Atlantic are receiving government subsidies. Then, there are already so many trade liberalization rules implemented under WTO. So, the benefits might not be as rosy as expected, and the agreement is met with strong oppositions from unions, charities, NGOs, and environmentalists, especially in the EU.

The agreement was intended to be finalized in 2014. Fourteen rounds of talks since produced not even one chapter of agreement out of 27 chapters presented for negotiations. Sigmar Gabriel, German Vice Chancellor and Economy Minister, said on August 28, 2016: "In my opinion, the negotiations with the United States have de facto failed, even though nobody is really admitting it". With the Brexit a reality, it further dampens the chance for TTIP to success.

Another American project is promoting the Trans-Pacific Partnership consisting of Australia, Brunei, Canada, Chile, Japan, Malaysia, Mexico, New Zealand, Peru, Singapore, the U.S., and Vietnam. TPP, comprising 40% global GDP, is the largest trading block in the world. The goal is to enhance trade and investment, to promote economic growth, and to create jobs. The negotiations were supposed to wrap up in 2012 but were bogged down by the issues of agriculture, intellectual property, services, and investments. The negotiation was finally concluded in October 2015 and is awaiting approval by each of the member countries. It certainly will play a positive role, enhancing economic activities among the member nations. However, it is not exclusive, limiting members' ability to engage in economic activities outside the organization; as well the treaty also duplicates or overlaps so many bilateral, multilateral, and international trade agreements in the same area so that the ultimate benefits are substantially reduced.

The U. S. Democratic congressmen voiced strong opposition to TPP based on labor unions' rights, the environment, and other concerns. In the 2016 U.S. presidential election, major candidates Bernie Sanders, Hillary Clinton, and Donald Trump all opposed TPP. Japanese farmers are upset about lowering tariffs, and the Australian Conservative Party lost seats in July elections. Both situations pose additional uncertainty for the passage of TPP. On January 23, 2017, right after the inauguration, President Trump issued an executive order to terminate U.S. participation in TPP, thus effectively ending TPP's existence. Observers believe that the Regional Comprehensive Economic Partnership promoted by China and India will replace TPP, with all TPP members, excluding all 5 American nations and adding 9 Asian nations. The 16 nations' RCEP is also duplicating most of the existing free trade agreements. Nonetheless, it is a step forward in the right direction and will enhance regional economic cooperation and integration.

Although the European Union has the world's largest economic output, the member states still retain their sovereignty in economic decisions, lacking unified collective policies and actions. In the practical sense, they do not constitute a single economic entity. So they have to compete among themselves and the countries outside the EU as well. The 2008 fiscal crisis caused the most trouble in the EU and several governments needed to practice austerity budget cuts. Although these measures will weaken consumption, the EU's vast market is conducive to economic development and will strengthen economic cooperation with other European countries. And, there is at least €315 billion European Fund for Strategic Investment in three years. By the end of 2015, only 50 billion have been dispensed. The recent economic accords between China and the U.K., Holland, Germany and France will further enhance European economic activities in the next decade.

Back in the 1970s and 1980s, Japan recorded economic booms, technological advance, and rapid social progress. Japan seemed destined to become an economic superpower, surpassing the United States not only in its economy, but in other areas as well. Meanwhile the Japanese people had circulated the belief among themselves that in World War II, Japan failed to beat the U.S. in the battlefields; it would now conquer America with economic power. However, the ambition turned to nothing by the

1990s. Not only did the Japanese economy register no growth but recorded a regression since 1996. Not until 2010 did Japan's GDP surpass that of 1995, lasting for 15 years.

Japan's economic booms before the 1990s were mainly powered by the wars in Korea and Vietnam. Japan was a major U.S. military supplier, and its military personnel station and recreation centers in Asia greatly benefited its business and enhanced its economy. Once the wars concluded, it was the end of the Japanese rope. Currently, Japan is facing similar economic dilemmas as the United States, i.e., high labor costs, low competitiveness, factories relocated abroad, product outsourcing, and the highest national debt to GDP ratio (245%) among the major nations. From 2000 to 2009, GDP grew by 8.57%, averaging less than 1% annually. Therefore, most experts do not expect that Japan's economy will have a great leap forward in the next decade.

The major developing economies of China and India enjoy the low wage advantage as compared with the advanced economies. India and Brazil incur a trade deficit, i.e., production lagging behind consumption requires debt and investment to foster economic stability and growth. The foreign direct investment statistics for the three nations taken from UNCTAD, between 2004 and 2013, are as follows:

2004-2013 Foreign Direct Investment, China, India, Brazil			
2004-2013, FDI	China	India	Brazil
Inflows, million $	903,579	257,890	402,109
Outflows, million $	510,138	121,411	62,208
Net inflows, million $	393,441	136,478	339,901

India's newly elected Prime Minister Narendra Modi, a commoner representing the poor, shaking off almost 70 years of elite families' grasp on Indian politics since its independence in 1947, gives a ray of hope that the era of the people may have arrived. It raises much optimistic expectation of improvement in living standards, education, economic development, and social progress. But in reality, India imports more than its exports, i.e., consumption is greater than production or producing not enough to support its own people, relying heavily on investment to make up the slack and to stimulate economic growth. The above table shows that India's ability to attract foreign private capital in 2004 to 2013 has been only 64% (257,890/402,100) of Brazil and 29% of China.

However, in 2015 India became the most favorite FDI Greenfield project destination, mainly attributable to liberalizing its FDI policies in sectors, ownership percentages, use of local resources, government approvals, etc. It's 100% foreign ownership of FDI in most sectors, including some defense industries in India vs. 49% cap in key sectors in China. Moreover, it might not be that simple to shake off the culture of bureaucracy and the habit of democratic debate that have been there since its independence, as well as the thousand years feudal tradition.

As the table in this section indicated, Brazil has the lowest merchandise trade to GDP, 27.2%, among the major economies and the highest service sector to GDP, 69.3%, except for the advanced economies, which most likely came from the Brazil's big government and large welfare programs. With exports lagging imports and consumption overrunning production, Brazil, too, needs investment to prod its economic activities to compensate for the big government and welfare spending. The president of Brazil, Dilma Rousseff, who won her reelection in 2014, pledged to practice budget austerity in order to revive the economy but met with protests over welfare cuts and corruption. Corruption is rampant; as discussed in Section 5.8, just 11 months into 2011, six government department ministers in Brazil resigned due to corruption. On May 12, 2016, President Rousseff's powers were temporarily suspended as she faced impeachment proceedings. She was impeached by the senate on August 31 removing her from office.

In 2016, manufacturing labor costs were $9.88 per hour in Brazil, probably the highest in the developing nations, uncompetitive in most general production. The growth of the economy was mainly powered by the commodity boom and government spending which accounted for 20.55% of GDP in 2012. Brazil has the Venezuelan syndrome and is very much following the Venezuelan social development path; it hinges on investment to sustain its economic growth. Brazil hosted the Summer Olympics in 2016 which should have boosted economic activities. The development of the Union of South American Nations will accelerate regional integration providing a positive economic effect to Brazil.

On May 19, 2015, China's Premier Li was in Brasilia witnessing the signing of 35 accords in production capacity, infrastructures, and finance, etc. as well as the construction or renovation of the Olympic facilities.

China will provide $27 billion in financing. Additional needs may come from the New Development Bank established by China, Russia, India, Brazil, and South Africa (BRICS nations) or other international institutions. These activities will help stimulate the economy.

At the end of 2015, the Association of Southeast Asian Nations formally declared the existence of Asian Economic Community (AEC) which comprises Thailand, Malaysia, Indonesia, Singapore, the Philippine, Borneo, Vietnam, Laos, Myanmar, and Cambodia. In their treaty signed in 1997, the first five funding nation's alliance affirmed that they will respect each other's independence, self-determination, equality, national and territorial integrity, non-intervention in each other's domestic affairs, and peaceful means of solving disputes as principles governing their relationship. The alliance is modeled after the European Economic Community and set tariff reductions by 10-40%, as members see fit, as its initial plan. In the 2003 alliance decision, they aimed to totally eliminate tariffs, to realize the free flows of labor, finance, and other services by 2020, but now they have moved up to the end of 2015 for a total economic integration. It is estimated the regional output will double in 15 years to $5.2 trillion, and per capita GDP increase from $4,130 to $6,618. Based on the last three years of records, seven nations in this group had an average GDP growth rate higher than 5.4%, so it is a reasonable expectation that the group growth rate will be at least 5% (2016/1/2). It is a shot in the arm to the global economy.

The Bank of America conducted a survey of 173 financial fund managers who oversee $449 billion of assets, about the current world economy. A whopping 92% of the respondents believe that there will not be any improvement, slow growth in 2016. A majority indicates that the world economy is in the bust stage of the economic cycle since 2008 which means a possible negative growth. Forth-five percent of respondents say that China's economic growth will be slow down, the greatest risk to the world economy. This same pessimistic sentiment was aired by business and government attendees at the 2016 Davos World Economic Forum, who have lost confidence in China's economic development. Their concern is based mainly on the financial and monetary mismanagement. For example, the uncertainty of Yuan exchange rate made by the Chinese officials since August 2015 caused a massive exodus of funds from China; $1 trillion in 2015 cited previously, which shocked stock markets around the world. Second, the volatile mismanagement of Chinese stock markets led to a negative effect on the world stock markets (2016/1/24). However, the western stock market professionals contended that the Chinese market was due for a major correction because the price earnings ratio was so much higher than the average in other markets. And then, a 7% market price fluctuation triggered the panic alarm to halt stock trading set by the Chinese security regulatory officials was certainly an incompetent policy. Finally, the transparency issue: The government never made it clear about the Chinese currency exchange policy nor on the reform of local government debt and excessive production capacity of state enterprises.

The above pessimistic observation about the Chinese economic future was basically directed at the financial mismanagement in recent years, which certainly will have a negative impact on the economy. However, it is not the major factor; the global Chinese economic activities such as aid to Africa, Belt and Road plan, and other infrastructure construction in addition to its domestic economic development plan will be the additional driving force to push for a higher export and higher economic growth for China. China's economic performance in the next decade compared to its past record during 2013-15 is likely to improve. If China maintains a 7.6% vs. 2.2% for America growth rate during 2012-2014, by year 2021, China's total output will likely be double that of the United States GDP in real value, i.e., adjusted for both PPP and LRP.

China's economy, adapting to its needs and reality, is in the mode of constant evolution. For example, to foster domestic consumption, wages and salaries were raised, giving people more purchasing power. Thus, losing cost advantages led to some factories to be relocated to lower labor cost areas, such as to Bangladesh or Vietnam. As a result, the policy also reduced exports and employment, causing foreign trade to shrink. The urbanization policy has several objectives besides promoting the service sector for healthy economic growth. In the last three years, an average of 11 million jobs per year was added to urban employment, which enhanced the service sector as well as the consumer purchasing power (2016/2/16). The next major economic policy promoted by China is infrastructure construction, especially One Belt One Road, HSRS for international, and CRRT for Chinese cities, which will accelerate resources flows, stimulate economic growth, and improve social conditions around the world.

In the next decade, the signed global economic development agreements with China run in the trillion dollars, financed by Chinese government, international banks, and Chinese private businesses, spreading over most continents on earth. Some development projects are already under way, such as the China-Pakistan infrastructure development corridor, linking China to Europe and Africa. In addition, China put the One Belt One Road plan into action with the formation of the Asian Infrastructure Investment Bank, which received international enthusiasm. This plan will provide economic activities and growth around the world as it has been expanded. Together, the Chinese economic accords reached with the Caribbean, Latin American, European and African countries since 2015 will enhance economic activities and growth in China and round the world. Taking the Africa development plans as an example, in 2016-18, the three years $60 billion investment mainly in infrastructural construction will require lots of manpower and material from local sources and large amounts of material, parts, machinery, equipment, etc. to be shipped out of China or other parts of the world to those construction sites. It will create jobs and stimulate business activities for all economies involved. China will have to step up production to satisfy these additional demands, enhancing employment, exports, and growth of GDP. The tremendous amount of natural resources required for these projects will help to revive the sagging commodity industries around the world and to utilize China's surplus production capacity. It is a winner for all.

The 2016 G20 Summit was held in Hangzhou, China, on September 4-5 under a heavy cloud of trade protectionism and the anti-globalization movement. This public sentiment is mainly due to factory relocations and product outsourcing abroad by the multinationals of the advanced economies in the recent decades; this in turn caused high unemployment, huge trade deficit, and economic downturns at home leading to a greater gap of income and wealth between the poor and the rich. Thus, it softens economic demand and slows down economic activities in the advanced economies. At the Summit, besides other monetary and fiscal policies, industry innovation and infrastructure investment are suggested as major tools to promote economic growth. Other consensus includes improving governance and restructure of global economics, financials, trade, and investment systems. The agenda on world affairs which includes sustainable economic growth directed by the UN, Paris climate agreement, industrialization and improving living standard of underdeveloped world set this Summit apart from its predecessors. It was especially welcome news to Africa and other poor countries around the world.

In summary, the advanced economies, because of wage rigidity, have nowhere to go but to take up the high-tech intelligence industry transformation; however, the path is not so easily pursued and may not necessarily benefit the domestic economies. The advanced economies, except Germany, would still need to be powered by debt, government spending, and investments for economic stability and growth. Some developing nations like Vietnam and Indonesia will duplicate China's economic success, contributing to global economic growth. However, the main factor influencing global economic growth will depend on China's economic development, i.e., expanding domestic consumption, domestic and global infrastructure investment activities as well as U.S. and other major economies' performance. Despite all of the pessimistic observation about China's economic development, China went on to record the second highest GDP growth rate among the major economies. Most international agencies give 6.7%, 1.6%, and 0.6% of the GDP growth rate in 2016 for China, America, and Japan respectively. Thus, their contribution to the world economic growth will be 41.3% for China, 16.3% for the U.S., and 1.4% for Japan, based on 2015 price as determined by the China National Statistics Bureau (*wenweipo.com*, 2017/1/14).

8.7. International Military Movements

Pacific territorial disputes heated up in recent years, involving Russia, Japan, Korea, China, Vietnam, the Philippines, Malaysia, and Brunei. Military exercises in the East China Sea and South China Sea are frequently held. A report released by the U.S. Strategic and International Studies indicated that in 2011 a total of $224 billion was spent on the military in Asia. China, Japan, and India led the pack, with $89.9, $58.2, and $37.0 billion respectively, but all are dwarfed by American military spending. The U.S. military budget in 2011 of $670 billion accounted for 40% of global military expenditure, more than double that of 2001 (2012/10/16).

The U.S. based website, "We are the mighty", predicts that by 2020 there will be 10 major military conflicts around the world. The conflicts involve the following parties: NATO and Russia in Eastern Europe; U.S.

and China in the Western Pacific; Saudi Arabia and Iran in the Middle East; India and China; Southeast Asia nations and China; Israel and Muslim radicals; and civil wars in Iraq, Turkey, and Afghanistan, with the Kurdish independence movement escalating as well. The North Korea's increasing nuclear threat poses another possibility for a large-scale military confrontation.

The U.S. and Russian nuclear arsenals are equally shared, and each has the capability to destroy the Earth several times. The U.S. has 10 active aircraft carriers and numerous warships, its naval power without a rival in the world. In addition to having the advantage in military aircrafts, with missile offensive and defensive systems continually upgraded, the space and the Internet warfare capacity have also been aggressively pursued. Then, there are global networks of embassies, consulates, the Central Intelligence Agency and National Security Agency providing intelligence and surveillance capability on all matters of interest to America. With no doubt, the United States is now the world's only military superpower. But with the economy stagnation and budget cuts, the national policy driven by the laboring class, if followed through by the government elite, America will deemphasize the armament and space programs and keep people's welfare and other social benefits as items of priority. This will certainly weaken America's military super power posture.

China successfully launched a hypersonic glide vehicle (HGV) on January 9, 2014, with up to 10 times the speed of sound (7,680 mph), dubbed WU-14. HGV is capable of evading any missile defense system and performing precision strikes. Currently, the U.S. and China possess the HGV working technology; India and Russia are close behind. According to the experts, if successful, HGV could significantly alter global military positions, and the U.S. military superiority could meet serious challenges. According to the Tokyo based The Diplomat magazine quoted sources from U.S. government intelligence that China conducted two successful tests on November 1 and 15, 2017, a new missile, DF-17 which was equipped with HGV intended for operational deployment. It was the first of its kind and will be operational by 2020, ahead of similar projects under development by the U.S. and Russia. The HGV can take out any missile defense system such as THAAD, and performing precision strikes with nuclear or conventional payload. Thus, it will pose a new challenge to the U.S. defense (thedipromat.com 2017/12/28). In addition, unconventional warfare, such as the 9/11 Al-Qaeda attack, the Internet, and space warfare are growing rapidly and will likely also affect the U.S. military position.

Earlier in 2012, the Obama administration announced a policy to reemphasize Asia, adjusting the Pacific and Atlantic military strength to 60 vs. 40 ratios. American troops have long been stationed in Japan and South Korea since the end of World War II. Recently, Thailand and Singapore have made air and naval bases available to the American military, and the U.S. intends to return to its old bases in the Philippines and Vietnam. Meanwhile, the United States actively participates in various activities in the Asia-Pacific organizations and will send its Secretary of Defense, for the first time, to attend the 11th Asian 28-nation Security Summit, proclaiming to safeguard maritime navigation freedom and regional security and stability, as a counterweight to China's growing military power.

The chairman of the U.S. Global Strategy and Transformation Consulting Company comments on the U.S. intensifying its military presence and alliance in the Pacific for containing Chinese expansion and influence as follows: "America lacking financial resources, the Asia-Pacific alliance with loose allies has neither a common threat, nor a concept of the common areas interest, very vulnerable. Japan places undue reliance on America; South Korea is concerned only with the threat from North Korea; India worries about its border with China and Pakistan; the Philippines is a U.S. fiscal burden; despite all the potential in Vietnam, Hanoi does not want to annoy Beijing" (2012/5/30). Of course, the Asia-Pacific countries welcome the American presence for providing free military protection so that they can strengthen their bargaining position with China, and at the same time, they may profit from the American military expansion in the region, such as the Thai and Singapore bases' rental and other military related income.

There are more differences than similarities between the U.S. and Asia-Pacific countries, whether they are in the cultural, educational, economic or social aspects. The majority of them do not need America's latest technology, do not appreciate American customs, and are entirely out of tune in religion, especially in Indonesia, Malaysia, Bangladesh, Pakistan, and other Muslim regions, as they fiercely demonstrated against the United States for smearing the Muslim prophet by one of its citizens. China has a long relation with Asia-Pacific countries: cultural affinity, similar lifestyle, and close trade relationship. In recent years, China has strengthened its ties in the area, some with aid or loans in economic and social development, such as the construction of the Pan Asia high speed railway system. It improves the host country as well as the Chinese economy: an all winner relationship.

America gets no protection fees from these Asian nations, and there seems to be no other benefits to be made. On the contrary, the U.S. has to dig into its pockets to pay for base rental and other military expenditure for a military presence in the region. Does that mean America is getting a lousy deal? The main purpose is to suppress China's expansion and growth, because currently only China poses a potential challenge to the U.S. as the only global superpower. Maintaining that status will provide much leeway for the U.S. in determining and controlling world affairs and their development; it will also help to maintain the dollar's global supremacy and unlike, Greece, the ability to float national debt in the international market at a relatively low cost without mandatory fiscal austerity constraints while maintaining government spending and economic stability. In the meantime, the implementation of the monetary easing policy will devalue the dollar and reduce the actual debt. Backed by the United States' huge military forces, this leaves the creditors no choice but accept its mercy.

In order to maintain the superpower status, the United States has very strong reasons to engage China in the East China Sea or South China Sea, weakening China's strength and delaying its ability to challenge. Besides, costly U.S. weaponry can be put to use; otherwise, after ten years, most of them will become useless scrap metal. However, China is not Afghanistan or Iraq; there is no UN or Western powers' support for the American military action; moreover, America does not have overwhelming military superiority over China. As a result, both may suffer substantial casualties, and the conflict may escalate into an all-out war that would include attacks launched from both sides in the Internet, space, economic, and financial areas. Since both parties are heavily interwoven in each other's economic and financial interests, and a war's adverse consequences spells out huge losses to the parties involved followed by global economic recession, there might not be a winner. Then, the international agenda, such as global warming, North Korean nuclear development, etc. requires mutual assistance and cooperation from the U.S. and China. The stakes are extremely high; the parties must evaluate the consequences carefully before launching into action.

The RAND Corporation made its study available to the public in July 2016, "War with China, Thinking through the Unthinkable." The research was sponsored by the U.S. Army and conducted by the RAND Arroyo Center's Strategy, Doctrine, and Resources Program, a federally funded R&D center sponsored by the U.S. Army. The authors of the lengthy report assumed a time frame from 2015 to 2025 in the western Pacific Ocean. The conventional warfare without nuclear weapons may be mild to severe in intensity or short to long in duration, giving four scenarios. The U.S. wishes that its allies, especially Japan, would get involved in the conflict with China.

According to the report, China possesses the anti-access and area denial system (A2AD) that prevents American gaining control and destroying its defenses. Then there are China's East Wind 21D missiles capable of sinking an aircraft carrier. Together, America is denied an outright military victory. Both sides will suffer heavy military losses. Economic damages from a one year long war may be to the tune of a 25-35% GDP decline for the Chinese and a 5-10% for the U.S., according to the study's estimate. The war may incite political protests and demonstrations in the U.S. and may revive anti-Communist party factions and minority independent forces to challenge the current Chinese regime. Finally, the war would inevitably reduce the parties' global strength, making them less effective in international affairs. Overall, the losses to the Chinese are expected to be higher than the U.S. and heavier in 2015 than in 2025 because the Chinese economy and technology are supposed to get bigger and stronger as time goes on.

Since the war spells catastrophic losses to the parties, as the report authors contend, leading to a world economic recession and impeding global construction and progress, a Sino-U.S. war should be a very high priority to avoid for both countries. The authors of this study go on to suggest that the Chinese counterpart should make a similar study so that a more realistic assessment on the cost and effect of a Sino-U.S. war could be ascertained, avoiding unreliable speculation. The report further suggests avoiding or minimizing the war for both governments to include crisis management, better communication between military leaders, and civilian control of the military, and instant and unfiltered hot line for top leaders before or during the war. However, the study did not cover aftermaths of the war that entail cost, extent, and speed of economic and social recovery for the parties involved and the new world order after the war as well.

In the Middle East and Africa, social unrest and civil wars will continue, especially with the presence of ISIS, which poses a real threat to the Baghdad regime. The Yemeni civil war has intensified and may develop into a confrontation between Saudi Arabia and Iran. The U.S. anti-terrorist officials said that although the top leaders were eliminated, Al Qaeda has branched out to Yemen, Somalia, Iraq, and North Africa, and its organization has become more complex and unpredictable. The situation has not improved and threats remain (2012/4/29). August 2, 2013, the U.S. State Department issued a warning that Al Qaeda may launch attacks and ordered the closure of 24 embassies and consulates in 17 Middle Eastern countries (2013/8/3). A report prepared by a team of analysts from the CIA, Defense Intelligence Agency, NSA and others was submitted to the White House after the Paris attack by ISIS on November 13, 2015. This report contradicts President Obama's earlier claims that ISIS is basically contained. Even dropping thousands of bombs and deploying 3,500 U.S. troops and other coalition trainers by the West it did not prevent ISIS's expansion and their recruiting more followers. Then globally, there are many nations and organizations who are sympathizers, followers, or supporters of ISIS. Unless ISIS suffers a major defeat in Iraq and Syria, it is likely to strengthen its forces and influence around the world (2015/12/7). This is another source of war and social unrest.

IX. Democracy in Crisis, New World Order Needed

At the end of World War II, in order to prevent the expansion of international Communism, U.S. Secretary of State George Marshall proposed to Congress to rebuild the European economy, improving people's living conditions, because poverty is the best breeding ground for Communism. The European Recovery Program, also known as the Marshall Plan, quickly passed Congress. The U.S. provided $13 billion in financial and technical assistance to non-Communist countries in Western Europe, lasting from 1948 to 1951. The plan focused on recovery from wartime destruction, modernization of industries, reducing tariff barriers, promoting economic growth, and improving people's living standards. By 1951, the GDP of all plan participants increased by more than 35% from 1938. Politically, Germany, Italy, and Spain abandoned their authoritarian regimes, establishing constitutional parliamentary governments. Western Europe enjoyed political stability and economic prosperity, filled with social freedom and optimism that has lasted for some 60 years. Goodwill, cooperation, and reality promoted the desire for uniting into one large entity, thus the European Union was born in 2000. However, since the financial crisis in 2008, many EU members have high national debt and face financial austerity, leading to economic recession, political and humanitarian crises, and a democracy crisis.

9.1. National Debt Mounting: Democracy is in Trouble

On a Tuesday election afternoon, chatting with colleagues in the faculty lounge about whom we should vote for, one of my colleagues said, "I voted for my pocket-book". This statement really is the gist of the democracy election system. People are not choosing the virtuous and capable leader to improve society for the benefit of the country but mainly selecting the best fighter who can fight for their best interests and more rights. Members of Congress are elected in this manner, so is the president. This is based on an assumption that those interests favored by individuals are bound to benefit society and the nation as well. True, in many cases, the interests of the individual and society are consistent. For example, improving one's education enhances personal status and is also conducive to social progress. However, in lots of situations, personal interests conflict with society, such as an increase in welfare which puts a burden on society.

Over the past 40 years, European politicians have been relying on providing people with more welfare benefits, higher retirement pensions, and better health care to get elected. Therefore, the current crisis in Europe is not only financial and economic; many people worry that democracy is also in peril (2012/5/16). Currently, Greece, Italy, Ireland, Portugal, and Spain's governments have been reorganized, some more than once. Greece has the worst situation. Just like the aforementioned teamster said most clearly: The two Greek political parties in the past 30 years each offered voters higher welfare as a mean to win votes, resulting in debt piling up higher. Now it is not only an economic and political crisis, but also a humanitarian crisis (see 7.2).

Although the United States is not Greece, it also needs to follow the rules of the democratic election system. The president, who is no emperor, is the people's servant and must comply with the people's wishes. Lawmakers from both parties also have to fight for the voters' rights as their No. 1 priority in order to get elected. Early in August 2012, President Obama went beyond the legislative powers of Congress, ordered a halt to the repatriation of non-criminal illegal immigrants, and accepted applications for residency and work documents. Pew Research estimated 1.7 million people benefited from the order, among them 75% from Mexico, the other mostly from Central America (2012/8/8, 24). Three months before the election, President Obama promulgated this executive order; the motive is self-evident. Therefore, the nature of the U.S. political problem is no different from that of Europe; in addition to expanding welfare benefits, medical and social services, vast resources are devoted to the military buildup and weaponry research and development. Now, the U.S., by virtue of its superpower status, can continue to survive on debt; however, sooner or later, it will have to face the reality of a $19.25 trillion national debt as of April 26, 2016 (USdebtclock.org). This is the self-destructive cocoon process of the democratic election system. For a period of less than 70 years, European and American democracies have encountered an unsolvable problem, nearing the end of an erratic path. There is nowhere to go. Democracy is in serious trouble.

Secondly, the social policy decisions under a democratic system are based on the majority's choice. Although hard-work and being thrifty are the main forces to get rid of poverty and make progress, human nature tends to favor leisure over work, spending over savings, so that there always will be more poor people than rich. Humanity is also somewhat selfish in its own interests (partially our self-preservation nature) so that demonstrators are all chanting for more welfare benefits and opposing tax increases. In 2011 the French government raised the retirement age, causing millions of workers to take to the streets in protest (2011/11/21). Greece, Spain, and the United Kingdom had repeated demonstrations against government austerity measures, and the United States had the Occupy Wall Street movement spreading to major cities. These demonstrations and movements lead to political unrest and social instability.

Politicians catering to voters' desires will only increase the financial burden on the rich. Yet, taxes must be fair and reasonable, not stifling motivation to earn more income; otherwise, they would cut off sources of tax revenue, tantamount to taking the eggs by killing the bird. Lack of wealth and minimal investment will lead to economic stagnation, rising unemployment, and the suffering of the whole society. Unless the wealth is ill-gotten gains, taxing the rich is not Robin Hood behavior but a legal means employed by the majority to rob the minority. It is an unjust act which runs contrary to the concept of fairness and justice.

9.2. Renouncing the Interest Group Struggle: Electing Capable and Ethical Leaders

The one person, one vote electoral system deciding major social and national issues, at first glance, seems to be the most equitable and fair principle. In reality, it is the most unfair system. Let us tentatively group all voters based on their contribution to society into three categories. The first group voters are self-disciplined, nurturing of their children to be useful to society and have a healthy and happy family. They also are dedicated workers, law-abiding citizens, charity volunteers, and they prompt business, government and society to complete their plans. This group of voters pay taxes, donate to good causes, volunteer service to the community, are the foundation of social stability and the sources of national prosperity and progress. They make significant contributions to society.

The second group of voters cannot keep jobs for long, are unable to make ends meet, abandon their families, and the whole family, young and old, depend on government welfare benefits for a living. This group of voters also includes the disabled, old, and sick, who are unable to make a living. Society should extend compassionate assistance to them. But, this second group is a burden on society and the country.

The third category of voters commits all kinds of evils, destroys public property, robs and murders. They are frequent visitors to the court and residents of the prison. This group of voters not only makes no contribution to society but causes significant social unrest and destruction. All three groups of people have the same voting rights (decision making power) on their own interest such as welfare benefits and common social issues; it is an utmost unfair and unreasonable phenomenon.

The power of decision making should be based on contribution to society. Those who make more contribution should have more say. Additionally, those who undermine social orders and violate the laws should be deprived of their voting right (decision making power). Today, some people pay taxes, volunteer services, support and improve society. Some, except the disabled, old, and sick, have no employment and enjoy the fruits made by others. Some violate law and order, destroying public facilities, increasing the burden on taxpayers. With the exception of a few whose voting rights are forfeited by the court, all have the same voting rights, leading to the above Robin Hood phenomenon. It is in essence one group of people using legitimate processes to rob another group of people. Therefore, redistribution of decision making power based on contribution to society is in order. It is fair and reasonable. And more importantly, it can prevent the self-destructive cocoon making process leading to the destruction of democracy.

In principle, the contribution to society should be used to determine how much decision power each voter should have. Contribution include: (1) experience, work or other qualifications; (2) knowledge, specialist education or above; (3) skills, technology, art, literature, or music creation, etc.; (4) dedication, paying taxes, donations, and volunteering. For example, if the voting rights of ordinary citizens is 10 points, then nurses, college students, volunteers, add 1 point per year; paying taxes, charity donations, add 1 point per thousand dollars per year; unlimited accumulation. On the other hand, those lacking a high school diploma or in prisons subtract 1 point per year, cumulated in the same manner to determine voting power. Detailed scoring rules should be drawn up by an independent committee, soliciting public opinion, and revised every two years before an election. Therefore, one person's voting power may be greater than hundreds or even thousands of people combined, so that democratic elections are no longer contests of giving out welfare benefits and fighting for each voter groups' interest but become the collective will of social contributors and their expressed social ideals and mean to achieve them. It is a progression from a simple quantity election to a quantity and quality electoral system. It is true implementation of equality and human rights.

Furthermore, the electoral system should adopt the conflict of interest rule, because when personal interests are involved, few people are able to remain calm and objective, resulting in bias in decision-making. Therefore, when the interests of any segment of society is the beneficiary of a vote, including ethnic, regional, community, or parts of business, the beneficiaries' votes should be set aside to be fair and impartial. Of course, the election process should not be used to penalize any part of the population or business because it constitutes an act of discrimination. A prime example is the recent proposed legislation, SCA 5, by a California Latino state senator which limits Asian-American students in the California State university system to provide room for Latino and African American students.

9.3. Reforming Remuneration System: Encouraging Employee Initiative

Since the financial crisis, more economic problems continue unabated. Yet, Congressmen can vote to raise their own pay and business CEOs can provide for them generous golden parachutes if they lose their jobs. In addition to a sound and effective control system, there is a need to strengthen people's vigilance and initiative so that justice can be done to reverse the unhealthy trend.

U.S. federal government agencies don't have to worry about profit or loss, being subject only to budget constraints. Generally, the remuneration of federal employees is double that of private enterprises, and members of Congress can also set their own salary standard, almost completely losing its objectivity and fairness. For example, since 1946 congressional pay has seen an increase of nearly 25% per year for more than 60 years in a row (see 5.8). Therefore, it is necessary to establish an independent remuneration committee which will determine all federal government employees' salaries, benefits, and retirement standards, from the president and judges down to clerks and laborers. Modifications of remuneration must first be initiated by an independent committee, approved by Congress and then the president. Selection of the committee members shall be nominated by the Supreme Court and agreed to by Congress and the president to ensure members' independent and impartial stance to achieve fair and reasonable goals.

Early in March 2013, a referendum limiting CEOs' salaries and generous compensation for loss of office (Golden parachute) was presented to the Swiss voters. A 68% of the electorate voted in favor of the proposal, and the banking center of Zurich got as high as 71%, which showed the extent of people's disgust toward this unjust practice employed by global business executives.

Private enterprise is almost completely losing control by allowing executives to make decisions as they wish without any oversights. The board of directors is window dressing, just executives' cheerleaders and their rubber stamps. The board does not fulfill its duty and obligation of setting business policy and overseeing its operations. The main reason is that the function of the board was not modified followed by changes in stockholders' composition so that executives monopolize corporate operation without the need to answer to anyone.

When securities' trading was not popular, corporate investors, mostly a few large shareholders were involved in the business operation and management themselves. In contrast, today there are few large investors and mostly small shareholders who are unable to participate in business management, delegating their rights of selecting directors to the company, leading to executives monopolizing the board activities. As a result, the board is no longer representing shareholders but has become the executives' operating tools.

Today, it is believed that businesses not only need to be responsible to their owners but also need to serve social interests so that capitalism may survive. This need includes taking care of their employees, customers, suppliers, and government at all levels as well as stock market interests besides shareholders. Even some social groups not directly related to the business, such as environmental organizations, human rights activists, investment funds, securities brokerages, and local communities, etc., are concerned with the business interests and have legitimate reasons to participate in the business decision-making process.

In addition to business executives on behalf of the shareholders, the board of directors should also include interest groups, inside and outside of the company, in response to the current needs. Each interest group should nominate and elect its own director so that the board is no longer an agent of company executives but represents all interest groups of the business. Each director should be elected independently and vested with legal authority so that the board can discharge its responsibility of corporate policy decisions and operational oversight. Then, businesses under capitalism may achieve the goal of serving the owner as well as discharging their social responsibility and prevent being overrun by socialism.

Functional details of the board would be prepared by the relevant professionals, especially the Financial Industry Regulatory Authority (FINRA). Of course, congressional legislation is required to achieve the necessary reforms. In the implementation of the new policy, any controversial or unclear items should have a public hearing before the Securities and Exchange Commission makes the final decision.

Corporate financial statements are important documents, providing the company's financial condition and operating results. Businesses use this information to measure the effectiveness of their policies and as a basis for future planning. Shareholders and employees, based on operating results, demand the proper profit share they deserve. Governments apply the reports to determine all kinds of taxes levied as well as for economic planning. Investors review the statements and related information to decide the flow of funds in the financial markets. Therefore, the accurate and timely reporting of corporate financial statements is a vital concern for all interested parties. To assure accurate financial statements and not mislead investors, the Securities Exchange Acts require that all published financial statements must be audited and signed by a Certified Public Accountant (CPA). So, it creates a lot of business opportunities, but it also brings a plight to accountants who are difficult to escape (serving two masters at the same time).

Currently a company hires accountants (CPAs) to audit its financial statements and to provide audit opinions for the benefits of investors. The company is a customer of the accounting firm and the U.S. business motto is "the customer first". Under this circumstance and within legal limits, accountants will always try to accommodate the wishes of company executives. They may whitewash unfavorable conditions or glorify operating results. Unless it violates the law, the accountant is unlikely to voluntarily reveal to the public and to follow up on the company's operating problems or financial scandals. Otherwise, it is bound to lose a client, which is a self-defeating act. As a result, the accountant will have to overlook the interests of investors.

To avoid a conflict of interest by accountants and to encourage accountants to report the company's financial reality, there must be a change in accountants' relationship with the company. If accountants concentrate on serving investors, it will be possible for accountants to pursue any financial irregularities or illegal behavior of the company and to expose them to the public. Accountants' auditing compensation must be borne by the investors, by a fund replenished from the securities trading surcharge, which is the logical arrangement, because investors are the primary beneficiaries of published financial statements.

Since the Enron and WorldCom scandals, Congress passed the Sarbanes-Oxley Act in 2002, which established the Public Company Accounting Oversight Board empowered to audit the auditors, subjecting the accounting industry to unprecedented scrutiny for their work results and escalating the cost of published financial statements. Also, currently major accounting firms have separated auditing as a special division from other management services to avoid the appearance of conflict of interest. However, these changes do not alter auditors' fundamental relationship with the businesses being audited. The problem remains the same.

Auditors should be nominated by the investment community and agreed to by the board of directors. Operational details of the auditors' appointment should be formulated by all concerned parties and the American Institute of CPAs.

To prevent military suppliers presenting the government with doctored bills, the U.S. Congress enacted the False Claims Act in 1863, also known as the Lincoln Law, because President Abraham Lincoln signed the Act during the Civil War. The Act provides an informer statutory protection and a bonus of 15-30% of the losses recovered by the government. The purpose was to encourage people's enthusiasm in exposing illegal conduct so that losses to society could be minimized.

After 1986, 2009, and 2010 amendments, it has had remarkable success in recent years. Between 1987 and 2008, the federal government recovered $22 billion from providers who made bogus claims, mostly medical providers and military suppliers. Meanwhile, 29 states also have similar laws, to avoid the wasting of public funds. Currently, almost all larger corporations are involved with public interest. Like Tyco International, as mentioned earlier, not only did the company suffer a loss of $600 million, all related parties, such as governments, would have tax revenue reduced, equivalent to a community loss. Hence, there is a need to extend this law to include all large private enterprises, especially those whose stocks are traded publicly so that violations may be exposed sooner, preventing more and larger losses. This is not intended to encourage employees to conduct mutual surveillance, especially in their private life, because it is an invasion of privacy, an illegal act. But often when employees perform their daily duties, they would discover these illegal transactions. Like the Tyco CEO who misappropriated funds to pay for his wife's birthday party, for an example, the company's finance and accounting departments should identify the purposes of $2 million bill or bank fund transfer to properly account for the item. Promptly reporting this illegal conduct would likely have avoided a huge loss of $600 million. If the finance staff knowingly fails to report the misconduct, they would have neglected their duty, and this is a breach of the law, too.

In recent decades, the economic development in China as observed by economists shows that Chinese efficiency and economic achievement have overtaken the records of the past. For example, in 30 years, China had completed industrialization and urbanization faster than Japan and South Korea by 20 years. The major difference is the enterprise decision-making and supervision processes. China's state-owned enterprises are collective state capitalism, the efforts by the government for the people's national interests. Before China's economic reform in 1980, many state-owned enterprises were corrupt, wasteful, with low efficiency, and operating losses were pervasive, like many bureaucracies around the world. Economic reform called for shutdowns, sales, or joint public-private partnerships of state-owned problem enterprises and streamlined operations in addition to stricter regulatory scrutiny. The survivors were mostly healthy and competitive businesses. Therefore, the key is not only what kind of doctrine is being touted, but also the presence of a sound, strictly enforced regulatory and oversight system.

Western business enterprises are private capitalism, mainly for the purpose of enriching investors. Today, this objective is being hijacked by corporate executives to enhance their own interests so that the effect on the national economy is deplorable. The severely adverse effect of iphone outsourcing on both domestic and foreign economies is a good example. If there is no fundamental change soon, the Occupy Wall Street and socialist movements will inevitably develop to a large extent coupled with the rise of the laboring class. Private capitalism in its current state will not be able to survive and sooner or later will be replaced by another economic system.

The above reform policies will promote equitable income distribution, narrowing the wealth gap, strengthening control and supervision of public entities and private enterprises, encouraging employee initiative so that the public and private workers will also serve society's interest. Democracy and capitalism may survive.

9.4. Restoring Family Function: Establishing a Sense of Responsibility

Rapid technological progress over the past century has dramatically improved living conditions and changed the way of life, but there are no significant innovations in the structure of society. As mentioned earlier, the family remains the most important social unit responsible for nurturing the younger generation, including physical and mental health, good character, moral standard, knowledge and skills, and willingness to assume responsibility. So, if family is dysfunctional, it would be difficult to expect a stable and progressive society.

Currently, the biggest threat to healthy families in America is the lack of stable marriages. Families with both parents account for only 48% of the nation's households. It was 78% in 1950, a drop of 30% in 60 years (see 5.6). The majority is single-parent families; lacking one parent and having one income, adversely affects children's upbringing and family finances. Secondly, with sexual liberation, fidelity in marriage is no longer the norm. The report shows that of fathers under the age of 45, nearly one half have an illegitimate child and that does not include those without a child just having mistresses alone (see 5.6); it is bound to cause marital difficulties and increased financial burdens, resulting in broken marriages. Neither congressional legislation nor public demonstrations can save marriage. Society must reaffirm the marriage institution and condemn all extramarital sexual relationships, exemplified by the leaders in all walks of life, working together with concerted and long-term unremitting effort so that the adverse trend may be reversed.

Unfortunately, moral standards have greatly declined in recent decades, as a former president was implicated in a sex scandal and a well-known pastor acknowledged having an illegitimate child. Society is in dire need of models for the masses to follow. This is partly the result of the democratic election system, because peoples are not choosing a virtuous leader but the most capable fighter for their interests. Only when the emphasis is on character, choosing virtue in addition to ability, will there be exemplary leaders who can lead the masses, turn the tide, and change the status quo. Then, the family will be able to restore its function of nurturing and educating its children.

The United States is a heaven for young people because they are the future masters of society, determining the nation's prosperity or failure, showered with love and respect. America is also a paradise for children who enjoy all kinds of privileges without corresponding required obligations. Right now, a lot of young people regard their home as a bank, restaurant, and hotel, but need not pay nor sign an IOU. Generally, American families make a very early transition from a father-son to a brother relationship as children are paid for helping with housework until they reach adulthood (between 18 to 21 years old); parents have no parenting obligation. This might be the reason why high school graduations are solemnly celebrated by the family much more so than university commencements.

The strong suit of this tradition is that children will learn about work and finance in early life preparing them for independent living. At the same time, it will also reward children by forming an industrious habit. The biggest downside is that it leads children to believe that they are entitled to a living and education, and there are no reciprocating duties required. This have-rights no-obligations concept deeply rooted during childhood is likely why so many workers are irresponsible, with a dereliction of duty, causing serious accidents; many welfare recipients demand their benefits, as though society owes them a living. As everyone knows, the world cannot just have rights without obligations; the two co-exist, indispensable to each other. Giving out benefits without obligations is charitable distribution, which equals the laboring fruits of others.

Therefore, children should be told that housework is their duty and the source of their rights.

Secondly, the lack of filial piety in Western culture means children do not return the upbringing efforts of their parents. Most of the old, disabled, and widowed are being sent to nursing homes, mostly becoming a group of non-persons, wanted by nobody, paid for mainly by the government. This is another social phenomenon that rights (benefits) and obligations (responsibilities) do not go hand in hand; it is grossly unfair.

The Eastern World piety concept should be promoted. Children have a moral and legal obligation to take care of their parents when these parents are unable to live by themselves. Singapore in 1995 enacted a parents' support law which provides government loans and other benefits to assist children living with their disabled parents. Offenders will be sentenced to one year in prison or a fine of 10,000 SD (US $7,964). Currently, it has reached 70% of the elderly living with relatives, and the government is planning to build housing that would accommodate three generations, taking into account convenience, family fun, and privacy, hoping to reach a higher policy goal (2012/2/25). China recently issued regulations requiring regular visiting to parents to provide emotional support by their children; it is especially needed in a one child per family society. The Singapore policy is a winner on several fronts: It improves the quality of life of the elderly; with the elderly present, it may help with child care; it enhances family happiness; it saves on medical costs; it reduces government funding for the old and disabled; and it strengthens the concept of social responsibility. Especially when the United States has budget shortfalls, with deficits in Medicare and Social Security funding, it needs workable solutions. This program provides more advantages than flaws and should be vigorously pursued. Moreover, it can also put an end to some family immigration which totally depends on government benefits for living and becomes an unfair burden to taxpayers.

Stable marriages and healthy families improve children's physical and mental well-being and education, and reduce drug abuse and criminal activities. It is the first step in moving toward social improvement, but also an indispensable step.

9.5. Legalizing Drug Trade; Strictly Prohibiting Firearms

President Nixon in June 1971 asked Congress for an additional $155 million as an emergency budget to fund a war on drugs. In 40 years and seven more Presidents who also vowed to fight the drug trade, it is estimated that the total cost of the war on drugs is over $1 trillion, with 40 million people detained or jailed in the U.S. for drug law violations. The United Nations Committee on Global Drug Policy issued a statement announcing the failure of global anti-drug efforts (*Kitsap Sun Daily*, Columnist Leonard Pitts Jr., 2011/6/19), not to mention the staggering loss of life related to drug trafficking and use of drugs.

Just in the first five months in 2012, Chicago had 203 homicide cases, almost all related to drug incidents (2012/7/11). When President Calderon of Mexico took office in December 2006, he stepped up the fight against drug cartels. In the five and a half years since, more than 47,500 Mexicans have died in drug-trafficking violence. Mexico blames the U.S. for its insatiable demand for drugs requiring a large quantity of drug inflow. Meanwhile, relaxation on arms sale control on the American side led to a flood of illegal weapons into Mexico. Drug lords killed each other as a result of interest disputes or suffered casualties caused by fighting against the anti-narcotics officers (2012/5/14). In short, the cost of fighting drugs is huge and the war on drugs has been lost on both fronts. Neither the suppliers nor the users of illegal drugs have been diminished but have increased.

Narcotics distribution and drug abuse in the Western world took a turn and developed into a new social pandemic: prescription drug abuse. According to the UN-linked International Narcotics Control Board's report in February 2016, almost all global supply of opioids, synthetic drugs capable of suppressing pain just like opium, are consumed in the developed countries. In 2015, the global opioids market was $34.9 billion and demand for the drug will grow 3.2% annually to the year 2021. From 2011 to 2013, the U.S. led the world by consuming 43,879 defined daily doses, a unit measuring drug consumption per million people, followed by Germany 23,352, Canada 22,941, U.K. 5,227, world average 3,027, and China 91. Projection of this drug used in 2016 is 1.36 billion grams in America and 76.86 million grams in China. The Chinese shunning away from opioids may be caused by the historical opium addiction rampancy which triggered the Opium War with the British leading to a century of disaster to China. The epidemic of prescription drug abuse has taken its toll in the U.S. Death due to opioid overdoses was higher than that of traffic accidents. President Obama told the audiences of the summit on prescription drug abuse on March 29, 2016: "You see an enormous ongoing spike in the number of people who are using opioids in the ways that are unhealthy, and you're seeing a significant rise in the number of people being killed." (*Bloomberg Businessweek*, 2016/4/4). This legalized narcotics trafficking, of course, requires participation from the medical personnel and its related professions. Numerous doctors and medical personnel have been convicted for abusing prescription drug. It is the same as the old drug trafficking for high profit; the problem will not go away.

With all these years' efforts, there seems to be no end in sight, and the war on drugs seems un-winnable. Then, why not change the course and adopt the popular American strategy -- If you cannot fight them, join them. That is, legalize the drug trade and levy high taxes on both users and traders. Earmark the tax revenue for anti-drug education, prevention, and addict rehabilitation and employment counseling. This will alleviate the financial burden of anti-drug campaigns, surveillance, detention, and conviction of drug traders and users. Furthermore, it will save hundreds of thousands of lives each year.

The federal government has proclaimed that the use of drugs is no longer a crime, but a disease. Since 2012 the states of Alaska, Colorado, Oregon, Washington, and the District of Columbia have legalized the use of cannabis, and 23 states have approved medical marijuana. The Department of Justice announced in October 2014 that Indian tribes could legalize cannabis use the same as the states do. This is the beginning of the policy change; it should go further to make a thorough and complete reform on legalizing drug trade and use.

In the 14th century, Western Europe relied on knowledge of gunpowder and firearms coming from China to make portable guns. Since then, guns became the most lethal weapons in fighting. It was also the most important weapon that the Europeans used to colonize the world. Before the founding of the United States, local governments required pioneers to carry firearms to fight off Indians. Since independence, the U.S. Constitution guarantees people the right to bear arms, so that owning firearms has become an undeniable American right and tradition. Even after the Sandy Hook School massacre on December 14, 2012, a Gallup poll showed 74% of people are against a ban on gun ownership. The

National Rifle Association (NRA) has become the most politically influential lobbyist for gun ownership rights.

Americans own a total over 270 million guns; almost everyone has a gun, including babies, the highest per capita gun ownership in the world. Every year more than 100,000 people are killed or injured by firearms, and 30,000 people died in gun-related incidents in 2010 (2012/4/14, 7/24). Massacres occurred all over the world, but the United States had the most. On July 20, 2012, a shooting took place in a small town cinema in Colorado; 12 people were killed and 58 wounded. These movie fans and the murderer had never met before, no score to settle. In 1999, also in Colorado, not far from the cinema carnage, two Columbine High School students killed 12 schoolmates, one teacher, injured 21 people, and then committed suicide on the school campus.

A brutal shocking massacre took place in Newtown, Connecticut, on December 14, 2012. A 20-year-old, Adam Lanza, committed matricide at home, then carrying automatic rifles, broke into Sandy Hook Elementary School, killing 20 children, the principal, and two teachers. He committed suicide when the police closed in. The tragedy triggered national mourning. President Obama attended the memorial at the city's high school, consoled the victims' families, and ordered the country's flag at half-mast. He also designated Vice President Biden as Chairman of an ad hoc committee to propose legislation preventing similar tragedies from happening again. Gun control sparked another round of heated debate nationwide; preliminary polls showed more than half of the people in favor of banning the automatic high-capacity rifle. The NRA became the target of gun critics, forcing the NRA to take a stance, but it still advocated violence against violence, arming the nation's school campuses as the most effective policy.

Again, on October 1, 2017, a solo gunman, Stephen Paddock took a position on the 32nd floor of the Mandalay Bay Resort and Casino which was overlooking a crowd of 22,000 funs of the country music festival. He possessed a total 32 guns; 12 of which were equipped with bump-stock or rapid fire devices. In less than 15 minutes, shooting by Paddock from his hotel window took 58 lives and 527 persons injured, surpassing 49 deaths occurred in June 2016 in the Orlando, Florida massacre. It set a record high in the American history for one shooting incidence. President Trump ordered flags at half-staff and visited the wounded a few days later declaring the act from a pure evil. Who and what do we blame for such senseless massacre? And how do we prevent these incidences from repeating again? These same questions have been asked for numerous times, but no effective action has been taken yet.

The gun violence epidemic prompts increasing casualties in civilian encounters with law enforcement personnel. In the first six months of 2016, civilian deaths caused by the police action registered at 491, an increase from 465 for the same period in 2015 (2016/7/9). Almost in the same period, policemen killed on duty numbered 26 in 2016 as opposed to 18 in the first six months in 2015 (*USA Today*, 2016/ 7/9). When the violence involves police and African American, it is not just a case of homicide. It is a racial conflict, a case of police brutality against the black community as condemned by the civil rights activists. On August 9, 2014, a white policeman while on duty shot a black youth to death in Ferguson, Missouri, causing protests and demonstrations. When a grand jury consisting of nine whites and three blacks announced no criminal charge against the officer on November 24, 2016, it triggered further violence. Protests and demonstrations became a daily ritual and turned into arson, vandalism, looting, riots, and gun fighting lasting several months in Ferguson.

After the Ferguson incident, shooting deaths involving a policeman and a black person occurred in New York, Louisiana, Minnesota, Oklahoma, and Charlotte, North Carolina. Protests and riots were seen in Charlotte beginning September 22, 2016, and lasting more than seven days. Shootings have become a part of the Black Lives Matter movement which stresses riot first, ask questions later, thus ignoring the merits of the shooting in each case.

The movement might have inspired the assassinator who ambushed a group of policemen maintaining the orderliness of a protest organized by Black Lives Matter in Dallas, Texas on July 7, 2016. The police department suffered five deaths and nine injured, the highest number of law enforcement personnel casualties since 9 /11. The killer voiced his intention to kill more policemen, especially white officers. The same intention is echoed by some radical black groups. There is no trust but hatred and different expectations between law enforcement and black communities. And with the American gun culture, it adds insult to injury making the situation worse. It has torn the American community fabric apart. President Obama on the night of the Ferguson grand jury's verdict addressed the nation, urging the public to be calm and accept the decision by the judicial system, to renounce violent action. He also said: "We need to recognize that the situation in Ferguson speaks to broader challenges that we still face as a nation". This challenge is nothing less serious than terrorism attacking America. The Charlottesville, Virginia violence on August 13, 2017 caused one young live which was the result of a head-on confrontation between the white supremacist and the anti-racist protesters. It speaks to the fact again that the race-relation problem in America is far from over.

Eliminating undesirable violent cultures, prohibiting firearms, improving social and economic justice, living standards and education, and nurturing various realistic expectations to form a consensus may reduce the fundamental causes of mistrust, ease racial tension and conflict, and thus, pave a road to racial peace and harmony.

Outrageous gun massacres happen so frequently in the country, but that still does not convince people of the need to prohibit firearms, because the belief is they are necessary to protect personal and family safety. However, today is not the pioneering era, except in wilderness areas; there are police or security personnel to maintain public safety. Criminals would find it harder to succeed if they didn't have firearms, but others believe that people need guns to protect freedom and democracy, to rally and combat against dictators. A group of amateurs is neither organized nor trained. Common sense shows that the amateurs' chance to win a battle against a regular army is near zero; and the chance to be killed is almost certain. Stricter control of gun trade and ownership, including examination of buyer identity, background, and mental fitness, were advocated as measures to end firearm abuses. The physical and mental states of gun owners are subject to change, and guns can also be transferred or borrowed. To manage 270 million firearms and their owners, hoping to achieve effective control goals, is almost impossible. Therefore, the only sensible way is to totally prohibit civilian firearm ownership so that massive killing and senseless loss of life can be avoided. It will greatly reduce the variety of criminal violence and racial tension because firearms also are the most lethal weapons; thereby, it improves social order and alleviates the government financial burden on public safety and imprisonment of criminals, one stone killing several birds. A central depository should be established to accommodate a sportsman's use of guns.

9.6. Renouncing Armament; Honoring Moral Superiority

The history of mankind is full of plunder, fighting, murder, violence, and war, mainly due to greed. Those who have nothing desire to have something; they demand more after having something. It is an endless circle, never reaching contentment. When it applies to international relations, countries covet territory, resources, power and control. Thus, nations advocate weapons development and rally allies to strengthen their war posture. After World War II, democracy, human rights, and rationality were greatly promoted by the West as the new world orders. However, nations still resort to force, instead of reason, as the main way to solve disputes. Ultimately, they waste valuable resources, compete to kill, and do not benefit mankind.

Stockholm International Peace Research Institute in its 2012 annual report stated that global armaments costs reached $1,735 billion, accounting for 2.5% of world output. The U.S. tops the world with a total of $711 billion, accounting for 41% of global arms expenditure, 4.7% of its GDP; China comes in second, $143 billion, 8.2 %, and 2.0% respectively. (Using the same PPP and LRP adjustments in 7.2, they are $379 billion for the U.S. and $222 billion for China, which is 59% of U.S. expenditure.) Russia is the second runner-up with $71.9 billion, 4.1 %, and 3.9% respectively: Britain and France round out the top five; all are permanent members of the United Nations Security Council.

In addition to the commitment of valuable resources for armaments, world powers are actively forging various alliances to strengthen their military posture, fighting for global rights and control. After the collapse of the Soviet Union, the Warsaw Pact disappeared, and some Eastern European countries changed course, such as Poland, joining the North Atlantic Treaty Organization; others joined the Collective Security Treaty Organization, and the Shanghai Cooperation Organization.

The U.S.-led NATO was founded in 1949 and now includes Eastern European nations; it has a total of 28 member states, accounting for 70% of global total arms spending. Besides, the U.S. also has alliances with 22 Partnership for Peace countries and 15 nations with military liaison mechanism. America is the most active militarily in the world. Except in

Africa and South America, she is pervasive all over the globe and is either a member or an ally of bilateral or multilateral military treaties. As a result, the U.S. military spending exceeds the sum of the defense budget of all other major countries combined.

The African Union's Peace and Security Council coordinates military operations in Africa. There are 22 countries in the Middle East forming the Arab League. South America has its South American Defense Council. Almost every nation on earth belongs to certain defense groups or military alliances.

In the Diaoyu Islands dispute between China and Japan, although the United States has repeatedly advocated that peaceful means should be sought to resolve the difference, it stressed that the U.S. is bound by the military treaty to assist Japan in military action. Similarly, China has military alliances which may develop into a multinational war. It seems that the U.S.-Japan military alliance would equally apply to the Japan-Russia territorial dispute, but the U.S. never mentions it. Maybe the U.S. and Russia have a secret non-aggression treaty not known to the world.

International disputes should be resolved based on justice, fairness and reasons, and merits. Asserting the alliance as the grounds for military actions is tantamount to the World War II Germany, Japan, and Italy military alliance which violated humanitarian axioms and intended to dominate the world by force for its own interests.

The United States and Russia each has more than 7,700 nuclear warheads (bombs), enough to destroy the Earth several times. China, Britain, France, India, Pakistan, and Israel, each with 80-300 nuclear warheads, are also trying to strengthen their nuclear capabilities (2013/6/3). Iran and North Korea plan to join the ranks of the nuclear club but are met with international sanctions. Why can some countries have nuclear weapons, but others cannot? In fact, all this nuclear competition is sadly marching towards global destruction and human extinction.

In his Current Affairs show, Dmitry Kiselyov said that "Russia is the only country in the world that is realistically capable of turning the U.S. into radioactive ash". Isn't that a horrible condition? (Kiselyov was named by President Vladimir Putin in December as the head of a new state news agency (2014/3/18)). Since nuclear weapons are possessed by multiparty, once a nuclear war starts, it may be marching us down the road towards the end of world and mankind, a total destruction. The world is under the shadow of the U.S. and Russian nuclear arsenal, threatening the existence of mankind, the worst kind of terrorism. The third Nuclear Security Summit was held in The Hague, Holland, on March 14, 2014. The main agenda was how to exclude terrorists from the possession of nuclear arms. In fact, all countries which possess nuclear weapons are threatening human existence, and therefore, they are terrorists. Violations of human rights are no more fundamental than threatening human survival. The United Nations Commission on Human Rights should formally charge all nations possessing nuclear weapons with human rights violations, especially the U.S. and Russia.

The Treaty on the Prohibition of Nuclear Weapons was formally adopted by negotiators of 128 nations on July 5, 2017 at the UN New York headquarters. The ceremony of ratifying the treaty was held on September 20, 2017 by 51 nations excluding all nine nuclear powers, at the UN general meeting which was denounced by the Western nuclear powers. This treaty will become legal force 90 days after its signing. On October 6, 2017, the Norwegian Nobel Committee named ICAN, the International Campaign to Abolish Nuclear Weapons, as winner of the 2017 Nobel Peace Prize. These two events though symbolic are a step toward the right direction especially during the nuclear war tension between the U.S. and North Korea.

Many Americans, especially hawkish Republicans, advocate military superiority. Of course, no country is willing to be in an inferior position, leading to an arms race which increases chances of military confrontation and eventually the outbreak of world wars. Using force to resolve conflicts is a temporary solution because the loser is forced to accept the outcome. Therefore, in their mind, they are not fully convinced that the settlement is fair and just. Once they have a chance, the conflict may start all over again. Besides, use of force is basically an uncivilized, barbaric act. In a civilized world, fairness, justice, and reason should be sought to settle differences. This virtuous approach will make the parties involved full heartedly agree to a settlement which is peaceful, sustainable, and lasting. Therefore, instead of military confrontation, the virtuous approach should be used as the main mechanism to resolve international disputes. And this rational approach together with moral superiority should be promoted to resolve disputes and to foster world peace and harmony.

The U.S. has military installations around the world. The

government claims that large military facilities and defense budgets are needed to ensure national security, to protect interests abroad, and to maintain international stability and world peace. Furthermore, it claims that the armaments budget and policy are examined and approved by the appropriate parliamentary procedures and there is sufficient transparency.

Safeguarding national security should be confined to national boundaries, not extended to other areas; otherwise, all global affairs may affect national security, leading to war. Maintaining international stability and peace should be the task of the United Nations, not the United States. It is neither the responsibility nor the right of any country. Should the American military surround a border and even courageous objections raised, would there be any practical effect? If weakness faces power, could there be equality in their dealings? When U.S. forces arrested the Panamanian leader in his own country, used chemical weapons in Vietnam, and recklessly bombed Laos and Cambodia during the Vietnam War, were these actions executed in accordance with international legal procedures?

President Obama was in Vientiane, Laos, on September 6, 2016, attending the ASEAN Summit. He announced to the meeting that it was time to unveil the secret American war in Laos some 50 years ago and promised $90 million in the next three years as war reparation for destroying 80 million remaining ordnance. As America lost its battles against North Vietnam, the CIA instigated a covert action of bombing Laos and Cambodia in order to cut off supplies to North Vietnam. Between 1964 and 1973, over two million tons of ordnance was dropped in Laos, more than those dropped in Germany and Japan combined during World War II. Laos became the most heavily bombed country in world history, averaging 10 bombs per person. However, a significant number of bombs were not exploded when they were dropped. The death toll from these delayed explosive bombs was in the thousands per year when the war ended in 1975. From 1975 to 2008, over 50,000 had died and 15,000 were wounded survivors. The casualties continued to be recorded at 48 in 2014. In the last 20 years, the U.S. has contributed $100 million to help with the war damages.

This secret war against Laos on such a large scale was not publicly announced nor approved by Congress. Of course, there was no declaration of war to the enemy. It was clearly an abuse of unchecked military power in action. University students in America staged a nationwide demonstration against the war. Four students died and nine were wounded at Kent State University, Ohio, during the demonstration. The American conscience was alive and well.

Edward Snowden recently revealed that not only did the U.S. National Security Agency collect information on the nation's phone calls, emails, and letters, it also teamed up with the intelligence apparatuses of Britain, Canada, Australia, New Zealand and other countries to monitor world leaders. Even close allies are not spared. German Chancellor Angela Merkel's telephone was tapped for more than 10 years, and until October 2006, 35 world leaders were under surveillance by the NSA (2013/10/29). It caused a global outcry, especially in the EU community, forcing President Obama to make a public statement. He said that collecting intelligence is a routine matter for every country; our major purpose is to prevent terrorist attacks and it is different from stealing technology.

It set off a hot national debate about government power in monitoring people's lives and collection of private information. When Obama was sworn in as President, he vowed to establish the most transparent government in history, to set up a file decryption office, to promote government openness, to provide citizens information as needed, and to explain how taxes are spent. Another Obama government action, using national secrecy as a shield, refused to disclose the Foreign Intelligence Surveillance Court's (secret court) unfavorable rulings against the administration, not just limited to intelligence and national security, but covering all matters, and aggressively persecuted the dissents (2013/6/17). All in all, the government conducts itself under covert operations, secret court actions, surveillance of people's communications, and using drones to kill. The government's credibility has become a big problem (2013/7/14).

American Foreign Policy magazine reported that President Obama intended to build an Internet empire (2013/10/26). The U.S. National Security Agency was founded in 1996 and has the most mathematics PhDs in all federal agencies with generous funding and leading information technology worldwide. The Internet is a new frontier, and there are neither international conventions nor global regulations. America, having the technological superiority, does whatever it can, benefiting the most.

The NSA not only snatches other countries' military, political, economic and technological secrets, but also steals people's privacy and dignity. America, a guardian of democracy and human rights, publishes an annual report on the human rights abuses around the world, but by surveillance its own people and world leaders, it is in grave violation of fundamental human rights. People are unconvinced by the government's assertion of preventing terrorist attacks as a defense. Internationally, there is no faith or trust even among close allies. The time of moral integrity has yet to come.

Hollywood star Matt Damon used to be a diehard Obama supporter but now declares that he and the President are not comrades anymore because he questions the government's actions, such as using drones to kill people and the NSA universal surveillance operation, and whether these actions are agreeable to the concepts of democracy, human rights, and international law. Even former Democratic Party President Jimmy Carter echoed: "We do not live in a democracy" (2013/8/10). On October 2, 2013, a march organized by the Stop Watching Us Union and 100 business and community groups, including the American Civil Liberties Union, the Electronic Frontier Foundation, Libertarian Party, and the New York City Occupy Wall Street Movement, etc. and nearly 4,500 people went to Congress in Washington D.C. to submit a nearly 580,000 people Internet petition. They held banners: Stop mass surveillance, Thank you, Snowden, Stop secret government, and Stop lying. Following the EU summit, Germany and France requested the United States to sign a non-surveillance agreement. Germany and Brazil together with 19 other countries requested the UN General Assembly to adopt a resolution protecting the rights of Internet privacy and declaring that "No one can arbitrarily or unlawfully infringe of people's privacy, family, home, or communications, nor can unlawfully attack the dignity and reputation of others." which will become a part of the International Covenant on Civil and Political Rights. In addition to Cuba and Venezuela, signers of the draft include Mexico, France, Sweden, Norway, Austria, etc (2013/10/27).

Pew Research Center released on August 1, 2017 its findings on global major threats from 30 countries not including China and Taiwan. America is seen as a threat to their countries more than Russia and China. A 38% of poll taken, an increase from 25% in 2013, considered America as a major threat as opposed 30% to the other two major powers. Even its allies or partners were uneasy about America; 72% Turks, 70% South Korean, 62% Japanese, and 61% Mexican felt the America as a major threat to their national security. Among the 30 countries polled, people in 23 countries expressed an increasing threat from America, 3 neutrals, and 4 decreases as compared with the last poll.

Who can read the President's mind to ensure that he does not follow Genghis Khan or the British Empire's ambition to rule the world by force? More importantly, checks and balances is the fundamental principle of a democratic system that prevents a totalitarian dictatorship to emerge. People are not gods or saints, whether individuals, groups, or nations and whether in military, technology, politics, or business, if there are no checks and balances in place for a long time, corruption and an abuse of power will inevitably occur. Tyco International, mentioned earlier, bombing in Cambodia and Laos, and the surveillance conducted by National Security Agency are prime examples of how unchecked powers were abused. Therefore, maintaining a large military force without checks and balances will instead threaten international security and world peace, and destroy democracy among nations. Bullying the weak and minorities is an act of injustice and a violation of human rights.

Armaments and military alliance not only waste valuable resources, but also threaten world peace and human survival. All nations should remember the bitter experience of World War II, renounce using force, subscribe to international laws, justice, and rationality in resolving disputes, treat neighboring countries well, and promote moral superiority. Armed forces should be terminated in their entirety except those needed to maintain public safety. The resources saved could be used to improve people's livelihood and education. In a timetable, those nations which failed to meet the reduction targets would have imposed a military tax, contributing to an international peace fund which will help developing countries to improve social conditions, living standards, and education.

An international travel site revealed its latest list of the most unwelcome tourists. The Chinese come in second, with American getting the title. In addition to the language and custom barriers, visitors from China are often in large groups, noisy, spitting, unruly, with other bad habits, and are averted by the locals (2012/9/9). The bad impression given is understandable because for more than a century, the majority of Chinese people were struggling to subsist and illiteracy was widespread; discipline and manners were almost out of the question. Moreover, due to China's large population, huge crowds were everywhere with limited facilities; shouting, jostling for position, and scrambling to get ahead were essential survival skills that developed into bad habits. Living improvements and more education were the facts of the last few decades. Large groups of Chinese people traveling abroad were a newly developed phenomenon just in the recent five or ten years.

On the contrary, for over a century, America has been the world's richest country. American tourists mostly are the middle class people who know etiquette, have similar customs, no language obstacles, and plenty of cash. On top of that, as a world superpower with its foreign aid program over the years, it should have accumulated a lot of influence and goodwill around the world. However, Americans are considered the most unwelcome visitors, worse than the Chinese. It boggles the mind, almost unbelievable.

In fact, American tourists are scapegoats of U.S. foreign policy. Because of the U.S. military presence around the world, some people regard them as military occupiers who are deeply resented. Second, American TV, movies, and music flood the globe, and some local societies regard them as cultural invasions. Then, American multinationals monopolize some businesses and are perceived as economic predators. The repeated offenses to Islam, adding insult to injury, intensify the hatred of the United States. The local government and residents of Okinawa, Japan, staged numerous protests against the U.S. military bases there. Conflicts with Muslims are even more frequent; they have spread to the whole Islamic world. Recent exposure that the United States disregards human rights and moral standards by using advanced technology to monitor its own people and foreign leaders caused global outcry. Americans may have good intentions and want to uphold justice and human rights for all and to safeguard world peace and stability. But to most people in the world, America is violating their sovereignty, imposing unequal military occupation, and obstructing their freedom and human rights; America is deeply resented. The 9-11 incident was one of the expressions of that dislike. This is America's most serious policy mistake, a grave foreign policy failure. The issue should be addressed intensely with necessary national policy changes so that this, America's worst enemy, can be dispatched. And one of the most important changes for

America is emphasizing moral superiority instead of military superiority. This will benefit the world as well.

Moral superiority consists of the actions which encompass love, compassion, justice, honesty, sacrifice, bravery; and helping the poor, old, handicapped, and widowed from suffering as well as providing relief to those who suffer from natural and human disasters. Currently, although a lot of the rich and foundations offer philanthropic efforts around the world, there is still not enough to meet the needs. And in many cases, only the parties involved can be of help. For example, the recent Asiana Airlines accident in San Francisco showed that the wounded purser, Lee Yoon-hye, assisted passengers to evacuate while the aircraft was on fire, and then she went back to the cabin for a final inspection to ensure that all passengers were safely evacuated. Another petite stewardess, Kim Ji Yeon, carried an injured woman to safety. They disregarded the safety of their own lives, showing the utmost responsibility for the passengers. In stark contrast, the Italian cruise ship Costa Concordia ran aground on January 13, 2012, but the captain ignored any responsibility, abandoning the ship and its 4,000 passengers. He was the first to evacuate. What a huge difference!

In 2014, the youngest winner in the history of the Nobel Prize was named: Malala Yousafzai, 17, from Pakistan. She ignored the threat to her life against the Taliban's ban on girls from attending school. A murder attempt was made on October 9, 2012, by the Taliban. She was seriously injured and hospitalized at local facilities. Later, she was transferred to Birmingham, U.K., for further treatment; she has recovered since. The Malala story aroused people's consciousness around the world, supporting her aspiration for women's equal rights and her courage to challenge an evil authority. The Nobel Peace Prize was awarded to this worthy recipient, and she has become a global moral celebrity.

Promoting kindness and charitable actions and expanding their social influence is everyone's opportunity not just for the rich, foundations, and charities. Almost all people have the conscience of kindness, but most people need inspiration and encouragement to induce their actions. Therefore, to motivate and intensify the enthusiasm for actions of kindness, perhaps the Nobel Prize Award model could be adopted as a means to popularize the moral superiority trend.

Instead of just one prize per category, there could be local, state, national, and global winners, somewhat like beauty contests, giving the awards in categories such as love, justice, integrity, honesty, bravery and so on. Vigorously promoting winners' social recognition will make them moral celebrities, adored and loved by the public just like sports stars. Malala is an excellent example. The moral superiority awards should not be confined to individual contests, but also extended to competition among community groups and nations. This may lead to a new social trend; for this competition, unlike the arms race--military superiority, the more the better; there are very few negative effects. Moreover, this virtuous approach will help to promote interpersonal and international lasting peace and harmony.

9.7. Rising Horizons: Experiencing a New World of Living

Since its inception in 1983, the Internet quickly gained acceptance by worldwide users. Especially in the last decade, the development was very rapid, affecting every facet of people's lives. In addition to disseminating information and ideas, it has evolved into business, politics, the military, and other social fields. The Arabian Jasmine revolution and the aforementioned Muslim terrorists attacking U.S. banks were facilitated by the Internet. Chinese net users recently rallied on the net to expose corrupt officials, an avenue that proved to be rather effective. The Philippines and Taiwan fishing boat incident prompted their countries' Internet users to launch wars (word and sabotage) against each other's country.

The following shows global Internet development.

Worldwide Internet Users, 2011-2013

2012/6/30	Asia	Europe	N. Am.	L. Am.	Africa	M. East	Ocean	world
Users (millions)	1,077	519	274	255	167	90	24	2,406
Global share (%)	44.8	21.5	11.4	10.6	7.0	3.7	1.0	100.0
Area share (%)	27.5	63.2	78.6	42.9	15.6	40.2	67.6	34.3
Growth (%/2000)	842	393	153	1,311	3,607	2,640	219	566
Facebook users (2012/9, millions)	236	243	184	189	48	23	15	937

Most Internet Users (2013/6/30)	China	U.S.	India	Japan	Brazil
Users (millions)	538	245	137	101	88
Global share (%)	22.1	10.2	5.1	4.2	3.7
National popularity (%)	40.1	75.1	11.4	79.8	45.6

Language (2011)	English	Chinese	Spanish	Japanese	Portuguese	global
Users (millions)	565	510	165	99	83	2,100
Population share (%)	43.4	37.2	39.0	78.4	32.5	30.3

By mid-2012, data show over 2.4 billion Internet users worldwide. In 2011, consumer online shopping in the United States exceeded $142.5 billion, accounting for 8% of retail sales and 13% of women's clothing sales. On November 11, 2015, Single's Day, Alibaba online sales hit $14.3 billion and eclipsed last year's record, a single day's world sale record which was participated by merchants and buyers from 232 nations and regions. It is going to become an annual international sale event (2015/11/12). According to emarketer.com's estimate on August 16, 2016, world e-commerce retail sales in 2016 will reach $1.915 trillion representing 8.69% of global retail sales of $22.049 trillion. By the year 2020, the respective numbers will be $4.058, 14.64%, and $27.726. China is the big leader with expected internet retail sales of $899 billion in 2016, accounting for 47% worldwide sales. The U.S. comes in second, about half the size of China, and the U.K. is a distant third, half of the size of the U.S. Social Internet media grew even faster, such as Facebook, having more than 900 million users worldwide in 2012. E-mails of 144 million were sent a day, but nearly 70% of them were Spam (junk mail). In 2012, global Internet users browsed YouTube videos for up to 4 billion hours monthly. Retailers and banks are now developing the global market. Internet users will soon be able to shop in the morning in New York's Fifth Avenue department stores, visit the Forbidden City in Beijing in the afternoon, and attend the Moscow Bolshoi ballet show in the evening. Internet social media will soon develop with speech and image capability for better direct communication. Almost all of the activities around the world are available at one's fingertips.

People can exchange experiences all over the globe and ultimately promote the flow of thoughts and ideas, enhancing mutual understanding and friendships, leading to the improvement of social and racial harmony. Perhaps this trend may help to diminish conflict and war, and to reach toward the realm of world peace and harmony. Today, the government's various controls and language pose the biggest obstacles to realizing this dream. However, these obstacles are insufficient to withstand the force of the Internet globalization trend, and sooner or later, improvement will be made.

Today, the Internet is a very important tool. And like all tools, it has its constructive and destructive uses depending on the circumstances. Since this is virgin territory, there are no conventions governing Internet use. Thus, users do whatever they want and seek whatever they need. Of course, countries with high-tech superiority benefit the most and may use this tool to interfere with other countries' political and social affairs. Therefore, early development of internationally accepted conventions will foster the Internet's healthy growth and security, with global beneficial results.

The 2nd World Internet Conference on December 16-18, 2015, in Wuzhen, China, called for popularizing the Internet globally, fostering cultural diversity, sharing Internet technology, ensuring cyber security, and improving Internet governance. Internet sovereignty, safeguarding cyber security, and cooperation and governance of the Internet by the world community were also emphasized by China's President Xi in his speech to the conferees. And a preliminary agreement on Internet security was reached by the U.S. and China when their two leaders met in September 2015 in Washington, D. C.

The unprecedented cyber-attack affecting 230,000 computers in 150 countries occurred on May 12, 2017. British hospitals, the Russian Interior Ministry, Spain's Telefonica, U.S. FedEx, and Deutsche Bahn were among the victims. Both government and private security experts were powerless to stop the spread of the WannaCry ransom ware. It infected local networks and the Internet for a week until dying down on May 19. The culprit, North Korea is speculated, has not been identified. It is a wake-up call to corporate boards, legislative chambers, and the international community that the time for action on cyber security is now. As suggested by the 2nd World Internet Conference, global cooperation and coordination are urgently needed to propose regulation and enforcement to safeguard cyber security.

9.8. Accommodating Diversity: Fostering Peace and Harmony

Years ago, I met a missionary family who spent years in China and was back in the United States for good. Of course, religion was the inevitable subject of conversation. The wife said, "Jesus Christ is the only God, others are idolatry". Indeed, some people even consider the Catholic Church as not the orthodox religion, holding an extremely narrow point of view. In other areas, some also regard themselves as the world standard and cannot accommodate different ideas, traditions, and lifestyles. They consider other cultures backward and isolate themselves from the rest of the world; more importantly, they lose touch with reality and the ability to communicate with the rest of the world.

The practice of polygamy in Muslim countries is criticized by human rights activists in the Western world. True, whether it is multiple wives or multiple husbands, polygamy as compared with monogamy violates the man and woman equality axiom. However, nowadays it is popular to have lovers or mistresses in the Western world, in fact polygamy. These are almost the same, whether the bottle is half full or half empty. The main difference is that there is no legal recognition for lover or mistress status. Therefore, once they break up, there is no legal recourse on either side in sharing their offspring and property. More importantly, extramarital activities will inevitably result in marital difficulties, increasing family financial burdens, and cause marriage breakups. In a polygamist society, wife and concubines share certain legal rights, keep peace with each other under established social traditions, and likely enjoy a relatively stable marriage and family relationship. Which marital relationship is inferior or superior than the other under the current conditions? The answer requires further study.

Democracy, freedom, human rights, equality, tolerance, fraternity, honesty, and diligence are humanistic ideals, some timeless, but all affected by interpersonal relationships. Thus, human behavior is unlike the principles of natural phenomena, without time and space constraints, immutable. To love, for example, whether today or in the past is love; at home or abroad, one should show loving care, not just to one's relatives and friends, but strangers as well, no exception. It is the consensus of universal ideals. However, does one show the same attitude towards the enemy in the battlefield? The answer may be different.

The U.S. State Department annual report on human rights to Congress may be a noble intent to show concern for humanity, justice, and social development around the world. But it has become an annual report card based on U.S. standards to measure human rights activities in other countries around the world. Moreover, the ideal of human rights is one of America's founding principles, but American women had to wait until 1920 to claim their voting rights, and African Americans, only after the Civil Rights Act of 1964 were able to exercise their full citizenship. Why did these violations of human rights and inequality last for nearly 200 years?

Since the September 11, 2001 terrorist attack leading to the war in Afghanistan, the U.S. military death toll has exceeded 2,000 people in addition to a $36 billion military expenditure each year and $10.4 billion economic aid per year until 2008. Due to logistical necessity, the United States has committed many resources in Pakistan, too. From 2001 to February 2012, the U.S. military and economic aid to Pakistan totaled $20.7 billion. After more than ten years of effort and all the resources invested in these two countries, the U.S. not only did not win over the friendship of the local people but recently turned them into enemies. As of August 2012, there were 30 cases of defections of Afghan soldiers or policemen, resulting in 45 U.S. or coalition personnel killed.

On May 2, 2011, without notice or authorization, the American military intruded into Pakistan killing Al Qaeda leader Osama bin Laden. On November 26th of the same year, the U.S. military in Afghanistan crossed over into Pakistan killing 24 Pakistani soldiers by mistake, triggering fiery, nationwide protests in Pakistan, closing the only pass to Afghanistan for up to seven months, and causing extreme hardship for the U.S.-needed military supplies in Afghanistan. Early in 2012, U.S. troops at the Afghanistan air base in Bahgram burned the holy Koran; despite the U.S. Defense Secretary's apology, it still incited massive nationwide protests.

Monetary aid and relief supplies are sometimes seen as charity from the rich or as a favor given by the boss; heartfelt thanks, but no friendship exists. Feelings fade away with the departure of the emergency. To establish a long-term, durable friendship, both material and human factors are indispensable. The American military focused on the material but almost completely neglected the human element so that years of effort became wasted.

Interpersonal relationships must be sincere, not doped with personal interest; be polite, respectful to others; do not look down on people but regard them as equal; be tolerant of other religions, political systems, and lifestyles; be a good listener and negotiator, not a commander; be sympathetic to others' circumstances and make joint decisions; don't use economic and military advantages to demand contributions by others; and have the courage and virtue to recognize others' good qualities and achievements. Moreover, Americans generally lack foreign language skills and cannot communicate effectively with the local population, thus it intensifies the difficulties in forging a good relationship with local people.

The lack of ability to manage interpersonal relationships is one of the biggest U.S. enemies. The motto of diplomats says: There are no permanent friends and permanent enemies in the world, because as circumstances change, the relationship between friends and foes also changes. But the enemy of interpersonal relationships is unlike other enemies; it is embedded in people's hearts and minds, just like the body and its shadow, inseparable. Only when people abandon their prejudices and accommodate differences, these enemies may be converted into friends.

X. Establishing New World Order and Creating a world Paradise

World War II caused extensive destruction and wiped out most industries in Europe. Goods of all kinds were scarce, especially before the economic recovery. So the quickest way to solve the severe shortage was to promote trade, exchanging the extra for the scarce, which set off an upsurge in international trade. In addition to the General Agreement on Tariffs and Trade and its successor the World Trade Organization, many similar regional associations and bilateral trade accords have been reached since.

With rapid trade development, international economic competition intensifies, resulting in the survival of the fittest. It also brings out a variety of trade-related issues, such as import and export controls, dumping and monopoly, currency exchange rate manipulation, tariff barriers, trade deficits, government subsidies, factories relocating abroad, product outsourcing, economic recession, high unemployment, etc. These issues are the normal development of international trade and flow of goods across national boundaries, but, overall, the trade promotes world economy growth and improves people's standard of living.

If goods are allowed to flow freely around the world, people are not bound by national borders, moving and working freely as they choose; if the governments do not impose controls on monetary flows, world economic activities will adjust as to where and how the production will be carried out. If this trend receives global support, eventually it will reach the domain where goods are best utilized; workers perform to their best capacity; and capital is applied where it is most needed. The world will become a big family, human equality prevailing, eliminating most of the desire to possess and control, and terminating all weapons and military preparation against each other. Mankind will enter into a new realm where nature's bounty will be share by all; brotherhood will prevail universally; prosperity and peace will endure; and finally everyone on earth will arrive in paradise. Wouldn't that be wonderful!

10.1. Implementing Free Flow of Goods: Sharing Providential Grace
People are restricted by their living region and are unable to fully enjoy the gifts of nature. Bananas grown in the tropical region were not often seen in the north before transportation facilities flourished. Through

transportation, demand and supply may be matched up. For nations to protect their industry, resources, employment, and favorable trade balance, etc., a host of restrictions and measures are enacted, as just mentioned above. As a result, it hampers the free flow of goods, reducing production efficiency, slowing down global economic development and improvement of people's livelihood. It also makes it difficult to achieve the goal that nature's bounty is best used and enjoyed by all in the world.

Some may think that this is propaganda to sell products for the advanced economies. Because once the market is open to outsiders, advanced countries rely on their technological superiority and higher production efficiency which inevitably will out-compete others. For example, agricultural mechanization greatly improves efficiency and increases farmers' productivity; therefore, this increases their competitiveness. So, the advanced countries may have an absolute advantage for all industries. If markets of developing countries are open to the outsiders, it will eventually lead to economic recession and serious unemployment. True, this is the possible downside after the local markets are open, allowing free inflow of goods from the advanced economies. For this very reason, the World Trade Organization has provisions to protect underdeveloped countries' infant enterprises, giving them the opportunity to mature so that they can successfully compete with advanced countries. Second, most developing countries have abundant labor resources which is a competitive strength. Finally, by implementing international trade, both the developed and underdeveloped countries are likely to benefit from economic growth and improved living standards. This mutually beneficial trade phenomenon is not easily understood. The economists called it "comparative advantages" which was first pointed out by the British economist David Ricardo in his 1817 thesis. Here is a simple example of comparative advantage to illustrate how mutual benefits may derive from international trade by nations under different stages of economic development.

Nation A and Nation B both need 10 cars and 2,000 pairs of shoes. A has advanced manufacturing technology for both products and an absolute advantage relative to B. However, under certain circumstances, if they divide the work and trade between each other, both nations can save production costs and achieve mutual benefits. The following table shows a simplified illustration of the effect on their economies with and without trade between these two countries.

Illustration of Economic Comparative Advantages

	Car	Shoe	Total
1. No trade, self-sufficient			
A: Quantity needed	10	2,000	
Production hours, each	1,000 hrs.	7 hrs.	
Total hours required	10,000 hrs.	14,000 hrs.	24,000 hrs.
B: Production hours, each	3,000 hrs.	10 hrs.	
Total hours required	30,000 hrs.	20,000 hrs.	50,000 hrs.
A and B, no trade. Total hours required			74,000 hrs.
2. With trade, division of labor			
A: Production hours, each	1,000 hrs.		
Quantity needed	20		
Total hours required	20,000 hrs.		20,000 hrs.
B: Production hours, each		10 hrs.	
Quantity needed		4,000	
Total hours required		40,000 hrs.	40,000 hrs.
A and B, with trade. Total hours required			60,000 hrs.

Without trade, country A needs 24,000 hours of labor to produce both products. If A concentrates on making 20 vehicles and using 10 of them in exchange for 2,000 pairs of shoes from B to meet the needs of both products, it saves 4,000 hours of labor. Country B takes 50,000 hours to make 10 cars and 2,000 pairs of shoes. If B makes only shoes, trading 2,000 pairs of shoes for 10 cars from A, it satisfies the need of both products with a net saving of 10,000 labor hours. The total savings of 14,000 labor hours can be used in other endeavors to enhance output or social improvement, which is a win for both countries. The effects of comparative advantage exist in countless millions of free trade situations. Therefore, when goods are allowed to flow freely with certain restrictions, such as anti-dumping rules, whether they are developed countries or developing countries, all will likely benefit from increased production, economic prosperity, and the ultimate effect of improving people's living standard.

After World War II ended, world leaders began discussing how to eliminate manmade trade barriers, to facilitate the smooth flow of goods, to promote economic growth, and to improve people's living standard. After two years of intensive negotiations, in 1948, 23 countries signed the

General Agreement on Tariffs and Trade. In 25 years of its existence, GATT promoted an annual global trade growth of 8% and the member countries' economy annual growth of 5 %. By 1994, there were 123 member countries, including all major global economies, and in early 1995 the World Trade Organization was established to replace GATT. In addition to goods (covered by GATT), services and intelligence industries were included. Currently there are 157 signing member countries, representing 81% of the 193 countries in the United Nations, and 27 observers who can apply for membership in five years.

The goals of WTO are eliminating trade barriers, mediating trade disputes, ensuring fair trade, accelerating trade flows, promoting economic growth, and improving living standards worldwide. In 2011, world trade tripled the amount recorded in 1990; except for inflation and economic growth, it was mainly the outcome of the WTO's effort.

After World War II, economic cooperation, integration, and development organizations have flourished, such as Europe's EU, Asia's ASEAN, North America's NAFTA, South America's UNASUR, Latin America's ALBA, and the Organization of Petroleum Exporting Countries. Except OPEC, all subscribe to the WTO's ideal, strengthening and supporting the WTO policies, eliminating artificial barriers to trade, and promoting free flow of goods, to achieve the goal of the best use of nature's bounty, to be enjoyed by all mankind.

10.2. Ending Oil Market Monopoly: Ensuring 100% Free Trade

The Organization of Petroleum Exporting Countries was founded in 1960. The organization's announced goal is to coordinate and unify oil exporting countries' policy and to promote stability of the international oil market to ensure: (1) Safe and economical oil supply to consumers; (2) the producing countries' stable income; and (3) the oil companies' fair profit. Currently, there are 12 member nations which are Algeria, Angola, Ecuador, Iran, Iraq, Kuwait, Libya, Nigeria, Qatar, Saudi Arabia, United Arab Emirates, and Venezuela. According to a November 2010 estimate, the 12 OPEC members account for 79% of global oil reserves and 44% of oil production, pivotal to the world oil supply.

Oil can be used as energy and fuel, and also as raw material for chemicals, pesticides, pharmaceuticals, fibers, fertilizers, plastics, and other products. It is one of the most important widely used raw materials, having a significant impact on the global economy. So, oil supply with a stable market price is vital to world economic stability and growth. OPEC claims that in order to maintain international oil market stability, it is necessary to set production quotas for its members, so as to balance market supply and demand, thus maintaining stable oil prices in order to achieve the above three objectives.

Another war between Israel and Arab countries broke out in 1973. Because the United States supported Israel, Saudi Arabia and Iran instigated an oil embargo against the U.S., causing oil prices to quadruple. Since then oil prices have risen more often than declined, and the margins of price changes were also getting larger and larger. The oil price has skyrocketed from $3 per barrel in the early 1970s to a record high of $145 a barrel in July 2007. In 2010-dollar value, to eliminate the effect of inflation, the average prices per barrel were as follows: During 1947-1972 was under $20; from 1973 to 1986 increased to $76; from 1987 to 2003 backed down to $30; then in 2004-2011 set a record of $96 a barrel. Drastic changes in oil prices, of course, affect the income of oil exporting countries. In 2005 dollars, OPEC's total oil revenues peaked in 1980, reaching $572 billion and bottomed out in 1998 to only $120 billion, a drop of nearly 80%. The data testify that before the establishment of OPEC, oil prices were basically stable, with few fluctuations in the international oil market. After the alliance was formed, oil supply was manipulated to promote high oil prices. Thus, it enabled oil-exporting countries and oil companies to make outrageous financial gains at the expense of oil importing nations. OPEC did not achieve its three objectives as it set out to do, i. e., to ensure economic and security of oil supply to consumers, stable income to oil exporting countries, and fair profits to oil companies.

On the other hand, oil exporting countries benefited from the free trade of low priced agricultural and manufactured products, resulting in cheap import prices and expensive export prices, which is also grossly unfair to oil exporting countries. Oil prices fluctuating drastically hamper global economic development and bring a major threat to people living because heating oil prices are sky high. That is the evil effect of the oil exporting countries' market monopoly.

The WTO should face reality and deal with this serious violation of the principle of free trade as an uncompromising policy. Based on the gap between the petroleum and other products price index since 1970, taxes should be levied on all net oil exporters at a progressive rate for five to ten years as the transitional period. If such artificial barriers to free trade still exist, the tax rate will be a full 100% of the difference between the oil market price and its indexed price. Funds collected from oil taxes will be used to reimburse oil net importers so that oil prices and supply will gradually be stabilized, which will help global economic development and improvement of people's livelihood.

In 2011, the sum of OPEC 12-nation GDP was only 4.4 % of the world total. The tax on oil would affect the interests of all net oil exporters, including Russia, Norway, Canada, Mexico, etc., which can form a strong opposition force and inevitably present a stubborn resistance that could interrupt oil supply and adversely affect the world economy. Therefore, most of the nations' support should be attained to mount a strong united front to overcome this reactionary force.

In recent years, the development of new energy sources such as solar, wind, etc. have made considerable progress, and massive oil and gas reserves have been recently discovered. At the same time, new technology accessing shale oil will make the U.S. the world's largest oil producing country and an oil exporter. And then there is a concerted effort worldwide to be environmentally friendly, encouraging saving energy and reducing consumption. So, the pressure on energy importers has been eased somewhat. On the other hand, some oil-exporting countries are not self-sufficient relying heavily on imports for daily necessities. The big oil exporter Saudi Arabia, for example, is highly dependent on imports for survival because its agriculture sector accounts for only 2% of the nation's total output, requiring the import of essentially all food stuff for its people's need. As a result, Saudi Arabia needs foreign products more than foreigners need their oil. Therefore, the embargo of daily necessities may be adopted as a measure against non-compliance.

The oil price plunged in late 2014 and continued on to 2015. In early 2016, it was down to under $30 a barrel, the worst since the 1980s price slump. The sharp oil price drop was attributable to several important factors. Since the 2008 financial crisis, the advanced economies did not recover economically, and developing economies slowed down their economic pace. As a result, demand for oil since then was greatly reduced. Second, the U.S. shale oil production rose dramatically during the period of high oil prices. In 2013 and 2014, America produced more oil than Saudi Arabia or Russia and exceeded its oil import need. And then great global effort and enthusiasm arose for developing green energy and practicing conservation, thus, reducing oil consumption.

When the oil price dropped to $50, it rendered shale oil producers to be unprofitable. The U.S. shale oil industry was paralyzed by operations shutting down or bankruptcy. It was the OPEC strategy to drive out shale oil producers from the market to maintain its monopolistic power. Saudi Arabia has initiated talks with Russia to control production preventing oil prices from declining further. These facts indicate that when oil prices are above $50, there are plenty of willing producers in the oil market, and OPEC has no power to limit oil production. When oil prices drop below $50, there are incentives for OPEC to reduce output quota to jack up prices. However, cheating by OPEC members and un-cooperated non-OPEC producers will make the quota ineffective. So, under the current global oil economics, OPEC is losing its real monopolistic power to manipulate oil market prices, no longer a viable entity. The timing to dismantle OPEC is now.

10.3. Promoting Labor Free Movement: Maximizing People's Potential

Religions, customs, habits, languages, and government regulations lay restrictions on human movement. Peoples are also subjected to union regulations so that supply and demand of manpower is difficult to match up. Although the U.S. has high unemployment, there is a shortage of scientists and technicians as well as farm workers. It requires the U.S. government to issue special work visas and relies on illegal immigrants to fill the gap. Most wage rates are fixed by laws and labor unions' contracts. They are not determined by the force of demand and supply in the labor markets like other resources. As a result, the wage rate fails as an adjuster to balance the demand and supply of labor, resulting in a big wage gap and demand/supply imbalance among nations.

The U.S. Labor Department data show that China's manufacturing wages in 2002-08 averaged $0.57 to $1.36 an hour, equal to 2.1% to 4.2 % of U.S. labor rates, or 48 to 24 times lower than the United States. Because wages are too high, American manufacturers lose their competitiveness, leading to plants relocating abroad or products outsourcing, which cause high unemployment, trade deficits, and economic recession at home. American workers accuse Chinese workers of stealing their jobs. In fact, it was their bosses who believed that they were paid more than the international exchange value they produced, resulting in a competitive disadvantage and hence unemployment. In the meantime, this unequal pay for the same work is unfair and violates basic human rights and the concept of equality, un-democratic.

Some people may worry that a world open door policy, allowing people to flow freely, provides advantages to the poor and undeveloped countries because their people could move into the rich nations to share their wealth and other resources. In fact, the property and resources would still belong to the original owner or country, under their disposal; no changes will occur at all.

People may also think that this is tantamount to inviting outsiders to come in replacing local workers. The facts show that job protection finally depends on economic competitiveness, unrelated to the free flow of people. Back in 1979, the United States had 21,040,000 manufacturing workers, but by 2010 there were only 11,500,000 factory employees, a net loss of 9.5 million, or 45.3% jobs lost in 30 years. During this same period, the Detroit Big Three automakers experienced high wages and poor product quality problems, and lost their competitiveness to imported cars, resulting in the shutting down of some operations and relocating others to the Southern States or foreign countries. The United Auto Workers Union (all Detroit auto workers must be union members) had 1,500,000 members in 1979; the number dwindled to 355,000 in early 2010 (2011/2/22). In 30 years, UAW members were reduced by 1,140,000, about 76% jobs lost, including those moved to the right to work Southern States. The union and government were working vigorously to protect the industries and their jobs, and there was no free flow of people during this period, but so many jobs were gone.

Even before World War II, Detroit was the world capital of the auto industry, a prominent world class city. There were excellent public facilities, such as museum, concert hall, theater, hotel, stadium, etc., attracting political and business elites, well known at that time. Not anymore. Detroit has become a deteriorating city with a population declining from nearly 2,000,000 people in the postwar era to the current 700,000 people. There are 78,000 abandoned buildings, criminal rampage, 28.4% unemployment rate (June 2009, highest since 2008; 9.8%

in December 2016), and a $20 billion city debt. Just in the last 30 years, auto workers have been reduced by 1.14 million people whose work was concentrated in Detroit, resulting in a population exodus and sharp reduction in government tax revenues. And over the past decade, the city mainly relied on debt for survival. On July 18, 2013, the city applied to the federal court for bankruptcy protection, setting a record for the largest U.S. city bankruptcy (2013/7/19). This is the most obvious case of how wage control and trade unions' impact on a city's economy. It has done to Detroit, so the United States is no exception. Unless one adopts a closed door policy, with no foreign trade, jobs will inevitably flow to the region with high economic competitiveness, just like the force of ocean waves; sooner or later they will even out global sea level. Therefore, without making improvements in economic competitiveness, the efforts of job protection by the unions and government may only delay, but may not prevent the eventual loss of jobs.

On March 28, 2013, the Right to Work Law, signed earlier by Republican Gov. Rick Snyder, went into effect. Michigan, a stronghold of labor unions and headquarters of the UAW, became the 24th state in America to disfranchise the labor unions' monopolistic power. For Detroit, it is probably 20 years too late though, but a giant step in the right direction. The law will prevent businesses from leaving the state and will entice new industries to set up shops in the state because of labor union considerations. It provides a ray of hope to the city as well as the state that the rust belt economic deterioration might be near an end and an economic and social revival will be forthcoming.

In the case of the United States, there is no need for factories to relocate or product to outsource abroad because cheap foreign labor will man the plants, keeping the factories operating as usual, restoring the local economy and providing more revenue to the government; the trade deficit and economic recession will be averted. More importantly, the world becomes a single labor market. Jobs are shared by global workers, and workers are free to compete without national distinction, eliminating the slave wage practice, achieving equal pay for equal work globally, and developing workers' full potential. This is putting democracy, equality, and human rights to work in the real sense. It also provides the opportunity for people to choose where in the world they want to reside. The displaced and unemployed will have more employment opportunities in the global labor market or can participate in the job training programs offered by the government to supplement those occupations which experienced worker shortages. Second, it will alleviate the financial and political issues associated with illegal immigrants, such as detention, repatriation, final settlement, health insurance, etc. The labor unions' resistance to change may prove to be the most difficult stumbling block to overcome because they will not easily give up their vested rights. However, if America continues to maintain the status quo, it will reinforce the plight of the cocoon, making it thicker and thicker, no workable solution in sight. Therefore, opening up the markets allowing all resources to flow freely, including goods, labor, and capital, will be a viable option to America.

Currently, there are 104 nations giving visa exemption to American passport holders to stay in their countries for periods ranging from 14 to 180 days, but limited to travel or visiting, not for work or business. The U.S. reciprocates with 37 nations and 11 regions by granting the same privileges. The latest information shows that passport holders of Finland, Sweden, and England, without a visa, are permitted to enter 176 of 219 countries surveyed, more than 80% of the total. Even for the most un-favored nation, Afghanistan, its people are freely welcomed into 28 nations without a visa (2014/4/23). It is a good start to the free movement of people; it should be carried one level higher so that all countries in the world will allow the free flow of people, free choice to reside, and free choice to work without regard to their nationality so that human resources will flow to the areas where they are most needed to perform their work to their maximum potential.

In order to assist the development of people's movement, the government should provide personnel information (people seeking jobs and jobs to be filled) in the main languages on the public websites. Immigration service centers should be established to assist immigrants with living arrangements and employment, preventing their being victimized, and providing local language and culture programs to ensure immigrants early integration into the local community. More importantly, the creation of a universal language and currency would facilitate communication and movement of people.

At present, there are 1,213 million people worldwide who use the Chinese language, followed by Spanish, with 329 million people, than

English with 328 million people. The Chinese language users are concentrated on the Chinese mainland; Spanish is commonly used in Spain and Central and South Americas. In addition to North America, English is the main language of Britain, Australia, New Zealand, and a lot of areas around the world. Geographically, it is the most widely used language. However, the most important feature to be considered for a universal language is its simplicity, ease to learn and ease to use, emphasizing first its communication capability to facilitate the flow of people.

The open door policy giving people the freedom of movement in the world not only concerns business but also affects community security, health, education, housing, etc. And a policy which harmonizes people with different cultures and customs to avoid social conflicts and maintains economic and social orders is a must. Without proper controls, it may lead to the influx of people into rich countries for welfare and social benefits, immediately causing problems for the local government. Therefore, detailed immigration regulations must be understood and agreed to by the governments and their people around the world; then they must work together according to the rules to achieve the expected benefits. Immigration regulations should be formulated by the experts. Here are a few major items to be considered: (1) Immigration limits should be placed on the carriers of serious infectious diseases, serious law offenders, and long term recipients of social welfare benefits, to prevent transferring national burdens; (2) Immigrants should possess two-way transportation, local health insurance, as well as living costs; job contract holders, tourists, and tour groups exempted; (3) Welfare benefits are only provided to a country's own citizens. If immigrants need welfare, they must apply for it in their own countries. Children born to immigrants cannot automatically become local citizens. Contribution or potential contribution to local society is required of immigrants to be eligible for citizenship; (4) As long as self-sustaining, immigrants are allowed to reside anywhere they choose, employment is not required; (5) Non-citizens and their dependents have to share the cost of educational services, including job training; (6) Equal employment opportunities are provided to all, whether a citizen or not, fair competition, no discrimination, and the abolition of labor union restrictions. Preference should be given to local workers if the same qualifications are submitted;

(7) Controls on the purchase and leasing of real estate should be instituted to prevent foreign capitalists' speculation and monopoly of the local real estate market leading to hardships for local residents and merchants, thus preventing completely transforming the original local landscape.

Overall, the free flow of people has the benefits of improving employment, maintaining economic and social stability, eliminating global slave wages, practicing democracy and human rights among nations, reducing international tension, and providing a favorable foundation for world harmony and peace.

10.4. Eliminating Financial Restrictions: Achieving Capital Efficiency

People in economically underdeveloped countries generally consume more than they produce, have no savings, are unable to borrow money from external sources, and lack capital, which results in long-term economic stagnation because capital or money is one of the important ingredients of production. After World War II, various international financial institutions were established to fulfill global capital needs. These included the World Bank, International Bank of Reconstruction and Development, International Development Association, International Finance Corporation, International Investment Insurance Agency, and International Monetary Fund, etc. Although each agency has its own mission and specific operating scope, all subscribe to the goals of economic development and improving people's livelihood. In addition, there are many regional financial organizations having the same objectives.

Financial assistance to underdeveloped countries mainly was achieved though aid and loans provided to the government. In Africa, for example, since 1950 up to $300 billion in loans were provided by international financial institutions to build infrastructures, to develop water supply, to improve agriculture, and to eliminate AIDS, etc. But this could only meet the partial capital requirements for public enterprises; the vast private sector was under-funded. Therefore, removing unnecessary financial restrictions on currency, foreign exchange, opening up capital markets to foreign investors, and promoting the flow of funds so that funds will flow to the most needed region will achieve the lowest cost and highest efficiency of capital usage.

Financial assistance should be provided to all entities, public and private, which need capital to develop the economy and to improve people's living standard. Of course, borrowers must meet the minimum conditions for loan repayment. On the other hand, the capital market also needs appropriate regulations, so as to avoid capitalists manipulating foreign exchanges, commodities, real estate markets or preventing corruption. Finally, the early introduction of a global currency, thereby eliminating currency exchanges, will not only help capital flows but also will promote the flow of goods and people.

In addition to the elimination of all government restrictions, the above-mentioned various international financial organizations play an important role in the flow of the world's financial resources. However, most of these institutions were established at the end of World War II, nominally affiliated with the United Nations, but chartered separately. Therefore, any changes in the UN have no direct impact on them. With 70 years of world evolution, the existence and operation of many financial institutions require a fundamental evaluation and reform to meet the needs of current and future international economic development. Elimination or integration of duplicate services and institutions that are no longer needed will reduce waste and increase efficiency. Special attention should be directed to institutional governance reform (just as the needed reform of the United Nations discussed later) so that the principle of fairness and global interests may be better served, thus leading to popular support by its members and achieving more and better operational results.

The Brookings Institution's paper, "Reform of Global Governance: Priorities for Action", published on October 18, 2007, voices the same concern for changes and makes some recommendations for IMF, World Bank, UN, and G8. For example, readjusting voting power among the members and eliminating the U.S. veto power will improve the operation of these organizations. However, because the report was done before the financial crisis in 2008, the extent of global economic and financial problem was less obvious; the recommendation did not go far enough to make a fundamental change so that the basic problems remain. Besides, all new governance structure should have a built-in periodic adjustment mechanism to adapt for changes taken place because world affairs are evolving daily.

One of the most important agencies, the International Monetary Fund, for example, was criticized by the Overseas Development Institute

(ODI), asserting that IMF uses the capitalist market economy as the standard of measurement, thus lacking objectivity; often without thorough understanding of local conditions, leading to diagnostic errors; one principle applied to all, a simplistic bureaucracy approach; internal disagreements, unclear policies; and focusing only on theory with lack of practicality. Perhaps this is a subjective opinion of ODI. Let's take a look at the IMF governance structure. IMF has 188 state members, among them seven major industrial countries (G7) which consists of the United States, Japan, Germany, France, Britain, Italy, and Canada, hold 43.09% (United States alone has 16.75% and a veto power) of the voting power, deciding on fund policies and major personnel appointments. This does not reflect the current world economic reality. G7 accounted for only 32.6% of world GDP in 2013 with PPP adjustment (World Bank data), even less if labor rate parity and other adjustments are taken into account. Then, they tend to use their country's interests as a basis for decision-making, resulting in biased decisions.

IMF was founded in 1945, aiming at the reconstruction of the international payment system, and now includes policies to promote international monetary cooperation, international financial stability, world trade development, global economic prosperity, etc. Loans to help member states with financial difficulties and financing projects are its main operation, making it a financial creditor institution. Currently, the U.S. is a heavy borrower and the world's largest debtor nation, but in the IMF, the U.S. becomes the largest creditor, inconsistent with reality. That is, the United States' capital in the IMF may be borrowed, not America's own assets. Furthermore, the United States is in economic and financial difficulties, and needing financial relief. Therefore, it may be making self-serving arrangements leading to conflicts of interest. So, reform is needed in its core principles.

The members of IMF did reach an agreement on quota and governance reform in 2010. However, after six years, the U.S. Congress is still holding the treaty without ratification rendering the reform ineffective. This is one important reason in addition to the country's own interests why all world major nations except Japan and Mexico joined the China-led Asian Infrastructure Investment Bank, despite the U.S. advice to the contrary. China is the promoter and pledges to contribute $50 billion initially to the bank, which is slated for operation by 2016 with its headquarters in Beijing. To its surprise, the bank received enthusiastic support not just from Asia, but also from Europe, Africa, South America, and Oceania. By the application deadline of March 31, 2015, 57 nations have become charter members. On March 25, 2016, after the bank is in operation, 30 more countries are intending to join the bank, well representing the world. An estimate of $800 billion is needed every year in Asia for infrastructure improvement. Therefore, the new bank is welcomed by the established world financial institutions, including the International Monetary Fund, World Bank, and Asian Development Bank, to supplement capital needs in Asia.

The BRICS (China, Russia, India, Brazil, and South Africa) alliance's dissatisfaction with the status quo of the current international financial setup decided to reinvent the wheel. On July 15, 2014, the group announced the creation of a New Development Bank, headquartered in Shanghai, with initial capital of $50 billion contributed equally by the members to finance infrastructure construction in the developing countries and $100 billion Contingency Reserve Arrangement fund for emergencies, financial difficulty relief, maintaining financial stability, etc. The 6th BRICS summit from July15 to 17, 2014, was held in Brazil; 11 countries from South America were invited to attend the meeting. Argentina, Egypt, Iran, Nigeria, and Syria also expressed interest in joining the BRICS alliance. Perhaps the additional competition may lead to progress and improvement in international financial development.

In 2004, a U.S. Internet company created bitcoins, also known as Bitcoin. And soon Bitcoin was welcomed by Internet users all over the world. Just in nine years, a total of 12 million coins were issued, and businesses in many countries are accepting Bitcoin as a medium of exchange. Canada claims to have the world's first Bitcoin ATM, and the German government considered it as private money. U.S. Federal Reserve Bank Chairman Ben Bernanke said that Bitcoin facilitates money laundering and terrorist activities, but there is a long-term unlimited potential. Currently, the Internet has also been used by terrorists as a tool to raise money, allowing users to donate Bitcoins anonymously for the reward of assassinating politicians. Ben Bernanke became the No. 1 target, cumulating 124.14 Bitcoin, more than President Obama.

Bitcoin was less than $14 by the end of 2012, but in 2013 the price skyrocketed to $200 by the end of October and by November 19th climbed to $900. On May 26, 2017, the coin set a new high, at $2,791.70 (*Wenweipo*.com). In recent years, the Chinese market showed a significant increase in Bitcoin trading volume. In 2013 by September 30, 59,611 coins had been traded, accounting for 30% of the world volume, dominating world trading, higher than the United States. At the same time, Chinese users who download the Bitcoin software also top the world. Possibly the Chinese regard the coins as favorable savings and investment vehicles, a better choice than U.S. bonds, and an international trade and exchange media (2013/11/20). *Bloomberg Businessweek* reported on January 11, 2016, that the nonprofit Bitcoin Foundation has seen $7 million evaporate in the last two years, and its total assets were less than $13,000 at the end of November 2015. When the Executive Director called a board meeting on December 15 to raise funds, director Olivier Janssen suggested the foundation may not be "fixable." Another director said, "Asking for money is just throwing money away". The foundation may be on the brink of collapse.

Clearly from the current development, Bitcoin lacks any government support, doesn't have a reasonable value reserve standard, or an effective regulatory system. It merely becomes the object of speculation in the financial market in which its value fluctuates with the speculators' operation. It does not meet the stable value standard of global currency and could not replace the dollar's status. In early September 2017, the Chinese government suspended the Bitcoin trading on the ground that there is no asset to back up the value of Bitcoin but an internet financial fraud. The regulation also required all traders to liquidate their accounts relating to Bitcoin, a big blow to Bitcoin survivability. The creation and circulation of Euro since 2002 providing rich experiences in its planning, implementation, management, and related issues, is a vital source of information for global currency development.

The flow of capital was greatly impeded by the national monetary systems because there was no global currency to facilitate international transactions; all had to rely on world dominant currencies. By 1920, the U.S. dollar replaced the British pound (sterling) as the dominant medium for international account settlement. As the time went on, the U.S. gained greater world influence, as did the dollar's supremacy. Up until 2002 the Euro, another major currency, was introduced in the EU. And in the recent decade, the regional economic and trade alliances, one after the other, were formed coupled with the declining of American economic global influence; so did the dollar lose some of its glitter.

In the past, most currencies issued by the central banks in the world were backed by the value of the precious metals, gold or silver standards. But most countries abandoned the standards before World War II. The U.S. Congress also suspended domestic (people) currency conversion to gold on June 5, 1933. Even though the gold standard was kept by the Bretton Woods International Monetary Agreement of 1944, domestic convertibility from currency to gold was non-existent. Gold and currencies were the medium of settlements of international balance of payment accounts. The U.S. dollar became the choice currency by the international community prompting many central banks to keep dollars instead of gold in their reserves. Thus, the demand for dollars was pushed to a higher level, as was the dollar's prominent stature, almost becoming the global currency. Some countries even adopted the dollar as their national currency.

The dollar international exchange rate for global central banks was $20.67 per oz. of gold in 1933, devalued to $35.00 in 1934 (exchanges for gold not available to business or individual). Due to the war in Vietnam and declining American economic prowess resulting in persistent balance of payment deficits, President Richard Nixon suspended the gold convertibility on August 15, 1971, and international gold conversion was never occurred since, not to any central bank. The dollar was further devalued nominally to $38.00 in December 1971 and to $42.22 in October 1973. The U.S. government removed the link of dollar value to gold from statues in 1976; thus, the international monetary system was made of pure fiat money. This change provides the U.S. with the ability to print as many dollars as needed to finance its national debt and budget deficit, and to maintain economic stability and growth. American control and influence over international financial institutions offer much leeway for the U.S. so that the financial crisis was rode out without fatal damage even with a national debt at $12 trillion by September 30, 2009. The Soviet Union was unable to weather its financial crisis leading to a total collapse. Greece and other European countries also faced many more difficulties than the American in dealing with the financial crisis. They all lack the American advantage: the dollar supremacy and the support of international financial institutions.

The dollar is the most popular denominator of economic value in international transactions, statistics, debt contracts, etc. Most of these uses may require no actual dollar at all. For example, a purchase contract of $10,000 will be settled when due with local currency at the time of the dollar exchange rate. The use of the dollar for these purposes will continue until another dominant currency emerges or a global currency is adopted. Therefore, the nominal uses of the dollar will not affect the global financial market.

The dollar is also most commonly used for international accounts settlement that prompts the world central banks to keep the dollar in their reserves. In addition, there is demand of dollars for individual and business needs, such as for travel or purchases in a foreign country. And there is a 16 nations/areas U.S. dollar currency union with 339 million people using the dollar. These add up to a huge demand for the dollar worldwide.

When a government practices deficit spending and monetary easing policies, the usual outcomes would be inflation and currency devaluation because more quantity of currency are in the market leading to more demand for goods and services. But this was not true in the U.S. after the government implemented the fiscal policies of more than one trillion dollars in 2009 to combat the financial crisis. The U.S. consumer price index remained stable, and the dollar gained its ground against other major currencies. Even though the amount of government spending added up to over a trillion dollars, it was a drop in the basket--a tiny fraction of the total dollar outstanding worldwide; thus, its effect was diluted, almost nil. Second, the other major currency countries may have practiced the same fiscal policy; this canceled out the effect on the exchange rate. However, the dollar supremacy is under increasing pressure by currency unions, regional economic and trade alliances, and increasing economic power of the developing nations.

In the recent several decades, regional economic consolidation, trade alliances, and international infrastructure investment have accelerated. These activities prompted changes in global monetary and financial systems. Some created their own money to facilitate regional resource flows. Others designate currencies other than the U.S. dollar as the terms of settlement. Thus, these changes reduce the actual use of the dollar and consequently its global supremacy.

In 1993 the European Union was formed to promote trade and economic development aiming for a political integration. Then in 2002, the Euro was introduced and has been adopted as the official currency to replace the existing money by 18 countries in the union and six non-union members with a population of near 329 million. The Euro also serves as a supplemental currency alongside the local currency in other EU member countries. Another currency, the SUCRE, was adopted in 2004 as a medium for trade without replacing the existing currencies by the Bolivian Alliance for the Americas, which consists of nine member countries and two associate members. Then, there are many currency unions which use a single currency to facilitate transactions in a region with/without a formal national agreement. Notable unions include the CFA franc which was set up in 1945 with 14 Central Africa countries and near 152 million people, Pound sterling in 1939 with 10 nations/areas and 62 million people, Australian dollar in 1966 with 11 nations/areas and 23 million people, Russian ruble in 2008 with three nations and 142 million people, South African rand in 1974 with four nations and 53 million people. In addition to the Chinese Yuan, Japanese yen, Swiss franc, etc., these currencies serve as a medium of exchange for intra-regional or some external transactions bypassing the necessity of using the U.S. dollar.

In the last decade, there were many bilateral and multilateral economic and trade agreements being reached. And China launched a massive infrastructure development plan that will involve trillions of dollars worldwide. Most of these international agreements are signed in the U.S. dollar. However, few actual dollars would be involved when it is time for account settlement. For example, the Asian Economic Community, consisting of 10 ASEAN countries, will not have a common currency for internal and external transactions. Since China is the major economic partner of the community members, they all need to settle the accounts with China. Hence, the Chinese Yuan would be more convenient to use among members and final settlement with China. Thus, it renders the dollar to the sideline. China's $60 billion economic and social development aid to Africa for 2016 to 2018 will be delivered to the countries as the programs call for. However, the aid would primarily be in goods and services either from China, the local community or other nations; few items would be in Yuans or dollars. Also, the major trading groups, such as the EU, Russia, and China, would designate their own currencies be used in settlement, further reducing the need for the dollar.

The U.S. dollar currency union is the largest, established in 1904 with Panama; now it has 16 nations/areas with 339 million people plus many unilateral users, such as Zimbabwe. The dollar is also popular in the Middle East and North Africa, and parts of South America. The international organizations in the world mostly conduct their business with the dollar, and each global entity's final account settlement with America uses the dollar, too. So the demand for the dollar is still strong. However, with developing economies growing at high rates and with their own global financial institutions, like the Asian Infrastructure Investment Bank, it will relatively reduce the dollar's supremacy and American global financial influence as time moves on.

10.5. Discarding Animosity: Reviving European Glory

At the completion of the Marshall Plan, Western Europe experienced economic prosperity, rising living standards, joy, and social harmony, but no one country became a dominant world power anymore. Any European nation is dwarfed when facing the U.S. or the Soviet Union, each with over 200 million people and vast resources and markets. With this new reality, they realized that to restore the dignity and glory of Europe, they must bury past feuds, forget old grudges, and work together to form a united force in order to deal with these two super powers.

Belgium, France, Italy, Luxembourg, the Netherlands, and Germany signed the European Coal & Steel Community and European Economic Community treaties in 1951 and 1958 respectively, consolidating heavy industries of all six states to avoid repeated fighting among themselves and establishing the Customs Union to eliminate custom duties, promoting logistics flow and integrating regional economic development. Then in 1960, Austria, Denmark, Norway, Portugal, Sweden, Switzerland, and the United Kingdom also formed the European Free Trade Association. As its name suggests, it also promoted the logistics flow and strengthened economic cooperation. Subsequently, the European Economic Community continued to expand, adding six more countries until 1993, laying down a favorable foundation for the European Union.

Five nations in the European Economic Community signed the Schengen Agreement in 1985, abolishing border restrictions so that the people could move freely. The Agreement was amended in 1990 to accommodate more countries, expanding the free movement area, but this has been a treaty only between the individual nations involved. In 1997, it was incorporated into the EU legal system, which now covers all EU countries except Bulgaria, Cyprus, Croatia, Ireland, Romania, and the U.K. and adding Liechtenstein, Iceland, Norway, and Switzerland. People in the Schengen area can now move freely to anywhere without a passport, visa, checkpoint, and other immigration procedures. The free flow of people has been achieved, but there are many European trade unions which hinder the normal development of the labor market. This obstacle cannot be easily overcome.

All EU 28 states including some former Soviet Union members have a population of 500 million, accounted for 7.3% of the world total and an area of 4,312,099 sq. km. with 2011 GDP of $17.6 trillion, 20% of the world GDP. In the EU, national barriers no longer exist, and the goal of logistics and people's free flow has been fully realized. In 2002 a single currency, the Euro, was adopted by 12 member countries and six more states have joined since. Currently, the European Central Bank is making plans to unify monetary control and financial market systems for facilitating the capital flow.

To sum it up, the EU member countries opened up their arms and hearts to accommodate each other by eliminating borders, man-made restrictions, international disputes, and the century old Franco-German feud, accelerating the flow of goods, people, and capital, leading to economic prosperity and social harmony which have the effect of promoting universal brotherhood and world peace. The EU is quite worthy to be a Nobel Peace Prize winner. This excellent model has been diligently copied by the Bolivian Inter-American Alliance, the Asian Economic Community, and the South American Union. The Asian Economic Community has realized its 10-nation economic integration by the end of 2015. The South American Union plans to achieve the free flow of goods, people, and capital by 2026 so that the people of 12 nations are free to choose work and residence anywhere in the vast region.

10.6. Determining Purposes in Life: Focusing on Happiness Building

Most people are busy getting an education, making a living, having a family, and taking care of the home. They all require money. Besides, money is the most versatile medium of exchange; with few exceptions, almost everything can be purchased. The Chinese have a saying that money can make ghosts help you turn the grinding stone which converts wheat into flour. It describes profoundly the magic power of money for even ghosts cannot resist its temptation. Therefore, people are busy chasing after money. Then, there are fame seekers. As a result, there was an attempted assassination of President Ronald Reagan so that John Hinckley would become well known and win affection from the actress Jodie Foster. And hundreds of thousands of people participate in eating contests around the world, like the Nathan's Hot Dog Eating Contest held on Coney Island, New York, every 4th of July. The winners of these competitions not only derive the psychological satisfaction of public recognition but also make possible financial gains for themselves. These, too, are avenues of money chasing.

People are in a hurry with living and making money; few take time to think about their life. What are the real goals or purposes in life? Moreover, each of us came into this world empty handed and will leave this world in the same manner; even the kings and the rich cannot take treasures with them when they leave the world. Money is the means not the end of life. Therefore, life is neither a money-making machine nor a fame generator; it should be a happiness builder.

Happiness may mean a lot of hamburgers, a pretty car, or a nice home. True, without basic necessities, people won't be happy, but that is not all there is to it. Can people feel happy if their family, neighbors, or countrymen suffer from misfortune? So, do hunger, disease, earthquakes, and other disasters occurring in the country or in other parts of the world make people happy? A happiness builder should not stop short at the family level but should include concern for the community, country, and world.

Individual good fortune will be insufficient to eradicate hunger, disease, ignorance, and provide people with security and dignity of life in the world. A socially concerted effort should be called for to achieve the goal of a prosperous and harmonious world. Thus, enhanced production and a better organized society will be able to meet the demands of a growing world population and improvement of humans' well-being which calls for people to make contributions in three major areas.

The first area is to discover the truth in nature and in society so as to improve production technology and interpersonal relationships. Emphasis should be given to maintaining a balance between nature and mankind, encouraging conservation so that the planet will not be overburdened, and developing science and technology that will do more with fewer resources. Global cooperation in space and deep ocean exploration should be forged to expand the territory and resources for mankind. Efforts should also be directed toward the improvement of interpersonal relationships which concern the political, economic, social, and other organizations. Especially, the reforms on organization governance should be carried out based on equitable, fair, reasonable, and efficient principles to satisfy the current and future needs; these include board of directors in business, the democratic electoral system, and governance of the UN and other national and international organizations to incite members' enthusiasm in achieving a higher goal of serving people.

The second area is promotion of charitable activities, through personal effort, foundations, or organizations, to supplement the inadequacy of the government welfare programs, achieving the goal of people's well-being and dignity. The moral superiority program, which is detailed in 9.6, should also be vigorously promoted to incite people's voluntary contribution.

The third area is perfection of everyone's profession in all walks of life whether doctors or janitors, so that maximum efficiency and innovation may be attained for the utmost benefit to society in terms of goods and services produced. As a result, it is possible to meet the needs of the growing world population and a higher living standard at the same time without moving toward earth's destruction.

10.7. Forming Global Consensus: Establishing World Citizenship

The Western culture is more outward looking to meet the desires of life, focusing on the pursuit of the material and encouraging pro-action to promote economic prosperity and social progress. But, after all, resources are limited and desires are insatiable. If desires are not properly managed, this will inevitably lead to the individual's discontent or corruption and nations scrambling to gain control of power and resources leading to wars. The global warming since the industrial revolution moving the earth toward destruction is the result of this unlimited material desire and acquisition. And, if pure materialism is the only emphasis, it will overlook mental and spiritual needs in pursuit of truth, charity, and perfection in the real world as well as eternity in the future life.

The 14th century's Renaissance liberated the European mind from the church's bondage. Society promoted experiments, gathering evidence, and proving assumptions as the scientific method of dealing with nature. Thus, worldly business has been conducted according to the scientific principles leading to technological advance, industrial revolution, improvement of production, and economic progress. As to the interpersonal conduct, even with laws and statutes, the church still holds the ultimate behavioral and moral authority in the Western culture. Thus, regardless of one's conduct in business or politics, personal salvation depends on the church's doctrines, e.g., sins could be forgiven by the church. So, in the West, science governs worldly business; churches still hold the authority over people's behavioral and moral standards.

Beginning in the mid-18th century, technological advances leading to the Industrial Revolution, coupled with rising standards of living, accelerated natural resource usage and waste generation, which have intensified in the last century. Drinking water and forests are seriously depleted; air and water pollution are more common. The Orb Media research report on 10 nations indicated that drinking water averaging 83% was contaminated with micro plastic, America leading the pack with 94%, followed by India and Lebanon. England, France and Germany were the least with 72%. Global warming causes sea levels to rise, threatening coastal cities and islands, and more extreme weather creates drought, flooding, wide fires, hurricanes, and tornados. The model of current economic and social development seems unsustainable, and civilization is moving toward global destruction. True, natural bounty is meant for people's enjoyment, but we must use it wisely so that we will not run out of it or cause environmental disaster and unsustainable economic progress.

Since the Industrial Revolution, the West, including Japan, has enjoyed rising standards of living, an expanding middle class, economic prosperity, social stability, military expansion, colonizing the rest of the world, and practicing imperial aggression. At the end of World War II, the world powers changed their courses, advocated democracy, freedom, equality, and human rights, ended imperialism, and encouraged colonies to become independent. In the last 70 years of world development, colonies changed to republics and are no longer under world powers' political control. However, the people of these newly established republics are still poor and ignorant, few becoming healthy nations. In reality, world powers still practice imperialism, dictate world orders, and subjugate developing nations and their people. For example, the Soviet Union dominated Eastern Europe and America dictated around the world. Capitalism's exploitation, as practiced by the advanced nation, intensified in the last few decades as discussed previously in the iPhone case. There is no democracy among nations, no equality among world workers, and slave wages are paid to the people of developing countries, e.g., undocumented farm workers in the U.S. and Indonesian manufacturing workers 50 cents hourly pay.

In other words, over the last 70 years, there was a lot of talk of democracy, equality, and human rights but very little in their substance was achieved in real life, especially in the third world. World powers compete to build up their military, to strengthen global control, and to enhance their national interest. Not much attention in the last few decades has been paid to the real political goals of improving people's living standard, enhancing people's well-being, and harmonizing society in the world. This inequality and injustice social condition fostered the growth of international terrorism such as the ISIS.

Currently, with welfare expansion and national debt rising, democracy is in crisis; the wealth gap is widening, income disparity is worsening, and capitalism is facing a serious threat. On January 19, 2015, just before the Davos World Economic Forum commenced its proceedings, the non-profit organization Oxfam issued its latest finding that the world's 1% super rich, about seven million people, amassed 48% of global wealth in 2014 and will exceed the other 99% combined by 2016. And, there are one billion people, over 14%, living under the $2 per day poverty line worldwide. This grave condition is the result of the current world orders established by the West and led by the U.S. In the 2016 U.S. presidential election, income inequality became a hot topic; Nobel Prize Economics laureate Joseph Eugene Stiglitz declared "The American economy is a failed economy. We have to once again rewrite the rules of the economy for the 21st century" (2016/3/3).

Europe and America have different national conditions and the degree of poverty's effect on society are not the same. However, the overall trend is that the laboring class will dominate the political decision-making process and will follow the footsteps of the recent political development in Venezuela, i.e., welfare growth, nationalization of major industries, heavy taxes on the rich, economy withering, class antagonism, and social unrest. Therefore, even if the underdeveloped countries can successfully duplicate the democratic system, ultimate consequences will be the same as the developments in Europe and America. The democratic system requires a fundamental change in order to achieve its political goals. The goals are to ensure the people's livelihood, to improve people's education, and to safeguard people's security and civil liberty.

Looking back to the last several decades of world development, China's one-party dictatorship coupled with state capitalism achieved phenomenal economic growth, popularized education, and fostered national revival, social stability, and economic prosperity. Even though there are limits in human rights and civil liberty, as criticized by the West, there are great accomplishments nonetheless; moreover, other political systems, including democracy, had failed miserably in China in the past. Now the experience is getting attention from other developing countries. Will Brazil, India, Indonesia, Egypt, Nigeria, Cuba, etc. be able to duplicate China's success story? Or, is it worthy for them to follow the Chinese approach?

In Eastern culture, the teaching of Confucianism and Buddhism advocates self-cultivation, seeks inner peace and satisfaction, and conduct good deeds to enrich one's life. Confucius' political doctrine begins with cultivating oneself in establishing moral values and a sense of responsibility, extended to family, society and national governance. It asks man to follow the virtuous and impartial principles that eliminate scrambling for personal gain and reducing power struggles; to uphold laws and take responsibility seriously to rectify poor performance and corrupt motives, thus leading to social progress and prosperity. The emphasis is that personal conduct and political life are inseparable and integral parts of a person. If one is not a good person, he/she cannot be a good parent, administrator, or any office holder.

In the social sphere, Confucius' ethical and moral ideology will help to provide proper interpersonal relationships, to restore family function, to correct corrupted culture, and to promote social harmony. These are much needed solutions to problems in today's world. More importantly, ethics and morals are the compass in life and society. Lacking them means losing direction, with advanced technology, resulting in greater destruction and being farther away from propriety and goodness.

The Pew Research Center estimates that in 2012 the world's religions and their followers were as follows:

World Religion Membership, 2012

Religion	Christianity	Islam	Hinduism	Buddhism	others	atheism	world
Member, millions	2,212	1,629	1,053	499	484	1,145	7,022
% of world population	31.5	23.2	15.0	7.1	6.9	16.3	100.0

Christians cover the most extensive regions, almost all over the world. Muslims are concentrated in the Middle East, North Africa, and parts of South Asia. Hindus, implied by its name, reside mainly in India. Buddhists populate East Asia and Southeast Asia. Generally, orthodox religions promote good behavior and staying away from evil, brotherly love, dedication, and public charity; arouse the public conscience to practice good deeds; and emphasize reward and retribution in a future life. It is a guide to human life, providing spiritual sustenance and comfort to the soul, having the effect of fostering social harmony and progress, essential institutions of society. Most major religions focus their attention on the whole universe and the entire human race, and are not limited to a particular country, region, or race. They are pioneers of the globalization concept and also the effective promoters of universal brotherhood. However, in the history of the outward expansion of Western hegemonies, religion was also employed as a tool of cultural invasion, most notably in Central and South America. Aboriginal religions and languages were almost replaced by Catholicism and Spanish. In addition, missionaries were also used for intelligence gathering or other illegal activities, paving the way for the invaders.

Christians view the entire human race as sinners, even newly born babies, because they inherited original sin from their ancestors, Adam and Eve, who committed a sin. To save human beings, God sent His Son, Jesus Christ (4 BC-30/33 AD), to the world, creating churches and spreading the Gospel. If people do not believe in Jesus as their Savior, they will never be saved and be in heaven, even if they are perfect philanthropists. So, for Christians, the only way to heaven, eternal life, and freedom from destruction is to believe in God and recognize Jesus as their savior.

The Buddhism founder, Shakyamuni (563/480 BC-483/400 BC), although a prince, was not immortal. As long as human beings practice good deeds and abandon all desires and passions (a very difficult realization), even a non-believer in Buddhism can become a Buddha in the future life. Buddha is also a realm of consciousness, free from worldly worries, no pain forever, eternal comfort and ease, no birth and death, and eventually in paradise. There is no God and human, or master and servant distinction in Buddhism, more equality. As long as the words and deeds are achieved at a high standard of awareness, even a non-Buddhist can become a Buddha, based on essence not formality, more fair and reasonable than Christianity. The Buddhism's major drawback is their overemphasis on individual salvation in the future life, almost neglecting the importance of today and society. Attempts to correct this shortcoming have been made by some Buddhist organizations to actively participate in social activities such as disaster relief efforts in the recent decades.

During World War II, the movement of a large number of troops in addition to international refugees accelerated the pace of people's flow. In the Korean War, the American overseas personnel, including military forces, exceeded 2.4 million people (1953); even today (2012), there are no less than 1.2 million oversea Americans. Although most settled in military bases, their presence constitutes an opportunity for cultural exchange, and the most recognized phenomenon was international marriages. Between 1942 and 1952, there were about 300,000 war brides from Europe alone.

In recent decades, with the booming world economy, global trade between 1990 and 2011 recorded a triple growth. According to the United Nations Educational, Scientific, and Cultural Organization report, international students number more than 5 million (2011). The United Nations Tourism Organization reported in 2013 a total of 1.087 billion international tourist trips, an increase of 5% over last year, providing $1.4 trillion in tourism revenue. Coupled with the private business activities as well as cultural and diplomatic exchanges, a substantial increase in the global flow of people and cultural exchanges has taken place which has the effect of promoting international understanding and integration.

According to the Economist Network report, in 2010 almost half of marriages in Switzerland were international couples, and international marriages in Singapore were close to 40%. Meanwhile, by years of legal and illegal immigration, the 2010 U.S. census shows a total immigration population of 39.9 million people, accounting for 12.9% of the total U.S. population, the highest proportion since 1920. As a result, currently many families have overseas relatives and dear friends.

Over the past centuries, the rapid advances in technology accelerated global integration, such as the Internet crossing national boundaries and satellites covering global activities in addition to the old modes of communication and transportation. The world is getting smaller, and interpersonal and international contacts accelerate at a high speed. In the meantime, global warming, air pollution, natural disasters, and nuclear accidents extend beyond national borders and become international issues. It is not a problem any one country can solve alone, and it is difficult to distinguish where national interest and responsibility exist. Insisting on national interests and racial viewpoints is bound to bring more and heated disputes, conflicts, and eventually wars.

The age of isolation and fending for oneself is history. There is no national security if the world is at risk. So, global interests and mutual benefits must be positioned ahead of national interests, and it is necessary to establish a world citizenship leading to a consensus on common ideals and behavior. The idea would be to accommodate and absorb the advantages of different cultures and integrate them into an international common conscience, using axioms and justice to resolve disputes and conflicts; and then world harmony and peace could be attained. This is not intended to suggest that people renounce their nationalities, but to subscribe the world citizenship as an additional responsibility. Should the spirits of these two citizenships collide the basis for choice people make should be subscribing to the universal principles, loyal to the ideals, and standing on fairness and justice for all.

Faced with a new environment and new challenges, one must recognize the targets clearly, having courage to accept different ideas and systems, to abandon prejudices, to discard the useless, to adopt the advantageous, and to blend them all together so that something better can be found or created. This will not only apply to politics, economics, technology, religion, academic, and other institutions, but is also equally useful in customs and cultural aspects which benefit mankind and promote social harmony and world peace.

10.8. Promoting Mutual Benefit: Enjoying Lasting World Peace

Looking back to the disastrous experience World War II brought to mankind, the leaders of 51 nations signed the Declaration in San Francisco in 1945 to establish the United Nations. The objectives of the UN were: Promoting international cooperation, seeking collective security, fostering economic development, improving social conditions, advocating human rights and equality, eliminating war, and safeguarding world peace. Currently, except the Vatican, all 193 global regimes are members of the UN. In its 70 years of existence, the UN has made significant contributions to the world, such as relieving disasters, eradicating diseases, improving people's livelihood, promoting education, and maintaining regional truces. But for disarmament and world peace, the UN seems powerless, with few achievements. Because soon after the signing of the Declaration to establish the UN, the United States and the Soviet Union became enemies, and each superpower was a Security Council permanent member vested with veto power, rejecting any motions that did not agree with their interests. The United Nations was unable to function effectively and to carry out its responsibilities required by the Charter.

With the passage of time, the basic UN governance structure no longer meets the needs of current world development. For example, the five permanent Security Council members, each with veto privilege, monopolize UN policies and often become obstacles to solving global problems. In recent decades, Germany, Japan, India, and Brazil requested to become permanent Security Council members, opposed by the Uniting for Consensus and met with rejection. In the end, what are the qualifications of a permanent Security Council member? On the other hand, the United States and other countries share excessive UN fiscal responsibility, leaving some nations without fulfilling their obligations. All these unfair rights and obligations structures greatly dampen the enthusiasm of most its members, seriously affecting the implementation of the UN missions. The recent UN General Assembly elected Saudi Arabia to the Security Council. It was considered an honor, but was turned down by Saudi Arabia, apparently displaying a negative attitude toward the United Nations.

As with the case of the democratic electoral system, the power structure of the United Nations needs to adapt to new world developments and make reasonable and fair reforms to encourage members' active support and to achieve its missions. The UN governance reform, including the Security Council, was discussed at the 2005 World Summit. The complete organization reform was called for to provide more voice for the developing nations, to promote efficient operation, and to meet increasing global challenges in many kinds and areas. Afterward, foreign ministers of China, Russia and India issued a joint communiqué to support the reform. However, the summit results became a well-documented historical paper, not much action has been taken since.

Some big nations enjoy veto power, unfair; and all countries have the same voting rights, also unreasonable. The decision making/voting right should be determined by each nation's basic rights, fulfillment of its obligations, and contributions to the international communities. There are: (1) Basic human rights, according to the size of population and quality of its people, i.e., life expectancy and literacy; (2) contribution to people's well-being measured by national economic output (GDP) reduced by the non-economic expenditures such as military and administration, adjusted for prices and wages differentials, values of barters, and value of self-produced and consumed, because non-monetary economic activities constitute a substantial part of the less developed economies; (3) international contributions, including support, financial or otherwise, to the United Nations and its sponsored institutions and projects, such as the International Red Cross, Haiti earthquake relief, peacekeeping efforts, as well as international moral superiority records. It should be periodically adjusted to reflect reasonable and fair voting power changes, to win a consensus and enthusiastic support of all its members, to maximize its effectiveness, and to promote more and better missions of the UN.

Recently, military exercises conducted by various parties in the East China and South China Seas stirred up a dense cloud of war. Israel and Palestine continue to trade air bombings with missile strikes. Nuclear programs are actively pursued by the North Koreans. As well, there are the crises in Ukraine and ISIS' rise in the Middle East, the Taliban's resurgence in Afghanistan, the intensified fighting in Syria and Iraq, and escalation of the Yemeni war, with a large-scale war highly possible. Perhaps, the promotion of the free flow of goods, people, and capital throughout the world, as well as global total disarmament, will make the world a large administrative region, with no more national boundary restrictions, tolerating and cultivating different political systems, cultures, and religions, moving towards the universal ideal of global brotherhood and harmony so that wars may be avoided. But international disputes are inevitable; the WTO mediation process can be modeled with its basis of justice and reason, providing a satisfactory solution to all parties. Otherwise, an appeal can be made to the United Nations.

In summary, if there are no manmade barriers, enterprises are attracted by the location which offers the best conditions for operation; goods, labor, and capital tend to flow to the place where they have the highest bidder. These natural/eternal forces, just like ocean waves, will erase the differences around the world to achieve the goals of goods being utilized in their best way, people working to their full potential, and capital being provided to the most needed endeavors. Thus, a new world order will be attained whereby nature's bounty is shared by all and the world becomes a big family where love and goodwill are prevailing. Military superiority and attempts to control territory and resources by the world powers are no longer necessary. And with the advancement of technology, both time and space become shorter and smaller; the Internet eliminates national boundaries and accelerates global interpersonal contacts. Satellites provide intercontinental activities; global warming affects everyone; nations are closely related and the era of seclusion, minding one's own business, has gone for good and will never return.

The world needs wise leaders making concerted efforts to promote moral superiority and advocate mutual benefit, not self-interest, as the only option. Self-interest is a prime mover of social progress and should be encouraged; but it should be limited to the extent that it will not put other parties/nations in any harm way, thus it prevents creating conditions of conflict of interest or war. Without jeopardizing national security, people should accommodate different political systems, cultures, religions, and customs; bury selfish and greedy desires; extend goodwill to neighbors; and promote the free flow of goods, people, and capital. The smooth flow of these resoueces will provide people of all races with equal opportunity which allows them to pursuit happiness, fulfillment of life, and a better social condition. Thus, it promotes brotherhood and equality among people in the world providing a solid foundation for peace and prosperity in the world. Mankind will march on the broad boulevard toward prosperity, harmony, eternal peace, and, finally, arrive in paradise.

Appendix: About China

AI. China's Significant World Contacts

A1.1. The Chinese Cultural Circle
China was unified in 221 B.C. by Chin Shih Huang, who also set up government offices in the northern parts of Korea and Vietnam. Meanwhile, Hsu Fu, an occultist, took 500 boys and 500 girls, provisions, books, and other supplies on ships out to sea in search of an elixir of life, ordered by Chin Shih Huang. He never returned and landed in Japan, as has been suggested. So in the early days, the Chinese culture and written language were adopted and modified by Korea, Japan, and Vietnam to suit their local needs.

The Chinese influence in these three nations achieved its height in the Tang Dynasty (618-907) including political, economic, education, and social systems as well as ideology and religion. Buddhism originated in India and then made its way to China and from China to Korea and Japan, flourishing and becoming the major religion in all three East Asian nations.

In the late 8th century, Japan introduced two sets of symbols to supplement the written language but still kept the Chinese characters in its writing. France colonized Vietnam in the late 19th century and also replaced the Chinese characters with a new language for Vietnam. In 1948, the Korean government banned the use of Chinese words in its official communications, and a total ban on its use was enacted in 1968. In recent years, Chinese language users in business, government, and tourism have surged in Korea, leading the government to ease its policy toward the ban on the Chinese language.

Then there was the Kingdom of Ryukyu, islands situated between Japan and Taiwan, which had long been accustomed to the Chinese way of life and written language. After the Ming Dynasty came in power in 1368, the Kingdom requested trade and cultural relations with the Ming government and wished to be recognized as a satellite state of China. The friendly relationship was maintained for 510 years until 1879 when Japan conquered the island chain. Singapore, with its profound Chinese heritage, declared independence from the Federation of Malaysia in 1965, becoming the newest nation member of the Chinese cultural circle. People of these six nations have much in common, from ideology such as Confucianism and ancestor worshiping to the use of chopsticks and tea drinking.

The Chinese culture incorporated many foreign elements such as Buddhism, grape wine, the clock, etc., but the main ideology and practices were developed by the Han Chinese. The AryanWisdom website posted on January 21, 2016, shows the five largest ethnic groups in the world: Han Chinese accounting for 17.3% of the world total population, 1,253 million people; Indo-Aryan 12.6%, 911 million; White 7.4%, 536 million; Dravidian 4.3%, 313 million; and Black/African 4.1%, 297 million. The Han would have been 400 million more if there were no one child per family population control for Han families in China in the last 30 years. Han probably is the most populous group in the history of mankind. Early civilization and continuity of social structure providing favorable living conditions and less community destruction may partially explain why the Han outgrew all other ethnic groups in the millions of years of human evolution. The cultural, environmental, and genetic factors might also have played important roles in the high population growth.

The Chinese written language and use of chopsticks were two unique characteristics among world cultures. Most written languages in the world use a set of phonetic symbols like the English alphabet, to record the spoken languages; so, the written and spoken languages are related, facilitating language learning. There is no alphabet in the Chinese written language; each character is one word; and they were developed under principles in addition to the spoken language. Tsang Chieh, a court minister of the first emperor of China Huang Ti, in 4200s B.C., reviewed the existing signs, symbols, and methods of recording, observed the natural and social phenomena, and analyzed the concrete and abstract aspects in devising a recording system, which was adopted by the emperor and has been used in China ever since. Over thousands of years there have been changes, but the basics written language remain the same. The latest counts of 91,251 different characters (words) were in use over the years. However, 3,000 words would cover 99% of today's common usage, and 1,000 words are sufficient for 92% of the time.

Although ethnic Han represents the overwhelming majority in China, there are 55 ethnic minorities; together more than 80 dialects are used in China today. The Han people alone use eight major dialects including

Mandarin, Wu, Hsiang, Gann, Hakka, Min south, Min north, and Cantonese. With so many dialects in use by the Han, this might explain why the Chinese avoided the common approach of using the phonetic symbols to record the spoken language because the peoples who did not use the dialect would not be able to understand the meaning of it. Since the founding of the Republic of China in 1911, to facilitate learning Mandarin, the official national language, by other non-native speakers, a set of phonetic symbols were devised and marked alongside each word to designate its pronunciation. These symbols might have been referred to by foreign language teachers as Chinese alphabets which provided a sound only, but several words may have the same sound, so they are not alphabets -- written languages. From a language standpoint, China is very much like the European continent. There are a few major and lots of minor language except China is dominated by more than 850 million Mandarin speakers.

The use of chopsticks is unique to the Chinese. No similar practice is found in any culture in other parts of the world. Tree branches, wood, or bamboo could be used to make a pair of chopsticks. Forks and knives compared with the chopsticks were much more expensive to make and harder to come by especially before the Industrial Revolution; most people in the world resorted to using fingers to facilitate eating. Evan today, using fingers for food is prevailed in some functions.

It takes less than one minute to learn how to use chopsticks, but it takes practice to become competent. It is an extension of the fingers, but it outperforms the fingers almost in all applications except the tender loving care fingers provide. For example, chopsticks can resist heat or cold, can go into a narrow neck jar, can puncture things, etc. which fingers are unable to do. And most importantly, by using chopsticks it avoids fingers from direct contact with food, thus preventing gems from spreading. Because the hands make most physical contact with other things, it is the most contaminated part of human body. To prevent gems from spreading, today, hospitals, nursing homes, and many public places offer hand cleaning towels or lotion for people to use.

The proper Chinese table manner requires using chopsticks instead of fingers for eating. Such practice may have prevented spreading of the communicable epidemics such as cholera which could wipe out the entire village population in one season. And over thousands of years, using chopsticks would had greatly reduced population fatality from such epidemics and contributed to making the Han the world's largest ethnic group.

The inventor of chopsticks and when it became popular in use are subjects to further research. The earliest record shows King Chou of Ying Dynasty, 1,144 B.C., used a pair of chopsticks made of ivory. Therefore, this Chinese cultural specialty has been around for at least 3,000 years.

Tea, another aspect of ancient Chinese custom, may also contribute greatly to making the Han Chinese the world's most popular human race.

Tea was the only adult drink besides wine and liquor in China years ago. It was customarily served with meals and after the meal. The earliest record traced tea leaf to Shen Nong (3245-3080 B.C., 165 years old?), founder of Chinese agriculture and herb medicine who used tea leaves as antidotes when tasting toxin herbs. In the early days, tea was used raw or cocked as soup or with other foods. The processed tea as we know today commenced in the Three Kingdom Period (220-280 A.D.). The arts of tea production and appreciation were developed, refined, and matured during the Tang and Song dynasties (618-1,279 A.D.). Green tea was the original and there were seven more major varieties of tea today.

Scientists have discovered green tea's health beneficial effect in recent years. "It's the healthiest thing I can think of to drink", proclaimed Christopher Ochsner, PhD, a research scientist in nutrition at the Icahn School of Medicine at Mount Sinai Hospital in New York City. Green tea contains rich antioxidants that fight and may even prevent cell damage leading to cancer. It also helps to improve blood flow and lower cholesterol, thus preventing related heart disease (webmd.com).

Tea has the property of breaking down grease, facilitating food digestion. It was also used by Chinese households to clean kitchens and wash cloths before soap was popular in China a century ago. Before oral hygiene technology was developed, drinking tea probably was the best mouthwash. Boiled water was needed to make tea, thus eliminating water contamination, and ensuring a healthy lifestyle. Multiple health benefits including cancer prevention, safe water, food digestion, and oral hygiene might have derived from drinking tea, thus enhancing a person's overall health.

A1.2. The Hun (not Han) and the Great Wall of China

China's east coast is the vast Pacific Ocean, and the west is bounded by the world's tallest mountain ranges that include the Himalayas and Tian Shan. Therefore, in the early history of China, the major outside contacts and conflicts took place on the northern and southern borders. Due to geographic conditions, the neighbors to the north were nomadic people depending on livestock, mainly horses, cattle, and sheep for their livelihood. The southern neighbors were earthbound farmers, the same as the Chinese. That was the main reason why there were more skirmishes and battles on the northern borders than in the south.

Many nomadic tribes were inhabited the Mongolian and Manchurian areas, north of China. The Huns (Xiongnu in Chinese) became the largest and most powerful group. In the very early days, they were mainly looters of the Chinese farmers in the northern borders. With their horses they could move in and out swiftly; the Chinese farmers were basically sitting ducks as their prey. The earliest Chinese record shows that in the King Yu era (795-771 B.C.) of the West Chou Dynasty, the burning torch on top of the Great Wall tower was used to alert the adjacent areas that the looters were coming so that a collective action could be taken. Gradually, the Huns moved inside the Great Wall, which was the barrier built by each border state to ward them off. At the height of its prosperity (209-128 B.C.), the Hun total population was estimated at a high of three million people.

The first large scale battle between the Huns and Chinese occurred in 246 B.C. General Li Bo (in Chinese, the family name comes first followed by the first name and second name) of the Chao state commanded 1,300 fighting vehicles, 13,000 cavalry, 50,000 warriors, and 100,000 archers using different strategies and soundly defeated the Hun's 100,000 cavalry. Then, in 215 B.C., six years after Chin Shih Huang unified China, an army consisting of 300,000 troops was dispatched to the northeast of China to drive the Huns back to the Mongolian Plateau and linked each segment of the Wall built by each state to become a complete line of defense.

After Chin Shih Huang's death in 210 B.C., the regime was shaken; civil wars followed. China's strongest military dynasty in its 5,000 year history lasted the shortest time, just 15 years (221-206 B.C.). In 201 B.C, five years after another Chinese dynasty, Han was established; the Huns saw an opportunity to launch 400,000 plus cavalry and besieged the Chinese Han emperor for seven days, forcing the Chinese to pay tributes, open borders for trade, and agree to royal family intermarriages. But that did not satisfy the Hun, and incursions continued on and off. China regained its strength after some 70 years of recuperation. During the Han Wu Di regime (140-87 B.C.), coupled with diplomatic effort in the neighboring states, four major military campaigns were launched to drive the Huns back to the north.

Infighting among the Hun's leaders was a main cause that substantially weakened their power. The fatal dispute over the succession to be Sunyu (king) began in 58 B.C., causing the Huns to split into north and south factions. In seeking asylum in China by the pursuing northern Huns, the southern Huns were reduced to a vassal state. The Chinese and southern Huns' military alliance drove off the northern Huns from the eastern region in 91 A.D. The final deadly blow to the northern Huns by the alliance took place two years later at the Altai Mountain region, causing them to move into Asia Minor. But that did not end their dream for a comeback; four major incursions were launched until their defeat in 151 A.D.; with that they finally gave up and moved on, never again to return to China.

The Huns disappeared from the historical record for almost 150 years because they had no contact with a major civilization during this period. The Chinese record cited in 290 A.D. that the Huns reached Asear (Azar) in Central Asia and in 350 A.D. conquered the kingdom of Asear. In 374 A.D., the record shows that Ostrogothic people engaged in battles with the Huns at the Dniper River. The Huns went westward, expanded their power and conquered most territory as they moved toward Rome, Italy. As they marched westward, it hastened the downfall of both the Eastern and Western Roman Empires. The Huns Empire was established near Budapest, Hungary, and ended its dynasty in 468 A.D.

The Huns probably were not as savage and brutal as the Mongols which came later. They destroyed and killed as they moved westward causing great social chaos and the first big population movement in Europe. On a positive note, the Huns served as transmitters of civil and cultural ideas from Asia to Europe, eventually strengthened the Silk Road commercial effect, even though they had blocked the passage for a number of years.

A1.3. The Silk Road to the East and West Interactions

The Silk Road was first developed for diplomatic reasons for getting the states on the west of China to join the military campaign against the Huns. It began in about 100-200 B.C. for a total length of 7,000 km. Chinese records show that during the Han Wu Di era (140-87 B.C.), a Chinese diplomat was dispatched to Alexandria, Egypt. And in 166 A.D., an envoy for the Emperor Trajan of Rome traveled the Silk Road and arrived in Loyang, the Chinese capital, to submit his credentials to the imperial court. It was the first diplomatic relation between two major nations representing the East and the West. The route also has a southwestern section which connected to India, having a significant impact on the East Asian culture.

Trade and cultural exchanges also flourished along the route. Jade and precious stones preceded silk as the major trading merchandise. So it was named the Jade and Stones Road before the German geologist Ferdinand von Richthofen coined its current name in the 19th century. Precious stones such as jade and lapis lazuli, mined in Xingjian and Afghanistan at that time, were distributed to China, India, the Middle East, and Europe. Merchandise exported from China consisted of silk, china, tea, metalwork, gold, silver, and herbs. Goods imported to China mainly included gold, silver, precious stones, glassware, spices, medicine, fabric, plants, and exotic birds and animals. Major technological exchanges were information about making paper, glass, printing, gun powder, the compass, grape wine, and, of course, silk. Buddhist teachings were also transmitted from India through the southwestern route to China and then to Korea and Japan which became the major religion in East Asia. Although modification had been made to adapt to the local conditions, Buddhism became an important religion of these societies.

In 605 A.D., Emperor Sui Yang Di embarked on a huge project excavating waterways to connect two segments of the Grand Canal which was built in 486 B.C. Thus, it provided waterway transportation from the capital, Loyang, to the northeast grain plain ending near Beijing and to the southeast region, the home of silk, china, and tea producers, terminating in Hangchow, with a length of 2,700 km. After its completion in 610 A.D., the waterway facilitated in increasing the volume and speed of goods movement while at the same time greatly reducing the cost of transport, leading to a commercial boom.

The Emperor staged a trade fair extravaganza in Loyang after the canal expansion was in operation. Some 40 foreign heads and tribal chiefs and their entourage, foreign dignitaries and merchants were invited to attend the fair. The government required shops in the three major capital markets to be open until dawn and provide free food to the foreign guests. Also, 18,000 musicians and show performers were furnished to entertain the fair goers. The fair lasted for an entire month, netting abundant trade contracts for both foreign and domestic merchants and leading to booming traffic along the Silk Road until the mid-Tang dynasty, about 750 A.D., lasting a total of 140 years.

With tribes like the Mongols, Turks, and Manchu gaining strength, northern China became a battleground again, causing political instability and social unrest and adversely affecting the Chinese economy and trade. The Silk Road traffic declined for some 500 years. Not until 1279 when the Mongols completed their conquest in Asia and Europe, and with the entire Silk Road under its control, was it made a thoroughfare with government protection. It took exchanges between the East and the West to a new height whether it was for government, business or other activities. As Marco Polo, a Venetian merchant, described in his book, merchants converged in Datu (Beijing) because any precious or rare goods were available in bountiful quantity, unsurpassed anywhere in the world. And there were so many hotels to accommodate travelers that those who came from different countries were housed in separate quarters according to their race.

Before the Mongols came to power, all the trade missions along the road were regional or segmental, like a relay race, causing the price of merchandise to increase multi-fold at the other end. Increased safety of the journey also contributed to the cost reduction and travel surged on the route during the Mongol rule. The division and eventual fall of the Mongol empire around 1370 reversed traveling conditions back to its old status. States and warlords took charge again in each section of the Silk Road which made it more difficult to travel and costly to trade, giving rise to sea traffic.

A1.4. The Sea Silk Route and Zheng He Expeditions

Beginning in the 1st century, the Chinese merchants traded along the South China Sea coast. Sea trade accelerated after the Three Kingdoms period (220-280 A.D.) in which China experienced a major civil war. The civil war, unlike many previous wars with northern invaders, was mainly taken place either on the Yangtze River or along the river, promoting naval development and related ship building and navigation technology. As a result, it extended the Chinese sea merchant's reach to 15 countries in India, the Persian Gulf, and the Red Sea. From there, the local traders resold the goods to Alexandria, Egypt, which in turn moved on to the Greek and Roman empires. Silk was the main staple.

The sea route was a supplemental alternative to land transportation in the early era. In the mid-Tang Dynasty, 750 A.D. when China, Asia Minor, and the Middle East experienced political instability and social unrest creating perilous conditions along the Silk Road, the sea route began to flourish. With the advancement in navigation, astronomy, and shipbuilding, the sea route became the main connection between Asia and Europe and Africa through the Song and Yuan Dynasties. Then expeditions conducted by Zheng He (a eunuch) of the early Ming Dynasty took China's world exploration to its highest level.

Thirty-seven years after chasing the Mongols from the Great Wall, the Ming Dynasty made considerable economic progress, especially in ship building which had seen a lot of improvements during the Mongol era for invasions of Japan and Java, Indonesia. Between 1405 and 1433, Zheng He led the Chinese ship flotilla seven times, visiting Southeast Asia, South Asia, the Arabian Sea, the Persian Gulf, and the Red Sea. Gavin Menzies, an English naval expert, contended in his recent book that Zheng He had also visited Oceania and America in 1421.

Zheng He's voyages covered 39 nations and over 100,000 Chinese miles. Twenty-one different sailing routes were mapped, the longest taking 22 days and the shortest just one day. Each expedition required an average of over 200 ships and 27,000 naval personnel. The flotilla consisted of five types of ships, namely Treasure (the command ship), Horse, Provision, Seating, and Battleships. The largest ship, Treasure, 63 of them, measured 151.18 meters long by 61.6 meters width, or 460.79 feet x 187.76 feet, accommodating up to 1,000 people with nine masts and 12 sails. The Battle was the smallest, measuring 61.6 meters x 23.27 meters or 187.76 feet x 70.93 feet apparently for its military maneuverability.

At each port of call Zheng He, the emperor's special envoy as well as the commander of the flotilla, proclaimed Emperor Ming Chen Zu's (alias Yuen Lo Di) decree that world peace, prosperity, international trade, and cultural exchanges must be safeguarded and promoted and a wish that other nations will establish or improve relations with China. A sizable gift, consisting of gold and silver art crafts, silk, porcelain, and tea, was usually provided to the local ruler. Zheng He also surveyed and studied local conditions, traded in local markets, served as mediator sometimes for political disputes and hosted foreign dignitaries and merchants to and from China for free. For example, on his 6th return voyage in 1422, there were 1,200 foreign guests on board including envoys and merchants, their families and aides from 16 nations. By 1424, the year Yuen Lo Di died, over 60 nations had diplomatic relations with China. The nation's treasury was empty at that time, so the new ruler called for a cessation of exploration. Zheng He made his final voyage in 1430. China made a 360 degree turn around, adopting an isolationist policy, closing all sea ports except one in Guangzhou until the 19th century when China was forced by world powers to open up ports for international trade.

The historians attributed the main motive of these unprecedented expeditions to the ultra-ambition of Yuen Lo Di, who desired to do big things. Besides the overseas adventures, imperial court scholars were ordered to compile a comprehensive Chinese dictionary, which was later published in his honor. It was the first in thousands of years of Chinese history. An unconfirmed speculation pointed out that Zheng He's voyages were also intended to eliminate the emperor's political foes because he snatched power in a palace coup. The survivors of the royal family might be hiding overseas and may pose a challenge to his political legitimacy.

The main reasons for the complete change of policy in Chinese overseas trades were summed up by scholars as follows:

1. It was costly. The cost of seven expeditions amounted to two years of national budget, not including the cost of ships. The construction and maintenance cost for each ship required 1,600 Chinese oz. of silver annually on average, and there were 260 of them.

2. Not much economic benefit. Except for gold and silver, the importing of spices and exotic birds and animals did not have that much market in China. The Chinese emperor, showing off his generosity, usually reciprocated with foreign gifts, tributes, or government trades that were 20 times more than their value which cost the treasury, too.

3. The Chinese had no colonial ambition. China had no colonial desire as demonstrated by the Zheng He's 3rd expedition in Sri Lanka (Ceylon) in 1409. When the king of Sri Lanka noticed the tremendous amount of treasure in Zheng He's ships, he had Zheng He and his senior officers attend a royal banquet at his palace and blocked their return path. At the same time, the king dispatched an army of 50,000 troops to surround the flotilla in an attempt to rob the treasure. As Zheng He became aware of the situation, he summoned 2,000 elite troops, and taking a shortcut, they attacked the palace and captured the king and his family. When the royal troops learned of the trouble in the palace, they returned to rescue the king. The troops, attacked on both sides, suffered a fatal defeat and surrendered to Zheng He.

The king was taken to Nanjing, the Chinese imperial court, in 1411 for a trial. All senior government officials recommended the death penalty, but the emperor, Yuen Lo Di, spared his life believing that the king was merely incompetent, but stipulated that Sri Lanka selected a new, competent ruler. The deposed king was sent back accompanied by the Chinese envoy who proclaimed the new king's coronation in Sri Lanka. It would have been a perfect pretext for China to annex Sri Lanka as a colony.

Zheng He was engaged in many battles with pirates during his expeditions, but Sri Lanka was the only knowingly military action with a foreign government. He died on his last trip home in the summer of 1433 while sailing along Indonesia at the age of 63 and was buried in Java, Indonesia.

Personal records from Zheng He's own writings about the expeditions might have been destroyed by several major fires at the imperial quarters. Also, loud opposition to the expeditions grew after the death of Yuen Lo Di. An official record keeper was implicated in the missing document, and the whereabouts of Zheng He's expedition records is still an unsolved mystery. So, Menzies' contention on Zheng He's 1421 voyage to America cannot be directly verified by his own writing.

4. There was no political benefit. Since the main threats to China's security were the northern invaders, the cordial relations with overseas nations did not improve Chinese national security.

5. The rampancy of Chinese coastal pirates. The pirates looted coastal Chinese residents, destroyed property and killed people in the

beginning and later on turned to occupying coastal islands or areas and becoming the lords of the land. The rampant pirate activities were mainly triggered by the civil war in China, transition from the Yuan to Ming Dynasties, and in Japan, the North and South split. The Chinese coastal area was lax in defense because of the civil war and became an easy target for the pirates. The Japanese soldiers displaced by the internal split ganged up with the Chinese outlaws to form the pirate groups in the early period.

Ming Tai Zu, the founding emperor of the Ming Dynasty, from 1370 to 1397, issued six decrees to ban private trade but allowed only government trade along the coast primarily to block the livelihood of opposition war lords and pirates. The policy set the precedent for most of the dynasty and backfired on several fronts. First, it displaced merchants, producers of all kinds of merchandises and ship builders by causing them to become unemployed and turned them into smugglers or pirates. Second, the great demand for Chinese products from overseas could not be fulfilled by government trade alone. As a result, smuggling proliferated and developed into a pirate operation similar to the illegal drug trade that exists today. With the relaxed policy of overseas trade and the efforts to combat piracy, the Ming government finally ended piracy on China's seacoast by 1562, almost 200 years after it stared.

One of the Zheng He expedition's byproducts was the invention of a card game, Mahjong (numbing general, the general will make sailors behaved and quiet). The game was intended for sailors to entertain themselves during their long monotonous voyages. The game consisted of four suits each with nine (1-9, and one with Chinese characters) cards and each had four identical cards for a total of 144 cards. There were only a few rules associated with the game which was easy to learn but difficult to become a master. Four players were required; each played their own hand independently, undisclosed; unlike the bridge card game which required a partner. To claim victory or completion of a hand in order to end the game, it required four sets of cards, either three of a kind or three in the run, e.g., 3 duos or 6, 7, 8, both in the same suit plus a pair for a total of 14 cards, one winner three losers. Initially, every player drew 13 cards. It required one more card to finish the game and to claim a victory. It was rare that the 13 cards would be in the right composition as in the above requirement, to claim a victory; therefore each player took turns to improve their hand either by taking the discarded card of other players or drawing a new one from the remaining 92 cards, and then discarding one. Thus, the process improved each hand toward the game's completion. Depending on the degree of difficulty, each completed game had its own value; an easy one may score 10 points, a hard to come by one may be worth 100 points agreed upon by the players before the game started. As a result, all players strived for high scores, but if it was not completed first, it was all done in vain regardless of how valuable the hand would be. Therefore, it required each player to constantly guess what the other players' hands held as to the value and the timing of completion so as to beat them before their completion. Since each move by a player may improve their hand, it also altered other players' game plans. Thus, the game was constantly evolving, changing all the time, unlike a bridge game where each player got 13 cards at one time and no more. It was one of the most fascinating and challenging games in the world and became the most popular card game in China where it was enjoyed by men and women, intellectuals and laborers, alike. It was not uncommon for game addicts who were plentiful in China, to play the game non-stop, day and night, having meals at the game table for three or four days, which caused health hazards to players as well as neglected their worldly duties. Mahjong is a popular gambling device as well. Thus, the game was denounced as a no-good vice banned by the authorities and looked down upon by society. In the last 40 to 50 years, public opinion changed and began to recognize the positive attributes of the game. For example, the game provides entertainment and mental exercise and requires very little physical movement. It is the best thing for senior citizens to kill time and reduces the progression of dementia. Its popularity is soaring again.

A1.5. Manchu's Ignorance and Incompetence Led China to Disaster
The Manchu, a northern tribe, was a powerful group that threatened the Song Dynasty before the Mongols did. In 1115, the Jin Kingdom (1115-1234, established by Manchu) had conquered northern China, forcing the Song regime to move south. Before they realized their ambition of becoming the rulers of China, they were defeated and chased away by the Mongols. The Manchu's dream was realized some 500 years later when they replaced the Ming Dynasty in 1644.
The Manchu regime was perceived by the Chinese as a northern

invader, not just passing the baton from one dynasty to another, but they were widely resented. They also committed atrocities during the conquering process that was even worse than the Mongols. In the 1645 Yangzhou massacre alone, 800,000 civilian corpses were collected for burial. Then, right after establishing their regime, the Manchu proclaimed a forced assimilation rule that required all males to follow the Manchu's custom to shave their head and to keep a braid of hair or a pigtail. A beheading penalty was imposed if anyone violated the rule. A popular slogan at that time was "saving your head by losing your hair or saving your hair by losing your head; the choice is yours".

Today, the pigtail is gone for good, and it is not easy to spot a Manchu anymore, except those living in the northeast mountain areas. Since the regime was established in 1644, voluntary assimilation had been practiced by both groups, Manchu and Han. For example, every Qing (Manchu dynasty) emperor, except the first few, was well versed in Chinese literature; Chien Leong, reigned from 1711 to 1799, was also a well-known Chinese calligrapher. Tsao Hsueh Chin, 1715-63, the Manchu authored *The Dream of the Red Chamber* which is one of the four best Chinese novels of all time. On the other side, Chinese ladies embraced Chi Pou, a Manchu original, as their own, becoming the modern Chinese lady's formal evening dress. Mandarin, the national language, is basically a dialect of Beijing, which was founded 3,000 years ago long before Manchu was known and was a national capital for 860 years. However, the dialect is profoundly influenced by and incorporated in many Manchu languages because Qing's central government had been seated in Beijing for 260 years. The Manchu's atrocity cannot be prosecuted; it can only be blamed on the savagery of war.

Zheng Chen Kon, 1624-62, a Ming navy officer, refused to surrender to the Qing government, taking his men to sea. As the anti-Qing movement grew, so did Zheng's force. In an alliance with Chang Hon Yuan in 1659, they launched attacks along the Yangtze River, captured several cities and besieged Nanjing, but ended up with failure. Two years later, he gathered his force to defeat the Dutch East India Co. in Tainan, Taiwan which was captured by the Dutch in 1624, restoring Chinese sovereignty and controlling the island until 1683. It served as a strong base for the anti-Qing/restoring Ming movement, leading to extreme restrictions on sea traffic imposed by the Qing government and cutting off all connection with the outside world along the coastal line for the purpose of starving Taiwan.

After eliminating the last major opposition force in Taiwan, the Qing government in 1684 opened up seaports for trade until 1717. Due to the increased piracy and colonial activities by the West, the ban to and from southeast Asia was re-imposed for another 10 years and re-opened in 1727 until 1757. Beginning from Chien Leong reign year 47 (1757), all ports were closed to foreign traffic except Guangzhou and restricted foreigners' activities within the city. Besides, the ban extended to include ship building of a certain size, weaponry, and oversea travel. Commodities such as grain, gold, silver, copper, and raw silk were banned or limited for export. A custom duty was also imposed to discourage exports.

After the British sent a large trade delegation to China, trying to convince Emperor Chien Leong about the advantages of international trade, in his 1793 reply to King George III, Chien Leong cited that China had abundant products, no shortage of anything, and there was no need to expand foreign trade. This was a true statement to a certain extent because the British had a constant unfavorable trade balance with China up to the early 1820s. If everything remained the same, exports increased demand which led to inflation, which was another reason for the Qing government officials to advocate the closed-door policy. And finally, the feeling of a foreign threat was growing, so no foreign contact might be the best policy. This mentality of the ruling elite led China to an unprecedented disaster that lasted until 1945, ending the imperial aggression by foreign powers for 105 years, resulting in almost the total destruction of China, and reducing China from having one of the highest living standards to one of the poorest in the world.

In retrospect, the Japanese ruling elite faced American intrusion with a different reaction. Meiji Restoration was advocated to catch up science and technology with the West. Japan, too, became a world power joining the imperial aggression.

A1.6. Imperial Invasions and Civil Wars: China's Century from Hell

Since ancient times, the West yearned for silk, porcelain, and tea from China. Marco Polo's writing triggered Christopher Columbus to seek a shorter sea route to China instead of going around the African continent which caused him to land in America. And after the disintegration of the

Mongol empire, the Silk Road became perilous to travel, leading to the rise of the sea trade again. The development of steamboats in the early 1700s accelerated the sea traffic directly from Western Europe to the Far East. By the early 1800s, sea transportation technology has advanced immensely, so it took sea trade to new heights.

China had always enjoyed a trade surplus with the West despite its restriction on exports and lack of modern technology; thus, it created an influx of gold and silver into China from the West. In the beginning, the British tried to convince the Chinese to open more ports for trade so that there might be a chance for them to turn around the trade deficit, but without success. Then, the British came up with the opium trade idea that turned the tide of in its favor.

Opium is an ancient medication as well as a recreational substance. It is highly addictive and causes health problems for long term users. The British East India Company secured an opium sale monopoly in 1773 and monopolized opium production in 1797. Thus, the company accelerated the production and distribution of opium to every corner of the world and accumulated huge profits for the company and for the British monarchy. In 1817, the cost of opium production per case was between 200-300 rupees, auctioned to the merchant for 1,785 rupees in India, and sold in China for 2,618 rupees, which was more than 10 times its average production cost.

Since the early 1800s, the British opium trade to China escalated from 3,000-4,000 cases to 10,000-20,000 cases per year. The British worldwide opium trade income in 1829 amounted to one million pounds, 10% of government revenue. Meanwhile, China's trade balance had a dramatic change from surplus to deficit. Just opium imported from Britain balanced out all of China's exports to that country. Cash outflows to the West escalated from 3.5 million ounces of silver in 1826-27 to 5-6 million ounces per year in the 1830s. After legalization of opium in 1858, opium imports skyrocketed every year, and in 1879 the total import of 104,900 dun (about 100 lbs.) accounted for 50% of the value of China's total imports.

Opium addiction became an epidemic, leading to the ban of the opium trade and becoming the pretext for the British invasion. In 1725 and 1796, the Qing government had forbidden the import of opium, but the bans were defeated by the smugglers and corrupt government officials.

Consumption of opium by the Chinese soared by the 1830s. Emperor Dao Kwan ordered a crackdown on the British trade, confiscating and burning 20,000 cases of opium, and discontinuing trade with Britain in 1838. After several negotiations without success, in June 1840, the British sent 47 war ships manned with 4,000 soldiers and 15,000 sailors to attack ports near Guangzhou and capture the city later. While negotiating and fighting, the British moved northward along the coast, overran Xiamen in Fujian province and seized several cities before threatening Nanjing on August 4, 1842. Although the Qing military and people put up fierce resistance, without modern weapons and organization, it was a losing battle in every encounter, prompting the Qing government to seek a ceasefire.

On August 29, 1842, the Nanjing Treaty was signed. China's first unequal treaty provided the following concessions to Britain: (1) Ceding Hong Kong; (2) opening five seaports; (3) paying 21 million Yuan as an indemnity; (4) joint decision on trade tariff; (5) allowing trade with private parties; and (6) having extraterritorial jurisdiction. Since then, all world powers demanded the same privileges, competing for spheres of influence on Chinese soil. For example, the U.S. signed the Wangxia Treaty with China in 1844 demanding the same privileges as the British but, as a goodwill gesture, agreed with the Chinese that opium trade was harmful and denounced opium trade as illegal and promised to hand over any violators to China for prosecution, even though American merchants were the second largest opium traders after the British. China was carved up like a melon.

The opium trade was the most lethal colonial policy. It drained China's financial resources while paralyzing its people so that the country could be colonized, without firing a shot. It was estimated that 25% of adult males in China by 1905 were still addicted to opium.

The misery for the Chinese was not over yet. The following were the major events that occurred in chronological order.

1850-64, Taiping Kingdom revolution, almost toppled the Qing regime. Death toll estimated to be 20 million people.

1858-60, Anglo-French Alliance looted and burned several palaces in Beijing.

1858-60, Aifei and Beijing Treaties with Russia, ceding over one million square miles of northeast territory almost the size of France and

Germany combined.

1862-77, Dungan Revolt, death toll 12 million.

1895, Sino-Japanese War, ceded Leo Peninsula, Pan He, and Taiwan to Japan.

1898-1900, Eight-Nations Alliance (The Boxer Rebellion) invaded Beijing, 450 million ounces of silver indemnity. (At 2017/6/27 market price of $16.65 per once, it is nearly $7.5 billion)

1910-11, Qing Dynasty overthrown, establishing a republic, death toll 12 million.

1927-37, civil war between the Nationalists and Communists. The Communist was forced to move from the southeast to the northwest of China. Death toll 7.5 million.

1937-45, Sino-Japanese War, total Chinese death estimated 18-30 million, the Nanjing Massacre alone was 300,00 people.

1946-50, Communists drove off Nationalists from the mainland, about 5.5 million casualties.

1950-53, Korean War, 183,108 deaths in addition to many wounded.

1958-61, the Great Leap Forward, 21 million deaths according to official records.

1966-71, the Cultural Revolution, official data in million: 4.2 prosecuted, 2.1 deaths, 7.0 wounded, 7.1 homes destroyed, costing Y800 billion (US$80 billion).

1989, the Tiananmen incident, estimated 300-2,000 deaths in the square.

After the end of World War II, imperialism was rigorously denounced, and all unequal treaties were declared invalid. However, China is still trying to recover some of its territory and lots of its national treasury that were lost in the past. China has been savagely beaten down many times, but don't count China out just yet.

AII. How China's Economic Miracle was Made Possible

When the People's Republic of China was established in 1949, China had experienced more than 100 years of suffering. By the turn of the 19th century, China was weak and incompetent, becoming easy prey for the world powers that were carving up China to satisfy their imperial aggression. China was practically reduced to semi-colonial status. Then it followed the civil war, deposing the Manchurian ruler, followed by another civil war between various factions of war lords. The four years of fighting between the Communists and Nationalist government after the end of World War II was preceded by eight years of Japanese invasion and occupation. China was nearly the poorest nation on earth and was confronted with the challenging of a prodigious population. Few believed that China would be able to regain its footing and become relevant once more.

The Communist regime at first provided people some hope that life might be improving because in the past everything had been going downhill and there was no place to go but up; this was the first time in nearly a century that China was unified and the central government had real control over the country. Soon the government proclaimed a public ownership system that covered practically everything, including real property, personal property, businesses, and factories. Except personal belongings and a few Yuans of pocket money, nothing else was allowed to be owned. People began to organize communes and dined in community halls. This was followed by a series of political campaigns that included land reform, purging evil elements, the Great Leap Forward, and the Cultural Revolution.

The social reforms enticed people's enthusiasm about a brand-new society that was in the making. But the Great Leap Forward's plunging economic output was a catastrophe, causing the deaths of at least 21 million, estimated by officials. Total eradication of traditional Chinese values as well as physical heritage was the end result of the Cultural Revolution. It also created political turmoil and almost toppled the government. It was really practicing Communism throughout the first 30 years since 1949. The Chinese people had plenty of experience with poverty and misery but never before encountered the emptiness of having no material possessions as well as the hope to have something called their own.

A2.1. Unleashing the Powerful Self-Interest Instinct

Economic reform was first promoted by Premier Deng Xiaoping in December 1978. From 1980, the reform program gradually introduced the market economy and private property ownership to the population. Four economic special districts were approved as an experiment to implement the new economic policy, most notably the city of Shenzhen which was incorporated on August 26, 1980, which now has the 4th largest GDP in China and the only city with a stock exchange in the country beside Shanghai. The reform stirred up much excitement and anticipation because people, so desperate for a good life and something to call their own, denied to them for so long, unleashed their powerful self-interest instinct. Everyone was eager to get started making progress, but lacked all the key elements, i.e., skilled labor, technology, capital, and organization for production. Especially capital, with the exception of the government, communes and co-ops, people practically owned nothing.

To promote economic growth, the government enticed all public organizations and all levels of government to participate in this endeavor. However, the province, city, county, and township lacked any funding because in China only the central government had the taxing authority. A revenue sharing scheme was introduced to alleviate the local government funding problem. The sharing scheme provided 75% and 25% from land sale and 25% and 75% of property taxes on newly constructed plants to the central and local governments respectively. Thus, essentially the entire nation's population belonged to one of the production units that consisted of communes in the rural regions, co-ops in the urban areas, and all levels of government. So, except for the disabled and aged, every one of the 1.3 billion people in China was on the economic growth bandwagon. Grow the GDP became a popular slogan. GDP also became the key measurement for performance and success. People's tremendous desire for improvement of life and for possession of property was put into action that drove the economy swiftly into a higher and higher gear. As Adam Smith suggested, the invisible hand not only fulfills individual interests but also benefits society as a whole.

A2.2. Revitalizing State Capitalism: Strengthening Economic Planning and Control

Before the economic reform, all enterprises in China were owned by the commune, co-op, or government, with no private ownership. The purpose of enterprises was to serve people's economic needs and national interest as opposed to private capitalism, whose purpose is for shareholders' profit as its original theory.

Bureaucracy, corruption, and abuse of power were the common pitfalls which associated with public-owned enterprises in China. The economic reform policy re-examined all state enterprises and made a painful decision to shut down or consolidate the problem ones so that most survivors were healthy enterprises. Then the government introduced a public-private joint ownership system to attract foreign businesses, which offered a complete business package, including capital, technology, and management, to come to China. Various incentives were offered but required a joint venture with the state enterprise, limited foreign interest up to 49% in key sectors, and required foreign businesses to transfer technology to the local business. During 1982-2013, the average foreign direct investment flowing into China was nearly $80 billion annually as the following table indicates, contributing significantly to the 32 years of rapid economic growth.

Since 1980, seven economic Five-Year Plans were introduced to determine the goals, to emphasize the key sectors, to coordinate development, and to adjust the imbalance, thus helping to launch the economy smoothly toward its targets. Also, a manager's responsibility system involving Communist party supervision, i.e., a party member served as a key supervisor, was instituted to ensure the enterprise met its goal of profitability as well as serving the national interest. In the meantime, China was aware of the socialist Economic Planning flaws that caused the Soviet Union to collapse. Consequently, China delegated the details and development to the market economy and introduced private business ownership to its people as soon as possible. At the same time, its policy prevented foreign economic invasion, capitalist lootings, and other free market economy negative effects. China selected the type of foreign investment, paced its development tempo, adjusted sector/regional imbalance and assisted industries in accomplishing its economic transformation.

The following table shows the economic data taken from the World Bank and the UN Conference on Trade and Development.

Select China Economic Indicators, 1980-20

Economic indicators and years, in US$	Average	High	Low
Per capita GDP annual growth, 1980-2013, $	$1,482	6,807	193
GDP growth per year, 1980-2013, %	9.9%	15.2	3.8
Export as % of GDP, 1982-2013, %	21.4%	39.1	7.7
Net merchandise trade balance, 1980-2013, m$	$62	298,126	-14,902
Savings as % of GDP, 1982-2012, %	42.5%	53.0	35.0
Capital formation as % of GDP, 1980-2013, %	39.8%	49.0	34.0
Foreign direct investment, inflow, 1982-2013, b$	$ 79.9	347.8	0.4
Foreign direct investment, outflow, 2003-2013, b$	$46.4	104.5	2.9
Personal foreign remittance, inflow, 1982-2013, b$	$10.8	40.0	0.2

A2.3. Controlling Population Growth: Diverting Resources for Social Improvement

Population, like everything else, has two sides to its story. When the population exceeds what society can comfortably support, it sets back social progress. On the other hand, too few people caused labor shortages and also dragged down social improvement. Most economically underdeveloped countries suffer from either under production or over consumption. Or, the country simply did not produce enough to support its people's consumption. Living on a subsistence level without adequate sanitation and health care means the premature death rate tends to be very high. High birth rates and high death rates are characteristically associated with underdeveloped countries.

In order to turn around this undesirable condition, a population policy must be established as a precondition for any social progress plan. An optimum population mix should take into consideration factors such as gender, age, health, education, occupation, geography and the environment in addition to social aspiration. It is a very complex issue involving ethical, political, economic, and social considerations. The discussion here is mainly to show what effects the population policy has on the economy. It is not intended either to support or to discredit the Chinese population policy.

Between 1840 and 1949, China suffered many foreign invasions and civil wars, a period of vast devastation and severe social turmoil and poverty; total growth in population in 109 years was recorded at 130 million people. From 1949 when the Communist regime was established to 1979, with a stable government and effective social control, notwithstanding the Korean War deaths of 150,000-400,000 and early 1960s' famine deaths of more than 21 million attributed to the Great Leap Forward and severe poverty, in the 30 year span, the population registered a net gain of 430 million people, which is 35% more than the total U.S. population in 2014. Without putting population growth in check, feeding all these people would prove to be an insurmountable task. As a consequence of China's population policy, China ended its merchandise net import trend of over $12 billion in 1993, i.e., production of merchandise was insufficient to meet the need for domestic consumption and investment.

China promulgated the one child per family policy on 1980/9/25 that affected everyone in the country except 55 ethnic minorities who were permitted to have as many children as they wished, to avoid a genocidal effect on ethnic minorities. According to the official data released at the end of 2011 for the past 30 years, this one child per family policy resulted in a net birth decrease of more than 400 million since its implementation. Again this total figure is considerable more than the total American population today. As a result, China bypassed expending the resources and effort needed to care and educate 400 million people for at least 15 years. Thus, population control diverted the tremendous resources and energy to raise the standard of living and to improve social condition. It also helped to produce an average savings rate of 42.5% of GDP in 1982-2012, a key factor contributing to the last 30 years of phenomenal economic growth leading to an income per capita increase of 104% (6,807/193/34) annually and a GDP gain of 9.9% per year.

A2.4. Internal and External Efforts Fulfilled Capital Need

In most economically underdeveloped countries, consumption outpaces production, and no savings are realized. Most of these countries have no ability to borrow from outside sources; without capital to invest, the country's economy tends to be stagnant or recessed. Therefore, capital is an essential ingredient of economic growth.

The earlier table shows that during 34 years, China's average GDP consists of 42.5% savings, 21.4% exports which leaves 36.1% for personal consumption and government spending. It is quite different from the current U.S. GDP makeup which is composed of 70% personal consumption, 20% government spending, and 10% investment. This implies that the savings in America is no more than 10%. In fact, in 2015 U. S. GDP registered a 2.8% deficit (see 7.1) and explained that it was financed by public and private debts. The ultra-high savings rate in China provided the major internal source of capital formation. People were not spending freely as they became affluent because a hard life had become the norm in China for over 100 years and people had a tendency to save for rainy days. Furthermore, since people had to forfeit property ownership for more than 30 years, and they were yearning to possess some big ticket items such as a car or house, it is likely that they were saving to make these purchases. Regardless of their motives, savings contributed to internal capital formation, and thus propelled the growth of the GDP.

There were three major external sources of capital for China during 1980-2013, namely foreign direct investment, personal remittance from overseas, and a favorable trade balance. The FDI was the most important item among the three. It provided nearly $80 billion annually to economic investment. A major part of this capital contribution paid for the land sale and property tax to the Chinese local and central governments by foreign investors. These funds fulfilled the need for capital by the government to launch economic projects in the early period of the economic reform, which were instrumental in the development of China's economic success story. The enthusiasm of foreign capitalists was primarily motivated by the extensive labor cost savings in the early period and the immense market and futures prospects in China in recent decades. Since China has the world's largest vehicle market (sales in 2016, China 27.8 million vs. U.S. 17.6 million), all major world carmakers have established car manufacturing plants in China. GM's operation in China is vital to the corporation overall profitability.

Personal remittance, contributing over $10 billion per year, was mainly due to overseas Chinese earnings being sent back to families. However, in recent years it included business and investment income as well. The controversial favorable trade balance accounted for a tiny third, averaging only $62 million per year, less than 8% of FDI.

The internal savings coupled with the external sources of capital helped to produce a 39.8% of GDP capital formation annually, serving as a powerful catalyst behind the GDP growth.

A2.5. Transferable Technology, Abundant Labor, and Worldwide Market

Economic globalization provides an easy transfer of plant, equipment, and operating technology with a few exceptions, such as very high-tech products. Most of the early foreign business transplants in China were in low tech and labor intensive operations involving very little tech secrecy. The Chinese government also stipulated transfer of tech information by foreign businesses to local joint ventures. As a result, it left only plant operation and skilled labor issues to tackle.

Most of today's mass manufacturing processes use assembly line or segmental operations. Workers are required to be familiar with a few tasks instead of the entire production process that turns out the finished product. Therefore, with adequate education, which was popularized before the economic reform, Chinese workers were able to gain competency in a short period of time. Since the economic reform also called for urbanization, millions of peasants poured into the cities in search of work. The government had to use residency ID to curb the overflows. Thus, an ample supply of workers was available. Thousands of workers could be assembled in a matter of hours.

During 1982-2013, China's exports accounted for more than 21% of its GDP. China was heavily dependent on foreign markets for its economic activities. It coincided with global trade liberalization promoted by the General Agreement on Tariffs and Trade, succeeded later by the World Trade Organization. China joined the WTO in 2001, enhancing its international trading position. Thus, Chinese goods have worldwide market appeal and accessibility. All the factors needed were in the right places at the right time helping the Chinese to complete its economic success story.

A2.6. Price China Paid for its Economic Progress

China has succeeded the U.S. and Japan as the world's leading factory and all three countries have one thing in common -- air and water pollution. Back in the 1950s and 1960s when America held the title, the Los Angeles smog was a hot topic that triggered the passage of the Clean Air Act of 1963 and led to the establishment of a brand new

Environmental Protection Agency. In the 1970s and 1980s, when Japan had the honor, it, too, suffered serious environmental damage. Three of the four major pollution diseases originated in 1956, 1961, and 1965, leading to the creation of the Environment Protection Agency in 1971. But, neither polluter can compare with the environment damage caused in China, relative to its magnitude and severity.

A report on China's environment was prepared jointly by the Asian Development Bank and field experts in 2013. The findings of the report concluded that seven out of ten of the world's most polluted cities are in China, and fewer than five of China's 500 largest cities meet the recommended air quality standard set by the World Health Organization. It was reported by the British Broadcasting website that in 2013 premature deaths caused by inhaling PM2.5 were estimated at 257,000 people in 31 cities in China. As air pollution has become worse, people in Beijing, the capital, have begun installing air filters at home and in the office and they wear mouth filters whenever they are outdoors. The authorities instituted odd and even day alternate traffic controls to reduce automobile air pollutants, especially when bad climate conditions exist and when major public events are held outdoors. In 2015, China accounted for 22% of new cancer cases worldwide, and total deaths due to cancer increased 74% from 2006 to 2015 (*Bloomberg Businessweek*, 2016/4/4).

Water pollution has been even worse than air pollution in China. Every major river is contaminated. Only 3% of city underground water is declared basically safe, 64% is considered unsafe. There have been 1,700 water pollution incidents reported every year. The World Health Organization reported 95,600 deaths due to using contaminated water in 2002. The assistant minister of the Land Resource Ministry announced on December 30, 2013, that 50 million acres of agricultural land in the nation were severely contaminated and could not be used for cultivation without major long term rehabilitation. Water pollution has seriously affected the availability of clean water for drinking, irrigation, as well as recreation activities, thus adversely impacting people's well-being and economic growth.

The nation's policy makers have been trying hard to contain the spread of pollution. In recent years, industrial pollution has been reduced, accounting for 35% of the problem. The majority came from people's waste, mainly due to sanitation and treatment facilities that did not keep up with urbanization and people's affluent living. It will take a long term, concerted effort to repair the damage. Ten years will not be sufficient time to get rid of the smog in the major cities, as expressed by a former meteorology official.

Economic progress and raising the living standard means more production and consumption. More economic activities lead to more waste, and more waste also produces more pollution. It is an unavoidable consequence. Therefore, the problem becomes one of minimizing pollution within tolerable limits. Recycling waste is one possible approach, but sometimes the cost may outweigh the benefit, and not all wastes are 100 % recyclable. Conservation, i.e., doing more with less resource in production and consumption, and practicing a simple life style by using less resource, could potentially be more effective in achieving the objective.

The one child per family policy coupled with the male favored tradition in China produced a lopsided gender imbalance in population. According to the Chinese National Statistics Bureau, the gender gap was 3.2% male compared to female in 1980 and 3.8% in 2016. The birth rate of 121.2 males vs. 100.0 females was recorded in 2004, declining to 113.5 in 2015. These conditions will make a lot of unhappy bachelors and exacerbate social as well as population problems. One child only families, without the prospect for having more children, had a negative effect on the child. It often made the child self-centered, unsociable, and selfish. Parents felt like they were simply raising a young emperor. When they enter society, one can only imagine what kinds of social conflicts these young emperors will create. Recently the Chinese authority made some changes to the one child per family restriction and instituted a new population policy.

The upheaval in the last 100 years in China brought extreme poverty and social dislocation, and uprooted most of the treasured Chinese traditions observed by the general population. During the first 30 years of the Communist regime, the trend was intensified; the party's doctrines became gospel. The Cultural Revolution went further to destroy all traditional Chinese values. All religious establishments required government approval and the teachings of Confucius were denounced as being pro-feudalism and anti-revolutionary; thus, people lost their moral compass in thinking, conduct, and belief in a future life. The vacuum was filled by worship of the GDP growth of the nation and individual wealth accumulation after the economic reform in 1980. Getting rich became the latest craze so that the popular advice "People should always look forward" became "People should always look at the money" because the words "forward" and "money" sound exactly alike in Chinese. With rapid economic growth and sudden affluence leading to rampant government official corruption and people's pompous attitude, money became the common denominator for life. It rules society. Lavish consumption and rude behavior of Chinese tourists who traveled overseas often became local newspaper headlines. A few years ago, the authorities started a campaign to crack down on the corrupt culture and to honor again Confucius' teachings, but it may take several generations before the traditional social values and civil conduct will be restored. The price of economic progress apparently is not cheap, but the choice has been made.

The Chinese economic success story stirred up lots of interest and criticism, and it has a monumental impact around the world. The question now being asked is whether developing countries with large populations like India, Brazil, Indonesia, Egypt, Nigeria, Mexico, etc., will be able to duplicate the successful Chinese economic development model if they choose to do so. The answer is that they will need to provide the very same factors that were used to create the successful Chinese economy. These factors not only included skilled labor, technology, capital, and management, but also required people's enthusiasm, population control, and the absence of a big social welfare program. When the economic reform began in 1980 social welfare in China was provided only to the aged and disabled, otherwise almost everyone in the country could meet the eligibility requirement if poverty was the qualifying standard. As a result, there was no big welfare roll draining the country's savings and economic output. The population policy and other intangible social factors, such as the people's enthusiastical embrace this goal, their commitment and full participation, coupled with their literacy, etc., may present the greatest challenge to other developing nations which intend to replicate the Chinese success story.

www.ingramcontent.com/pod-product-compliance
Lightning Source LLC
Chambersburg PA
CBHW071250220526
45468CB00001B/65